NINTH EDITION

Managing Stress

Principles and Strategies for Health and Well-Being

Volume 1

Brian Luke Seaward
Paramount Wellness Institute
Boulder, Colorado

World Headquarters
Jones & Bartlett Learning
5 Wall Street
Burlington, MA 01803
978-443-5000
info@jblearning.com
www.jblearning.com

Jones & Bartlett Learning books and products are available through most bookstores and online booksellers. To contact Jones & Bartlett Learning directly, call 800-832-0034, fax 978-443-8000, or visit our website, www.jblearning.com.

Substantial discounts on bulk quantities of Jones & Bartlett Learning publications are available to corporations, professional associations, and other qualified organizations. For details and specific discount information, contact the special sales department at Jones & Bartlett Learning via the above contact information or send an email to specialsales@jblearning.com.

13796-5

Production Credits
VP, Executive Publisher: David D. Cella
Publisher: Cathy L. Esperti
Editorial Assistant: Carter McAlister
Director of Production: Jenny L. Corriveau
Senior Production Editor: Nancy Hitchcock
Director of Marketing: Andrea DeFronzo
Production Services Manager: Colleen Lamy
VP, Manufacturing and Inventory Control: Therese Connell
Composition: S4Carlisle Publishing Services
Cover Design: Kristin E. Parker
Director of Rights & Media: Joanna Gallant
Rights & Media Specialist: Wes DeShano
Media Development Editor: Troy Liston
Cover Images (Title Page): © Inspiration Unlimited. Used with permission.
Printing and Binding: LSC Communications
Cover Printing: LSC Communications

Library of Congress Cataloging-in-Publication Data
Names: Seaward, Brian Luke, author.
Title: Managing stress : principles and strategies for health and well being / Brian Luke Seaward.
Description: Ninth edition. | Burlington, MA : Jones & Bartlett Learning, [2018] | Includes bibliographical references and index.
Identifiers: LCCN 2017010699 | ISBN 9781284126266
Subjects: | MESH: Stress, Psychological--therapy | Adaptation, Psychological | Mind-Body Therapies--methods | Psychophysiology--methods
Classification: LCC RA785 | NLM WM 172.4 | DDC 616.9/8--dc23
LC record available at https://lccn.loc.gov/2017010699

6048

Printed in the United States of America
24 23 22 21 20   10 9 8 7 6 5 4 3 2 1

To all my friends and family,
and to the many great people I have encountered
who have served as dynamic inspirations in my own life journey,
thanks for making this a better world in which to live.

A portion of the royalty derived from the sale of
this book will be donated to several nonprofit
organizations dedicated to environmental conservation
and health promotion.

"No problem can be solved from the same level of consciousness that created it."
— Albert Einstein

"Your time is limited, so don't waste it living someone else's life. Don't be trapped by dogma, which is living with the results of other people's thinking. Don't let the noise of others' opinions drown out your own inner voice. And most important, have the courage to follow your heart and intuition. They somehow already know what you truly want to become. Everything else is secondary."
— Steve Jobs

Brief Contents

PART 1
The Nature of Stress 1

1 The Nature of Stress 2
2 The Sociology of Stress 27
3 Physiology of Stress 44
4 Stress and Disease 61

PART 2
The Mind and Soul 97

5 Toward a Psychology of Stress 98
6 The Stress Emotions: Anger, Fear, and Joy 125
7 Stress-Prone and Stress-Resistant Personality Traits 146
8 Stress and Human Spirituality 167

Contents

Foreword .... *viii*
Preface .... *ix*
Acknowledgments .... *xiii*
How to Use This Book .... *xiv*
Student & Instructor Resources .... *xvi*
Praise for Managing Stress .... *xx*
Introduction .... *xxii*

PART 1
The Nature of Stress 1

1 The Nature of Stress 2
Times of Change and Uncertainty 2
Definitions of Stress 5
The Stress Response 6
Tend and Befriend 7
Types of Stress 8
Types of Stressors 10
Bioecological Influences 10
Psychointrapersonal Influences 11
Social Influences 11
Social Stress in America: A Twenty-first Century Look 11
The General Adaptation Syndrome 13
Stress in a Changing World 15
Stress and Insomnia 15
College Stress 17
A Holistic Approach to Stress Management 19
Summary 24
Study Guide Questions 24
References and Resources 25

2 The Sociology of Stress 27
Technostress 29
Digital Toxicity, FOMO (Fear of Missing Out), and Digital Dementia 32
A Decline in Civility 33
Environmental Disconnect 35
Occupational Stress 39
Race and Gender Stress 40
Summary 42
Study Guide Questions 42
References and Resources 42

3 Physiology of Stress 44
The Central Nervous System 45
The Vegetative Level 45
The Limbic System 45
The Neocortical Level 46
The Autonomic Nervous System 47
The Sympathetic and Parasympathetic Nervous Systems 47
The Endocrine System 50
The Neuroendocrine Pathways 52
The ACTH Axis 53
The Vasopressin Axis 54
The Thyroxine Axis 55
A Parable of Psychophysiology 55
Three Decades of Brain Imaging Research 56
Summary 58
Study Guide Questions 58
References and Resources 59

4 Stress and Disease 61
Theoretical Models 62
The Borysenko Model 63
The Pert Model 67
The Lipton Model 69
The Gerber Model 70
The Pelletier Premodel 78
DNA, Telomeres, Stress, and Aging 82
Target Organs and Their Disorders 82
Nervous System–Related Disorders 84
Immune System–Related Disorders 87
Summary 91
Study Guide Questions 91
References and Resources 92

PART 2
The Mind and Soul 97

5 Toward a Psychology of Stress 98
Freud and the Egg 99
Jung and the Iceberg 102
Elisabeth Kübler-Ross: The Death of Unmet Expectations 106
Viktor Frankl: A Search for Life's Meaning 108
Wayne Dyer: Guilt and Worry 110
The Sin of Guilt 111
The Art of Worrying 111
Leo Buscaglia: The Lessons of Self-Love 112
Abraham Maslow: The Art of Self-Actualization 115
Martin Seligman: Optimism and the Art of Being Happy 118
A Tibetan Perspective of Mind and Stress 120
Some Theoretical Common Ground 121
Summary 122
Study Guide Questions 122
References and Resources 123

6 The Stress Emotions: Anger, Fear, and Joy 125
The Anatomy of Anger..................... 126
Gender Differences.........................127
Physiological Responses 129
The Myth of Catharsis 129
Anger Mismanagement Styles................131
Creative Anger Strategies....................132
The Anatomy of Fear 134
Basic Human Fears.........................135
Fear, Vulnerability, and Shame 137
Strategies to Overcome Fear 138
Depression: A By-Product of Anger or Fear?.............................. 138
Joy, Eustress, and the Art of Happiness 139
Summary................................ 142
Study Guide Questions 142
References and Resources................... 143

7 Stress-Prone and Stress-Resistant Personality Traits 146
Type A Behavior 148
Hostility: The Lethal Trait of Type A's 149
Behavior Modification for Type A Behavior.....150
Social Influences on Type A Behavior 150
Did Someone Say Type D Personality? 151
Codependent Personality Traits.............. 151
Helpless-Hopeless Personality 155
Resiliency: The Hardy Personality 156
Survivor Personality Traits.................. 158
Sensation Seekers......................... 160
Self-Esteem:The Bottom-Line Defense 161
Summary................................ 164
Study Guide Questions 164
References and Resources................... 165

8 Stress and Human Spirituality 167
A Spiritual Hunger? 168
A Turning Point in Consciousness 169
Definition of Spirituality.................... 171
Theories of Human Spirituality.............. 172
The Path of Carl Jung........................173
The Path of M. Scott Peck 175
The Path of Hildegard von Bingen 177
The Path of Black Elk 177
The Path of Matthew Fox 179
The Path of Joan Borysenko 181
The Path of Deepak Chopra 182
The Path of Jesus of Nazareth................184
The Path of Joseph Campbell 186
The Path of Lao Tzu 188
The Path of Albert Einstein..................189
Common Bonds of Human Spirituality 191
Centering Process (Autumn).................192
Emptying Process (Winter) 192
Grounding Process (Spring)..................193
Connecting Process (Summer)................194
A Model of Spirituality for Stress Management...194
Internal and External Relationships...........194
Personal Value System 196
Meaningful Purpose in Life..................197
The Divine Mystery 199
Spiritual Potential and Spiritual Health.........199
Roadblocks and Interventions................199
Current Research on Spirituality and Health 200
Summary................................ 203
Study Guide Questions 204
References and Resources................... 204

Glossary *547*

Foreword

Courtesy of Larry Dossey, MD.

"After ecstasy, the laundry!" This ancient saying can be applied to our current understanding of health and illness. During the past 50 years, we have discovered that, beyond doubt, the mind has an enormous impact on the body. Our emotions, thoughts, attitudes, and behaviors can affect us for good or ill. Now that we have glimpsed these lofty insights, it's time to get down to practicalities and apply them. It's time, in other words, to do the laundry. But the task isn't simple. How, exactly, can we bring mind and body into harmony? How can we alleviate the stressful effects of modern life? How can they be turned to our advantage? Can we learn to benefit from these changes? Can we become wiser and healthier in the process? Advice is not difficult to find, as self-proclaimed experts are everywhere. They tout the latest formulas for stress-free living and personal transformation from tabloids, talk shows, and a plethora of self-help books, giving the entire area of stress management a bad name.

It is refreshing, amid all this blather, to discover Dr. Brian Luke Seaward's *Managing Stress: Principles and Strategies for Health and Well-Being*. In clear, uncluttered language, he takes us on a gentle walk through the territory of mind–body interaction. From cover to cover you will find that he is a very wise guide and possesses a quality almost always missing in stress management manuals: humor. Dr. Seaward knows the field well—he has taught it and lived it—and he provides scientific documentation at every step. But perhaps most importantly, Dr. Seaward daringly goes beyond the usual approach to the subject to speak of the soul and of human spirituality. He realizes that stress management and maximal health are impossible to attain unless the questions of life's meaning are addressed.

Since *Managing Stress* first came out in 1994, the pace of life has certainly quickened. With this change, Americans have begun to embrace a host of complementary healing modalities, which underscores the importance of seeking a sense of inner peace from the winds of change.

As a physician who has long advocated the integration of mind and body for optimal health, I find it a pleasure and honor, therefore, to recommend this work. It is a fine contribution to the field of stress management and will serve as an invaluable guide to anyone seeking harmony in his or her life. A new day is dawning in medicine and health promotion, and Dr. Seaward has awoken early to watch and share the sunrise.

— Larry Dossey, MD
Executive Editor, *Explore: The Journal of Science and Healing*
Former Executive Editor, *Alternative Therapies in Health and Medicine*
Author of *Reinventing Medicine, One Mind,* and *Healing Words*

Preface

STRESS: THE NEW NORMAL?

Young adults today are growing up in a world that is very different from not only that of their parents, but also that of their older siblings. Since the first edition of *Managing Stress* came out two decades ago, experts agree the world has become a much more frenetic place to live. In the approximately 20 years that this book has been in print there have been cultural revolutions in daily life, including significant changes to the music industry (iTunes), the news industry, the job market, the banking industry, the communication industry, the hotel industry (Airbnb), and the cab industry (Uber), not to mention daily changes in social media and the emergence of new ways to share information. Add to this layer of complexity various health issues, including the increase in autism, the Zika virus, obesity, diabetes, teen suicide, and opioid addiction, as well as the increase in population and shifting demographics, such as increased Latino, Asian, and Muslim populations and the growing number of senior citizens. There is a great quote from Roy Blixer stating that "the only person who likes change is a wet baby." By and large, people don't like change, particularly change that they cannot control. Magazine headlines that once suggested various ways to decrease stress now tell us that stress is here to stay (so get used to it). Stress is the new normal. Despite the rapidly changing dynamics on planet Earth, what hasn't changed are the means to find your center, your sense of inner peace.

Experts from a host of disciplines have been commenting on the state of information processing today in the Wi-Fi digital age. The prognosis is not necessarily good. People are spending the vast majority of their time, perhaps all of it, in what has become known as "short-form information processing" and "short-form messaging." In simple terms, this means cherry-picking information for specific facts, without taking time to process the larger context of the facts or taking time for critical thinking, synthesis, creative thinking, and memorization. Metaphorically speaking, people today are missing the entire forest because they are staring at one or two trees.

The proliferation of iPads, smartphones, and other electronic devices, coupled with instant access to information and decreased attention spans, has begun to change (some say decrease) the intellectual capacity of the twenty-first–century citizen. What is being lost is what is now called "slow, linear thinking skills," along with intuitive-based knowledge. *Knowledge* (a domain of mental well-being) is the ability to gather, process, recall, and communicate information. *Wisdom* is the alchemy of knowledge and experience (real, not virtual) accrued over time. Time, however, is a rare commodity today, and more and more experience is viewed through a computer screen. People are opting for information rather than knowledge. As a result, wisdom becomes ever more rare.

Stated simply: There is a big difference between information gathering (for example, facts and figures) and the application of deep-seated wisdom. All-too-common examples include people who venture into national parks for a day's hike unprepared, without proper equipment or supplies. Such people often have cell phones and GPS tracking devices, which they then use to call for help when stranded on a mountaintop or when they have fallen down cliffs. Facts and figures cannot replace common sense (accrued wisdom), nor is a reliance on technology an excuse for ignorance. Stressful times, such as those in which we are living, necessitate wisdom.

Managing Stress is a synthesis of wisdom: accrued knowledge and personal experience over time. More than just a collection of facts and figures, *Managing Stress* connects the dots for nearly all aspects of stress through the ageless wisdom of the mandala template of mind, body, spirit, and emotions. *Managing Stress* is also a process of transformation, in which one moves from a motivation of fear toward a motivation of love and compassion. Mountains are a symbol of strength in times of change, which is why this symbol was chosen as the cover art for this ninth edition.

A quick glance at any headline makes it obvious that dramatic change is in the air. Global warming, energy demands, terrorism, personal bankruptcy, water shortages, advances in technology, and new diseases are a few of the many changes sweeping Earth as we speak. As planetary citizens, we are not immune to change. Moreover, with change comes stress, and humans are not immune to stress either. But with each change we encounter we have a choice to view it as a threat or an opportunity for growth. This new edition offers a unique synthesis of timeless wisdom from various world cultures, combined with new insights, research studies, and practical approaches to empower you to become resilient to stress during these times of dramatic change.

Many of the multicultural concepts in this edition are considered to be ageless wisdom, also known as *common sense*. But as the expression goes, "Common sense is not too common when people are stressed." As newly initiated members of the Wi-Fi generation, people not only expect instant information retrieval but also perfect sound bites of wisdom to accommodate their every need (rarely does a sound bite solve a life problem). As such, experts have coined the term "disposable knowledge" to describe the Internet mentality of failing to dig beyond the surface (or the first ten listings of a Google search) to really gain a handle on information content. This book digs beneath the surface to reveal an alchemy of ageless wisdom, current research, and practical tips for you to have the best skills and resources for your personal life journey. As several students have said to me, "*Managing Stress* not only connects the dots; it builds a bridge to a better life."

When *Managing Stress* was first published in 1994, it broke new ground. Never before had the focus of a college textbook presented such a holistic perspective of health and well-being under the influence of stress. Twenty years ago, you would have been hard pressed to find the word *spirituality* in a college textbook, yet today it would seem awkward not to address this aspect of health. Indeed, many of the topics and aspects that were considered at the vanguard a decade ago are now so familiar that they have become household words: t'ai chi, hatha yoga, echinacea, Pilates, meridians, and chakras, to name a few. As the global village knocks on your doorstep, insights from Asia, Africa, and Latin America offer a multicultural approach to seeking and maintaining balance in our lives. Perhaps it's no secret that as the pace of life continues to increase, so does the hunger for credible information to create and maintain a sense of balance in these times of change. As the first edition of *Managing Stress* found its place on bookshelves across the country, it became known as the "Bible" of stress management. I am happy to say that I continually hear it described that way. I am also happy to hear so many comments on the writing style, layout, and production of the textbook: aesthetically pleasing to the eyes, easy to read and understand. A lot of work goes into the selection of photographs, cartoons, and artwork to make this book visually appealing and engaging. As with all previous editions, a conscious decision was made not to include stress-inducing photographs. The television news and the Internet are saturated with these types of images, and my intention is to maintain a positive energy between the covers of this book.

WHAT IS NEW AND IMPROVED IN THIS NINTH EDITION?

The topic of stress and stress management (now called *resiliency*) is quite dynamic, and as such there is always new information to add to the ever-growing body of knowledge. Here are some things added to place this ninth edition on the cutting edge of this colossal topic.

Chapter 1: The Nature of Stress

- Social Stress in America: New research by the American Psychological Association as well as the Harvard School of Public Health now highlights the issues of stress and health well beyond the work of Holmes and Raye. Additional studies on stress by NPR and Kaiser Health also point to what they call the burden of stress in America, from big life changes to daily hassles.

- Stress and insomnia have been linked for a long time, and now this new edition adds seven ways to improve your sleep hygiene for better sleep.

Chapter 2: The Sociology of Stress

- *Technostress* may not be new, but new research highlights the problems with repeated use of screen devices, including the outsourcing of our memory to technology. New terms in the lexicon of technostress include *digital toxicity* and *digital dementia*. This section highlights a few studies about the dangers of being distracted time and again by our screen devices, thus causing more stress.
- The environmental disconnect continues to grow as more news reveals the problems nationwide with our drinking water (e.g., Flint, Michigan) and the serious climate change flooding precautions, which add to one's stress level.

Chapter 3: Physiology of Stress

- A Closer Look at Panic Attacks—from Physiology to Treatment: Many students experience their first panic attack in college, and more and more people across the country seem to be experiencing this phenomenon. Often described as the "Stress response on steroids" this section takes you through the experience and how to deal with it.

Chapter 4: Stress and Disease

New to this chapter are several topics that beg for attention regarding stress and disease; these are topics that are likely to be in the news for quite some time.

- The Human Microbiome & Stress: The secret life of healthy gut bacteria. New research suggests that understanding the gut is essential to understanding health. With more than 70 percent of our immune system in the gut, the connections between stress and disease are overwhelming.
- Lyme Disease and Stress: New studies indicate that Lyme disease (and its co-infections) is an emerging national epidemic and the connections to stress are powerful and serious. This section takes a closer look at this debilitating autoimmune disease.
- DNA, Telomeres, Stress, and Aging: Nobel prize–winning research on the topic of telomeres and stress is now headline news, with implications for health and longevity.
- Stress and Inflammation: Inflammation seems to be tied to a great many health issues. This section reveals the connection between stress and inflammation.

Chapter 6: The Stress Emotions: Anger, Fear, and Joy

- Fear: Vulnerability and Shame (Brene Brown)

The stress emotions are complicated, yet researcher Brene Brown has made it a lot less complicated by shedding light on the aspects of vulnerability and how this can perpetuate fear rather than resolve it.

- Happiness: More ways to understand and pursue eustress. Studies on the topic of happiness reveal that we can have a positive effect on our state of mind by the choices we make and the perceptions we hold.

Chapter 10: Healthy Boundaries: Behavior Modification

- Because the term "behavior modification" sounds boring, and because so many issues with stress involve poor boundaries, the title of this chapter was updated to reveal the need to create healthy boundaries.

Chapter 12: Expressive Art Therapy

- A small section was added to include the new trend with adult coloring books, now used as an accepted coping technique for stress.

Chapter 13: Humor Therapy (Comic Relief)

- A small section was added to include the topic of Laughter yoga, a coping technique for stress that combines humor and support groups for a more powerful means to cope with stress.

Chapter 14: Creative Problem Solving

- A small section was added to the obstacles of creativity from best-selling author, Elizabeth Gilbert (*Eat, Pray, Love*) about fear as a destructive role in the creative process. A human feature story (Stress with a Human Face) was added to this chapter to show students that one of their own used the content of this chapter to resolve stress in her life.

Chapter 17: Additional Coping Techniques

- Hawaiian Forgiveness: Ho'oponopono

With so much anger in the world today, learning to resolve it is essential to finding a sense of inner peace. One of the newest takes on coping with stress is the Hawaiian modality of forgiveness called *Ho'oponopono*.

Chapter 19: Meditation and Mindfulness

- A small section was added about the executive function of the brain and how this compares to the left brain/right brain understanding of consciousness.

STRESS MANAGEMENT IN A RAPIDLY CHANGING WORLD

As with each new edition, this revision contains highlights of the latest state-of-the-art research on all aspects of stress management. This book strikes a fine balance between highlighting the landmark research on health psychology, psychoneuroimmunology, and holistic healing and the newest research studies, theories, and applications of effective stress management in our rapidly changing world.

Although it may seem like health care is in a state of flux, from a different perspective it appears to be on the cusp of a new revolution where mind, body, and spirit are seen as equal parts of the whole. Once again, *Managing Stress* stands at the vanguard as the premier resource for holistic (mind–body–spirit) stress management.

Since the creation of the Office of Alternative Medicine at the National Institutes of Health in 1993 (now called the National Center for Complementary and Integrative Health), more money and more research has been focused on a host of healing modalities that fall under the domain of complementary or "integrative" medicine. Every technique for stress management is considered at some level to fall into the category of complementary or alternative medicine. Although at best the conclusions can only be drawn from outcomes due to the dynamics of the mind–body–spirit paradigm, the interest in this field only continues to grow. This book bears the collective fruit of this growing body of knowledge.

I urge readers to consider *Managing Stress* as an invitation to further explore all of the many topics highlighted in this book in greater depth through other books, articles, and experts in each respective field. No one book can contain all of the information on any topic, let alone this one, but it is my hope that this book sets you on a path toward a well-balanced life.

Acknowledgments

When Maureen Stapleton won her Oscar for Best Supporting Actress in 1982 for her role in the movie *Reds*, she walked up to the podium and said, "I'd like to thank everyone I ever met." At times writing this book, and working on all its many editions, I have felt much the same way. In fact, I would like to include many people I have never met but whose work and wisdom have found their way into this book. While I would like to share my gratitude with everyone—and you know who you are, including Joe Pechinski, Dave Clarke, Candace Pert, James Owen Mathews, and my invaluable mentors Elisabeth Kübler-Ross and Larry Dossey—there are simply too many friends, colleagues, scholars, and luminaries to list here. A very special thanks to Mark Ellison and Sally Cadman for their insightful feedback on Chapter 28, *Ecotherapy: The Healing Power of Nature*. Heartfelt gratitude to Randy Glasbergen and Brad Veley for the use of their wonderful cartoons. Huge thanks also to all my students, friends, and colleagues too numerous to mention, who were so kind to allow me to use their art therapy pieces or pose for countless photos used in this book. I am forever grateful. Special thanks go to Cathy Esperti, Carter McCalister, Nancy Hitchcock, and Wes DeShano at Jones & Bartlett Learning, who are simply awesome. Thanks for making this *Ninth Edition* the best ever. The phrase "it takes a village" certainly applies here, so thanks to everyone who has been and continues to be part of my "village."

How to Use This Book

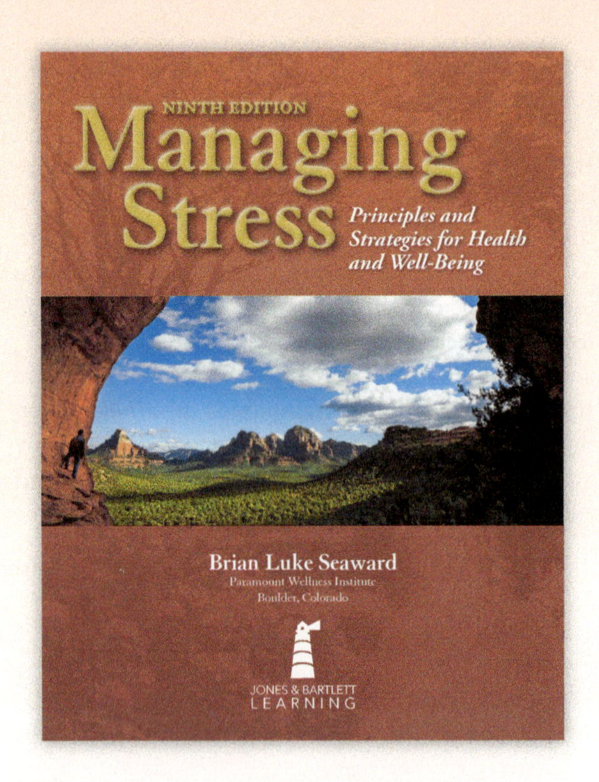

Based on the concept of holistic wellness, where the whole is always greater than the sum of the parts, *Managing Stress*'s content and format uniquely offer insights on the integration, balance, and harmony of mind, body, spirit, and emotions throughout each section and in various chapters (for example, the concept of entrainment can be found in Chapter 4, *Stress and Disease*, and Chapter 22, *Music Therapy*). Like the wellness paradigm it is based on, *Managing Stress* is formatted in a mandala of four parts:

- **Part 1: The Nature of Stress** (physiology, stress, and disease)
- **Part 2: The Mind and Soul** (mental, emotional, and spiritual aspects as they relate to stress)
- **Part 3: Coping Strategies** (promoting insights and resolution of stressors)
- **Part 4: Relaxation Techniques** (promoting physical homeostasis)

This book integrates all four components of the wellness paradigm. First, because it is so visible, we will look at stress from the physical point of view, including both the dynamics involved in fight-or-flight and the most current theories attempting to explain the relationship between stress and disease. We then focus on mental and emotional factors, outlining pertinent theoretical concepts of psychology: the stress emotions, anger and fear, as well as specific personality types that are thought to be either prone or resistant to stressful perceptions. (More cognitive aspects are covered in Part 3.) The much-neglected component of spiritual well-being will round out the first half of the book, showcasing selected theories of this important human dimension and its significant relationship to stress. The remainder of the book will focus on a variety of coping strategies and relaxation techniques, and come full circle to the physical realm of wellness again, with positive adaptations to stress promoted through the use of physical exercise. As you will surely find, true to the wellness paradigm, where all components are balanced and tightly integrated, there will be much overlap among the physical, mental, emotional, and spiritual factors in these chapters, as these factors are virtually inseparable. And just as the word *stress* was adopted from the discipline of physics, you will see that some other concepts and theories from this field are equally important to your ability to relax (such as entrainment).

True to the nature of holistic stress management, there is no separation or division between mind and body, emotions and spirit, or any of these four aspects. As such, you will see cross-referencing between chapters to help you connect the dots so that your understanding of the mind–body–spirit connection is solid. You may find it best to start with Chapter 1, *The Nature of Stress,* and continue straight through to the end of Chapter 8, *Stress and Human Spirituality*, to gain the best perspective of this colossal topic. From there you can cherry-pick information on which coping techniques and relaxation techniques work best for you. Keep in mind that the best approach is to try them all to find which is most effective for you.

Each chapter of the text has a number of pedagogical devices designed to aid in the mastery of the material, including feature boxes, surveys, key terms, exercises, and checklists.

Case studies titled Stress with a Human Face illustrate how real people deal with a variety of stressful situations.

Stress with a Human Face

Courtesy of Juliet Simbo.

Society, and the culture it creates, is often described in metaphors. A common one is "the social fabric." For Juliet, a more apt metaphor might be a carpet, one that was pulled right from underneath her feet as a child. Juliet Mamie Simbo now lives in Denver, Colorado, but at the age of 13 she and her family fled from Sierra Leone, a small country on the west coast of Africa. She begins her story with a Hollywood reference:

"If you have seen the movie *Blood Diamond*, starring Leonardo DiCaprio and Jennifer Connelly, then you have witnessed a realistic portrayal of the horrors of civil war in Sierra Leone. I lived in this world. I witnessed my dad held at gunpoint on our porch on January 10th, 1999, by a rebel who told all of us that he was going to kill my father and suck his blood because of his vocal opposition to the atrocities being committed in my country. The gunman spared my father's life; however, in a defiant move, he turned and shot and killed our family dog. Because of greed and hatred amongst the people of my country, death came to many in Sierra Leone for seemingly no reason. I was changed forever by these events, knowing that my life was kept alive by the slimmest of margins."

As an immigrant to the United States, she had to adapt quickly to a whole new culture, one with superhighways, fast food, snowstorms, power shopping, abundant lifestyle opportunities, high technology, and crumbling family structures. "Initially, I felt lost and lonely as I tried to merge into the fast lane that is the American lifestyle," she explained. But over time, Juliet became less shy and more assertive, adapting successfully to a new way of life in a new culture. With college graduation months away, her eyes are now set on new sights. One day Juliet hopes to return to Africa and use her knowledge, skills, and experience to help make the world a better place, beginning with the severe hunger issues known in this part of the world.

Juliet has used her experience of cultural differences in a positive way and hopes that others will do the same. As she said in her high school graduation speech, "I say to you, open your eyes to the world beyond your country's borders. Feel the presence of humanity around the world and learn about them, even experience their culture. I hope that one day, you can be as grateful as I am for what you know about a different land and people. I thank you for being a part of my world, and I welcome you to visit mine."

Key terms are clearly defined in the text where the term first appears to help with comprehension and expand your professional vocabulary.

Walter Cannon: Twentieth-century Harvard physiologist who coined the term "fight or flight."

Fight-or-flight response: A term coined by Walter Cannon; the instinctive physiological responses preparing the body, when confronted with a threat, to either fight or flee; an evolutionary survival dynamic.

Stress reaction: The body's initial (central nervous system) reaction to a perceived threat.

Freeze response: Part of the stress response, where the individual neither fights nor flees but freezes like a deer caught in the headlights, paralyzed as if the person has forgotten to run.

Homeostasis: A physiological state of complete calmness or rest; markers include resting heart rate, blood pressure, and ventilation.

Stress response: The release of epinephrine and norepinephrine to prepare various organs and tissues for fight or flight.

End of chapter summary appears at the end of each chapter and contains a comprehensive summary of the main points in the chapter along with study guide questions and references for further study.

SUMMARY

- Physical exercise is a form of stress: the enactment of all the physiological systems that the fight-or-flight response triggers for physical survival.
- Physical exercise is classified as either anaerobic (fight) or aerobic (flight). Anaerobic (without oxygen) is a short, intense, and powerful activity, whereas aerobic exercise (with oxygen) is moderately intense activity for a prolonged period of time. Aerobic exercise is the better type to promote relaxation.
- The body adapts, either negatively or positively, to the stress placed upon it. Proper physical exercise will cause many adaptations that in the long term are thought to be effective in reducing the deleterious effects of stress by returning the body to a profound state of homeostasis. Physical exercise allows the body to use stress hormones for their intended purposes, detoxifying the body of stress hormones by utilizing them constructively.
- To get the benefits of physical exercise, four criteria must be met: intensity, duration, frequency of training, and mode of exercise. Together they are called the all-or-none principle, meaning that without meeting all four requirements few if any benefits will be gained. It takes between 6 and 8 weeks to see significant benefits in the body.
- The positive effects of physical exercise are lowering resting heart rate, resting blood pressure, and muscle tension, and a host of other functions that help maintain or regain physiological calmness.
- Exercise evokes not only physiological changes, but various psychological changes (e.g., runner's high) as well, again suggesting that mind and body act as one entity. Habitual physical exercise produces both physiological homeostasis and mental homeostasis. Individuals who engage in regular physical exercise report higher levels of self-esteem and lower incidences of depression and anxiety.
- Although the primary purpose of food is as a source of nutrients, many people use food as a means to fill an emotional void created by stress.
- Because of the global condition of soil depletion, even a healthy diet is considered deficient in the essential vitamins and minerals so that supplementation is encouraged.
- A malnourished diet—one that is deficient in essential amino acids, essential fats, vitamins, and minerals—is itself a stressor on the body.
- Research has shown that some foods actually induce a state of stress. Excess amounts of sugar, caffeine, salt, and foods poor in vitamins and minerals weaken the body's resistance to the stress response and may ultimately make a person more vulnerable to disease and illness.
- Not all supplements are created equal. Check to see that the processing does not destroy what it is intended to promote. Taken in excess, supplements can do more harm than good by inhibiting the proper digestion and absorption of essential nutrients.
- Food you eat can either boost or suppress the immune system.
- Food affects not only the physical body, but the mental, emotional, and spiritual aspects as well. The concept of spiritual nutrition suggests eating a wide variety of fruits, vegetables, and grains that nurture the health of the seven primary *chakras*. In addition, spiritual nutrition suggests ensuring a balance in all aspects of food, including the acid/base balance.
- Eating disorders are emotionally rather than physiologically based, ranging from bulimia and anorexia to overeating—all of which have serious consequences if not resolved.
- Change various aspects of your diet, including reducing or eliminating the consumption of caffeine, refined sugar, sodium, and fats, to reduce the risk of stress-related problems.

Box features throughout the chapters provide unique current and historic perspectives on key topics, questionnaires, and things to consider.

BOX 27.2 Insomnia and Physical Exercise

One of the benefits of exercise that has been touted by exercise physiologists for years is the fact that regular rhythmical (cardiovascular) exercise promotes quality sleep and decreases symptoms of insomnia. The very nature of physical exercise increases one's metabolic activity, thus increasing one's body-core temperature. As the body returns to homeostasis after a vigorous workout, body-core temperature drops. During sleep, the body-core temperature is at its lowest point as a result of decreased metabolic activity. Research shows that the drop in body-core temperature that occurs when bedtime is four to six hours after a vigorous workout promotes drowsiness and deeper (delta waves) sleep than in nonactive individuals. For this reason, it is suggested *not* to engage in strenuous physical activity shortly before bedtime. According to *Power Sleep* author James Maas, the best time to schedule a workout is around the noon hour or late afternoon, with morning exercise having the least effect on sleep quality. The best type of exercise to ensure a good night's sleep is cardiovascular in nature, including vigorous walking, jogging, swimming, or biking that elevates the heart rate to one's specific target zone for the desired duration. All types of rhythmic exercise utilize the cocktail of stress hormones for their intended purposes and help the body metabolize what's not used in this process as waste products for elimination.

Student & Instructor Resources

NAVIGATE 2 ADVANTAGE ACCESS

Each new book comes complete with a dynamic online resource packed with instructor and student resources! Navigate 2 Advantage Access provides an interactive eBook, workbook activities, audio engagement with the author, meditation audio and video, as well as assessments, knowledge checks, learning analytics reporting tools, and more.

Relaxation Media and Audio Introductions

In his own words, the author, Brian Luke Seaward, introduces each of the four sections in the book. He provides a summary of each chapter in the section and explains why the information is so important to the understanding and management of stress. This is a great resource for students and instructors!

The author also includes four relaxation audio files as well as a relaxation video—perfect to listen to while studying, meditating, or simply relaxing.

The Art of Peace and Relaxation Workbook, Ninth Edition

The new edition of the workbook is now available only through our Navigate 2 product. Worksheets are included as printable and/or writable PDFs.

Lesson Plans

This edition includes 26 lesson plans and class exercises created specifically for students and participants in the author's holistic stress management certification workshop. The lesson plans have been adapted for instructors who use *Managing Stress* as a college textbook.

Interactive Lectures

The following 16 unique audio and closed-captioned visual interactive lectures contained in Navigate 2 provide a powerful, comprehensive exposure to the holistic (mind, body, spirit, and emotions) approach to stress management, including both cognitive (coping) skills, a host of relaxation techniques, and personal life skills for optimal health and well-being (also known as mind-body-spirit homeostasis). In each weekly lesson, these online lectures combine both theoretical and experiential learning through a series of exercises to give the user the life skills to promote peace, relaxation, and optimal health.

Lesson 1: Welcome to the Stress of Life

Stress knows no demographic boundaries. It affects everyone and is often called the "equal opportunity destroyer." We begin by looking at the nature of stress, various types of stress, and stressors, followed by some definitions of stress and some classic background from experts who first studied the concept of stress. This lesson then progresses to expand your comprehension beyond the Western "mechanistic" approach to a complete wellness dynamic, including the mental, emotional, physical, and spiritual aspects, known collectively as the *holistic perspective*. Combined with this content is an introduction to a very basic relaxation technique called *diaphragmatic breathing*.

Lesson 2: SOS: Message in a Bottle

Is the world in deep trouble? Perhaps! Stress may be a perception, but many external factors are coming together in an unprecedented way that influence these perceptions. This lesson looks at several social factors that can so greatly fan the flames of personal stress. We conclude with a time-tested coping skill: journal writing as a means to release stress-based emotions and gain clarity in one's thoughts.

Lesson 3: The Stress or Relaxation Barometer

To really know what effects stress has on the body, you must first understand the basics of stress physiology. This lesson takes a closer look at the physiology of stress (both short term and long term). It also explains a classic relaxation technique, progressive muscular relaxation, that can help you understand stress physiology.

Lesson 4: Headaches, Lupus, and Hemorrhoids, Oh My!

The association between stress and disease is colossal. From tension headaches to cancer, our thoughts and the associated emotions can directly affect our health. Is the physical body the first or last place that the symptoms of disease and illness manifest? This lesson explores two perspectives of the stress and disease dynamic through several models of the stress and disease phenomenon: a holistic and a mechanistic approach. By understanding the mind–body connection, you become empowered to maintain or return to homeostasis.

Lesson 5: Reprogramming the Software of the Mind

By and large, stress begins as a perception—an interpretation of some event that we perceive as a threat. As such, it is essential to understand the framework of the mind (thoughts, perceptions, attitudes, beliefs, opinions, and emotions) to manage stress effectively. By becoming familiar with various theories of psychology, one can better achieve this goal to turn the perceived threat into a nonthreat and move on with one's life. This lesson begins with some basic fundamentals of psychology, through the eyes of stressful perceptions, and then highlights a formidable tool, cognitive restructuring (also known as *reframing*) to use in everyday life.

Lesson 6: Feeling the Stress, Feeling the Love

In simple terms, there are two stress emotions: anger (fight) and fear (flight). But nothing is simple about stress. There are actually hundreds of stress emotions, including joy and happiness (eustress). This lesson takes a closer look at the two primary stress emotions (anger and fear) as well as ways to deal creatively with each so that you control your emotions rather than having them control you. We also look at the emotions associated with good stress (eustress) followed by specific aspects of personality that can either promote stress or help buffer against it.

Lesson 7: Minding the Body, Mending the Mind

Art therapy is a formidable coping technique that serves as an emotional release (catharsis) for unresolved emotions. Through the use of various media, feelings and thoughts can be expressed in ways that verbal language simply cannot articulate, thus opening the door to resolution and inner peace. Muscle tension is the number one symptom of stress. Physical relaxation is also a powerful stress reducer. Hence, massage is accepted as a much-desired relaxation technique. This lesson also explores bodywork (massage therapy) as a relaxation medium.

Lesson 8: Health of the Human Spirit

Spiritual well-being is very much a part of health and wellness, but it is so often ignored in dealing effectively with stress. Left unaddressed, stress can choke the human spirit. For this reason (and many others), human spirituality is very much a part of stress and stress management. In fact, spirituality is considered by many to be the cornerstone of holistic stress management regarding relationships, values, and a meaningful purpose in life, aspects that are related to every stressor. This lesson invites you to take a closer look at this often-ignored wellness component by exploring many different perspectives from various luminaries around the world.

Lesson 9: Change This!

We all have ideas on how we can improve our lives by tweaking some habits that throw gasoline on the fire of stress. Luckily, there is help. This lesson takes a look at several types of behavior that can push one over the edge and, equally important, ways to examine and change behavior for the better by becoming more assertive, more confident, and embracing change for the better.

Lesson 10: Be the Calm in the Eye of the Storm

Today, everyone is bombarded with sensory overload, from Facebook updates and YouTube links to thousands of text messages. How does anyone stay grounded in these cyber winds of change? The answer is meditation: a simple way to calm the mind of perpetual sensory bombardment and information overload, not to mention common emotional issues. Meditation is not a religion! It is a simple technique for mental training, and every athlete does it. Speaking of athletes, many athletes do a form of meditation called T'ai Chi ch'uan, often called a "moving meditation" that is also a great means of relaxation.

Lesson 11: Imagination Is More Powerful Than Knowledge

It has been said that we have the means to solve our own problems (stressors). We just need to use our heads. If stress can be disempowering, creativity is considered very empowering. Creativity allows you to have options. Einstein said that imagination was more powerful than knowledge. It was the empowerment aspect of creativity he referred to. We begin to explore the creative process and then see how it can help us solve problems (both big and small). The mind not only has the power to create options, it also has the power to promote relaxation and healing through the use of mental imagery and visualization, very effective relaxation skills.

Lesson 12: Good Vibrations

The sound of laughter and the sound of music may not seem to have much in common, but they are both regarded as ways to ease stress and lighten the heart. From an energy perspective, they are both known as "good vibrations." Humor, that which can promote laughter, is one of the finest coping techniques known to humanity. Music has been recognized for millennia as a soothing relaxation technique.

Lesson 13: Coping and Relaxation Techniques, Part I

It has been said often that time and money (more likely the lack thereof) are the causes of tremendous stress. Perhaps we have all felt this way at one time or another. By understanding the psychology of money and time, one can better navigate the shoals of stress. Good communication skills are also very important for this navigation because many stressors involve interactions with others. This lesson focuses on refining several effective coping skills essential for personal homeostasis. One of the most common techniques to promote relaxation is called *progressive muscular relaxation* (PMR). An exploration of this technique rounds out this lesson.

Lesson 14: Coping and Relaxation Techniques, Part II

There are hundreds of ways to cope with stress, from hobbies to dream therapy, all of which help give insights to our problems and help us to work toward resolution. This lesson examines some additional coping techniques that are important to include in your toolkit of stress management. Combined with this is a closer look at Hatha yoga as an essential relaxation skill. Hatha yoga has gone mainstream in the United States. More specifically, it has gone corporate (which is really the antithesis of Hatha yoga). We explore the basics of yoga as it was originally taught several thousand years ago.

Lesson 15: The Power of Suggestion

The mind has an incredible power to heal (make whole). This has been recognized the world over in many types of relaxation efforts, including autogenic training, clinical biofeedback, and ecotherapy. This lesson takes a closer look at these methods that can help the mind work with the body to achieve a greater sense of relaxation and homeostasis.

Lesson 16: A Healthy Body: Back to Basics

Stress begins in the mind but quickly ends up in the body. Perhaps the most effective relaxation technique is an activity that engages the stress response, which is exactly what physical exercise does. Exercise is stress to the body, but a controlled stress. We cannot talk about exercise without addressing nutritional habits. Moreover, we really cannot talk about stress without addressing nutrition as well. For this reason we discuss several important factors to consider when incorporating exercise and nutrition in your overall stress management program.

Additional Instructor Resources

- Test Bank
- Slides in PowerPoint format
- Instructor's Manual
- Discussion Questions
- Lecture Outlines
- Lesson Plans
- Grading and Analytics Tools

Praise for *Managing Stress*

PROFESSIONALS

Hi Luke,

Thank you so much for talking to the classes yesterday. It truly is so generous of you to do this for the students. Your answers to their varied topics were perfect, even the more challenging questions such as the GMO inquiry. The students said that they really enjoyed the opportunity to talk with you. They liked that you were so accessible and down-to-earth friendly. Also, we appreciated the extra info on Lyme disease and your reassuring words about optimism.

Teri Harbour
Frederick Community College
Frederick, MD

Hi Luke,

Thank you so much for volunteering your time and speaking with my class yesterday. It was wonderful for the students to have the opportunity to digitally meet and talk with you and gain another perspective on stress management. I appreciate you sharing more information for the student's question and sharing the letter from an AU student. It's a beautiful letter that nicely shows the impact you have on students. Thanks again for the opportunity to share yourself and work with my students!

Best wishes,
Ethan Mereish, PhD
The American University
Washington, D.C.

"This book helps students to approach stress management in a livable, realistic, and creative way. It recognizes the premise that coping with stress is a 'total' experience and Seaward's approach to spirituality and stress really opened the minds and hearts of both myself and my students. As one of my students reflected: 'This class has not only taught me an extreme amount of useful information, but learning effective ways to deal with it, coupled with the daily practice of relaxation techniques and journal writing skills, will encourage me to continue these practices after class ends.' Personally, this book has helped me refocus on taking time to practice the skills I teach and how these skills must be a part of my daily life."

— Jacqueline R. Benedik, MS, CHES, Health Educator

"Dr. Seaward's book is the best resource I have found for teaching a holistic approach to coping with stress. Whether I concentrate on one hour of cognitive restructuring for unemployed professionals, one day of stress and spirituality for nurses, or a semester course for university students, it provides the material I need. It's reader friendly, rich in references, and full of humor!"

— Paula LeVeck, RN, PhD

"Stress is at the heart of most all diseases that society faces today. Brian Luke Seaward's book goes right to the root causes of stress and communicates cutting-edge material. My hope is that more people will put this information to practice by tapping into their inner strength so that we can combat the disease crisis, including obesity, cancer, and coronary heart disease."

— Kelly Stobbe, MEd, Wellness Councils of America, Director of Council Affairs

"*Managing Stress* is the perfect textbook for my graduate course in stress management for advanced practice nurses. It blends beautifully the research, clinical, and educational components of each topic—a rare find! It is sophisticated enough for advanced students, yet accessible to first-time readers on this subject."

— Valerie Yancey, PhD, St. Louis, MO

"*Managing Stress* is a unique textbook in that it serves as an essential guide to the exploration of the interaction of the mind, body, and spirit. Dr. Seaward brings us an extensive, current, and well-researched review of approaches to stress management in a clear and uncomplicated style. This book, with its seamless blend of theory, skill building, and coping techniques, is a gift to us all."

— Elaine Matheson Weiner, RN, MPH, CHES, Manhattan Beach, CA

"Brian Luke Seaward's book, *Managing Stress: Principles and Strategies for Health and Well-Being*, is the most comprehensive text on stress management I've used for teaching. What makes this book so exceptional is the weaving of science, spirit, and individual stories into an organized, holistic format conducive to personal and professional learning. I would recommend this text for any educator interested in providing the most current research on a growing field that is having such an impact on the lives of individuals yearning to find balance in their lives."

— Jamie Damico, RN, MSN, CNS, Colorado Springs, CO

"I highly recommend Luke's text to any college professor who teaches stress management. It is a comprehensive and holistic approach to stress management in that one fully walks away with a clear and in-depth understanding of the wide variety of causes and effects, as well as the many wonderful adoptable options for managing stress. I have reviewed many stress-management books, and I have found this book to be unequivocally the best one."

— Susan Kennen, Professor, Health Education, Poughkeepsie, NY

"From humor to heart disease, history to holistic, physical exercise to prayer, *Managing Stress* covers all aspects of this worldwide epidemic. With its smorgasbord of techniques to manage stress, it's the perfect book on how to improve quality of life and increase joy, vitality, and inner calm. It's informative, fun, and best of all, it inspired this reader into action. It is a must-read for anyone interested in living a healthier, happier life."

— Conee Spano, Health Educator, Las Vegas, NV

STUDENTS

"The information I have learned from this book is definitely something I will remember and use the rest of my life. I found the exercises on breathing, yoga, and aromatherapy most beneficial."

— Christine S., University of Northern Colorado

"The chapter on time management was the best. Before this class I was extremely good at wasting time. Now I realize that time is an important resource that I need to make the most of. I do this by keeping a daytimer, prioritizing, and cutting out a lot of television. Thanks!"

— Jason A., Indiana University

"Just from reading the first chapter, I knew this was a book I wasn't going to sell back at the end of the semester. This book has been my saving grace. Thanks!!!"

— Bill G., Richland College, Dallas, TX

"The most valuable thing I got out of the whole book was dealing with my anger. I never knew I was holding it in. I now know how to let it go and not let my feelings ruin my life. The chapters on music therapy and breathing were excellent."

— Melanie B., University of Northern Colorado

"By far the most significant aspect of this book was the chapter on human spirituality. Even though I had heard most of the information before, it has never been presented to me in such a broad yet concise manner. It refreshed my desire to continue to grow spiritually."

— Ivette B., University of New Mexico

"I had no idea how beneficial keeping a journal is to help ease the tension that occurs in everyday life."

— Emily B., University of Vermont

"It is a great comfort to know there is more than one way to deal with stress. Many times in college, I have found myself very stressed out and in need of relief. I now have many techniques to promote a less stressful lifestyle."

— Aspen V., University of Maryland

"Like most textbooks, I thought this one was going to be boring. Boy, was I wrong! I learned a great deal about my body, my mind, and my spirit. As an athlete, I now have skills for a lifetime. The chapter on humor therapy was the best! Keep those jokes coming."

— Will C., University of Utah

Introduction

During the Renaissance, a philosophy shaping the direction of medicine in the Western world started taking hold. This philosophy, promulgated by René Descartes (1596–1650), stated that the mind and body are separate entities and therefore should be examined and treated differently. This dichotomy of mind and body advanced the understanding of the true human condition. Albert Einstein's revolutionary unified field theory, which at the time was regarded as ludicrous, began to lead Western science back to the ancient premise that all points (energy and matter) connect, each significantly affecting all others, of which the human entity (mental, emotional, physical, and spiritual components) is very much a part.

Only recently has modern science taken steps to unite what Descartes separated over 360 years ago. The unity of the body, mind, and spirit is quite complex, especially as it relates to stress management. But one simple truth is emerging from the research of the late twentieth century: The physical, mental, emotional, and spiritual aspects of the human condition are all intimately connected. Mental imagery, entrainment theory, *pranayama*, divinity theory, split-brain research, Jungian psychology, and beta-endorphins all approach the same unity, each from a different vantage point, and each supporting the ancient axiom that "all points connect."

Stress is a hot topic in American culture today. Its popularity stems from the need to get a handle on this condition—to deal with stress effectively enough so as to lead a "normal" and happy life. But dealing with stress is a process, not an outcome. Many people's attitudes, influenced by their rushed lifestyles and expectations of immediate gratification, reflect the need to eradicate stress rather than to manage, reduce, or control their perceptions of it. As a result, stress never really goes away; it just reappears with a new face. The results can and do cause harm, including bodily damage. Studies now indicate that between 70 and 80 percent of all disease is strongly related to, if not directly associated with, stress. So-called lifestyle diseases, such as cancer and coronary heart disease, are leading causes of death; both seem to have direct links to the stress response. Healthcare reform having become a major national issue, the ability of and the need for individuals to accept responsibility for their own health is increasing. But knowledge of the concepts of stress management alone is not enough. Continual application of this knowledge through both self-awareness and the practice of effective coping skills and relaxation techniques is essential for total well-being.

Thus, this book was written to acquaint you with the fundamental theories and applications of the mind–body–spirit phenomenon. More specifically, it offers more than sixteen coping strategies you can use as tools to deal more effectively with the causes of your stress, and twelve relaxation techniques to help you reduce or eliminate potential or actual symptoms associated with the stress response. It is my intention that collectively they may help you to reach and maintain your optimal level of physical, mental, emotional, and spiritual well-being in the years to come. For this reason, I would like to suggest that you revisit the book again and again as time goes by. What may appear today to be "some theory" to memorize for a final exam could one day take on great relevance in your life.

PART ONE

The Nature of Stress

Life is either a daring adventure or nothing at all.

– Helen Keller

CHAPTER 1

The Nature of Stress

I cannot and should not be cured of my stress, but merely taught to enjoy it.

—Hans Selye

Are you stressed? If the answer is yes, then consider yourself to be in good company. Several recent Harris and Gallup polls have noted an alarming trend in the psyche of the American public and beyond—to nearly all citizens of the global village. Across the board, without exception, people admit to having an increasing sense of anxiety, frustration, unease, and discontent in nearly every aspect of their lives. From the lingering effects of the Great Recession and subsequent job market challenges to fracking issues, genetically modified food allergies, increases in autism, overpopulation, climate change weather incidents (e.g., Hurricane Sandy and severe droughts), world banking issues, and gun violence and terrorist attacks (from Sandy Hook Elementary to the Boston Marathon), the symptoms of global **stress** can be found everywhere. Ironically, in a country where the standard of living is considered to be one of the highest anywhere in the world, the Centers for Disease Control and Prevention estimates that nearly one-quarter of the American population is reported to be on antidepressants, and current estimates suggest that one in three people suffers from a chronic disease, ranging from cancer and coronary heart disease to rheumatoid arthritis, diabetes, and lupus. Something is very wrong with this picture!

Stress: The experience of a perceived threat (real or imagined) to one's mental, physical, or spiritual well-being, resulting from a series of physiological responses and adaptations.

Furthermore, since the start of the Great Recession, a blanket of fear and anger has covered much of the country, if not the world, keeping people in a perpetual state of frustration and anxiety. Global problems only seem to intensify our personal stressors. It doesn't make a difference if you're a college student or a CEO of a multinational corporation, where you live, or how much money is in your checking account; stress is the equal opportunity destroyer! But it doesn't have to be this way. Even as personal issues collide with social and planetary problems, creating a "perfect storm" of stress, we all have choices—in both our attitude and behaviors. This text will help you connect the dots between mind, body, and spirit to create positive choices that empower you to navigate your life through the turbulent waters of the human journey in the twenty-first century.

Times of Change and Uncertainty

Today, the words *stress* and *change* have become synonymous and the winds of change are in the air. Changes in the economy, technology, communications, information retrieval, health care, and dramatic changes in the weather are just some of the gale forces blowing in our collective faces. By and large, the average person doesn't like change because change tends to disrupt one's comfort zones. It appears that the "known," no matter how bad, feels like a safer bet than the unknown. Change, it should be noted (particularly change one cannot control), has always been part of the human landscape. However, today the rate of change has become so fast and furious, without an adequate reference point to anchor oneself, that stress holds the potential to create a perpetual sense of uneasiness in the hearts and minds of nearly everyone. Yet it doesn't have to be this way. Where there is change, there is opportunity. Where there is opportunity, there is comfort.

At one time, getting married, changing jobs, buying a house, raising children, going back to school, dealing with the death of a friend or close relative, and suffering from a chronic illness were all considered to be major life events that might shake the foundations of anyone's life. Although these major life events can and do play a significant role in personal upheaval, a new crop of social stressors has added to the critical mass of an already volatile existence, throwing things further out of balance. Consider how these factors directly influence your life: the rapid acceleration of technology (from software upgrades to Internet downloads), the use of (if not addiction to) the World Wide Web (e.g., Facebook), the proliferation of smartphones and Wi-Fi use, an accessible 24/7 society, global economic woes (e.g., unemployment, food prices), global terrorism, carbon footprints, and public health issues (e.g., the latest epidemic of bedbugs or Zika virus). Times of change and uncertainty tend to magnify our personal stress. Perhaps the biggest looming concern facing people today is the issue of personal boundaries or the lack thereof. The advances of high technology combined with a rapidly changing social structure have eroded personal boundaries. These boundaries include, but are not limited to, home and work, finances, nutritional habits, relationships, and many, many more, all of which add to the critical mass of one's personal stress. Even the ongoing war on terrorism appears to have no boundaries! Ironically, the lack of boundaries combined with factors that promote a fractured society, where people feel a lack of community and belonging, leads to a greater sense of isolation, which also intensifies our personal stress levels. Believe it or not, life wasn't always like this.

The stress phenomenon, as it is referred to today, is quite new with regard to the history of humanity. Barely a household expression when your parents were your age, use of the word *stress* is now as common as the terms *global warming* and *smartphone apps*. In fact, however, stress in terms of physical arousal can be traced back to the Stone Age as a "survival mechanism." But what was once designed as a means of survival is now associated with the development of disease and illness that claims the lives of millions of people worldwide. The American Institute of Stress (www.stress.org) cites the following statistics:

- 43 percent of all adults suffer adverse health effects due to stress.
- 80 percent of all visits to primary care physicians are for stress-related complaints or disorders.

Stress has been linked to all the leading causes of death, including heart disease, cancer, lung ailments, accidents, cirrhosis, and suicide. Some health experts now speculate that perhaps as much as 70 to 85 percent of all diseases and illnesses are stress-related.

Government figures compiled by the National Center for Health Statistics in 2010 provide a host of indicators suggesting that human stress is indeed a health factor to be reckoned with. Prior to 1955, the leading causes of death were the sudden onset of illness by infectious diseases (e.g., polio, rubella, tuberculosis, typhoid, and encephalitis) that, in most cases, have since been eradicated or brought under control by vaccines and medications. The post–World War II era ushered in the age of high technology, which considerably altered the lifestyles of nearly all peoples of every industrialized nation. The start of the twenty-first century has seen the influence of high technology dramatically alter our lifestyles. Consumer products, such as the washer, dryer, microwave oven, television, DVD player, laptop computer, and even cell phones, were cited as luxuries to add more leisure time to the workweek. But as mass production of high-technology items increased, so too did the competitive drive to increase human effort and productivity, which in turn actually decreased leisure time, and thus created a plethora of unhealthy lifestyles, most notably obesity.

Currently, the leading causes of death are dominated by what are referred to as "lifestyle diseases," those diseases whose pathology develops over a period of several years, and perhaps even decades (FIG. 1.1). Whereas infectious diseases are treatable by medication, lifestyle diseases are, for the most part, preventable or correctable by altering the habits and behaviors that contribute to their etiology. Previously, it was suggested that an association existed between stress and disease. Substantial research, however, suggests that there may, indeed, be a causal factor involved

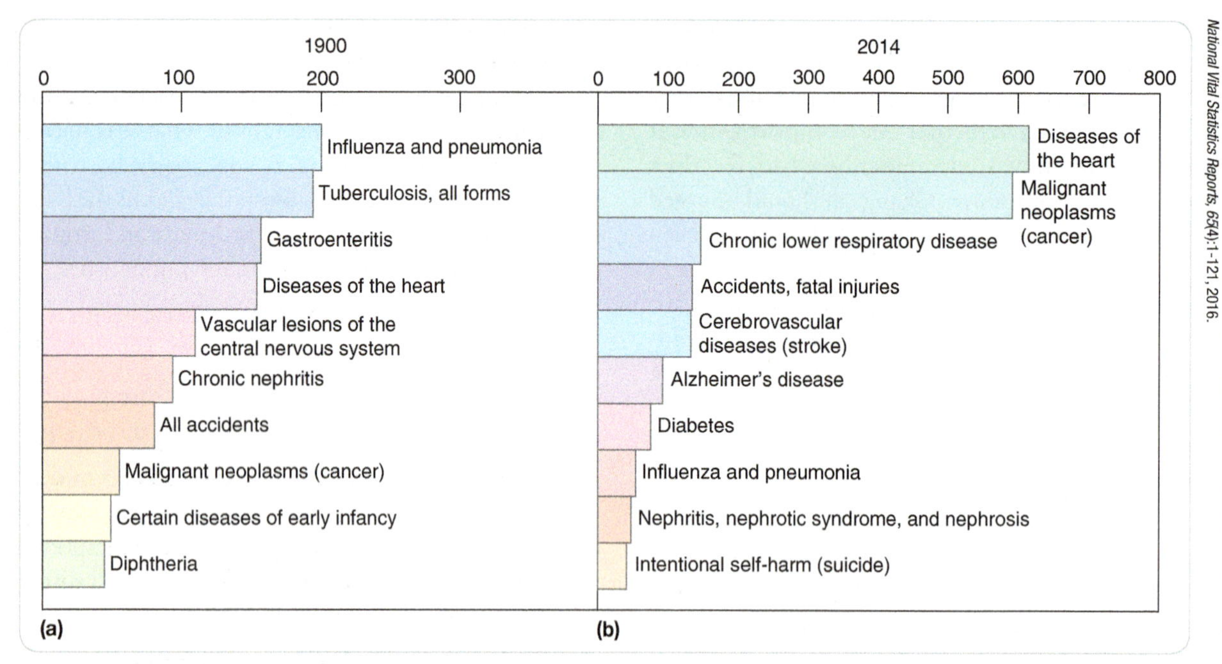

Data from (a) National Center for Health Statistics, Washington, D.C., 2010.; (b) Kochanek, K.D., Murphy, S.L., Xu, J., and Tejada-Vera, B., Division of Vital Statistics. Deaths: Final Data for 2014, *National Vital Statistics Reports, 65*(4):1-121, 2016.

FIGURE 1.1 Death rates for the ten leading causes of death per 100,000 population in the United States in (a) 1900 and (b) 2014.

with several types of diseases, particularly autoimmune diseases (Segerstrom and Miller, 2004). Regardless, it is well understood that the influence of stress weakens the body's physiological systems, thereby rapidly advancing the disease process. The most notorious lifestyle disease, coronary heart disease (CHD), continues to be one of the leading causes of death in the United States, far exceeding all other causes. The American Heart Association states that one person dies from heart disease every minute. Although the incidence of CHD has decreased over the past decade, cancer—in all its many types—continues to climb the statistical charts as the second leading cause of death. According to 2013 statistics from the American Cancer Society (www.cancer.org), cancer claims the lives of one out of every four people in the United States. Alarming increases in suicides, child and spouse abuse, self-injury, homicides, alcoholism, and drug addiction are only additional symptoms of a nation under stress. Today, research shows that many people maintain poor coping skills in the face of the personal, social, and even global changes occurring over the course of their lives.

Originally, the word *stress* was a term used in physics, primarily to describe enough tension or force placed on an object to bend or break it. Relaxation, on the other hand, was defined as any nonwork activity done during the evenings or on Sunday afternoons when all the stores were closed. On rare occasions, if one could afford it, relaxation meant a vacation or holiday at some faraway place. Conceptually, relaxation was a value, influenced by several religions and represented as a day of rest. The word *stress* as applied to the human condition was first made popular by noted physiologist Hans Selye in his book *The Stress of Life,* in which he described his research: to understand the physiological responses to chronic stress and its relationship to disease (dis-ease). Today, the word *stress* is frequently used to describe the level of tension people feel is placed on their minds and souls by the demands of their jobs, relationships, and responsibilities in their personal lives. Oddly, for some, stress seems to be a status symbol tied to self-esteem. Relaxation, meanwhile, has been transformed from an American value into a luxury many people find they just don't have enough time for. Despite the current economic crisis, some interesting insights have been observed regarding work and leisure. The average workweek has expanded from 40 to 60 hours. The U.S. Department of Labor and Statistics reports that with more service-related jobs being created, more overtime is needed to meet the demands of the customers. Not only do more people spend more time at work, they spend more time driving to and from work (which is not considered work time). Moreover, leisure time at home is often related to work activities, resulting in less time for rest and relaxation. Downtime is also compromised. Since

FIGURE 1.2 With rapid economic, ecological, and technological changes, the global village appears to have become a more stressful place, which is all the more reason to learn and practice effective stress-management techniques to maintain a sense of balance in one's life despite these winds of change.

2001, Expedia has conducted an annual survey on vacations (called the Vacation Deprivation survey). The 2012 results revealed that one out of every three Americans doesn't use all of his or her vacation time. One in five respondents cited work responsibilities/pressure as the primary reason for canceling a vacation. A new word entered the American lexicon in the summer of 2010—the "staycation," in which people simply stayed home for vacation due to financial or work constraints. Those who do head for the mountains or beaches for vacation often take their work (in the form of smartphones and laptops) with them—in essence, never really leaving their job. It's no surprise that staying plugged in doesn't give the mind a chance to unwind or the body a chance to relax. By comparison with other countries, Americans take less vacation time than other global citizens (Germans, on average, take 4 to 6 weeks per year). "The stress associated with the current economy makes the need for time away from work even more important than ever, and it's unfortunate that one-third of Americans won't use all of their vacation days this year," said Tim MacDonald, general manager of Expedia.com. The "dividend" of high technology has proven to be an illusion for many that has resulted in a stressed lifestyle, which in turn creates a significant health deficit (FIG. 1.2).

Definitions of Stress

In contemporary times, the word *stress* has many connotations and definitions based on various perspectives of the human condition. In Eastern philosophies, stress is considered to be an absence of inner peace. In Western culture, stress can be described as a loss of emotional control. Noted healer Serge Kahili King has defined stress as any change experienced by the individual. This definition may be rather general, but it is quite correct. Psychologically speaking, stress, as defined by noted researcher Richard Lazarus, is a state of anxiety produced when events and responsibilities exceed one's coping abilities. Physiologically speaking, stress is defined as the rate of wear and tear on the body. Selye added to his definition that stress is the nonspecific response of the body to any demand placed upon it to adapt, whether that demand produces pleasure or pain. Selye observed that whether a situation was perceived as good (e.g., a job promotion) or bad (e.g., the loss of a job), the physiological response or arousal was very similar. The body, according to Selye, doesn't know the difference between good and bad stress.

However, with new psychoneuroimmunological data available showing that there are indeed some physiological differences between good and bad stress (e.g., the release of different neuropeptides), specialists in the field of **holistic medicine** have expanded Lazarus's and Selye's definitions as follows: Stress is the inability to cope with a perceived (real or imagined) threat to one's mental, physical, emotional, and spiritual well-being, which results in a series of physiological responses and adaptations (Chopra, 2000; Dossey, 2004). The important word to emphasize here is *perceived* (the interpretation), for what might seem to be a threat to one person may not even merit a second thought to another individual. For example, not long ago a raffle was held, with the winning prize being an all-expenses-paid one-week trip for two to a beach resort in Bermuda. Kelly, who won the prize, was ecstatic and already had her bags packed. Her husband, John, was mortified because he hated to fly and he couldn't swim. In his mind, this would not be a fun time. In fact, he really wished they hadn't won. Each perceived the same situation in two entirely different ways. Moreover, with the wisdom of hindsight, our perceptions often change. Many episodes that at the time seemed catastrophic later appear insignificant, as humorously stated by Mark Twain when he commented, "I'm an old man and I have known

Holistic medicine: A healing approach that honors the integration, balance, and harmony of mind, body, spirit, and emotions to promote inner peace. Every technique used in stress management is considered to support the concept of holistic medicine.

a great many troubles, but most of them never happened." The holistic definition of stress points out that it is a very complex phenomenon affecting the whole person, not just the physical body, and that it involves a host of factors, some of which may not yet even be recognized by scholars and researchers. As more research is completed, it becomes increasingly evident that the responses to stress add up to more than just physical arousal; yet it is ultimately the body that remains the battlefield for the war games of the mind.

The Stress Response

In 1914, Harvard physiologist **Walter Cannon** first coined the term **fight-or-flight response** to describe the dynamics involved in the body's physiological arousal to survive a threat. In a series of animal studies, Cannon noted that the body prepares itself for one of two modes of immediate action: to attack or fight and defend oneself from the pursuing threat, or to run and escape the ensuing danger. What Cannon observed was the body's reaction to acute stress, what is now commonly called the **stress reaction.** Additional observations suggested that the fight response was triggered by anger or aggression and was usually employed to defend territorial boundaries or attack aggressors equal to or smaller in size. The fight response required physiological preparations that would recruit power and strength for a short duration, or what is now described as short but intense anaerobic work. Conversely, the flight response, he thought, was induced by fear. It was designed to fuel the body to endure prolonged movement such as running away from lions and bears. In many cases, however, it included not only fleeing, but also hiding or withdrawal. (A variation on the flight response is the **freeze response**, often noted with post-traumatic stress disorder, where a person simply freezes, like a deer staring into a car's headlights.) The human body, in all its metabolic splendor, actually prepares itself to do both (fight and flight) at the same time. In terms of evolution, it appears that this dynamic was so advantageous to survival that it developed in nearly all mammalian species, including us. (Some experts now suggest, however, that our bodies have not adapted to the stress-induced lifestyles of the twenty-first century.)

In simple terms, there are four stages of the fight-or-flight response:

Stage 1: Stimuli from one or more of the five senses are sent to the brain (e.g., a scream, the smell of fire, the taste of poison, a passing truck in *your* lane).

Stage 2: The brain deciphers the stimulus as either a threat or a nonthreat. If the stimulus is not regarded as a threat, this is the end of the response (e.g., the scream came from the television). If, however, the response is decoded as a real threat, the brain then activates the nervous and endocrine systems to quickly prepare for defense and/or escape.

Stage 3: The body stays activated, aroused, or "keyed-up" until the threat is over.

Stage 4: The body returns to **homeostasis,** a state of physiological calmness, once the threat is gone.

It is hypothesized that the fight-or-flight response developed primarily against threats of a physical nature, those that jeopardized the survival of the individual. Although clear physical threats still exist in today's culture, including possible terrorism, they are nowhere near as prevalent as those threats perceived by the mind and, more specifically, the ego. In a theory put forward by a disciple of Selye's, Simeons (1961), and repeated by Sapolsky (2009), it is suggested that, in effect, the fight-or-flight response is an antiquated mechanism that has not kept evolutionary pace with the development of the human mind. Consequently, the **stress response** becomes activated in all types of threats (mental, emotional, and spiritual), not just physical intimidations. The physiological repercussions can, and do, prove fatal. The body enters a state of physical readiness when you are about to receive your final exam grades or walk into an important meeting late, just as it does when you sense someone is following you

Walter Cannon: Twentieth-century Harvard physiologist who coined the term "fight or flight."

Fight-or-flight response: A term coined by Walter Cannon; the instinctive physiological responses preparing the body, when confronted with a threat, to either fight or flee; an evolutionary survival dynamic.

Stress reaction: The body's initial (central nervous system) reaction to a perceived threat.

Freeze response: Part of the stress response, where the individual neither fights nor flees but freezes like a deer caught in the headlights, paralyzed as if the person has forgotten to run.

Homeostasis: A physiological state of complete calmness or rest; markers include resting heart rate, blood pressure, and ventilation.

Stress response: The release of epinephrine and norepinephrine to prepare various organs and tissues for fight or flight.

FIGURE 1.3 Some of our worst stressors are fabricated in our minds.

late at night in an unlit parking lot. Moreover, this same stress response kicks in, to the same degree and intensity, even when the threat is wholly imaginary, in reaction to everything from monsters hiding under your bed when you were 4 (FIG. 1.3), to the unsubstantiated idea that your boss doesn't like you anymore and is out to get you.

Cannon noted the activation of several physiological mechanisms in this fight-or-flight response, affecting nearly every physiological system in the body, for the preparation of movement and energy production. These are just a few of the reactions:

1. Increased heart rate to pump oxygenated blood to working muscles
2. Increased blood pressure to deliver blood to working muscles
3. Increased ventilation to supply working muscles with oxygen for energy metabolism
4. Vasodilation of arteries to the body's periphery (arms and legs) with the greatest muscle mass
5. Increased serum glucose for metabolic processes during muscle contractions
6. Increased free fatty acid mobilization as an energy source for prolonged activity (e.g., running)
7. Increased blood coagulation and decreased clotting time in the event of bleeding
8. Increased muscular strength
9. Decreased gastric movement and abdominal blood flow to allow blood to go to working muscles
10. Increased perspiration to cool body-core temperature

Unfortunately, the metabolic and physiological changes that are deemed essential for human movement in the event of attack, pursuit, or challenge are quite *ineffective* when dealing with events or situations that threaten the ego, such as receiving a parking ticket or standing in a long line at the grocery store, yet the body responds identically to all types of perceived threats.

Tend and Befriend

Do women respond differently to stress than men? The answer may seem obvious.

Generally speaking, men are prone to act more hostile while women have a proclivity to be more nurturing. Yet until recently every source on stress addressed the fight-or-flight response as if it were the only human default response. It was the work of Shelley Taylor and colleagues who filled in the missing piece with regard to the female response to stress. Curious about why only men were studied to formulate the basis for the fight-or-flight response, Taylor hypothesized that the stress response needed to be reexamined, this time including astute observations of the female gender. In 2000, Taylor and colleagues proposed a new theory for the female stress response that they termed **tend and befriend.** Although both men and women have a built-in dynamic for the survival of physical danger, women also have an inherent nurturing response for their offspring as well as a means

Tend and befriend: A theory presented by Shelley Taylor that states that women who experience stress don't necessarily run or fight, but rather turn to friends to cope with unpleasant events and circumstances.

to befriend others. This in turn creates a strong social support system, an invaluable coping technique. Taylor suggests that the female response to stress is hardwired into the DNA and revealed through a combination of brain chemistry and hormones. The biological basis for tend and befriend appears to be the hormone oxytocin, now regarded as both the "trusting hormone" and the "social affiliation" hormone. Although oxytocin is found in both women and (to a lesser degree) men, estrogen is known to enhance the effects of oxytocin in the brain. The tend-and-befriend behavior is built on connectedness—a caregiving process, possibly triggered by a release of oxytocin in conjunction with female reproductive hormones, that may actually override the flood of stress hormones so pronounced in women's male counterparts. Generational social factors may support the tend-and-befriend behavior pattern as well (FIG. 1.4).

Not only do men and women have differences in their stress physiology, but there appears to be gender-specific behaviors for discussing and solving problems as well. Whereas men tend to think their way through by looking for solutions to problems, women like to talk about problems. Women bond quickly by sharing confidences. However, although talking may be beneficial, researchers note that merely talking about stressors tends to perpetuate rather than solve one's stressors. Researchers refer to stress-based conversations as **co-rumination**. Although talking may strengthen female friendships, it is also known to increase anxiety and depression if solutions aren't introduced quickly. Experts warn against "unhealthy rumination" and the emotional contagion that results from it (Stepp, 2007).

FIGURE 1.4 Fight or flight isn't the only response to stress. To cope with personal problems, women often feel the need to socialize and bond together in what is now known as the "tend and befriend" response.

It is fair to say that the concepts of survival are complex and perhaps not so neatly packaged by hormones or gender. Women are known to back-stab their "friends" and regrettably, on occasion, ditch their newborn babies in dumpsters and run away. Conversely, some men choose peace over violence (Gandhi and Martin Luther King, Jr., come to mind) and, when times get tough, some men are known to bond together over a beer or game of golf.

Types of Stress

To the disbelief of some, not all stress is bad for you. In fact, there are many who believe that humans need some degree of stress to stay healthy. The human body craves homeostasis, or physiological calm, yet it also requires physiological arousal to ensure the optimal functioning of several organs, including the heart and musculoskeletal system. How can stress be good? When stress serves as a positive motivation, it is considered beneficial. Beyond this optimal point, stress of any kind does more harm than good.

Actually, there are three kinds of stress: **eustress**, **neustress**, and **distress**. Eustress is good stress and arises in any situation or circumstance that a person finds motivating or inspiring. Falling in love might be an example of eustress; meeting a movie star or professional athlete may also be a type of eustress. Usually, situations that are classified as eustress are enjoyable and for this reason are not considered to be a threat. Neustress describes sensory stimuli that have no consequential effect; it is considered

Co-rumination: Stress-based conversations between women as a means of coping by finding support among friends.

Eustress: Good stress; any stressor that motivates an individual toward an optimal level of performance or health.

Neustress: Any kind of information or sensory stimulus that is perceived as unimportant or inconsequential.

Distress: The unfavorable or negative interpretation of an event (real or imagined) to be threatening that promotes continued feelings of fear or anger; more commonly known simply as stress.

neither good nor bad. News of an earthquake in a remote corner of the world might fall into this category. The third type of stress, distress, is considered bad and often is abbreviated simply as *stress*. There are two kinds of distress: **acute stress**, or that which surfaces, is quite intense, and disappears quickly; and **chronic stress**, or that which may not appear quite so intense, yet seems to linger for prolonged periods of time (e.g., hours, days, weeks, or months). An example of acute stress is the following. You are casually driving down the highway, the wind from the open sunroof is blowing through your hair, and you feel pretty good about life. With a quick glance in your rearview mirror you see flashing blue lights. Yikes! So you slow down and pull over. The police car pulls up behind you. Your heart is racing, your voice becomes scratchy, and your palms are sweating as you try to retrieve license and registration from your wallet while rolling your window down at the same time. When the officer asks you why you were speeding you can barely speak; your voice is three octaves higher than usual. After the officer runs a check on your car and license, he only gives you a warning for speeding. Whew! He gets back in his car and leaves. You give him time to get out of sight, start your engine, and signal to get back onto the highway. Within minutes your heart is calm, your palms dry, and you start singing to the song on the radio. The threat is over. The intensity of the acute stress may seem cataclysmic, but it is very short-lived.

Chronic stressors, on the other hand, are not as intense but their duration is unbearably long. Examples might include the following: being stuck for a whole semester with "the roommate from hell," a credit card bill that only seems to grow despite monthly payments, a boss who makes your job seem worse than that of a galley slave, living in a city you cannot tolerate, or maintaining a relationship with a girlfriend, boyfriend, husband, or wife that seems bad to stay in but worse to leave. For this reason, chronic stressors are thought to be the real villains. According to the American Institute of Stress (AIS), it is this type of stress that is associated with disease because the body is perpetually aroused for danger.

A concept called the **Yerkes-Dodson principle**, which is applied to athletic performance, lends itself quite nicely to explaining the relationship between eustress, distress, and health. As can be seen in FIG. 1.5, when stress increases, moving from eustress to distress, performance or health decreases and there is greater risk of disease and illness. The optimal stress level is the midpoint, *prior* to where eustress turns into distress.

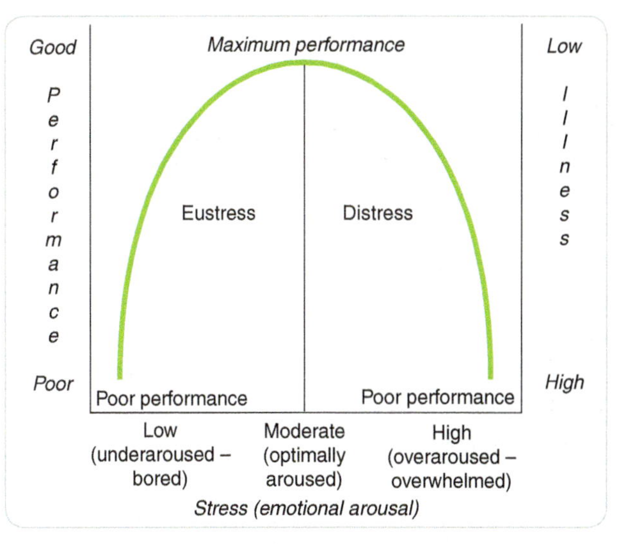

FIGURE 1.5 The Yerkes-Dodson curve illustrates that, to a point, stress or arousal can actually increase performance. Stress to the left of the midpoint is considered to be eustress. Stress beyond the midpoint, however, is believed to detract from performance and/or health status and is therefore labeled distress.

Studies indicate that stress-related hormones in optimal doses actually improve physical performance and mental-processing skills like concentration, making you more alert. Beyond that optimal level, though, all aspects of performance begin to decrease in efficiency. Physiologically speaking, your health is at serious risk. It would be simple if this optimal level was the same for all people, but it's not. Hence, the focus of any effective stress-management program is twofold: (1) to find out where this optimal level of stress is for you so that it can be used to your advantage rather than becoming a detriment to your health status, and (2) to reduce physical arousal levels using both coping

Acute stress: Stress that is intense in nature but short in duration.

Chronic stress: Stress that is not as intense as acute stress but that lingers for a prolonged period of time (e.g., financial problems).

Yerkes-Dodson principle: The theory that some stress (eustress) is necessary for health and performance but that beyond an optimal amount both will deteriorate as stress increases.

skills and relaxation techniques so that you can stay out of the danger zone created by too much stress.

Types of Stressors

A situation, circumstance, or any stimulus that is perceived to be a threat is referred to as a **stressor**, or that which causes or promotes stress. As you might imagine, the list of stressors is not only endless, but also varies considerably from person to person. Acute stress is often the result of rapid-onset stressors—those that pop up unexpectedly—like a phone call in the middle of the night or the discovery that you have lost your car keys. Usually the body begins to react before a full analysis of the situation is made, but a return to a state of calm is also imminent. Chronic stressors—those that may give some advance warning yet manage to cause physical arousal anyway, often merit more attention because their prolonged influence on the body appears to be more significant. Much research has been conducted to determine the nature of stressors, and they are currently divided into three categories: bioecological, psychointrapersonal, and social (Giradano, Everly, and Dusek, 2012).

Bioecological Influences

There are several biological and ecological factors that may trigger the stress response in varying degrees, some of which are outside our awareness. These are external influences, including sunlight, gravitational pull, solar flares, and electromagnetic fields, that affect our biological rhythms. From the field of chronobiology we learn that these factors affect three categories of biological rhythms: (1) **circadian rhythms**, fluctuations in physiological functions over the course of a 24-hour period (e.g., body temperature); (2) **ultradian rhythms**, fluctuations that occur over less than a 24-hour period (such as stomach contractions and cell divisions); and (3) **infradian rhythms**, changes that occur in periods longer than 24 hours (e.g., the menses). These biological changes are influenced by such natural phenomena as Earth's orbit and axis rotation, which give us periods of light and darkness as well as seasonal differences (FIG. 1.6). A prime example of a bioecological influence is **seasonal affective disorder (SAD)**, a condition affecting many people who live at or near the Arctic Circle. Many of these people become depressed when they are deprived of sunlight for prolonged periods of time. But technological changes are also included in this category, an example being jet lag as a result of airplane travel through several time zones. Electrical pollution, environmental toxins, solar radiation, and noise pollution are other potential bioecological influences. Genetically modified organisms (GMOs), petrochemicals, synthetic chemicals, and some types of nanotechnology are considered new bioecological threats. In addition, some synthetic food additives may trigger the release of various stress hormones throughout the body. Note that there is a growing opinion among some health practitioners that increased stress levels in the

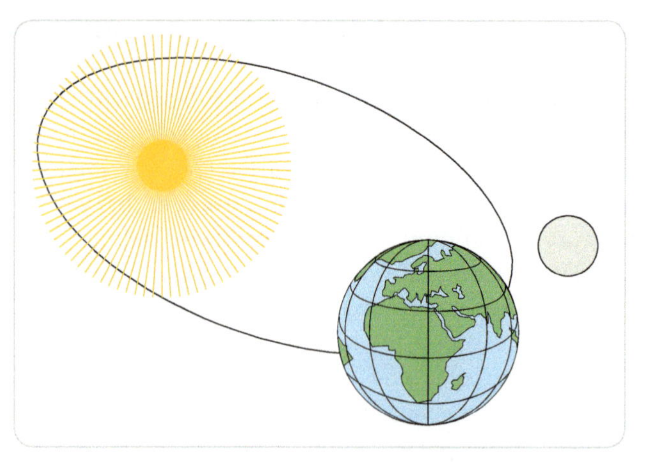

FIGURE 1.6 Because of the tilt of Earth's axis as it moves in its orbit around the sun, areas closest to the poles vary the most in the amount of daily sunlight they receive. Studies show that an inadequate amount of full-spectrum light is associated with depression, a phenomenon now known as seasonal affective disorder (SAD) or arctic winter madness.

Stressor: Any real or imagined situation, circumstance, or stimulus that is perceived to be a threat.

Circadian rhythms: Biological rhythms that occur or cycle within a 24-hour period (e.g., body temperature) that create the body's internal clock, also known as chronobiology. These can be affected by stress, causing a disruption that is even more stressful to the body.

Ultradian rhythms: Biological rhythms that occur many times in a 24-hour period (e.g., hunger pangs). These can be affected by stress.

Infradian rhythms: Biological rhythms that occur in periods longer than 24 hours (e.g., women's menstrual period). These can be affected by stress.

Seasonal affective disorder (SAD): The physiological response to lack of sunlight that results in feelings of depression.

twenty-first century may be a direct result of our being out of touch with the *natural* elements that so strongly influence our body's physiological systems. In any case, some of these bioecological factors can be positively influenced by lifestyle changes, including dietary habits, exercise, and the regular practice of relaxation techniques, which bring a sense of balance back into our lives.

Psychointrapersonal Influences

Our current understanding is that psychointrapersonal influences make up the greatest percentage of stressors. These are the perceptions of stimuli that we create through our own mental processes (perceptions and interpretations). Psychointrapersonal stressors involve those thoughts, values, beliefs, attitudes, opinions, and perceptions that we use to defend our identity or ego. When any of these is challenged, violated, or even changed, the ego is often threatened and the stress response is the outcome. Psychointrapersonal stressors reflect the unique constructs of our personality, and in the words of stress researcher Kenneth Pelletier, represent "the chasm between the perceived self and the ideal self-image." Because these influences are the most likely to cause stress, they are a major focus of this text. It is imperative to intercept the stress response in the mind before it cascades down as a rush of stress hormones into the body to cause potential damage.

Social Influences

Social influences have long been the subject of research to explain the plight of individuals who are unable to cope with their given environment. Most notable is the issue of overcrowding and urban sprawl. Classic studies conducted on several species have shown that when their numbers exceed the territorial boundary of each animal, despite an abundance of food and water, several seemingly healthy animals die off (Allen, 1983). This need for personal space appears to be universal in the animal kingdom. This includes humans, who likewise begin to show signs of frustration in crowded urban areas, traffic jams, long lines at checkout stands, or whenever their personal space is "invaded." The origin of this particular social influence may be instinctual in nature. Additional social causes of stress include financial insecurity, the effects of relocation, cultural assimilation issues, some technological advances, violation of human rights, and low socioeconomic status, to name but a few. New to the list of social influences are global warming concerns and water resource issues as the global population increases, taxing our very lifestyles with regard to scarcity issues.

Social Stress in America: A Twenty-first Century Look

The social influences linked to stress have been studied for decades, most notably by Holmes and Raye with the Social Readjustment Rating Scale (SRRS) and the concept of life-change units (LCUs). It was their work over 50 years ago that first highlighted the list of top life stressors, including the death of a spouse, the loss of a job, the death of a child, divorce, and high mortgage payments (even then). Although these types of stressors persist, the pace of society has moved to warp speed. With this rapid pace of change, additional stressors have reconfigured the proverbial list of stressors, as well as confirmed the deleterious impact of stress on one's health.

Comprehensive studies conducted by the American Psychological Association (APA) and the Harvard School of Public Health in 2014 and 2015 identified a host of stress indicators, suggesting that stress is indeed a health factor to be reckoned with. For the past 10 years, the APA has conducted a yearly survey titled "Stress in America: Paying with Our Health." Based on interviews with more than 3,000 people in various demographic populations (gender, income levels, generational groups, etc.), the results have not been promising. Key findings of the 2014 study, which was published in the spring of 2015, revealed the following:

- Although reported stress levels have decreased slightly over the past few years, over half of adults between the ages of 18 to 40 reported their stress level above 5 on a scale of 1–10.
- Seniors appeared to have the least stress, millennials the most.
- The top five reasons for stress were: (1) financial issues (money), (2) career responsibilities (work), (3) family responsibilities, (4) personal health issues, and (5) family health issues.
- Overall, women reported more stress than men (and the gap has been widening), and children appeared to model their stress behaviors from their parents (who are very stressed).

Effective coping skills appear to be in short supply according to this survey. The conclusions drawn from this study underscore the relationship between stress and disease/illness and highlight the need for people to harness better stress management skills.

Based on various factors, including the Black Lives Matter movement and the political aspects of sexual discrimination, the APA's 2015 survey specifically looked at the impact of discrimination on stress levels. Results revealed that perceptions of discrimination (based on race or ethnicity, age, disability, gender, sexual orientation, and gender identity) account for significant levels of personal stress, all of which impact personal health (APA, 2016).

Similar to the APA's "Stress in America" study, National Public Radio and the Kaiser Health Foundation conducted a series of surveys in 2014 and presented their findings under the title "The Burden of Stress in America." Here are some of their findings:

- Half of those questioned, more than 2,000 people, cited a major stressful experience in the past year.
- Health-related stressful experiences were the most frequently mentioned.
- Feelings of being overwhelmed with responsibilities and financial struggles topped the list of those who experienced the greatest stress.
- Additional stressors included work problems, health problems, family issues, and being unhappy with physical appearances.

The study also looked at common daily stressors/hassles. Topping the list were juggling family schedules, disillusion with government politics, watching/reading/listening to the news, household chores, running errands, car problems, commuting to work, losing cell phones, and using social media. Whether daily hassles or bigger issues, respondents reported both sleep patterns and eating behaviors as being greatly (negatively) impacted by stress.

Not all people reported having stress, and, among those who appeared to cope well, many credited their resilient personality traits, family and friends, spending time outdoors, hobbies, physical exercise, meditation, and time with pets.

FIGURE 1.7 Weddings are supposed to be a joyous occasion. However, they can rank near the top of one's list of stressors when planning this event, with stress lasting well after the reception when things don't always go as expected.

Although major life events like getting married (FIG. 1.7) or relocating for a new job may be chronic stressors to some, renowned stress researcher **Richard Lazarus** hypothesized in 1984 that the accumulation of acute stressors or **daily life hassles**, such as locking your keys in your car, playing phone tag, or driving to work every day in traffic, are just as likely to adversely affect one's health as the death of a spouse. These hassles are often based on unmet expectations that trigger an anger response of some type, whereas stressors of a chronic nature more often than not appear to have a greater association with fear and anxiety. Lazarus defined hassles as "daily interactions with the environment that were essentially negative." He also hypothesized that a balance of emotional experiences—positive emotions as well as negative ones—is necessary, and that people who have no exposure to life's "highs" or emotional uplifts (eustress) are also susceptible to disease and illness. Further research by Lazarus (1983, 1984), Ornstein and Sobel (1989), and

Richard Lazarus: Renowned stress researcher credited with the concept of daily life hassles.

Daily life hassles: Occasional hassles, like locking your keys in your car; when combined with many other annoyances in the course of a day, these create a critical mass of stress.

others has proved that his hypothesis has significant merit regarding stress and disease. As might be expected, the issue of lifestyle habits, changes, and hassles as social influences has come under attack by those who argue that perception or cognition plays an important role in the impact of stressors. Suffice it to say that all stressors, regardless of classification, are connected to human well-being in a very profound way. Over the past decade, the impact of social stressors on personal stress has become dramatically significant.

The General Adaptation Syndrome

Following Cannon's lead early in the twentieth century, Hans Selye, a young endocrinologist who created a name for himself as a leading researcher in this field, studied the fight-or-flight response, specifically the physiological effects of chronic stress, using rats as subjects. In experiments designed to stress the rats, Selye noted that several physiological adaptations occurred as a result of repeated exposures to stress, adaptations that had pathological repercussions. Examples of these stress-induced changes included the following:

1. Enlargement of the adrenal cortex (a gland that produces stress hormones)
2. Constant release of stress hormones; corticosteroids released from the adrenal cortex
3. Atrophy or shrinkage of lymphatic glands (thymus gland, spleen, and lymph nodes)
4. Significant decrease in the white blood cell count
5. Bleeding ulcerations of the stomach and colon
6. Death of the organism

Many of these changes were very subtle and often went unnoticed until permanent damage had occurred. Selye referred to these collective changes as the **general adaptation syndrome** (GAS), a process in which the body tries to accommodate stress by adapting to it. From his research, Selye identified three stages of the general adaptation syndrome:

Stage one: Alarm reaction. The alarm reaction describes Cannon's original fight-or-flight response. In this stage, several body systems are activated, primarily the nervous system and the endocrine system, followed by the cardiovascular, pulmonary, and musculoskeletal systems. Like a smoke detector alarm going off at night, all senses are put on alert until the danger is over.

Stage two: Stage of resistance. In the resistance stage, the body tries to revert to a state of physiological calmness, or homeostasis, by resisting the alarm. Because the perception of a threat still exists, however, complete homeostasis is never reached. Instead, the body stays activated or aroused, usually at a lesser intensity than during the alarm stage but enough to cause a higher metabolic rate in some organ tissues. One or more organs may in effect be working overtime and, as a result, enter the third and final stage.

Stage three: Stage of exhaustion. Exhaustion occurs when one (or more) of the organs targeted by specific metabolic processes can no longer meet the demands placed upon it and fails to function properly. This can result in death to the organ and, depending on which organ becomes dysfunctional (e.g., the heart), possibly the death of the organism as a whole.

Selye's general adaptation syndrome outlined the parameters of the physiological dangers of stress. His research opened the doors to understanding the strong relationship between stress and disease and the mind-body-spirit equation. In addition, his work laid the foundation for the utilization of relaxation techniques that have the ability to intercept the stress response, thereby decreasing susceptibility to illness and disease. Congruent with standard medical practice of his day (and even today), initial stress-management programs were geared toward reducing or eliminating the *symptoms* of stress. Unfortunately, this approach has not always proved successful.

General adaptation syndrome: A term coined by Hans Selye; the three distinct physiological phases in reaction to chronic stress: the alarm phase, the resistance phase, and the exhaustion phase.

Alarm reaction: The first stage of Selye's general adaptation syndrome, in which a threat is perceived and the nervous system is triggered for survival.

Stage of resistance: The second stage of Selye's general adaptation syndrome, in which the body tries to recover.

Stage of exhaustion: The third and final stage of Selye's general adaptation syndrome, in which one or more target organs show signs of dysfunction.

BOX 1.1 Post-Traumatic Stress Disorder 101

There is stress and then there is STRESS! Although most people claim (even brag) to live stressful lives, the truth of the matter is that few people encounter truly horrific events of death and carnage. The repeated horrors of war, however, have notoriously ranked at the top of every list as the most unbearable of all stressors that anyone can endure psychologically—and for good reason. To quote Civil War General William T. Sherman, "War is hell." Exposure to these types of events typically include those that threaten one's life, result in serious physical injury, expose one to horrific carnage, or create intense psychological shock, all of which are so strongly influenced by the intensity and duration of the devastation either experienced or observed first hand. The result is an emotional wound embedded in the unconscious mind that is very hard to heal.

Every war seems to have its own name for this type of anxiety disorder. Somber Civil War soldiers were described as having "soldier's heart." Affected military personnel returning from World War I were described as being "shell-shocked," whereas soldiers and veterans from World War II exhibiting neurotic anxiety were described as having severe "battle fatigue" or "combat fatigue." The term *post-traumatic stress disorder*—more commonly shortened to PTSD—emerged as a result of the treatment of returning soldiers from Vietnam who seemed to lack industrial-strength coping skills to deal with the hellacious memories that haunted them both day and night. This emotional disorder was first registered in the *Diagnostic and Statistical Manual of Mental Disorders (DSM)* in 1980 and has been the topic of intense investigation ever since. Sadly, the Iraq and Afghanistan wars have provided countless case studies for this anxiety disorder today.

Although mortal combat ranks at the top of the list of hellacious experiences, one doesn't have to survive a suicide bomber in the streets of Baghdad to suffer from PTSD. Survivors and rescue workers of the World Trade Center and Pentagon catastrophes are known to still be dealing with this trauma, as are several thousands of people still displaced from the wrath of Hurricane Sandy, and the devastation of towns in the paths of class 5 tornadoes. Violent crime victims, airplane crash survivors, sexual/physical assault victims, and occasionally first responders (e.g., police officers, fire fighters, and emergency medical technicians) are also prone to this condition. Given the nature of global warming and climate change and terrorism, it is suggested that PTSD may become a common diagnosis among world citizens with the ripple effect affecting legions of friends, colleagues, and family members alike. *Secondary PTSD* is a term given to family members, friends, and colleagues who are negatively affected by the ripples of strife from loved ones (even patients) who have had direct exposure to severe trauma.

The symptoms of PTSD include the following: chronic anxiety, nightmares, flashbacks, insomnia, loss of appetite, memory loss, hypervigilance, emotional detachment, clinical depression, helplessness, restlessness, suicidal tendencies, and substance addictions (MayoClinic .com). Typically a person suffering from PTSD has several of these symptoms at one time. Whereas the symptoms for some individuals may last months, for others PTSD becomes a lifelong ordeal, particularly if treatment is avoided, neglected, or shunned. The key to working with PTSD patients is to access the power of the unconscious mind by identifying deep-seated memories so that they may be acknowledged and released in a healthy manner rather than repressed and pushed deeper in the personal unconscious mind.

Specialists who treat patients with PTSD recommend that treatment begin as soon as possible to prevent a worsening effect. Initial treatment (intervention) is referred to as critical incidence stress management (CISM). The purpose of CISM is to (1) significantly reduce the traumatic effects of the incident and (2) prevent further deep-seated PTSD occurrences. Specific treatment modalities include eye movement desensitization and reprocessing (EMDR), counseling, and group therapy as a means to promote emotional catharsis. The Trauma Recovery Institute also cites art therapy, journal writing, and hypnosis as complementary coping skills for emotional catharsis. Many patients are also prescribed medications. Although medications may help reduce anxiety, it should be noted, they do not heal emotional wounds. Whereas the nature of this book is not specifically directed toward those who suffer from PTSD, the breadth and depth of content are found in all types of counseling and therapeutic modalities.

Stress in a Changing World

All you need do is read the latest Twitter feeds, Facebook updates, or the headlines on the homepage of your Internet browser to see what you already know: These are stressful times. Our world is changing rapidly, and with this change comes potential stressors that affect nearly everyone on the planet (FIG. 1.8). Today, stress has permeated the lives of nearly every person in every corner of the planet, permeating the borders of every country, province, and locale. And because people have to work for a living to put food on the table and a roof over one's head, job stress seems to be at the top of the list of common stressors across the globe. After investigating workplace absence due to stress, *The Daily Mail*, one of England's top-selling newspapers, quoted economic experts stating that stress is the Black Death plague of the twenty-first century (Barrow, 2011). According to the Chartered Institute of Personnel and Development, stress, as a public health issue, has eclipsed heart disease, strokes, cancer, and lower back problems. Daniel L. Kirsch, President of the American Institute of Stress, also refers to stress as America's New Black Death, explaining that stress is what's killing us most right now (Perman, 2013).

Stress, it seems, knows no age, race, gender, religion, nationality, or socioeconomic class. For this reason, it is called "the equal opportunity destroyer," for when left unresolved, stress can undermine all aspects of your life. Although it may seem that stress becomes a critical mass in your life once you leave home and go to college, the truth is that the episodes and behaviors associated with stress start much earlier than the college years. Pressures in high school, even grade school, as evidenced by school shootings, cases of self-injury, Facebook issues, and insomnia, are well documented. Combined with the stress of high technology, the effects are exponential.

FIGURE 1.8 Although most Americans admit to being very stressed, in comparison to half the planetary citizens who earn less than $2 per day and struggle to survive with substandard living conditions, we have it pretty darn good!

Which demographic group carries the most stress in the United States these days? If you said the Millennium Generation (people between the ages of 18 and 33), you would be right. Millennials are considered to be far more stressed than the baby boomer generation or even members of Generation X (ages 34–47). The backstory on this answer is a bit more complex than the daily statistics of unemployment figures and unpaid college loan debt. Experts often cite overprotective parenting styles (helicopter parents) of the millennials as a primary reason. Unlike baby boomers, typically, both parents of millennials have jobs/careers. The end result is less time with their children. Guilt kicks in, and parents overcompensate with poor boundaries. Campus counseling centers across the country see a theme among millennials walking in the door. "There is a generation of kids, now adults, who were given everything on a silver platter as they were growing up. Everything has been given to them, fostering a false sense of entitlement. These kids don't know how to fail successfully" (Neu, 2013). Millennials not only have poor coping skills when faced with adversity, but also feel that professional counseling would provide no lasting help (Ferri, 2013). In a cover story for *Time* magazine, reporter Joel Stein described the rampant impatient, narcissistic micro-celebrity status (i.e., 15 minutes of fame) as the gateway to entitlement (Stein, 2013).

Stress and Insomnia

Muscle tension may be the number one symptom of stress, but in our ever-present, demanding 24/7 society, insomnia runs a close second. **Insomnia** is best defined as poor-quality sleep, abnormal wakefulness, or the inability to sleep, and it can affect anyone. Overall, Americans get 20 percent less sleep than their nineteenth-century counterparts. According to a recent survey by the National Sleep Foundation, more than 60 percent of Americans suffer

Insomnia: Poor-quality sleep, abnormal wakefulness, or the inability to sleep.

from poor sleep quality, resulting in everything from falling asleep on the job and marital problems to car accidents and lost work productivity. Does your stress level affect your sleep quality? Even if you sleep well, it is hard these days not to notice the proliferation of advertisements for sleep prescriptions, suggesting a serious public health concern.

Numerous studies have concluded that a regular good night's sleep is essential for optimal health, whereas chronic insomnia is often associated with several kinds of psychiatric problems (Maas, 2001). Emotional stress (the preoccupation with daily stressors) is thought to be a primary cause of insomnia. The result: an anxious state of mind where thoughts race around, ricocheting from brain cell to brain cell, never allowing a pause in the thought processes, let alone allowing the person to nod off.

Many other factors (sleep stealers) detract from one's **sleep hygiene**, which can affect the quality of sleep, including hormonal changes (e.g., premenstrual syndrome, menopause), excessive caffeine intake, little or no exercise, frequent urination, circadian rhythm disturbances (e.g., jet lag), shift work, medication side effects, and a host of lifestyle behaviors (e.g., social media, Internet use, binge-watching, video games, alcohol consumption, constant cell phone use) that infringe on a good night's sleep.

How much sleep is enough to feel recharged? Generally speaking, 8 hours of sleep is the norm, although some people can get as few as 6 hours of sleep and feel fully rested. Others may need as many as 10 hours. New findings suggest that adolescents, including all people up to age 22, need more than 8 hours of sleep (Dawson, 2005).

Not only can stress (mental, emotional, physical, or spiritual) affect quality and quantity of sleep, but the rebound effect of poor sleep can, in turn, affect stress levels, making the poor sleeper become more irritable, apathetic, or cynical. Left unresolved, it can become an unbroken cycle (negative feedback loop). Although many people seek medical help for insomnia and are often given a prescription, drugs should be considered as a last resort. Many (if not all) techniques for stress management have proven to be effective in promoting a good night's sleep, ranging from cardiovascular exercise to meditation.

The field of sleep research began in earnest more than 60 years ago. Yet, despite numerous studies, the reason why we spend approximately one-third of our lives in slumber still baffles scientists. From all appearances, sleep promotes physical restoration. However, when researchers observe sleep-deprived subjects, it's the mind—not the body—that is most affected, with symptoms of poor concentration, poor retention, and poor problem-solving skills.

"If you have trouble falling asleep, lick your feet for a few minutes. It works for my cat!"

Insomnia is categorized in three ways: transient (short term with one or two weeks affected), intermittent (occurs on and off over a prolonged period), and chronic (the inability to achieve a restful night of sleep over many, many months). Although each of these categories is problematic, chronic insomnia is considered the worst.

All-nighters, exam crams, late-night parties, and midnight movies are common in the lives of college undergraduates, but the cost of these behaviors often proves unproductive. Unfortunately, the population of people who seem to need the most sleep, but often gets the least amount, are adolescents younger than age 20.

Although sleep may be relaxing, it is important to remember that sleeping is not a relaxation technique. Studies show that heart rate, blood pressure, and muscle tension can rise significantly during the dream state of sleep. What we do know is that effective coping and relaxation techniques greatly enhance one's quality of sleep.

Given the high rate of insomnia among Americans (including college students), here are a few suggestions to improve your sleep quality:

1. Avoid drinking any beverages with caffeine after 6:00 p.m., as the effects of caffeine on the nervous system promote a stress response rather than a relaxation effect.

Sleep hygiene: Factors that affect one's quality of sleep, from hormonal changes and shift work to excessive caffeine intake.

2. Daily physical exertion (cardiovascular exercise) is a great way to ensure a good night's sleep.
3. Keep a regular sleep cycle. Make a habit of going to bed at the same time every night (within 15 minutes) and waking up about the same time each morning (even on weekends).
4. Enhance your sleep hygiene. Create a sleep-friendly environment where bright light and noise are minimized or completely eliminated and sheets, pillows, and comforters easily lull you to slumberland.
5. Avoid screentime right before you go to bed. Instead, try reading.
6. Honor a media curfew by not using your screen devices after 8:00 p.m. to allow your pineal gland to make the sleep hormone melatonin.
7. Make your bedroom a tech-free zone. Avoid using your smartphone and/or tablet in the bedroom, even as an alarm clock, and turn off your Wi-Fi router before you crawl under the covers.

College Stress

What makes the college experience a significant departure from the first 18 years of life is the realization that with the freedom of lifestyle choices comes the responsibility that goes with it. Unless you live at home while attending school, the college experience is one in which you transition from a period of dependence (on your parents) to independence. As you move from the known into the unknown, the list of stressors a college student experiences is rather startling. Here is a sample of some of the more common stressors that college students encounter.

- ***Roommate dynamics:*** Finding someone who is compatible is not always easy, especially if you had your own room in your parents' house. As we all know or will quickly learn, best friends do not make the best roommates, yet roommates can become good friends over time. Through it all, roommate dynamics involve the skills of compromise and diplomacy under the best and worst conditions. And should you find yourself in an untenable situation, remember, campus housing does its best to accommodate students and resolve problems. However, their time schedule and yours may not always be the same. For those college students who don't leave home, living as an adult in a home in which your parents and siblings are now roommates can become its own form of stress.
- ***Professional pursuits:*** What major should I choose? Perhaps one of the most common soul-searching questions to be asked in the college years is, "What do I want to do the rest of my life?" It is a well-known fact that college students can change majors several times in their college careers and many do. The problem is compounded when there is parental pressure to move toward a specific career path (e.g., law or medicine) or the desire to please your parents by picking a major that they like but you don't.
- ***Academic deadlines (exams, papers, and projects):*** Academics means taking midterms and finals, writing research papers, and completing projects. This is, after all, the hallmark of measuring what you have learned. With a typical semester load of fifteen to twenty credits, many course deadlines can fall on the same day, and there is the ever-present danger that not meeting expectations can result in poor grades or academic probation.
- ***Financial aid and school loans:*** If you have ever stood in the financial aid office during the first week of school, you could write a book on the topic of stress. The cost of a college education is skyrocketing, and the pressure to pay off school loans after graduation can make you feel like an indentured servant. Assuming you qualify for financial aid, you should know that receiving the money in time to pay your bills can be challenging. Problems are compounded when your course schedule gets expunged from computer records because your financial aid check was two weeks late. These are just some of the problems associated with financial aid.
- ***Budgeting your money:*** It's one thing to ask your parents to buy you some new clothes or have them pick up the check at a restaurant. It's quite another when you start paying all your own bills. Learning to budget your money is a skill that takes practice. And learning not to overextend yourself is not only a skill, but also an art. At some time or other, everyone bounces a check. The trick to avoid doing it is not to spend money you do not have and to live within your means.
- ***Lifestyle behaviors:*** The freedom to stay up until 2 a.m. on a weekday, skip a class, eat nothing but junk food, or take an impromptu road trip carries with it the responsibilities of these actions. Independence from parental control means balancing

Stress with a Human Face

Joseph Ramos has just started his first year at the University of Colorado-Boulder. Like nearly every other freshman, a million thoughts filter through his mind daily regarding this stage of his life: the right college major, new friends, finding a girlfriend, grades, a tendency to procrastinate, roommate dynamics, budgeting his money, volunteer work, and time to do all the things that he loves when not studying. With a physique and body composition that most college men would envy, Joseph is already worried about packing on the "freshman 15" (undesired weight gain) and he is determined not to let that happen. In high school, Joseph played football, track, and cross-country. He also was involved in student government and was a member of the National Honor Society. He is well aware that being voted senior prom king probably won't carry much weight in college. For better or worse, the college years are a time to prove, if not reinvent, yourself all over again. Joseph welcomes this challenge. Currently, Joseph's strategy to cope with his stress levels includes running and lifting weights. He also has a passion for the martial arts. These activities have helped him get through high school and a few family crises, but he realizes that he will need a few more stress-management strategies to support his study habits in college if he is to achieve the desired grades to get into medical school so that he can achieve his lifelong dream of becoming a physician.

freedom with responsibility. Stress enters your life with a vengeance when freedom and responsibility are not balanced.

- ***Peer groups and peer pressure (drugs and alcohol):*** There is a great need to feel accepted by new acquaintances in college, and this need often leads to succumbing to peer pressure—and in new environments with new acquaintances, peer pressure can be very strong. Stress arises when the actions of the group are incongruent with your own philosophies and values. The desire to conform to the group is often stronger than your willpower to hold your own ground.
- ***Exploring sexuality:*** While high school is the time when some people explore their sexuality, this behavior occurs with greater frequency during the college years, when you are away from the confines of parental control and more assertive with your self-expression. With the issue of sexual exploration come questions of values, contraception, pregnancy, sexual orientation, AIDS/STDs, abortion, acceptance, and impotence, all of which can be very stressful.
- ***Friendships:*** The friendships made in college take on a special quality. As you grow, mature, and redefine your values, your friends, like you, will change, and so will the quality of each friendship. Cultivating a quality relationship takes time, meaning you cannot be good friends with everyone you like. In addition, tensions can quickly mount as the dynamics between you and those in your close circle of friends come under pressure from all the other college stressors.
- ***Intimate relationships:*** Spending time with one special person with whom you can grow in love is special indeed. But the demands of an intimate relationship are strong, and in the presence of a college environment, intimate relationships are under a lot of pressure. If and when the relationship ends, the aftershock can be traumatic for one or both parties, leaving little desire for one's academic pursuits.
- ***Starting a professional career path:*** It's a myth that you can start a job making the same salary that your parents make, but many college students believe this to be true. With this myth comes the pressure to equal the lifestyle of one's parents the day after graduation. (This may explain why so many college graduates return home to live after graduation.) The perceived pressures of the real world can become so overwhelming that seniors procrastinate on drafting a resume or initiating the job search until the week of graduation.

For the nontraditional college student, the problem can be summarized in one word: *balance*! Trying to balance a job, family, and schoolwork becomes a juggling act extraordinaire. In attempting to satisfy the needs of your supervisor, colleagues, friends, spouse, children, and parents (and perhaps even pets), what usually is squeezed out is time for yourself. In the end, everything seems to suffer. Often schoolwork is given a lower priority when addressing survival needs, and typically this leads to feelings of frustration over the inadequacy of time and effort available for assignments or exams. Of course, there are other stressors that cross the boundaries between work, home, and school, all of which tend to throw things off balance as well.

A Holistic Approach to Stress Management

When the stress response was first recognized, much attention was given to the physical aspects of the dynamics involved with fight-or-flight, specifically the symptoms of stress. As this field of study expanded to explore the relationship between stress and disease, it began to overlap, and to some extent even merge, with the fields of psychology, sociology, theology, anthropology, physics, health, and clinical medicine. What was once thought to be a physical response, and then referred to as a mind-body phenomenon, is now suggested to be a complex, multifaceted, or holistic phenomenon involving the mental, physical, emotional, and spiritual components of well-being. Looking at stress from these four different perspectives may explain why there are so many definitions of it. Ironically, this new insight continues to produce some tension within the community of health care professionals.

Medical science is slowly experiencing a **paradigm shift**. A paradigm is a conceptual model used to understand a common reality. A shift is a change in the perception of that reality. For the past 375 years or so, Western culture has adopted a mechanistic model of reality, influenced in large part by the philosophy of **René Descartes** that the mind and body are separate, and by the laws of physics created by **Isaac Newton**, some of which are believed to have been inspired by Descartes. The mechanistic paradigm compares the universe and all its components to a large mechanical clock, where everything operates in a sequential and predictable form. When it was first developed, the **mechanistic model**, also called the reductionist model, seemed to logically explain nearly every phenomenon.

The field of medicine, strongly influenced by Newtonian physics, applied the mechanistic model to the human organism, comparing the body to a clock as well. This applied paradigm, during what Dr. Larry Dossey called Era I medicine, focused on symptoms of dysfunction, and like a watch repairman, physicians were trained to fix or repair any parts that were broken. Drugs and surgery became the two primary tools forged in the discipline of clinical medicine. Prime examples of the fix-or-replace method include the prescription of penicillin and organ transplants, respectively. To no one's surprise, the application of this mechanistic model in medicine virtually stripped the responsibility of healing from the patient and placed it completely into the hands of the attending physician(s). There is no denying that many advances in clinical medicine have been nothing less than astonishing. Take, for example, heart and liver transplants and total hip replacements. Yet along with these magnificent achievements are significant limitations and hazardous side effects. Today, medicine is aptly referred to as an art as well as a science, but in the mechanistic model of reality, anything that cannot be measured or quantified is still virtually ignored. Moreover, anything that cannot be scientifically explained by cause and effect is dismissed as superstition and regarded as invalid. What this medical paradigm failed to include was the dimension of the human spirit, an unmeasurable source of energy with a potential healing power all its own. The human spirit is now considered so important by the World Health Organization (WHO) that it issued a statement saying, "The existing definition of health should include the spiritual aspect, and that health care should be in the hands of those who are fully aware of and sympathetic to the spiritual dimension."

However, the Newtonian paradigm was viewed as the ultimate truth until the turn of the twentieth century,

Paradigm shift: Moving from one perspective of reality to another.

René Descartes: A seventeenth-century scientist and philosopher credited with the reductionistic method of Western science (also known as the Cartesian principle). He is equally renowned for his influential philosophy of the separation of mind and body as well as the statement, "I think, therefore I am."

Isaac Newton: An eighteenth-century physicist who advocated the mechanistic paradigm of the universe, which was then adapted to the human body.

Mechanistic model: A health model based on the concept that the body is a machine with parts that can be repaired or replaced.

FIGURE 1.9 Sir Isaac Newton (along with René Descartes) is credited with what is now referred to as the mechanistic approach to scientific thinking, which is based on the idea that the universe operates like a large mechanical clock. Albert Einstein supported a different theory, called unified field theory, suggesting that the universe is a living web and validating the ancient whole systems theory in which everything is connected together and the whole is greater than the sum of the parts.

when a young physicist named **Albert Einstein** introduced his theory of relativity in 1905 (FIG. 1.9). In simple terms, Einstein said that all matter is energy, and furthermore, all matter is connected at the subatomic level. No single entity can be affected without all connecting parts similarly being affected. From Einstein's view, the universe isn't a giant clock but a living web. New ideas are often laughed at, and old ideas die hard. But as new truths unfold, they gather curious followers who test and elaborate on the original idea. Initially mocked, the complexities of Einstein's theory have gained appreciation among physicists today, leading to the frontiers of the new field of quantum physics and a whole new understanding of our universe in what is now called the *whole systems theory*. In his attempt to understand the big picture, one of Einstein's more colorful quotes states, "Gravity is not responsible for people falling in love."

Although current medical technology is incredibly sophisticated, physicians for the most part still view the human body as a clock with fixable or replaceable parts. In other words, the basic approach to modern medicine in the Western world has not changed in more than 375 years. Furthermore, the mind and body, so completely separate in the theory of Descartes, are still treated separately, not as one living system. The idea of a mind-body connection (which in rare cases appears powerful enough to make cancers go into spontaneous remission) is still as foreign a concept to many physicians today as the idea of a smartphone would have been to the founders of the United States more than 230 years ago. But new discoveries in the field of medicine have not fit so nicely into the concept of mechanical clock

Albert Einstein: A world-renowned theoretical physicist who revolutionized perceptions of reality with the equation $E = mc^2$, suggesting that everything is energy. His later years focused on a spiritual philosophy including pacifism.

or reductionist theory. Instead, they mirror Einstein's concept of an intricate network of connecting systems. As a result, standard concepts regarding health and disease are slowly beginning to give way to a more inclusive reality or paradigm. As an example, recently, medical researchers have learned that emotions can suppress the immune system, an idea thought to be inconceivable and ludicrous not long ago. The body-as-machine mentality no longer seems to answer all the questions posed about the human organism; and thus some issues, like subtle energy systems and the placebo effect, are being completely reexamined.

But old paradigms are not abandoned until new conceptual models are created and established. Ironically, some new paradigms are actually old concepts that have been dusted off and resurrected. Such is the case with a very old but newly rediscovered health paradigm strongly paralleling Einstein's theory and called the holistic **wellness paradigm**. This model suggests that total wellness is the balance, integration, and harmony of the physical, intellectual, emotional, and spiritual aspects of the human condition. These four components of total well-being are so closely connected and interwoven that it is virtually impossible to divide them. Although for the purposes of academic study these areas are best understood separately, in reality they all act as one interconnected living system, just as Einstein hypothesized about the universe.

The word *health* is derived from the Anglo word *hal*, meaning "to heal, to be made whole, or to be holy"; throughout the ages, wholeness has been symbolized by a circle. The wellness philosophy states that the whole is always greater than the sum of the parts and all parts must be looked at as one system (FIG. 1.10). When applied to clinical medicine, this philosophy indicates that all aspects of the individual must be treated *equally* and each considered part of the whole. Although advances have been made to integrate a host of mind-body-spirit healing modalities into Western health care, by and large, conventional medical practice still treats the physical component—the symptoms of stress—with drugs and surgery, often disregarding how the physical body connects with the mental, emotional, and spiritual aspects of well-being. Although the paradigm is slowly shifting, some physicians (because of their medical training) still refuse to fully acknowledge the link between stress and disease. Nontraditional approaches (of which stress management is a part), specifically biofeedback, meditation, massage therapy, and mental imagery, are commonly referred to as **alternative medicine** by the American Medical Association. Because the word *alternative* has a negative connotation to many practitioners in the field of holistic wellness, the words *complementary* and *integrative medicine* also are used to refer to additional healing modalities. Every technique for stress management falls within the domain of complementary medicine.

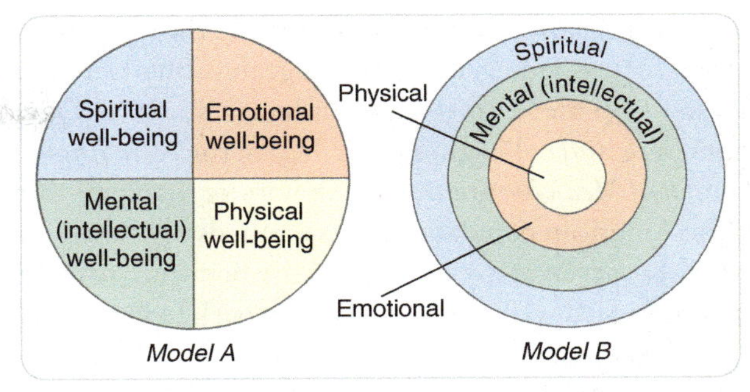

FIGURE 1.10 Two different approaches to the wellness paradigm. In Model A, expounded by Elisabeth Kübler-Ross, all components are present in the human organism, but each holds specific dominance at different phases of the individual's growth cycle. The emotional aspect is the first to develop; the spiritual aspect is the last. In Model B, each component is superimposed on the others in a holographic form, yet it is the spiritual component in which they are all contained.

Please note that healing and curing are two different concepts. Typically, the word *curing* means that the symptoms of a disease or illness are eradicated. Although in some cases healing techniques may cure a person of disease or illness, the concept of healing really means bringing a sense of inner peace to someone's life, even in the face of death. From this vantage point you can see that a person can be healed and yet still be ill. In the age of high technology and instant gratification, expectations are often placed on the curing aspects—eradicating the symptomatic problems—rather than the essence of true healing. This in itself has caused tension in the allied health fields because

Wellness paradigm: The integration, balance, and harmony of mental, physical, emotional, and spiritual well-being through taking responsibility for one's own health; posits that the whole is greater than the sum of the parts.

Alternative medicine: Modalities of healing (homeostasis) that include nearly all forms of stress-management techniques. Also known as complementary or integrative medicine.

many healthcare professionals trained in the mechanistic paradigm use both terms interchangeably. But the tension doesn't stop there. In 1993, a landmark study by David Eisenberg and colleagues published in the *New England Journal of Medicine* announced that more than one-third of the American population seeks methods of healing outside those accepted by traditional medicine because they are unsatisfied with the Western approach to health care. What makes this matter even more astounding is that most healing methods are not covered by medical insurance, meaning that people are paying for these services out of their own pockets. In the highly acclaimed PBS television series entitled *Healing and the Mind*, creator and host Bill Moyers distilled the trend in this way: "There is a deep yearning for a human (whole) approach to medicine." Stress-management techniques, which attempt to deal with the causes as well as the symptoms of stress, support and contribute to this holistic approach.

Statistics released by the National Center for Alternative and Complementary Medicine in 2008 indicate that as many as 50 percent (adults and children) of the U.S. population use various forms of integrative medicine. Many of these people pay out-of-pocket expenses (totaling in the billions of dollars) as only a few holistic modalities, such as acupuncture and some forms of bodywork, are reimbursable by insurance companies. Today, alternative healing practices have gone mainstream with acupuncture, hatha yoga, T'ai Chi ch'uan, aromatherapy, and many other modalities as common healthcare practices (Comarow, 2008).

Let us take a closer look at the components of the wellness paradigm and the effects that stress has on them. **Mental** (intellectual) **well-being** is regarded as the ability to gather, process, recall, and exchange (communicate) information. Exposure to stress tends to overload the cognitive "circuits," decreasing the processing and recall abilities needed to make sound decisions as well as the ability to communicate them. **Physical well-being** is described as the optimal functioning of the body's major physiological systems (e.g., cardiovascular, digestive, reproductive). From the observations documented in Selye's research, as explained in his book *The Stress of Life*, the inability to return to homeostasis can prove fatal to various organ tissues and eventually to the host organism. **Emotional well-being** is defined as the ability to feel and express the full range of human emotions and to control them rather than be controlled by them. Anger and fear act as "umbrella" emotions that can collectively overload emotional circuits, resulting in mental paralysis and often leading to states of depression. **Spiritual well-being** is described as the maturation of higher consciousness through strong nurturing relationships with both the self and others; the development of a strong personal value system; and a meaningful purpose in life. Stress can create a series of obstacles on the road to spiritual development, making the path to one's higher self difficult, if not entirely inaccessible. Over the past few decades, scholars (including Bill Hetler and John Travis) have included social well-being and environmental well-being as additional components of the wellness paradigm. Actually, what they have done is tease these aspects out of the mental, emotional, physical, or spiritual factors involved. If you take a closer look at the original four components, you will see that social well-being is a large factor of spiritual well-being. And environmental well-being demonstrates how interwoven these four components really are, integrating aspects of physical and spiritual well-being. Although the major focus of this book is self-reliance—working from within to achieve inner peace—remember that our ability to harmonize with people within our collective environments is paramount to total well-being. Thus, from a holistic perspective, to effectively deal with stress, all areas of the wellness paradigm must be addressed and nurtured equally; the whole is always greater than the sum of the parts.

Not long ago (and in some cases today), many stress-management programs were based on the mechanistic model and focused solely on physical well-being. Upon initial recognition of the association between stress and disease, courses designed to intervene in this process emphasized techniques to decrease the physical symptoms of stress. These classes consisted primarily of teaching one or two relaxation techniques to help decrease the most obvious stress symptom: muscle tension. These techniques, addressing merely the symptoms (the physical component), did nothing to relieve the causes of stress

Mental well-being: The ability to gather, process, recall, and communicate information.

Physical well-being: The optimal functioning of the body's eight physiological systems (e.g., respiratory, skeletal).

Emotional well-being: The ability to feel and express the full range of human emotions and to control these feelings, not be controlled by them.

Spiritual well-being: The state of mature higher consciousness deriving from insightful relationships with oneself and others, a strong value system, and a meaningful purpose in life.

FIGURE 1.11

(the mental, emotional, or spiritual components). As a result, people often experienced a rebound effect; their symptoms recurred. On a different front, coping skills (e.g., cognitive restructuring, time management, and journal writing) were taught by psychologists in private therapy sessions, and these coping strategies soon made their way into public awareness as well (FIG. 1.11).

Through the efforts of advocates of the wellness paradigm, attempts have been made to unite the practice of both relaxation skills and coping skills for a unique holistic approach to stress management. This implies viewing each person as more than just a physical body and dealing with the causes of stress as well as the physical symptoms. The primary focuses in the application of the wellness model are on the prevention of disease and illness and the enhancement of health. Furthermore, the underlying current of this empowering philosophy is to place the responsibility of healing back in the hands of the individual. Successful stress-management therapy programs have now begun to adopt the wellness philosophy and holistic approach, supporting the concept that the whole is indeed greater than the sum of the parts. A sound stress-management program does not attempt to merely reduce (fix or repair) stress, but rather to manage it efficiently. This management process attempts to focus on all aspects of one's well-being. This philosophy is implemented by attempting to both resolve the causes *and* reduce or eliminate the symptoms of stress. It is imperative to remember that, as an intervention modality, the wellness paradigm does not preclude the use of medications or surgery. Rather, it strongly suggests that there be a collaborative integration of several therapeutic techniques to produce the most effective healing process (e.g., chemotherapy and visualization). Equally important as preventive measures, coping skills and relaxation techniques are also advocated to *maintain* inner peace.

Stated simply, effective holistic stress management includes the following:

1. Sound knowledge of the body's reaction to perceived stress
2. Sound knowledge of mental, physical, emotional, and spiritual factors associated with stress
3. Utilization of several effective coping techniques to work toward a resolution of the causes of stress
4. Regular practice of relaxation techniques to maintain homeostatic balance of the body
5. Periodic evaluation of the effectiveness of coping skills and relaxation techniques

SUMMARY

- The advancement of technology, which promised more leisure time, has actually increased the pace of life so that many people feel stressed to keep up with this pace.
- Lifestyles based on new technological conveniences are now thought to be associated with several diseases, including coronary heart disease and cancer.
- *Stress* is a term from the field of physics, meaning physical force or tension placed on an object. It was adopted after World War II to signify psychological tension.
- There are many definitions of stress from both Eastern and Western philosophies as well as several academic disciplines, including psychology and physiology. The mind-body separation is now giving way to a holistic philosophy involving the mental, physical, emotional, and spiritual components of well-being.
- Cannon coined the term *fight-or-flight response* to describe the immediate effects of physical stress. This response is now considered by many to be inappropriate for nonphysical stressors.
- There are three types of stress: eustress (good), neustress (neutral), and distress (bad). There are two types of distress: acute (short-term) and chronic (long-term), the latter of which is thought to be the more detrimental because the body does not return to a state of complete homeostasis.
- Stressors have been categorized into three groups: (1) bioecological influences, (2) psychointrapersonal influences, and (3) social influences.
- Holmes and Rahe created the Social Readjustment Rating Scale to identify major life stressors. They found that the incidence of stressors correlated with health status.
- Selye coined the term *general adaptation syndrome* to explain the body's ability to adapt negatively to chronic stress.
- Females are not only wired for fight-or-flight, but also have a survival dynamic called "tend and befriend," a specific nurturing aspect that promotes social support in stressful times.
- Stress can appear at any time in our lives, but the college years offer their own types of stressors because it is at this time that one assumes more (if not complete) responsibility for one's lifestyle behaviors.
- The association between stress and insomnia is undeniable. The United States is said to be a sleep-deprived society, but techniques for stress management are proven effective to help promote a good night's sleep, including physical exercise, biofeedback, yoga, and diaphragmatic breathing.
- Previous approaches to stress management have been based on the mechanistic model, which divided the mind and body into two separate entities. The paradigm on which this model was based is now shifting toward a holistic paradigm, in which the whole is greater than the sum of the parts, and the whole person must be treated by working on the causes as well as the symptoms of stress.
- Effective stress-management programming must address issues related to mental (intellectual), physical, emotional, and spiritual well-being.

STUDY GUIDE QUESTIONS

1. How could you best define stress?
2. How does acute stress differ from chronic stress?
3. What is the general adaptation syndrome? List the stages.
4. Do men and women respond to stress in the same way? If not, how do their responses differ?
5. How does stress affect sleep? List as many ways as possible.
6. What is post-traumatic stress disorder (PTSD) and what is secondary post-traumatic stress disorder?
7. What is holistic stress management?

REFERENCES AND RESOURCES

Allen, R. *Human Stress: Its Nature and Control.* Burgess Press, Minneapolis, MN, 1983.

Alter, A. *Irresistible: The Rise of Addictive Technology and the Business of Keeping Us Hooked.* Penguin Press, New York, 2017.

American Cancer Society. *Cancer Facts & Figures 2007.* www.cancer.org/downloads/STT/CAFF2007PWSecured.pdf.

American Institute of Stress (AIS). *Homepage.* www.stress.org.

American Psychological Association. Stress in America: Paying with Our Health. February 4, 2015. http://www.apa.org/news/press/releases/stress/2014/stress-report.pdf.

American Psychological Association. Stress in America: The Impact of Discrimination. March 10, 2016. http://www.apa.org/news/press/releases/stress/2015/impact-of-discrimination.pdf.

Anxiety Disorders Association of America (ADAA). *2007 Stress & Anxiety Disorders Study.* www.adaa.org/stressOutWeek/study.asp.

Austin, J. Why Patients Use Alternative Medicine, *JAMA* 279:1548–1553, 1998.

Barrow, B. Stress Is Top Cause of Workplace Sickness and So Widespread It's Dubbed the Black Death of the 21st Century. Mail Online. October 5, 2011. www.dailymail.co.uk/health/article-2045309/Stress-Top-cause-workplace-sickness-dubbed-Black-Death-21st-century.html.

Becker, D. *One Nation Under Stress.* Oxford University Press, New York, 2013.

Beckford, M. Working Nine to Five Is Becoming a Thing of the Past, *Daily Telegraph*, May 4, 2007.

Cannon, W. *The Wisdom of the Body.* W. W. Norton, New York, 1963.

Carpi, J. Stress . . . It's Worse Than You Think, *Psychology Today* 29(1):34–41, 74–76, 1996.

Chopra, D. Personal conversation, June 22, 2000.

Comarow, A. Embracing Alternative Care, *U.S. News & World Report,* 31–40, January 2008.

Condon, G. Futurists Say World Is at Turning Point. *Chicago Tribune* (Section 5), April 9, 2003.

Cryer, B., McCraty, R., and Childre, D. Pulling the Plug on Stress. *Harvard Business Review* 81(7):102–107, 2003.

Damasio, A. *Descartes' Error.* HarperCollins, New York, 2006.

Dawson, P. *Sleep and Adolescents.* 2005. www.nasponline.org/resources/principals/Sleep%20Disorders%20WEB.pdf.

Dossey, L. Personal conversation, July 30, 2004.

Dossey, L. *Reinventing Medicine.* Harper, New York, 1999.

Dossey, L. *Space, Time, and Medicine.* Bantam New Age Books, New York, 1982.

Eisenberg, D., et al. Unconventional Medicine in the United States, *New England Journal of Medicine* 328:246–252, 1993.

Eisenberg, D., et al. Trends in Alternative Medicine Use in the United States, 1990–1997: Results of a Follow-up National Survey, *JAMA*, 280:1569–1575, 1998.

Expedia.com. *2012 International Vacation Deprivation Survey Results.* 2012. http://www.expedia.com/p/info-other/vacation_deprivation.htm.

Ferri, J. Millennials: The Most Stressed-Out Generation in America. Yahoo! February 8, 2013. http://shine.yahoo.com/work-money/millennials-are-the-most-stressed-out-americans-184318812.html.

Gerber, R. *Vibrational Medicine*, 3rd ed. Bear and Company, Inner Traditions, 2001.

Giradano, D., Everly, G., and Dusek, D. *Controlling Stress and Tension, A Holistic Approach*, 9th ed. Addison-Wesley, Boston, 2012.

Greenberg, J. *Comprehensive Stress Management*, 13th ed. McGraw-Hill Humanities, New York, 2012.

Hettler, W. *The Six Dimensional Wellness Model.* The National Wellness Institute. www.nationalwellness.org/index.php?id=391&id_tier=381.

Holmes, T. H., and Rahe, R. The Social Readjustment Rating Scale, *Journal of Psychosomatic Research* 11:213–218, 1967.

Huffington, A. *The Sleep Revolution.* Harmony Books. New York, 2016.

Kanner, A., et al. Comparison of Two Modes of Stress Management: Daily Hassles and Uplifts versus Major Life Events, *Journal of Behavioral Medicine* 4(1):1–37, 1981.

Kaplan, A., ed. *Health Promotion and Chronic Illness.* World Health Organization, Geneva, 1992.

King, S. K. Removing Distress to Reveal Health. In R. Carlson and B. Shield (eds.), *Healers on Healing*, Jeremy Tarcher Inc., Los Angeles, 1989.

Krugman, M. *The Insomnia Solution.* Grand Central Publishing, New York, 2005.

Kübler-Ross, E. Keynote Address, American Holistic Health Association Annual Conference, Lacrosse, WI, 1981.

Kuhn, T. *The Structure of Scientific Revolutions.* University of Chicago Press, Chicago, 2012.

Lazarus, R. Puzzles in the Study of Daily Hassles, *Journal of Behavioral Medicine* 7:375–389, 1984.

Lazarus, R., and DeLongis, A. Psychological Stress, and Coping in Aging, *American Psychologist* 38:245–254, 1983.

Levine, P. A. *Waking the Tiger: Healing Trauma.* North Atlantic Books, Berkeley, CA, 1997.

Levy, S. Facebook Grows Up, *Newsweek*, August 20, 2007: 41–46.

Lippmann, S., Mazour, I., and Shahab, H. Insomnia: Therapeutic Approach, *Southern Medical Journal* 94:866–873, 2001.

Luskin, F., and Pelletier, K. *Stress Free for Good: 10 Scientifically Proven Life Skills for Health and Happiness.* HarperOne, New York, 2005.

Maas, J. *Power Sleep*. Quill Books, New York, 2001.

Manning, G., Curtis, K., and McMillian, S. *Stress: Living and Working in a Changing World.* Whole Persons Associates, Duluth, MN, 2011.

Markes, J. Time Out, *U.S. News and World Report* 119 (23): 84–96, 1995.

Mayo Clinic. *Post-traumatic Stress Disorder*. www.mayoclinic.com/health/post-traumatic-stress-disorder/DS00246.

McGonigal, K. *The Upside of Stress: Why Stress Is Good for You, and How to Get Good at It.* Penguin Random House, New York, 2013.

Meyer, A. *The Common Sense Psychiatry of Dr. Adolf Meyer: Fifty-Two Selected Papers*. Ayer, Salem, NH, 1948.

Mitchum Report on Stress in the '90s. Research and Forecast Inc., New York, 1990.

Moyers, B. *Healing and the Mind*. Doubleday, New York, 1993.

Moyers, B. *Healing and the Mind*. Public Broadcasting System, 1993.

National Public Radio. Stressed-Out. 2014. http://www.npr.org/series/327816692/stressed-out.

Neu, S. Warderburg Health Center. University of Colorado, Boulder, CO. Personal conversation, March 2, 2013.

Ornstein, R., and Sobel, D. *Healthy Pleasures*. Addison-Wesley, Reading, MA, 1990.

Pelletier, K. *Mind as Healer, Mind as Slayer*, 2nd ed. Dell, New York, 2011.

Perman, C. Argggh! American Workers are at a breaking point. April 9, 2013. Business on NBCnews.com. http://www.cnbc.com/id/100624671.

Rahe, R., et al. Simplified Scaling for Life Events, *Journal of Human Stress* 6:22–27, 1980.

Rothschild, B. *The Body Remembers: The Psychophysiology of Trauma and Trauma Treatment*. W. W. Norton, New York, 2000.

Sapolsky, R. *Why Zebras Don't Get Ulcers*, 4th ed. W. H. Freeman & Company, New York, 2009.

Sateia, M. J., and Nowell, P. D. Insomnia, *Lancet* 364:1959–1973, 2004. www.sleepfoundation.org.

Seaward, B. L. *National Safety Council's Stress Management*. Jones & Bartlett, Boston, MA, 1994.

Seaward, B. L. *A Good Night's Sleep: Stress Insomnia and Digital Toxicity*. WELCOA, Omaha, NE, 2015.

Segerstreom, S. C., and Miller, G. E. Psychological Stress and the Human Immune System: A Meta-analytic Study of 30 Years of Inquiry, *Psychological Bulletin* 130(4):601–630, 2004.

Selye, H. *The Stress of Life*. McGraw-Hill, New York, 1976.

Selye, H. *Stress without Distress*. Lippincott, New York, 1974.

Shapiro, D. *Your Body Speaks Your Mind*. Sounds True Books, Boulder, CO, 2006.

Simeons, A. T.W. *Man's Presumptuous Brain: An Evolutionary Interpretation of Psychosomatic Diseases*. E. P. Dutton, New York, 1961.

Stein, J. The New Greatest Generation, *Time*, 28–34, May 20, 2013.

Stein, J. Tyranny of the Mob (Why We Are Losing the Internet to the Culture of Hate). *Time*. August 29, 2016.

Stepp, L. S. Enough Talk Already, *Washington Post*, August 21, 2007. www.washingtonpost.com/wpdyn/content/article/2007/08/17/AR2007081702267.html.

Taylor, S. *Health Psychology*, 9th ed. McGraw-Hill, New York, 2014.

Taylor, S. *The Tending Instinct*. Owl Books, New York, 2003.

Taylor, S., et al. Biobehavioral Responses to Stress in Females: Tend and Befriend, Not Fight or Flight, *Psychological Review* 107(3):411–429, 2000.

Travis, J., and Ryan, R. *Wellness Workbook*, 3rd ed. Celestial Arts, Berkeley, CA, 2004.

Wong, M. Vacationing Americans Have Given New Meaning to the Advertising Slogan, Don't Leave Home Without It, *Associated Press*, Sept. 1, 2000.

Zarski, J. J. Hassles and Health: A Replication, *Health Psychology* 3:243–251, 1984.

CHAPTER 2

The Sociology of Stress

Americans are the most entertained and least informed people on the planet.

—Robert F. Kennedy, Jr.

Today's world is a very different place from the one that existed when Walter Cannon coined the term "fight-or-flight response" and Hans Selye first uttered the words "general adaptation syndrome." Little did they know just how much stress would become a part of the social fabric of everyday life in the twenty-first century. Some experts argue that our collective stress is a result of our inability to keep up with all the changes that influence the many aspects of our lives. Simply stated, our physiology has not evolved at a comparable rate to the social changes of the last half-century. Perhaps it never will.

Futurist Alvin Toffler warned of these changes decades ago in his best-selling book *Future Shock*. In a 2010 National Public Radio (NPR) interview celebrating the fortieth anniversary of his book, Toffler stated that the "future shock" he described then is here now. *Future Shock* describes the stress that accompanies a proliferation of technology, urban sprawl, and a glut of information on the Internet.

Douglas Rushkoff is a social media theorist and author of the book *Present Shock*, a timely sequel to Toffler's *Future Shock*. Whereas Toffler described that rapid change was coming, Rushkoff states the whirlwind of change is here. Our society, he states, has become reoriented to the present moment with the likes of Twitter, Facebook, Tumblr, and Instagram. In Rushkoff's words, "Everything is live, real time, and always-on." Citizens with cell phones now post current events on YouTube quicker than CNN can get a camera crew to report the headline news (as was evident in the Boston Marathon bombing event in 2013). Emails have lost favor to instant messaging, blogs have given way to Twitter feeds, and the search engine Google includes the Google Now option. Linear time has become compressed into a collection of single moments, each forgotten as we become immersed in the next now moment. As someone with his finger on the pulse of social media, Rushkoff sees a new series of stressors and problems with the syndrome he calls present shock. They include the following:

1. *Narrative collapse:* Because so much attention is on the present moment, people cannot get a clear perspective on their lives (e.g., addressing problems of global warming or saving for retirement). Life events are reduced to myopic 140-character tweets or quick Facebook status updates, losing the bigger context of one's life.
2. *Digiphrenia:* The tacit permission to be in more than one place at a time with a variety of social media.
3. *Overwinding:* The ability to reduce big-time scales into small ones (as a result, getting less done).
4. *Fractalnoia:* The anxiety associated with rapid media grazing and jumping to conclusions with incomplete information in the absence of cause and effect perspective.

Moreover, the need for instant gratification mixed with voyeurism and ego grooming becomes a recipe for stress. People's eyes may have adapted to viewing multiple screens and fingers may adapt to smaller keypads finding multiple search engines, but the human nervous system interprets the bombardment of sensory stimulation as overload and adapts through the general adaptation system (GAS).

Author and physician Roberta Lee has a new name for this intense state of stress: "superstress." As a practitioner on the front lines of health care, she sees the result of superstress in patients who live a hectic and demanding lifestyle, in whom chronic stress ultimately translates into chronic disease. She predicts that this association will only increase if people don't take time to integrate effective stress-management skills—specifically meditation, exercise, and healthy eating habits—into their daily lives.

Holmes and Rahe, the creators of the Social Readjustment Rating Scale, were dead-on regarding various social aspects of life that can destabilize one's personal equilibrium, even with the best coping skills employed. Yet no matter what corner of the global village you live in, the stresses of moving to a new city or losing a job are now compounded by significant twenty-first-century issues. We are a product of our society, and societal stress is dramatically on the rise. A quick look at current headlines provides a window on the impact of societal stress on the individual:

- Pedestrians Killed by Texting Driver
- Florida Family Gets Micro-Chipped: Are You Next?
- Bedbug Epidemic Spreads to University Campuses
- Consumers Addicted to Smartphones
- Impact of the Great Recession to Last for Years to Come
- Obesity Epidemic Related to Artificial Sweeteners?

Experts who keep a finger on the pulse of humanity suggest that as rapid as these changes are now, the rate and number of changes are only going to increase.

It's not just the changes we encounter that affect our stress levels, but also how we engage with these new changes. Increasingly, this engagement is online. Unfortunately, the stress that is provoked is real, not virtual. The majority of interactive Web sites are littered with negative comments, frustrations, expletives, and rants, all of which suggest a malaise in the general public combined with an unparalleled freedom to honestly express oneself anonymously. While it's true that Facebook, Twitter, and YouTube played a significant role in the social changes of Arab countries, from Tunisia and Egypt to Libya, Yemen, Syria, and even Turkey, many people found themselves persecuted for expressing these freedoms publicly.

Sociology: The study of human social behavior within families, organizations, and institutions; the study of the individual in relationship to society as a whole.

Being overwhelmed with choices in communication technology for staying in touch with friends, colleagues, and employees leads to a whole new meaning of "burnout." Being tied to smartphones and tablets after work hours is bringing about a rash of lawsuits regarding unpaid overtime (Simon, 2010). And then there is the stress associated with the creative freedom gained or lost in cyberspace. True, freedom and creativity have been elevated to new heights by the Internet; however, in today's narcissistic and exhibitionist society, anybody can publish a book, release a single, be a critic, star in their own YouTube video, comment on any blog, and claim their full 15 minutes of fame. The rest of the world looks on in what is often described as "e-voyeurism."

The world is rapidly changing, and with it, the culture in which we live—all of which holds the potential to add layers upon layers of stress weighing on each individual. Simply stated, one cannot examine personal stress levels without looking at intertwining social mores and cultural trends, because whether we know it or not, we are greatly influenced by them all. As the expression goes, "Each of us is a product of our culture." As much as we might like, we cannot renounce the world and move to the nearest monastery or Amish community. En masse, we would only take all our cultural tendencies with us. In the words of John Donne, "No man is an island." The social fabric connects us all. There are, however, those who make a serious effort to change the fabric of the social culture, living examples of how to reduce the collective stress level. These, too, make the headlines, but mostly as curiosities:

- Organic Food Purchases on the Sharp Increase
- Man Escapes the Black Hole of his Smartphone
- Biking to Work Increases 60% in Past Decade
- Drop in Teen Suicide Linked to Legalization of Same-sex Marriage
- Pursuit of Happiness Still a Strong American Pastime

Physiology, psychology, anthropology, theology—the topic of stress is so colossal that it is studied by researchers in a great many disciplines, not the least of which is sociology. **Sociology** is often described as the study of human social behavior within families, organizations, and institutions: The study of the individual in relationship to society as a whole. Because everybody is born into a family and most people work for a living, no one is exempt from the sociology of stress. Revising John Donne's observation for the modern era, "No man or woman is an island." Whether we like it or not, we are all connected to each other.

What if it is not we who are stressed per se, but the society and culture we live in (or have created)? Poorly designed urban sprawl with no consideration of sidewalks or nature paths for exercise. Food deserts in our nation's cities. Poorly drafted legislation regarding working mothers. Perpetual issues of gender and race inequality that are so woven into the fabric of society that they are often hidden to those fortunate enough to even know what stress management is. This is the argument made by Dana Becker in her book *One Nation Under Stress*, which discusses what she calls stress and the biopolitics of American life. In an overview of the past several decades, Becker, a professor of social work at Bryn Mawr College in Pennsylvania, cites many examples of societal stress that contribute to personal strife, particularly affecting women, minorities, and the poor. She contends that for stress to be addressed fully, it must be reconciled from a societal perspective or what she calls the "wear and tear of society."

Perhaps the sociology of stress can best be acknowledged through the buzzword "social networking," which describes the likes of Facebook, Twitter, Facetime/Skype, YouTube, Snapchat, Instagram, and new social media and networking outlets looming on the horizon. Technology has even changed how people converse at a dinner party (e.g., one person asks a question and five people pull out their cell phones and Google the answer). Technology, the economy, and the environment have become significant threads of the social fabric. This chapter examines some of the most current issues and trends in the global society and their potential to increase stress for each of us personally.

Technostress

The tsunami of cyber information has been building for years, yet the first devastating wave seems to have hit the shores of the human mind in earnest at about the same time Facebook reached over half a billion users in 2010 (FIG. 2.1), which was the same year that the Swiss army knife included a USB drive as a necessary tool for "survival." The deluge of tweets, Facebook updates, Skype messages, text messages, and emails has led to annoyance and addiction for a great many people who are fed up with giving their lives over to technology. The growing dependence on technology has even inspired a term: "screen addiction." If it's not computer screens and smartphones, it's iPads, google glasses, and Bluetooth technology, none of which is bad, but all of which can become problematic if your life is completely centered around being plugged in all the time.

FIGURE 2.1 In 2013, the popular social networking site Facebook reached over 1 billion users. What was originally created as a means for college-aged students to meet each other is now cited by some as promoting loneliness and increasing social alienation.

Technology is meant to serve us, yet many people have turned the roles upside down and have become slaves to technology, hence the technostress phenomenon.

The perfect storm of stress related to the information age comes from the overwhelming amount of information available, the distractive nature of being plugged in 24/7, a sense of alienation, and the poor boundaries people maintain to regulate the information available. Examples of poor boundaries include college students who text during classroom lectures (Rubinkam, 2010) and the scores of people who bring all their technology with them on vacation, thus never separating work from leisure and possibly compromising both (FIG. 2.2). For example, it is not uncommon to find people plugged in to Wi-Fi technology at or near National Park campgrounds, a place people once went to get away from the trappings of modern civilization (Seigler, 2010). Similarly, fewer than half of all employees nationwide leave their desk or workstation during lunch hour, according to a Manpower survey, leading to higher stress levels and fatigue (Marquardt, 2010).

FIGURE 2.2 Copper Mountain Ski Resort in Colorado has some of the best slopes in the world to ski, but these days many people ski or snowboard one run and then check their emails and text messages. Vacations were once a way to escape from work, but now people bring their work with them via smartphones and laptops. People now say they cannot live without these accessories.

Many terms have been created for all the problems associated with this tsunami of information and the convenience of accessing it, but the one term that sums it all up is **technostress**, which is the feeling of being overwhelmed by technology. Factors contributing to techno-stress include, but are not limited to, privacy issues, identity theft, cell phone radiation, sensory bombardment, Internet scams, addiction to Internet gambling and pornography, and the problem of children having access to adult content. The Kaiser Family Foundation data suggest that 8–18-year-olds spend over 7 hours per day with entertainment media (video games, TV, apps, etc.).

Technostress: A term used to define the result of a fast-paced life dependent on various means of technology, including computers, cell phones and smartphones, personal digital assistants, texting, and email—all of which were supposed to give people more leisure time. Instead, people have become slaves, addicted to the constant use of these devices and technologies.

Perhaps the most widespread stress from technology that most people experience is the perpetual distraction of email and the replacement of face-to-face conversation with digital communications (FIG. 2.3). In one of a series of articles in 2010 for the *New York Times*, technology investigative reporter Matt Richtel noted that people check email up to 37 times an hour on average. Furthermore, some people feel an urge to respond to emails immediately and feel guilty if they don't. How many emails can push one over the edge, past the threshold of exhaustion? According to a Harris Interactive poll, respondents said that more than 50 emails per day caused stress, many using the phrase "email stress" to explain their frustrations. According to Pingdom, a Web-monitoring firm, over 90 trillion emails were sent over the Internet in 2009, with an average of 247 billion emails per day (Swartz, 2010).

In the age of digital anxiety, what impact does repeated interfacing with Wi-Fi technology have on our brains? Given the recent discovery that our brain tissue has the ability to adapt to a host of cognitive challenges and stimuli (a phenomenon known as *neuroplasticity*), the implications are significant. Susan Greenfield (2008, 2009), a professor of synaptic pharmacology at Oxford University, is concerned regarding how six to eight hours a day of computer interfacing will affect neuronal connectivity. Research from the University of California at Irvine reveals that the constant interruption of emails triggers the stress response, with the subsequent release of stress hormones affecting short-term memory (Richtel, 2010). And if you ever wondered why people, perhaps even yourself, seem addicted to checking emails, voice mails, or tweets, consider this fact: Research shows that the receipt of emails and tweets is accompanied by a release of dopamine. Dopamine, a "feel-good" neurotransmitter, is associated with chemical addictions. In the absence of dopamine release, boredom ensues, until the next fix (Richtel, 2010).

Whereas Greenfield and others are alarmed regarding sensory input and brain physiology, others are concerned with people's emotional maturity, intuition, psychological reasoning, memory processing, and moral compass (Dossey, 2009). Clay Shirky, author of the best-selling book *Cognitive Surplus*, cites a dramatic shift in society's relationship to technology, from primarily watching television to using online media. With this shift lies both promise and peril. The promise is the collective effort (sometimes called "digital consciousness" or "wiki efforts") to solve world problems. The peril is becoming self-absorbed in cyberspace with screen-addiction or being drowned out by the sheer amount of cyber noise (Alter, 2017).

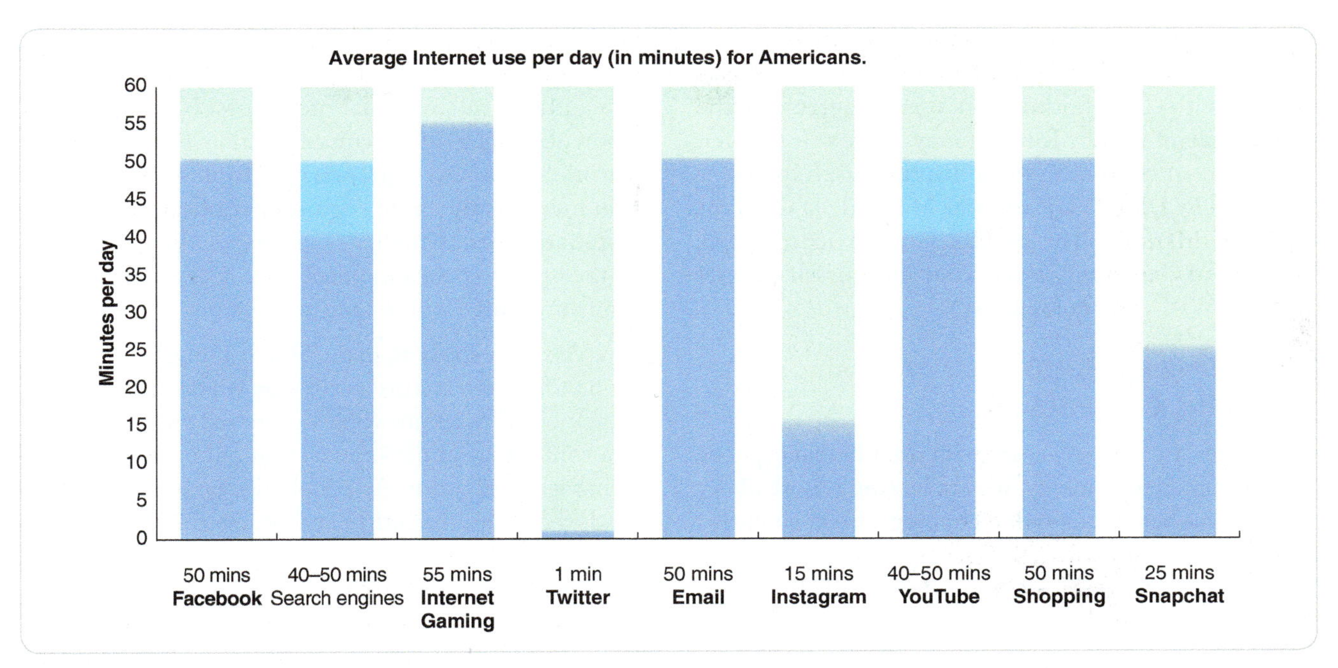

FIGURE 2.3 According to data collected by various organizations including Social Media Today, Amazon, Google, and the Entertainment Software Association for 2016, on average, people spend 8 hours per day on their screen devices, from gaming, shopping, and search engines to all kinds of social media posting. Teens (ages 12–18) spend as much as 9 hours per day. One billion hours of YouTube is watched every day. The impact of screen use and Internet interaction on society cannot be understated.

Every abrupt shift in the history of societies has had its associated stressors; for example, the shift from agrarian to industrial society was correlated with a dramatic increase in alcoholism, regarded as the "social disease" of its time. In today's abrupt shift to online technology and social media, the online technology is itself the addiction. This addiction is easy to observe: Check people's behavior inside an airplane cabin the moment the plane touches down, or in a movie theater once the credits appear on the screen—everybody reaches for their cell phone to check messages. Young people today who never knew life without a cell phone or iPad don't understand why older adults seem so concerned about their addictive tech habits, whereas adults notice that children and teens raised with screen technology may be well versed in cyber communications skills but are socially immature regarding face-to-face communication skills, including eye contact. Harvard psychologist Sherry Turkle notes these and other growing stressors in her book *Alone Together*, stating that people's social skills diminish with technology and artificial intelligence.

Another problem associated with constantly being "on" with technology is what experts describe as the **shallow effect**. According to Nicholas Carr, author of the book *The Shallows: What the Internet Is Doing to Our Brains*, information grazing is not the same thing as cultivating a synthesis of wisdom, yet superficial information grazing has become the norm, resulting in a shallow understanding of complicated issues. Not long ago, there was a clear line between information and entertainment. That line is quite blurry, if not non-existent, now—so much so that many people view these two aspects as one and the same, as illustrated by Jon Stewart's *Daily Show*, Huffingtonpost.com, and DailyBeast.com. Moreover, jumping from site to site and cherry-picking information seems to "rewire" the brain to deleterious effect; specifically, it compromises one's ability to concentrate or focus on something long enough to fully understand all its implications. Carr states that this rewiring of the brain not only weakens one's ability to cultivate one's memory (by always being reliant on an outside source of

Shallow effect: A shallow understanding of complicated issues that is caused by information grazing. Jumping from site to site and cherry-picking information compromises one's ability to concentrate or focus on something long enough to fully understand all its implications.

information), but also makes it more difficult for people to calm the mind and relax. Many social media experts disagree with Carr's findings, but they do agree with the obvious dilemma: The Internet may make you smarter, but beware of the multitude of distractions. Experts interviewed by *USA Today* reporter Marco della Cava for a story on this topic all offered the same advice to people aged 30 and younger: Learn to restrain yourself when it comes to Wi-Fi technology.

Digital Toxicity, FOMO (Fear of Missing Out), and Digital Dementia

As more research comes to light with regard to smartphone use and screen technology, we are learning more about how various behaviors with technology affect cognitive skills, including memory, as well as social skills (or the lack thereof). Sociologists, including MIT Professor Sherry Turkle, identify two of the biggest concerns with screen devices as being isolation and alienation, both of which lead to or perpetuate stress.

What effect does digital overload have on memory? Research conducted by Bill Thornton at the University of Southern Maine and published in the journal *Social Psychology* revealed that people who had their cell phones within easy reach were less efficient with a given task than those who did the same task without the presence of their cell phone (Freidman, 2014). Smartphones not only distract one's attention, but the constant anticipation of social media messages derails memory processing and perhaps other cognitive functions, keeping the brain in an alert state, one that is hard to turn off when preparing for sleep.

With the world of information at our fingertips, can having access to so much information be a hindrance to memory rather than an asset? The answer appears to be a definitive YES! In an article titled "A Smart Thing That Makes You Stupid," investigative reporter Ron Friedman cites a series of studies that reveals the problem with being online with a smartphone all the time. In the first study, two groups of people were given a task: one group was allowed to have their cell phones within arm's reach (on the table where they were working) and the second group had no access to their smartphones. When the results were tabulated, the group of people with access to their smartphones did 20 percent worse on the task than the control group. In a similar study, people were asked to participate in a face-to-face conversation. Those who had a smartphone within reach found the person they were in conversation with boring, whereas those without a smartphone did not.

The results showed that when one's focus is split (distracted) between a task and the anticipation of a text message, email, phone call, or social media post (the opposite of "undivided attention") memory function is compromised. For information to be transferred from short- to long-term memory, the brain requires periods of rest. When people are glued to their screen devices, there is no time for the brain to rest, and hence shift necessary information from short-term to long-term memory.

Likewise, in a study to determine if the process of taking handwritten lecture notes was superior or inferior to memory formation, when compared to taking notes on a computer, results showed that old fashioned note-taking is far superior. As people listened and wrote by hand, they were forced to synthesize the information rather than merely transcribe it digitally, and hence were better able to demonstrate memory recall. Freidman has these suggestions to avoid digital dementia: (1) keep smartphones off desks, (2) banish email and text alerts, and (3) schedule distraction-free periods each day.

The boom in the telecommunications industry and computer industry, pillars of the information age, has led to an overnight conversion of lifestyle in both American and global society. In their book *Technostress*, authors Weil and Rosen suggest that the rapid pace of technology will only continue with greater speed in the coming years, giving a whole new meaning to the expression "24/7." They predict, as do others, that the majority of people will not deal well with this change. The result will be more stress, more illness and disease, more addictions, more dysfunction, and a greater imbalance in people's lives (Alter, 2017). There is general consensus that the rate of change of technology has far outpaced the level of responsibility and moral codes that typically accompany the creative process. The following are some aspects of technostress as they currently affect our lives:

- *Information overload:* Given the flood of Facebook updates, text messages, emails, pop-up ads, smartphone apps, Web sites, and Pinterest posts, it is easy to become inundated by information. Reviewing and responding to a slew of text messages, emails, tweets, and voice mails, not to mention deleting spam and closing pop-up ads, can eat up several hours of one's time each day. Research reveals that too much information, coupled with all the means of accessing it, results in what is now called "brain freeze," "information paralysis," and "infostress," leading to indecisiveness, inability to focus, and poor memory recall (Begley, 2011).

- *Cyber bullying:* Bullying may be a perpetual pastime, but taking this behavior online to a global audience with online harassments, accusations, slurs, and rumors can destroy one's personal integrity. (Several people have committed suicide over cyber-bullying.)
- *Identify theft:* Well beyond bank account numbers and credit card access codes, identify theft now includes imposter Facebook and Twitter accounts. One's identity can be stolen in seconds, yet it may take months to recover.
- *Cyber hacking:* It's one thing to have someone hack into your online accounts (and this is stressful), but the stakes have been raised with international hacking, most notably overseas nationals infiltrating everything from online banking systems and news outlets to power companies that connect to the power grids that service the Internet.
- *Bandwidth and cloud issues:* If you have ever tried to download and watch a movie only to find out that there are issues with bandwidth, you know the meaning of technostress. And as more and more apps and software become available only through the cloud, stress looms when there are issues with cloud accessibility.
- *Boundaries:* Less than twenty years ago, there were clear-cut boundaries between one's personal and professional lives. Today the boundaries have dissolved to a point where it's hard to tell where one ends and the next begins. With smartphones, and tablets, a person can be accessed every minute of the day. People feel compelled to take these devices to movie theaters, plays, restaurants, vacations, and even to bed. Although the expression "24/7" was first coined to refer to retail shopping, it now conveys nonstop accessibility.
- *Privacy:* With constant accessibility, one forfeits privacy. Furthermore, with many purchases made on the Internet, each person develops a consumer profile, which then is sold to a host of other vendors. From cookies to bookmarks to cyber-bullying to identity theft, privacy has become a serious if not stressful issue in the information age. With advances in reducing the microchip to the size of a molecule, information storage is predicted to go from the smart card to biotech implants.
- *Ethics:* With the completion of the Human Genome Project, scientists may be able to identify persons likely to inherit genetic-based diseases. Although this information may provide insight into cures, fear arises at the prospect of this information falling into the hands of insurance companies that revoke policies based on genetic profiling. Scientific breakthroughs in genetic research raise other moral and ethical concerns, too, such as those surrounding genetic cloning and genetically modified foods.
- *Less family time:* Unlike television watching, which can be done as a family, surfing the Internet is a solitary activity. Thus, people are spending more virtual time on their computers and cell phones and less real time with each other.
- *Online dating:* As people spend more and more time plugged into their computers, they find less time for social activities. Many people are enlisting the help of Facebook, Match.com, and eHarmony for finding relationships. Although many are happy to have this new way to meet people and have great luck with it, some find their expectations unfulfilled by people who falsely represent themselves online.
- *Wi-Fi stress:* If you were to eavesdrop on conversations or scroll through social tweets, you would be quick to notice that issues such as net neutrality, cloud distortion, and bandwidth access are producing a great deal of stress for nearly everyone tied to the Internet. As more content becomes accessible online, these issues will result in higher service fees, stretching tight budgets even tighter.
- *Technology and the generational divide:* Are you constantly being asked by your parents to assist them with all things digital, such as helping to program their iPod and digital cameras, download music files, install software packages, upgrade operating systems, download apps, or set up Wi-Fi in the house? It's not an uncommon hassle among the younger generation, who feel as if they are constantly on call for "parental tech support."

A Decline in Civility

Have you noticed that people today seem quick-tempered, impatient, cynical, self-centered, and perhaps even rude at times? If you have, you are not alone. Once again, a review of some disturbing national headlines suggests a high level of restlessness in the American culture:

- Why We're Losing the Internet to the Culture of Hate
- Responsible Gun Owner Shoots, Kills Brother in Fight over Cheeseburger

- Churchgoer Killed in Fight over Seat at Sunday Service
- Internet Harassment Is Now the Norm
- Man Shoots Woman After He Runs Red Light
- Majority of College Students Text During Classroom Lectures

Civility, as expressed through social etiquette, refers to the practice of good manners and appropriate behavior. Many consider the basic rules of civility to be sorely lacking in today's culture. Nitsa Lallas, who authored the book *Renewing Values in America*, attributes the lack of civility to an alchemy of narcissism and a national lack of values, contributing not only to social unease, but also to the economic mess that created the Great Recession of 2008–2009.

Moreover, a revolution in the way people communicate with each other over the past few years has dramatically changed the social fabric of our culture, particularly how we relate, or fail to relate, to each other in face-to-face situations, as discussed earlier. Instant accessibility has sown the seeds for impatience. Politeness has given way to rudeness. The type of behavior used in Internet rants and talk radio phone calls carries over into face-to-face shouting matches at sporting events and political rallies. Social manners (e.g., appropriate behavior and thinking of others first) have become minimal, if not obsolete, for many people, particularly when bursts of anger perpetuate feelings of victimization.

Today's self-centered, narcissistic indulgences have hit an all-time high, many of which are directly related to political incivility (BOX 2.1). How did things go so wrong? Some people blame poor parenting skills. Many cite talk radio and various news media outlets that broadcast incivility. Others point their finger at the proliferation of technology and the constant self-promotion that seems to go along with it (Meyer, 2008). Many say the perfect storm of "uncivil Americans" is a combination of all these factors. Noting the serious issue of American incivility, Rutgers University has initiated a one-credit course called Project Civility for students, with topics ranging from cell phone etiquette and cyberbullying to civil sportsmanship and social responsibility (BOX 2.2). It is likely that other colleges will follow this trend (Lanman, 2010).

Civility: The practice of good manners and appropriate behavior.

BOX 2.1 Political Incivility

Political incivility reached new heights (or lows) with the 2016 U.S. presidential election, and experts suggest that this is the new normal. It was not uncommon to see fights breaking out at political rallies and candidates name-calling (e.g., "nasty woman") during the presidential debates. The political climate was so polarized that feuds broke out among friends and family members across the country. People seem to have less tolerance for those with differing opinions. Social media rants and bullying have reached an all-time high. Many blame candidates, social media, and the Internet for the rise of political incivility. Political incivility, in turn, can lead to other antisocial behaviors in various aspects of people's lives, adding to already increased stress levels (Richards, 2016).

According to a study by the *New York Times*, the average young American now spends every waking minute (with the possible exception of school classes) using a smartphone, computer, television, or other electronic device. Adults appear to be no different. It is not uncommon to see people texting while at movie theaters, talking on cell phones in restaurants (despite signs prohibiting their use), and texting while driving (despite the growing number of state laws banning this behavior). In 2006, researchers at the University of Utah were curious to see whether the distraction of cell phone use while driving was similar to driving while under the influence of alcohol. Using driving simulators, it was revealed that people on cell phones show a driving impairment rate similar to a blood alcohol level of 0.08%, the demarcation of drunk driving in the majority of U.S. states. Although many people may recognize the dangers of talking and driving, few offer to give up this social faux-pas mode of multitasking (Dossey, 2009).

Many people use technology to avoid stressful situations, which adds to a general lack of civility in society. Examples include quitting a job with a tweet, breaking up with a girlfriend or boyfriend via Facebook, or sending a derogatory email and blind-copying everyone in one's address book (FIG. 2.4). The modern lack of civility cannot be blamed entirely on technology, yet the

BOX 2.2 Civility 101

(Things Your Parents Should Have Taught You)

The following is a short list of commonly accepted polite manners that promote civil behavior. The premise of civility, as expressed through etiquette, is respect for your fellow human being (also known as the Golden Rule).

1. Always say "please" and "thank you."
2. Always look a person in the eye when addressing them.
3. Never interrupt when someone is talking; wait until they finish speaking.
4. Refrain from rude or vulgar language in public.
5. Stand when someone enters a room and greet people politely upon meeting them.
6. Shake hands when you are introduced to someone new.
7. Hold the door open for people upon entering or exiting through it.
8. Cover your mouth when you sneeze, cough, yawn, and/or chew food.
9. Wait for everyone to be served before eating.
10. Don't take cuts (e.g., airport gates, movie theaters, etc.).
11. Don't bring your cell phone to the dinner table.
12. Don't end a relationship with a text message, Facebook post, or email. Do it in person.

dramatic rise in the use of communication devices has played its part. How would you rate your current level of social etiquette?

Americans may be lacking in the social graces, but they are renowned the world over for giving generously to the needy (e.g., the Boston Marathon bombing victims, New York and New Jersey residents affected by Hurricane Sandy, and the victims of countless devastating tornadoes in the midwest). However, texting a donation for earthquake relief while watching the Super Bowl or The Voice is far different from face-to-face contact and polite social interactions. It's the direct social contact skills that are sorely lacking in American culture today.

FIGURE 2.4 People spend less face-to-face time with each other and more screen time talking to others, leading many experts to suggest that social skills and face-to-face communication skills are on the decline in America.

Environmental Disconnect

Even if you don't listen to the news regularly, it's hard to ignore the impact humanity is having on the state of the planet. The word "sustainable" has entered the American lexicon, even if the concept is largely ignored in practice by most people. From a sociological perspective, the earth may not be your family, an organization, or institute, but it is your home, and as such your relationship to it and with it is paramount. Modern society can be said to suffer from an **environmental disconnect**, a state in which people have distanced themselves so much from the natural environment that they cannot fathom the magnitude of their impact on it. The term **nature deficit disorder** was coined by award-winning author Richard Louv in his book *Last Child in the Woods* to describe the growing abyss between people and the outdoor world. Kids, as it turns out, would rather play

Environmental disconnect: A state in which people have distanced themselves so much from the natural environment that they cannot fathom the magnitude of their impact on it.

Nature deficit disorder: A term coined by Richard Louv to describe a now-common behavior (affliction) where people (particularly children) simply don't get outside enough, hence losing touch with the natural world and all of its wonder.

video games or surf online than play outside—where there are no outlets. A great many experts and luminaries have predicted over the years that as humanity distances itself from nature, people will suffer the consequences, primarily in terms of compromised health status.

Continuing our theme of current news headlines, consider these:

- 2016 Hottest Year on Record
- Children Spend Less Time Outdoors Than Prison Inmates
- Fracking Now Linked to Hundreds of Earthquakes
- Earth Just Passed the 400 PPM Climate Threshold
- Dangerous Depletion of the World's Aquifers
- Climate Change Puts 1.3 Billion People and $158 Billion at Risk, Says World Bank

An age-old question asks, "How many angels can dance on the head of a pin?" Today that imponderable question has become "How many humans can sustainably live on planet Earth?" It's interesting to note that some of the earliest studies on stress physiology involved placing an abnormally high number of mice in a cage. As their environment, personal space, food availability, and quality of life decreased with each additional occupant, tension significantly increased. The parallels between the environment and behavior of those mice and humans today are unavoidable, giving credence to the axiom, "As population increases, behavior decreases."

To support this premise, scientists recently reviewed over 60 studies regarding the relationship between increased global temperatures and increased violence. They concluded that as global temperatures increase, there is a corresponding increase in violence, hostility, and conflict (Kirwood, 2013).

Even if you think your drinking water is safe, you may be mistaken. Residents of Flint, Michigan, have been forced to drink bottled water for several years due to lead contamination. Lead, leaching into the drinking water from old pipes, is a well-known toxin associated with brain dysfunction, and the drinking water of Flint is full of it. Not only is the inconvenient lack of tap water stressful, so is the realization that many children may suffer the long-term effects of brain damage. People in Flint have been forced to drink bottled water for years, currently with no signs of improvement due to political squabbling. Residents of Flint may get the most headlines about toxic drinking water, but they are hardly alone with this concern. Residents from several cities and communities around the country have similar issues, not the least of whom are the Navajo Indians in Arizona.

In other water news, rising waters due to global warming are already having an effect in Miami, where city officials have begun to elevate highways in and around the city in an effort to deal with the loss of land due to flooding from global warming. Rising sea levels have also swallowed up land in Louisiana. In fact, it is estimated that the Bayou State is losing several hundred acres a year to climate change. Once shaped like a shoe, the map of Louisiana is a much smaller land mass now than it was even a decade ago.

By now everyone has not only heard of the issues on global warming, but also has experienced the preliminary effects first hand: violent storms, hotter summers, more intense droughts, and severe weather patterns. The problems of our dependence on oil were highlighted by the massive 2010 oil spill in the Gulf of Mexico. What has yet to become clear to the average person, however, are the looming problems of water shortages, an issue that will greatly affect everyone. Former United Nations Secretary General Ban Ki-Moon has repeatedly stated that wars will most likely be fought over water sources in our lifetime. So significant is this stressor that *National Geographic* dedicated its April 2010 issue entirely to the topic of water and our thirsty world. Environmentalist Lester Brown of the Earth Policy Institute states that when valuable drinking water is used for such things as fracking, and laws make collecting rainwater illegal, tension rises. Moreover, the variables of rapid population growth, increased energy demands, farming irrigation demands, depleted aquifers, and limited water supplies make water a dramatically stressful topic for a great many global citizens, including Americans. Here are some facts concerning water that will affect you now and in the years to come:

- 97.5 percent of the earth's water is salty, with only 2.5 percent of earth's water considered fresh.
- Two-thirds of all fresh water is frozen.
- Many Western states (e.g., Texas, Arizona, and California) are draining underground aquifers quicker than they can be naturally restored.
- Many freshwater streams contain hormones and antibiotics from prescription drugs flushed down toilets and petrochemical fertilizers from agricultural run-off.
- Americans use approximately 100 gallons of water at home each day, compared with 5 gallons per day in developing nations.

Stress with a Human Face

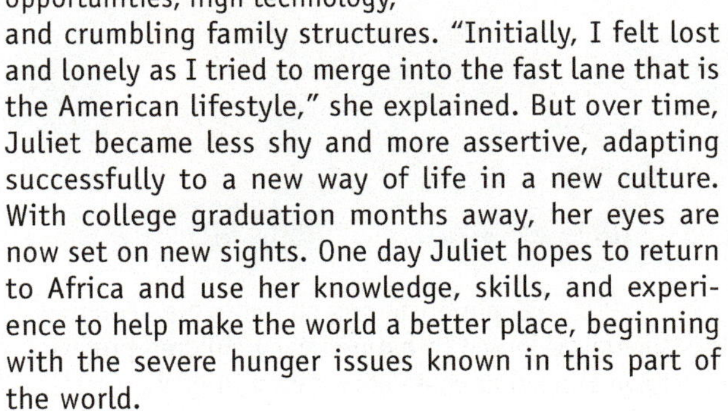
Courtesy of Juliet Simbo.

Society, and the culture it creates, is often described in metaphors. A common one is "the social fabric." For Juliet, a more apt metaphor might be a carpet, one that was pulled right from underneath her feet as a child. Juliet Mamie Simbo now lives in Denver, Colorado, but at the age of 13 she and her family fled from Sierra Leone, a small country on the west coast of Africa. She begins her story with a Hollywood reference:

"If you have seen the movie *Blood Diamond*, starring Leonardo DiCaprio and Jennifer Connelly, then you have witnessed a realistic portrayal of the horrors of civil war in Sierra Leone. I lived in this world. I witnessed my dad held at gunpoint on our porch on January 10th, 1999, by a rebel who told all of us that he was going to kill my father and suck his blood because of his vocal opposition to the atrocities being committed in my country. The gunman spared my father's life; however, in a defiant move, he turned and shot and killed our family dog. Because of greed and hatred amongst the people of my country, death came to many in Sierra Leone for seemingly no reason. I was changed forever by these events, knowing that my life was kept alive by the slimmest of margins."

As an immigrant to the United States, she had to adapt quickly to a whole new culture, one with superhighways, fast food, snowstorms, power shopping, abundant lifestyle opportunities, high technology, and crumbling family structures. "Initially, I felt lost and lonely as I tried to merge into the fast lane that is the American lifestyle," she explained. But over time, Juliet became less shy and more assertive, adapting successfully to a new way of life in a new culture. With college graduation months away, her eyes are now set on new sights. One day Juliet hopes to return to Africa and use her knowledge, skills, and experience to help make the world a better place, beginning with the severe hunger issues known in this part of the world.

Juliet has used her experience of cultural differences in a positive way and hopes that others will do the same. As she said in her high school graduation speech, "I say to you, open your eyes to the world beyond your country's borders. Feel the presence of humanity around the world and learn about them, even experience their culture. I hope that one day, you can be as grateful as I am for what you know about a different land and people. I thank you for being a part of my world, and I welcome you to visit mine."

- It takes 2,500 gallons of water to make 1 pound of beef and 1,800 gallons to grow enough cotton for a pair of blue jeans (TABLE 2.1).
- Clean water is a huge issue in China, so much so that the country tried (and failed) to license and export fresh water from the Great Lakes Region in the United States and Canada.
- The Three Gorges Dam in central China caused the earth's axis to tilt by nearly an inch.

TABLE 2.1 The Real Cost of Water

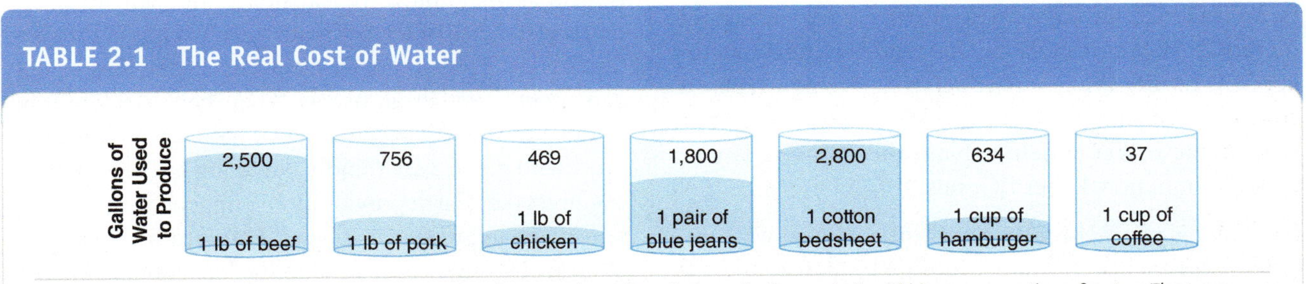

NOTE: Fresh water consumption is far more extensive than people realize. A closer look reveals the hidden consumption of water. The term "virtual water" is used to describe the amount of water used to create a product; in essence, a "water footprint."

Data from National Geographic Society. *Water: Our Thirsty World* [special issue], *National Geographic*, April 2010; and Water Footprint Network (www.waterfootprint.org). Accessed February 16, 2011.

FIGURE 2.5 People, including children, are spending less time outside and in nature. Many children prefer to be inside playing video games or surfing the Internet. Being disconnected from nature may be harmful to one's health, including inadequate exposure to natural sunlight for vitamin D absorption.

FIGURE 2.6 In every generation, there are people who predict humanity's demise. The world is not coming to an end, but our future will certainly depend on how we act now.

Perhaps the most subtle warning of a disconnect from our environment is the news that for the first time it has been noted that Americans are not getting enough vitamin D, as explained by nutritionist and *New York Times* reporter Jane Brody. Vitamin D deficiency is due to lack of exposure to sunlight and poor dietary habits. Sunlight is often referred to as the "sunshine vitamin" because, as sunlight reaches the skin, it reacts to help form vitamin D. Today, people spend little time outdoors, denying themselves exposure to adequate amounts of sunlight (FIG. 2.5).

Vitamin D isn't the only nutritional/environmental problem. People who saw the documentary film *Food, Inc.* (or who read the book by Karl Weber) are acutely aware that the move away from family farms to industrial farms in the last few decades has greatly compromised the quality of food, primarily chicken and beef, and encouraged the proliferation of products that use high-fructose corn syrup. Changes in the food industry, along with inadequate exercise, help explain the recent dramatic increase in national obesity levels.

Sadly, what we lack in the sunshine vitamin, we compensate for plenty with our exposure to plastic, and not just water bottles clogging our landfills. In her acclaimed expose on this ubiquitous substance, Susan Freinkel's book, *Plastic: A Toxic Love Story*, highlights a frightening bio-ecological stressor: many plastics (derived from petroleum and natural gas) once thought to be inert are now known to leak synthetic estrogens into the fluids and foods they contain to interfere with the hormones of our endocrine system that orchestrate growth, development, and the immune system, with phthalates being one of the biggest concerns to one's health.

Some of the world's leading scientists are not optimistic about the future of humanity, given the stresses we have put on our environment and, in turn, ourselves (FIG. 2.6). Physicist Stephen Hawking's outlook for humanity is grim at best, unless we learn to change our ways, and quickly. In a 2010 interview with the Huffington Post blog (Stuart, 2010), he stated, "We are entering an increasingly dangerous period in our history. There have been a number of times in the past when survival has been a question of touch and go. We are rapidly depleting the finite natural resources that Earth provides, and our genetic code carries selfish and aggressive instincts." Harvard biologist E. O. Wilson and others now refer to the loss of biodiversity in our modern era as the "sixth mass extinction" on Earth, with hunting and fishing, loss of natural habitat, and pollution as the primary causes (Eldredge, 2001). Meanwhile, sociologist Jared Diamond warns that if positive changes are not made with regard to our use of resources and our relationship to our natural environment, we too will face extinction.

Not all views of the future of humanity are so dire or fatalistic. Several, in fact, are quite optimistic—with the caveat that we must act now. Consider the viewpoint of cell biologist and philosopher Bruce Lipton. In his book *Spontaneous Evolution*, he states: "Society is beginning to realize that our current beliefs are detrimental and that our world is in a very precarious position. The new science (the nexus of quantum physics, psychology, and biology) paves a way into a hopeful story of humanity's potential future, one that promotes planetary healing." Lipton uses the model of holism (in which all parts are respected and come together for a greater purpose) as the template for his optimism. Lipton is among a growing group of social luminaries, including Barbara Marx-Hubbard, Jean Houston, Christine Page, Edgar Mitchell, Elizabeth Sartoris, and Gregg Braden, who share this optimistic paradigm of humanity's shifting consciousness (Schlitz, 2010). In the words of the rock musician Sting, "Yes we are in an appalling environmental crisis, but I think as a species, we evolve through crises. That's the only glimmer of hope, really" (Richter, 2010).

Another ray of hope shone brightly on November 5, 2016, when the Paris Agreement on Climate Change became official, instituting restrictions on CO_2 emissions, as well as other strategies to halt global warming.

When technostress, incivility (mixed with political instability), and environmental disconnect combine, they form a "perfect storm of stress." How do these aspects of the sociology of stress affect you directly? Consider this: As climate changes create more droughts, food prices will increase. As chemicals from discarded technology (smartphones, flat screen TVs, etc.) pollute water supplies, environmental stressors increase. As oil reserves decrease, increasing the price of a barrel of oil, all things tied to gasoline (food distribution, travel, consumer products) will increase in price, adding to an ever-growing sense of economic anxiety. The importance of learning and using effective stress management skills becomes even more essential in the twenty-first century.

Occupational Stress

Sociologists suggest that one's family is the first and often the most important social structure, providing social support, but also stress. Coming in a close second in both aspects is one's work environment. While ideally providing professional fulfillment, a creative outlet, and a path to wealth, work is also cited as a source of significant stress by a great many employees. Paul Rosch, M.D., director of the American Institute of Stress, notes that in American society today, **occupational stress**, or job stress, is at an all-time high (FIG. 2.7). He defines job stress as coming from "occupational duties in which the individual perceives having a great deal of responsibility, yet little or no authority or decision-making latitude" (Rosch, 1991).

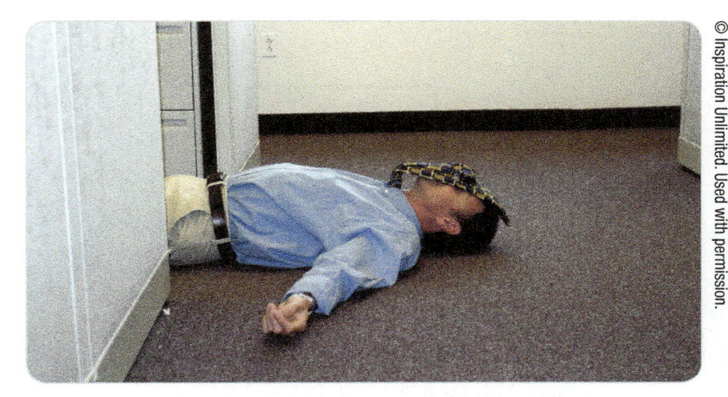

FIGURE 2.7 Worker burnout has reached epic proportions as people strive to personify the Puritan work ethic that deems that work equals worth.

According to a 2013 Harris survey, 83 percent of American workers claim to be stressed out, a 10 percent rise from 2012. Reasons for the rise in stress are attributed to low pay, unreasonable workloads, annoying co-workers, poor work-life balance, and the fear of being laid off or fired (Perman, 2013). Few of these people take advantage of employee assistance programs offered at the worksite (Scott, 2007). One of the first signs of stress at the workplace is burnout, followed by absenteeism. The term *presenteeism* was coined to describe the related problem of going to work but being unproductive and unmotivated, there in body but not in mind.

The cost of stress is not insignificant in terms of work productivity or the bottom line of corporate profits. Rosch noted that the fiscal consequences of occupational stress cost an average of $200 billion each year. Moreover, between 60 and 80 percent of all industrial accidents are stress induced,

Occupational stress: Job-related stress, which often comes from occupational duties for which people perceive themselves as having a great deal of responsibility, yet little or no authority or decision-making latitude.

FIGURE 2.8

as are over 80 percent of all office visits to primary care physicians. Perhaps most striking is that workers' compensation claims associated with stress are skyrocketing, with 90 percent of claims being awarded in settlements.

What are some reasons for job stress? (FIG. 2.8) Although perceptions will vary from person to person, the following is a list compiled by the National Safety Council (2011):

- Lack of job security
- Too much responsibility with little or no authority
- Unrealistic expectations, deadlines, and quotas
- Corporate downsizing, restructuring, or job relocation
- Inadequate training
- Lack of appreciation
- Inadequate time to complete job responsibilities
- Inability to voice concerns
- Lack of creativity and autonomy
- Too much to do with too few resources
- Lack of clear job descriptions
- Commuting and traffic difficulties
- Keeping pace with technology
- Inadequate child care
- Poor working conditions (lighting, ventilation, noise)
- Sexual harassment and racial discrimination
- Workplace violence

Rosch noted that the Public Health Service placed stress-management courses as its top priority in order to improve health standards at the worksite. However, Rosch, who surveyed several hundred existing stress-management programs in cooperation with the Office of Occupational Safety and Health, came to the conclusion that few stress-management programs currently taught in the corporate or industrial setting offer enough substance to make a positive influential change in lifestyle behaviors, because they are either too narrowly focused or too brief, or both. Those programs he did find to be effective showed reduced illness and absenteeism, higher morale, and increased productivity.

Unfortunately, stress in the workplace is not likely to decrease any time soon. In the next decade, more companies will merge, meaning more corporate restructuring. Companies looking to appease stockholders will look for ways to trim budgets, especially by letting go of senior employees and replacing them with a young and eager workforce, or by outsourcing jobs.

Race and Gender Stress

Several national events between 2014 and 2016 brought the issues of racial and gender stress to the forefront, including the Black Lives Matter movement and the 2016 U.S. presidential campaign.

The United States, a nation of immigrants, has often been described as a melting pot, but recently another metaphor has been used to describe the make-up of her citizens: a tossed salad, where assimilation meets head on with cultural diversity. Race and ethnic issues currently make headline news, such as illegal alien issues nationwide, disenfranchised black voters in Florida, poverty in New Orleans, and Muslim Americans facing episodes of discrimination, to name a few issues. Race and gender tensions, however, are not new. It could be argued that they are as old as humanity itself. Since time began, people have felt threatened by other people of different skin color, ethnicity, gender, religion, or sexual preference. The 2008 election of the first African American president has helped jump-start a national discussion on race, but it hasn't resolved intolerance.

Stress, you will remember, is defined as a perceived threat, a threat generated by the ego. These threats manifest in a variety of ways, including stereotyping, prejudice, discrimination, harassment, and even physical harm. Race and gender stress may begin early in life; many children can attest to being bullied in grade school or excluded and teased by social cliques because of their race or gender. The emotional stress associated with this type of angst includes low self-esteem, alienation, and anxiety. Everybody wants to be accepted.

How can society help alleviate race and gender stress? Anti-bullying programs are being implemented in many schools nationwide, helping raise awareness among kids and parents of the dangers of bullying and cyber-bullying. On television, many shows have tried to better reflect the demographics of American society with casts of various ethnicities and gender identity issues (e.g., *Glee*, *Transparent*, and *Sense*). The Women's March on Washington in January 2017 also made a strong statement regarding gender inequity issues. Although these are steps in the right direction, school curricula marches on Washington D.C., and television shows alone cannot change the world overnight. They are a start, however. Remember that when people demonstrate a bias toward your race, gender, ethnic background, or anything related to these concepts, they are projecting their fears onto you. A common reaction is to meet stress with stress, but the best answer is to rise above it and take the high road.

Experts remind us that the cultural fabric of society is in a tremendous transition, one unparalleled in recorded human history. Indeed, we are products of our society, and society is in a state of rapid flux regarding demographics, technology, economics, global warming, and several other factors that lead to an increasingly dynamic landscape. In the end, everyone will be affected. The best strategy for coping with these changes is to adapt to them.

SUMMARY

- Sociology is described as the study of human social behavior within families, organizations, and institutions. Societal stress is a force to be reckoned with in today's culture. Once called *future shock*, the tsunami of social issues is now referred to as *superstress*—the inability to cope with an overwhelming amount of change.
- No one is exempt from the sociology of stress.
- *Technostress* is a term used to describe the overwhelming frustrations of sensory bombardment and poor boundaries that result from the plethora of technological gadgets. Technostress began with personal computers but has evolved with the advent of and addiction to social networking. The body's physiology wasn't designed to be "on" all the time. The result is burnout and physical health issues.
- Social stress includes a decline in social etiquette. A lack of civility (demonstrated by rude, impatient behavior) is on the rise.
- Experts suggest that one aspect of societal stress is an environmental disconnect: a growing disregard of the environment by humanity, such that dramatic changes, from dwindling supplies of fresh water to declining food quality to environmental pollution, will have a significant impact on each individual's lifestyle and health.
- *Nature deficit disorder* is a term describing people's absence from the natural world. One result is inadequate amounts of sunlight exposure, which produces a vitamin D deficiency.
- Most people garner their self-worth from their jobs or careers, yet many Americans cite their job as being stressful, thus impacting self-worth, self-esteem, family relationships, and many other aspects of their lives in negative ways.
- Race and gender issues have always been part of the social fabric and continue to contribute largely to stress, especially as people express themselves with reckless abandon in the digital age.

STUDY GUIDE QUESTIONS

1. How would you define the term *sociology*? How would you describe the concept of the sociology of stress?
2. How would you best explain the concept of technostress?
3. What factors are associated with technostress?
4. What explains the attraction of (or addiction to) being plugged in all the time?
5. What effect does information overload and sensory bombardment have on brain function and cognitive abilities?
6. How does stress affect our relationships with others, in terms of social etiquette?
7. What factors are associated with environmental disconnect?
8. Give examples of ways in which society can help alleviate race and gender stress.

REFERENCES AND RESOURCES

Alter, A. *Irresistible: The Rise of Addictive Technology and the Business of Keeping Us Hooked*. Penguin Press, New York, 2017.

Becker, D. *One Nation Under Stress: The Trouble With Stress as an Idea*. New York, Oxford University Press, 2013.

Begley, S. I Can't Think, *Newsweek*, March 7, 2011: 28–33.

Brody, J. What Do You Lack? Probably Vitamin D, *New York Times*, July 26, 2010. www.nytimes.com/2010/07/27/health/27brod.html?_r=1&partner=rss&emc=rss.

Brown, L. "The Real Threat to Our Future Is Peak Water." *The Guardian*. July 6, 2013. http://www.theguardian.com/global-development/2013/jul/06/water-supplies-shrinking-threat-to-food.

Carr, N. *The Shallows: What the Internet Is Doing to Our Brains*. W. W. Norton, New York, 2010.

Davis, D. *Disconnect*. Dutton Book, New York, 2010.

Della Cava, M. Attention Spans Get Rewired, *USA Today*, August 4, 2010.

Diamond, J. *Collapse: How Societies Choose to Fail or Succeed*. Penguin Books, New York, 2011.

Dossey, L. Plugged In: At What Price? The Perils and Promise of Electrical Communications, *Explore* 5:5, 2009.

Eldredge, N. The Sixth Extinction, *ActionBioscience.org*, June 2001, www.actionbioscience.org/.

Freinkel, S. *Plastic: A Toxic Love Story*. Houghton Mifflin Harcourt, New York, 2011.

Garrett, T. Lack of Civility in America Brought to Light, *Canyon News*, September 19, 2009.

Glei, J. *Unsubscribe: How to Kill Email Anxiety, Avoid Distractions, and Get Real Work Done*. Public Affairs Books, New York, 2016.

Greenfield, S. *ID: The Quest for Meaning in the 21st Century*, London, Sceptre, 2009.

Greenfield, S. Perspectives: Reinventing Human Identity, *New Scientist*, May 21, 2008:48–49.

Kirwood, S. Climate Change and Conflict. Living On Earth. August 2, 2013. http://www.loe.org/shows/segments.html?programID=13-P13-00031&segmentID=1.

Lallas, N. *Renewing Values in America: Are You Ready to Do Your Part?* Mill Valley, CA, ArtisPress, 2009.

Lanman, S. Choosing Civility in the Face of Rudeness, *Rutgers Focus*, March 2010. http://news.rutgers.edu/focus/issue.2010-03-02.2969546649/article.2010-03-30.3504010889.

Lee, R. *The Superstress Solution*. Random House, New York, 2010.

Lewin, T. If Your Kids Are Awake, They're Probably Online. *New York Times*, January 20, 2010, www.nytimes.com/2010/01/20/education/20wired.html.

Lipton, B., and Bhaerman, S. *Spontaneous Evolution*. Carlsbad, CA, HayHouse, 3rd ed. 2010.

Louv, R. *Last Child in the Woods*. Algonquin Books, Chapel Hill, NC, 2008.

Marquardt, K. The Value of a True Lunch Break, *US News and World Report*, November 23, 2010. http://money.usnews.com/money/careers/articles/2010/11/23/the-value-of-a-true-lunch-break.

National Geographic Society. Water: Our Thirsty World [special issue], *National Geographic*, April 2010.

National Public Radio. Digital Overload: Your Brain on Gadgets, *Fresh Air*, August 24, 2010, www.npr.org/templates/transcript/transcript.php?storyId=129384107.

National Safety Council. March 31, 2011, http://www.nsc.org/safety_work/Pages/Home.aspx.

Page, S. Poll: USA Fed Up with Political Incivility, *USA Today*, April 4, 2010. http://www.usatoday.com/news/washington/2010-04-21-civility-poll_N.htm.

Perman, C. Argggh! American Workers Are at a Breaking Point. April 9, 2013. Business on NBCnews.com. www.cnbc.com/id/100624671.

Richards, M. D. How Much Incivility Will American Voters Tolerate in the Race to the White House? February 2, 2016. http://www.krcresearch.com/how-much-incivility-will-american-voters-tolerate-in-the-race-to-the-white-house/.

Richtel, M. Your Brain on Computers: Attached to Technology and Paying a Price, *New York Times*, June 6, 2010.

Richter, A. Sting, the Yogi Behind the Music, *Energy Times*, October 2010, www.energytimes.com/pages/features/1010/sting.html.

Rosch, P. Is Job Stress America's Leading Adult Health Problem? A Commentary, *Business Insights*, 7(1):4, 7, 1991.

Rubinkam, M. During Boring Classes, Texting Is the New Doodling, *Netscape Gadgets & Tech*, November 26, 2010, http://webcenters.netscape.compuserve.com/tech/story.jsp?floc=DC-headline&sc=f&idq=/ff/story/1001/20101126/5255.htm.

Rushkoff, D. *Present Shock: When Everything Happens Now*. Current Books/Penguin., New York, 2013.

Schlitz, M. Keynote Address, Healing Touch International, St. Louis, MO, September 12, 2010.

Scott, E. New Research on Employee Burnout, *About.com Stress Management Blog*, May 22, 2016. http://stress.about.com/b/2007/10/15/new-research-on-employee-burnout.htm.

Seaward, B.L. Sleep Wellness, Digital Detox, and Mindfulness. White paper. WELCOA, Omaha, NE, May 13, 2015.

Seigler, K. Tweeting with the Birds: Pitch Tent, Switch to Wi-Fi, *NPR*, August 3, 2010, www.npr.org/templates/story/story.php?storyId=128697566.

Shirky, C. *Cognitive Surplus: Creativity and Generosity in a Connected Age*. Penguin Press, New York, 2010.

Shirkey, C. *Cognitive Surplus: How Technology Makes Consumers into Collaborators*. Penguin Books, New York. 2011.

Simon, S. Using Your BlackBerry Off-Hours Could Be Overtime, *NPR*, August 14, 2010, www.npr.org/templates/transcript/transcript.php?storyId=129184907.

Smith, R., and Lourie, B. *Slow Death by Rubber Duck: The Secret Danger of Everyday Things*. Counterpoint, Berkeley, CA, 2011.

Stuart, H. Stephen Hawking to Human Race: Move to Outer Space or Face Extinction, *Huffington Post*, www.huffingtonpost.com/2010/08/06/stephen-hawking-to-human_n_673387.html.

Swartz, J. Survey Warns of E-mail Stress, *USA Today Technology Live*, July 16, 2010, http://content.usatoday.com/communities/technologylive/post/2010/07/e-mail-stress-when-is-too-much-e-mail-too-much/1?loc=interstitialskip.

Temple, J. All those tweets, apps, updates may drain the brain. Sunday, April 17, 2011. http://www.sfgate.com/cgibin/article.cgi?f=/c/a/2011/04/17/BUTO1J0S2P.DTL.

Tugend, A. Incivility Can Have Costs Beyond Hurting People. *The New York Times*. Nov. 19, 2010. http://www.nytimes.com/2010/11/20/yourmoney/20shortcuts.html?pagewanted=all&_r=0.

Turkle, S. *Alone Together*. Basic Books, New York, 2011.

Weber, K. (ed.). *Food, Inc.: How Industrial Food Is Making Us Sicker, Fatter and Poorer—And What You Can Do About It*. PublicAffairs, New York, 2009.

Weil, M., and Rosen, L. *Technostress: Coping with Technology @work @home @play*. John Wiley and Sons, New York, 1998.

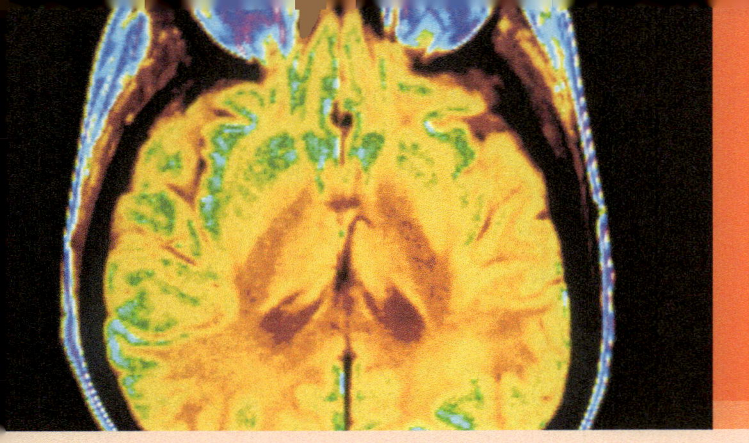

CHAPTER 3

Physiology of Stress

To understand the stress response, we must possess a fundamental knowledge not only of psychology but of physiology as well.

—George Everly

Hans Selye's discovery of a direct relationship between chronic stress and the excessive wear and tear throughout the body laid the foundation for a clearer understanding of how physiological systems work in an extremely complex and integrative way. Perhaps because of this discovery and the fact that physical deterioration is so noticeable, much attention has been directed toward the physiology of stress. This chapter will take you through some basic concepts that explain the physiological dynamics involved with the stress response—specifically, the immediate, intermediate, and prolonged effects on the body. These processes will be explained in terms of "pathways," which set in action the systematic and integrative steps of the stress response. Because physiology involves specific nomenclature outside the realm of your everyday vocabulary, you may find the nature of this chapter to be very specific and its contents very detailed. Most likely it will merit more than one reading to fully grasp, understand, and appreciate how the body responds to stress. The importance of a strong familiarity with human physiology as influenced by stressful stimuli becomes evident when the necessary steps are taken to effectively deal with the symptoms they produce, especially when using relaxation techniques. For example, it is important to know how the body functions when using specific imagery, visualization, music therapy, autogenic training, progressive muscular relaxation, and biofeedback.

In many circles, this topic of study is referred to as *psychophysiology*. This term reflects the fact that a sensory stimulus (perceived threat) that prompts the stress response must be processed at the mental level before it can cascade down one or more physiological pathways. In other words, the term **psychophysiology** suggests that there is a mind-body relationship and supports the theory that many diseases and illnesses are psychosomatic, meaning that their origins lie in the mind through the higher brain centers. Although the mind-body dualism suggested by Descartes is no longer a viable model for a complete understanding of human physiology, to hold an appreciation of the "whole person" we must first

Psychophysiology: A field of study based on the principle that the mind and body are one, where thoughts and perceptions affect potentially all aspects of physiology.

examine the parts to understand how they connect to that whole.

Three systems are directly involved with the physiology of stress: the nervous system, the endocrine system, and the immune system, all of which can be triggered by perceived threats.

The Central Nervous System

The nervous system can be divided into two parts: the **central nervous system (CNS)**, which consists of the brain and spinal cord, and the peripheral nervous system (PNS), comprising all neural pathways to the extremities. The human brain is further divided into three levels: the vegetative level, the limbic system, and the neocortical level (FIG. 3.1).

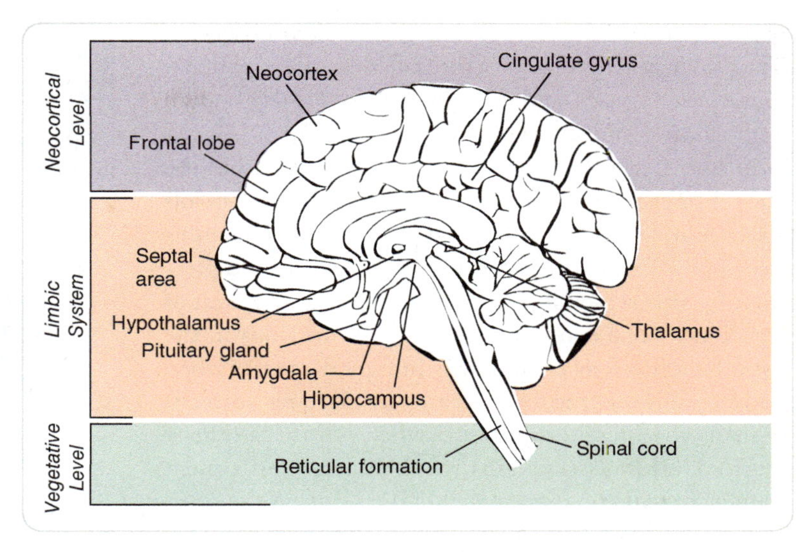

FIGURE 3.1 Three levels of the human brain: vegetative level, limbic system, and neocortical level.

The Vegetative Level

The lowest level of the brain consists of both the reticular formation and the brain stem. The reticular formation, or more specifically the fibers that make up the **reticular activating system (RAS)**, is the link connecting the brain to the spinal cord. Several stress physiologists believe that it is the bridge joining the mind (brain) and the body as one; this organ functions as a communications link between the mind and the body (FIG. 3.2). The brain stem, consisting of the pons, medulla oblongata, and mesencephalon, is responsible for involuntary functions of the human body, such as heartbeat, respiration, and vasomotor activity. It is considered the automatic-pilot control center of the brain, which assumes responsibility for keeping the vital organs and vegetative processes functioning at all times. This level is thought to be the most primitive section of the human brain because this portion is similar to those of all other mammals.

FIGURE 3.2 Brain physiology at work.

Central nervous system (CNS): Consists of the brain and spinal column, while the peripheral nervous system (PNS) comprises all neural pathways to the extremities.

Reticular activating system (RAS): The neural fibers that link the brain to the spinal column.

Limbic system: The midlevel of the brain, including the hypothalamus and amygdala, which is thought to be responsible for emotional processing.

The Limbic System

The second or midlevel portion of the brain is called the **limbic system**. The limbic system is the emotional control center. Several tissue centers in this level are directly responsible for the biochemical chain of events that constitutes the stress response Cannon observed. The limbic system consists of the thalamus, the hypothalamus, the amygdala, and the pituitary gland, also known as the master endocrine gland. These four glands work in unison to maintain a level of homeostasis within the body. For example, it is the hypothalamus that controls appetite and body-core temperature. The hypothalamus also appears to be the center that registers pain and pleasure; for this reason it is often referred to as the "seat of emotions." The combination of these functions in the hypothalamus may explain why hunger decreases when body-core temperature increases in extreme ambient heat, or why appetite diminishes when you are extremely worried. This also explains why tempers (and violent crimes) flare up on extremely hot days during the summer months, as crime statistics prove each year. Research evidence is clear that fear is first registered in the amygdala. When a threat is encountered, the hypothalamus carries out four specific functions: (1) it activates the autonomic nervous system; (2) it stimulates the secretion of adrenocorticotropic hormone (ACTH); (3) it produces antidiuretic hormone (ADH) or vasopressin; and (4) it stimulates the thyroid gland to produce thyroxine. All of these will be discussed in greater detail later.

The Neocortical Level

The neocortex is the highest and most sophisticated level of the brain. It is at this level that sensory information is processed (decoded) as a threat or a nonthreat and where cognition (thought processes) takes place. Housed within the neocortex are the neural mechanisms allowing one to employ analysis, imagination, creativity, intuition, logic, memory, and organization. It is this highly developed area of brain tissue that is thought to separate humans from all other species.

As Figure 3.1 illustrates, the positions of these structures are such that a higher level can override a lower level of the brain. Thus, conscious thought can influence emotional response, just as conscious thought can intercede in the involuntary control of the vegetative functions to control heart rate, ventilation, and even the flow of blood. This fact will become important to recognize when learning coping skills and relaxation techniques designed to override the stress response and facilitate physiological homeostasis.

> **Autonomic nervous system (ANS):** Often referred to as the automatic nervous system, the ANS consists of the sympathetic (arousal) and parasympathetic (relaxed) nervous systems. This part of the central nervous system requires no conscious thought; actions such as breathing and heart rate are programmed to function automatically.

BOX 3.1 The Amygdala Revisited

The brain has many regions involved with consciousness, stress, and behavior. In the past several years, the small almond-shaped portion of the brain known as the amygdala, a key structure in the limbic system, has proven to be of great interest with regard to functional magnetic resonance imaging (fMRI) research and stress. For decades scientists knew the amygdala was associated with aggressive behavior (anger) as well as feelings and behavior associated with fear and anxiety. Additionally, studies have found that the amygdala is responsible for the formation and consolidation of memories associated with events that provoked a strong emotional response (including anger and fear). It is suggested that these memories are imprinted via the neural synapses, perhaps as an ancestral survival dynamic (e.g., beware of the rattlesnake). Through a complicated dynamic between the amygdala and the hippocampus, specific memories of past events can reprise the fight-or-flight response, merely by thinking about them. More recent studies have also linked the amygdala to binge drinking, most likely associated with stress.

Separate from the CNS is a network of neural fibers that feed into the CNS and work in close collaboration with it. This neural tract, the peripheral nervous system (PNS), comprises two individual networks. The first is the somatic network, a bidirectional circuit responsible for transmitting sensory messages along the neural pathways between the five senses and the higher brain centers. These are called the efferent (toward periphery) and afferent (toward brain) neural pathways. The second branch of the PNS is called the **autonomic nervous system (ANS)**. The ANS regulates visceral activities and vital organs, including circulation, digestion, respiration, and temperature regulation. It received the name *autonomic* because this system can function without conscious thought or voluntary control, and does so most, if not all, of the time.

Research conducted by endocrinologist Bruce McEwen indicates that initially a stressful encounter is etched into the memory bank (so as to avoid it down the road), but that

BOX 3.2 A Closer Look at Panic Attacks

ABC's *Nightline* co-anchor Dan Harris didn't plan on starting a daily meditation practice. In fact, it was the furthest thing from his mind, until he experienced a series of on-air panic attacks. In his search for peace of mind (and as a way to keep his career intact) he stumbled upon mindfulness meditation. In his best-selling book *10% Happier*, he not only tells his story, but uses his position of national notoriety to explain that meditation is a skill that everyone should include in their list of daily habits. For Dan Harris, it was a panic attack, but everyone today is riding a wave of adrenaline-based information overload.

Anyone can have a rush of fear come over them, but some people are prone to a more severe experience, often called a "panic attack." A panic attack is often described as "the stress response on steroids." In short, it is the response of the sympathetic nervous system. Panic attacks can occur in any place, at any time, and often out of the blue. Physical symptoms of a panic attack include hyperventilation, a racing heart, sweating, chest pain, a choking feeling, nausea, chills, dizziness or feeling faint, tingling sensations, and muscle tremors or shaking. Some people describe it as feeling like they are having a heart attack. Other symptoms include a feeling of impending death, loss of sanity, or having a "nervous breakdown." Panic attacks are most common in early adulthood, but can occur at any age. Women are more prone to this condition than men (Smith and Segal, 2016).

Panic attacks occur abruptly. They may seem like they last forever to those who experience them, but the duration is typically about 10 to 20 minutes (in rare cases over an hour). What is the cause of a panic attack? Although they seem to come out of the blue, every panic attack is triggered by some decoded sensory stimuli (or memory) that creates an intense fear or apprehension about some future event. Ironically, some panic attacks are brought on by fearing another panic attack (Baker, 2011).

While some experts suggest that panic attacks may be hereditary, others suggest that they may be due to abnormalities (hypersensitivity) in the amygdala and/or hypothalamus that control the fight-or-flight response. Some panic attacks are associated with substance abuse, but the vast majority are caused by stress (the interpretation of an exaggerated threat).

What is the best way to cope with a panic attack? The best strategy is to bring yourself back into the present moment and ground yourself. Experts suggest to sit on the floor with your back up against the wall. Place your hands and your feet firmly on the ground and take several deep breaths. If you wish, repeat to yourself the phrase, "My hands and feet are firmly on the ground." If a panic attack occurs while driving, pull over, stop the car, place your hands down by your waist, and repeat the phrase, "My hands and feet are fully grounded." You can train yourself to avoid or minimize the effects of panic attacks by engaging in both effective coping skills and relaxation techniques (McDonagh, 2015).

repeated episodes of stress decrease memory by weakening hippocampal brain cells. Chronic stress is thought to wither the fragile connection between neurons in this part of the brain, resulting in "brain shrinkage."

Until recently it was believed that, unlike the voluntary somatic system involved in muscle movement, the ANS could not be intercepted by conscious thought, but now it is recognized that both systems can be influenced by higher mental processes. The ANS works in close coordination with the CNS to maintain a favorable homeostatic condition throughout the body. There are two branches of the ANS that act to maintain this homeostatic balance, the **sympathetic** and **parasympathetic** nervous systems, and these are activated by the hypothalamus. Most organs are innervated (stimulated) by nerve fibers of both the sympathetic and parasympathetic systems.

The Autonomic Nervous System

The Sympathetic and Parasympathetic Nervous Systems

The sympathetic nervous system is responsible for the responses associated with the fight-or-flight response (FIG. 3.3). Through the release of substances called

Sympathetic: The branch of the central nervous system that triggers the fight-or-flight response when some element of threat is present.

Parasympathetic: The branch of the central nervous system that specifically calms the body through the parasympathetic response.

Stress with a Human Face

George is 19 years old, yet the stress he has experienced in his first year serving as a Marine in Iraq makes him seem at least 10 years older—from the lines on his face to the tenor of his voice. I met George in Honolulu International Airport. We were both waiting to fly home to Colorado: me from vacation, George from the war. A delay in our scheduled departure allowed a friendly conversation at the gate's lounge, but for the most part, I just listened.

"You don't know what stress is until you are smack in the middle of a war. Your body is on alert 24 hours a day. You are constantly aroused even when you're trying to relax. You can never fully relax in a war zone. You can feel your heart pounding in your chest nearly all the time; a 24/7 adrenaline rush! I guess you just get used to it. All of your senses are heightened—never knowing what to expect, but always ready for something. This is my second visit home and I am on guard right now as we speak. When I go into a restaurant back home, the first thing I do is scout out all the exits. It's survival mode. You can never be relaxed completely in a war zone. Sadly, this mentality stays with you outside the war zone, like right now.

"The stress of war is incredible. It only gets worse when your patrol has encountered an IED [improvised explosive device]. I have lost several buddies to these. You go right into reaction mode: Stop the bleeding! They train us all in emergency first aid and you just pray you never have to use it. When one of these goes off you don't have time to be afraid. You just react. Stop the bleeding, whoever's bleeding, whatever's bleeding. Usually it's an arm or a leg blown off. I've seen stuff that would curl your hair. No matter what they tell you in basic training, there is nothing that can prepare you for war. I know several guys with PTSD (post-traumatic stress disorder). I didn't believe in PTSD until I got to Iraq. I have crazy dreams at night. They say having nightmares is part of PTSD, but how can you not? After all it is a war zone . . . your mind is processing all that's gone on in the course of the previous day. War is not the normal course of a typical day for most people, and definitely not Americans.

"Yes, they [the military leaders] hand out psychotropic drugs to keep soldiers up. Exponential Adrenaline Rush! I don't take 'em. I need all my wits about me when I am out there, outside the Green Zone . . . even inside the Green Zone. . . . Believe me . . . war is the ultimate stress zone."

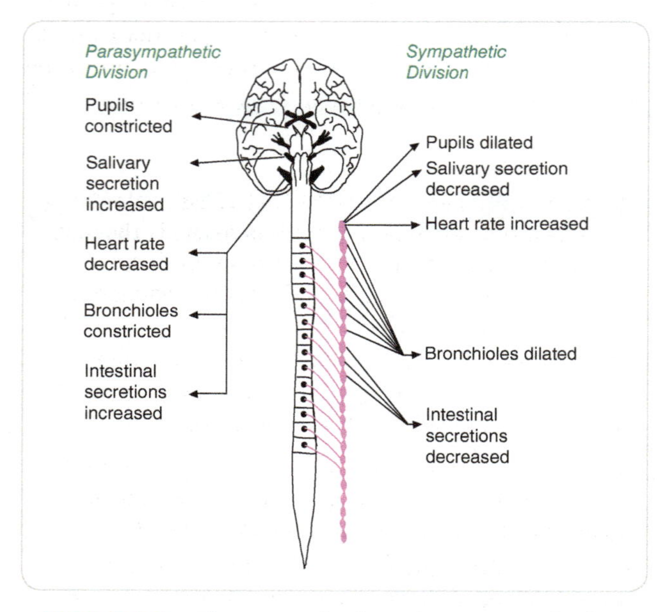

FIGURE 3.3 The sympathetic and parasympathetic systems. Internal organs are typically innervated by neural fibers from both sympathetic and parasympathetic divisions.

catecholamines, specifically **epinephrine** (adrenaline) and **norepinephrine** (noradrenaline), at various neural synapses, a series of events occurs in several organ tissues to prepare the body for rapid metabolic change and physical movement. Sympathetic drive is associated with energy expenditure (e.g., jogging), a process known as **catabolic functioning**, where various metabolites are

Epinephrine: A special neurochemical referred to as a catecholamine that is responsible for immediate physical readiness for stress including increased heart rate and blood pressure. It works in unison with norepinephrine.

Norepinephrine: A special neurochemical referred to as a catacholamine that is responsible for immediate physical readiness to stress including increased heart rate and blood pressure. It works in unison with epinephrine.

Catabolic functioning: A metabolic process in which metabolites are broken down for energy in preparation for, or in the process of, exercise (fight or flight).

BOX 3.3 Hormonal Imbalance

The endocrine system is an amazing yet delicate system of chemical properties aligned to ensure physiological homeostasis. The stress hormone dehydroepiandrosterone (DHEA), for example, is secreted from the adrenal gland. DHEA is also known as a precursor sex hormone that decreases in both production and secretion throughout the aging process. Speculation suggests that supplementation of DHEA might increase stamina and memory, and may decrease the aging process in much the same way as the antioxidants beta-carotene, vitamin C, vitamin E, and selenium. Results of a host of studies revealed that no significant changes in these aspects occurred in either animals or humans. Data published by the American Cancer Society reveals that increased amounts of DHEA, above what the body normally produces, might actually promote cancer. Supplementation is recommended only on the advice of your physician.

Serotonin and **melatonin** are not stress hormones, yet they do seem to have an effect on mood. Decreases in both serotonin and melatonin are thought to be related to bouts of depression. Many things affect serotonin levels in the brain—from the natural and synthetic chemicals in the foods you eat, to the amount of sunlight you receive in the course of a day, to perhaps things we still don't know. Research is inconclusive about how serotonin affects mood. Most likely, stress affects serotonin levels as well.

broken down for energy in preparation for movement. It is the release of epinephrine and norepinephrine that causes the acceleration of heart rate, the increase in the force of myocardial contraction, vasodilation of arteries throughout working muscles, vasoconstriction of arteries to nonworking muscles, dilation of pupils and bronchi, increased ventilation, reduction of digestive activity, released glucose from the liver, and several other functions that prepare the body to fight or flee. It is the sympathetic system that is responsible for supplying skeletal muscles with oxygenated, nutrient-rich blood for energy metabolism. Currently it is thought that norepinephrine serves primarily to assist epinephrine, as the ratio of these two chemical substances released at neural synapses is 5:1 epinephrine to norepinephrine during the stress response. The effects of epinephrine and norepinephrine are very short, lasting only seconds. Because of their rapid release from neural endings, as well as their rapid influence on targeted organ tissue, the effects of the sympathetic nervous system are categorized as **immediate**.

Just as the sympathetic neural drive is associated with energy expenditure, the parasympathetic drive is responsible for energy conservation and relaxation. This is referred to as **anabolic functioning**, during which body cells are allowed to regenerate. The parasympathetic nervous system is dominated by the tenth cranial, or vagus, nerve, which in turn is influenced by the brain stem. When activated, the parasympathetic nervous system releases **acetylcholine** (ACh), a neurological agent that decreases metabolic activity and returns the body to homeostasis. The influence of the parasympathetic drive is associated with a reduction in heart rate, ventilation, blood pressure, muscle tension, and several other functions. Both systems are partially active at all times; however, the sympathetic and parasympathetic systems are mutually exclusive in that they cannot dominate visceral activity simultaneously. These two systems allow for the precise regulation of visceral organ activity, much like the use of the accelerator and brake when driving. Sympathetic arousal, like a gas pedal pushed to the car floor, becomes the dominant force during stress, and parasympathetic tone holds influence over the body at all other times to promote homeostasis. In other words, you cannot be physically aroused and relaxed at the same time.

Question 10

Serotonin: A neurotransmitter that is associated with mood. A decrease in serotonin levels is thought to be related to depression. Serotonin levels are affected by many factors including stress hormones and the foods you consume.

Melatonin: A hormone secreted in the brain that is related to sleep, mood, and perhaps several other aspects of physiology and consciousness.

Immediate (effects of stress): A neural response to cognitive processing in which epinephrine and norepinephrine are released, lasting only seconds.

Anabolic functioning: A physiological process in which various body cells (e.g., muscle tissue) regenerate or grow.

Acetylcholine: A chemical substance released by the parasympathetic nervous system to help the body return to homeostasis from the stress response.

But there are exceptions to the dynamics of these biochemical reactions. For example, it is sympathetic nerves, not parasympathetic nerves, that release ACh in the sweat glands to decrease body-core temperature during arousal. And sympathetic and parasympathetic stimulation of salivary glands is not antagonistic; both influence the secretion of saliva. In addition, all blood vessels are influenced by sympathetic dominance, with the exception of the vasculature of the penis and clitoris, which is activated by parasympathetic innervation.

The Endocrine System

The endocrine system consists of a series of glands located throughout the body that regulate metabolic functions requiring endurance rather than speed. The endocrine system is a network of four components: glands, hormones, circulation, and target organs. Endocrine glands manufacture and release biochemical substances called hormones. Hormones are "chemical messengers" made up of protein compounds that are programmed to attach to specific cell receptor sites to alter (increase or decrease) cell metabolism. Hormones are transported through the bloodstream from the glands that produced them to the target organs they are called upon to influence. The heart, skeletal muscle, and arteries are among the organs most targeted by hormones for metabolic change.

The glands that are most closely involved with the stress response are the pituitary, thyroid, and adrenal glands. The **pituitary gland** is called "the master gland" because it manufactures several important hormones, which then trigger hormone release in other organs. The **hypothalamus**, however, appears to have direct influence over the pituitary gland (FIG. 3.4). The thyroid gland increases the general metabolic rate. Perhaps the gland that has the most direct impact on the stress response, however, is the **adrenal gland** (FIG. 3.5). The adrenal gland, a cone-shaped mass of tissue about the size of a small grapefruit, sits on top of each kidney. The adrenal gland (known as "the stress gland") has two distinct parts, each of which produces hormones with very different functions. The exterior of the adrenal gland is called the adrenal cortex, and it manufactures and releases hormones called corticosteroids. There are two types of

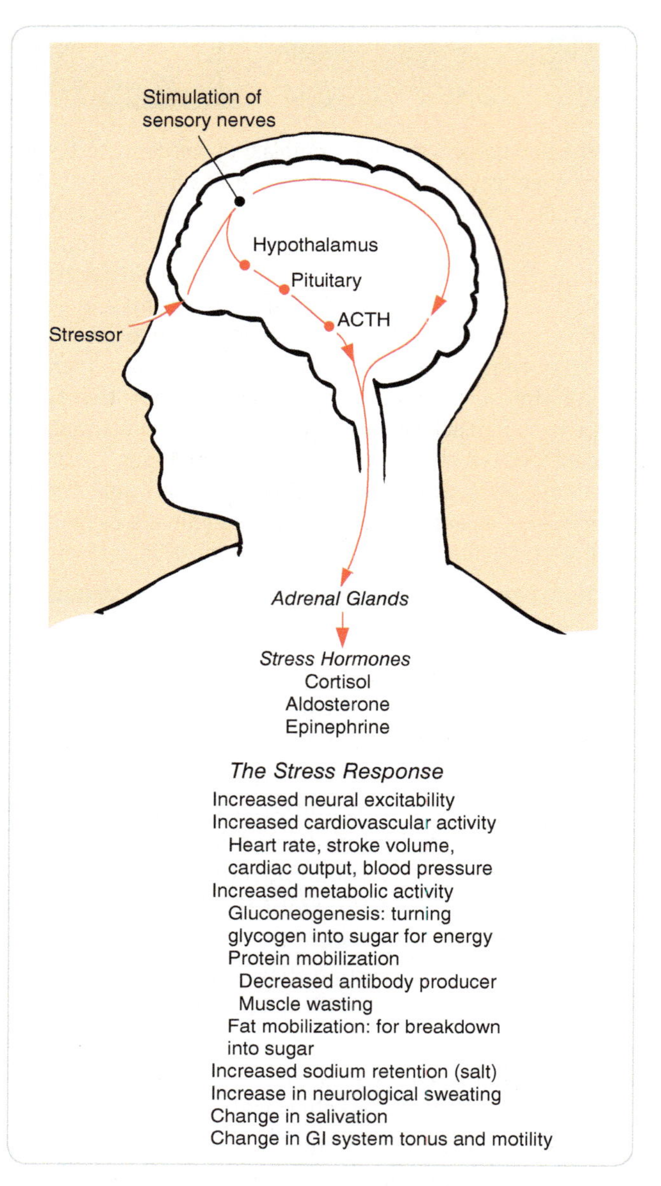

FIGURE 3.4 The physiological response to stress.

Pituitary gland: An endocrine gland ("master gland") located below the hypothalamus that, upon command from the hypothalamus, releases ACTH and then commands the adrenal glands to secrete their stress hormones.

Hypothalamus: Often called the "seat of the emotions," the hypothalamus is involved with emotional processing. When a thought is perceived as a threat, the hypothalamus secretes a substance called corticotropin-releasing factor (CRF) to the pituitary gland to activate the fight-or-flight response.

Adrenal gland: The endocrine glands that are located on top of each kidney that house and release several stress hormones including cortisol and the catecholamines epinephrine and norepinephrine. The adrenal gland is known as "the stress gland."

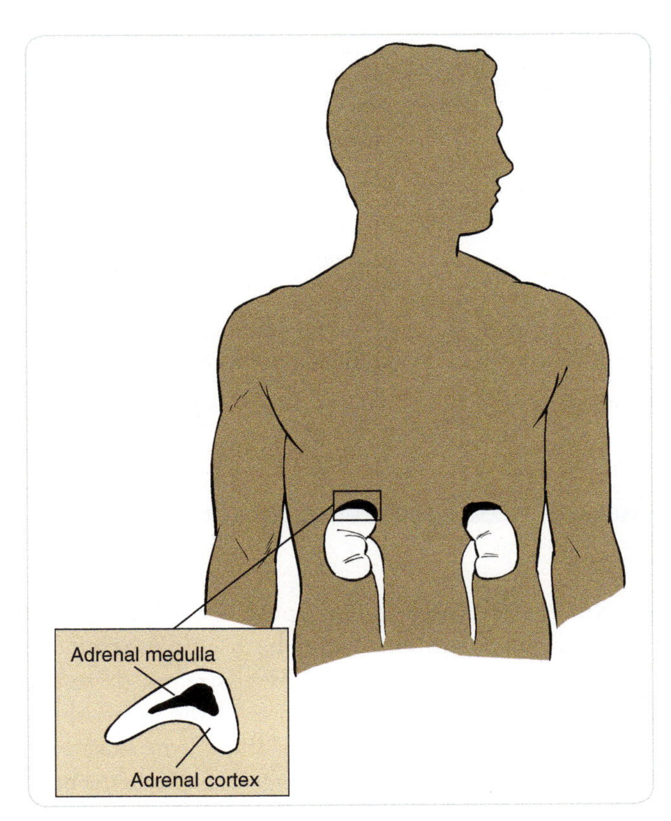

FIGURE 3.5 The adrenal gland, made up of the adrenal cortex and medulla, sits upon the top of each kidney and is cone-shaped in appearance.

BOX 3.4 Adrenal Fatigue and Adrenal Failure

With the alarming rate of chronic fatigue syndrome, the word in some medical circles is that many Americans suffer from adrenal fatigue as a result of prolonged stress. What is adrenal fatigue? Because of the amount of chronic stress many people admit to experiencing, the adrenal glands begin to work overtime. Signs of exhaustion and the inability to produce and release the host of catecholamines and hormones for fight or flight appear to give credence to Hans Selye's general adaptation syndrome. The symptoms of adrenal insufficiency include fatigue, dizziness, low blood sugar (resulting in cravings and subsequent weight gain), poor libido, and depression. Weak adrenals are associated with the incidence of autoimmune diseases, ranging from chronic fatigue syndrome and lupus to rheumatoid arthritis. Because of the complexities of human physiology, poor adrenal function is also associated with aggravated symptoms of menopause. Addison's disease is the name given to those with adrenal failure, a condition where the adrenal glands are no longer able to produce and secrete the necessary hormones for metabolic function.

corticosteroids: glucocorticoids and mineralocorticoids. **Glucocorticoids** are a family of biochemical agents that includes cortisol and cortisone, with cortisol being the primary one. Its function is to help to generate glucose, through the degradation of proteins (amino acids) during a process called gluconeogenesis in the liver, as an energy source for both the central nervous system (the brain) and skeletal muscles during physical exercise. A metaphor to illustrate this process is the situation in which you resort to burning the furniture to keep warm once you exhaust your supply of firewood. **Cortisol** is also involved in the process of lipolysis, or the mobilization and breakdown of fats (fatty acids) for energy. Clinical studies have linked increased levels of cortisol with suppression of the immune system. It appears that cortisol metabolizes (degrades) white blood cells. As the number of white blood cells decreases, the efficiency of the immune system decreases, setting the stage for illness and disease. It has also come to light that increased cortisol can direct excess amounts of cholesterol into the blood, thereby adding to associated artery plaque buildup and leading to hypertension and coronary heart disease. **Mineralocorticoids**, specifically aldosterone, are secreted to maintain plasma volume and electrolyte (sodium and potassium) balance, two essential functions in the regulation of circulation. (The exact mechanisms will be discussed later in this chapter.)

Corticosteroids: Stress hormones released by the adrenal cortex, such as cortisol and cortisone.

Glucocorticoids: A family of biochemical agents that includes cortisol and cortisone, produced and released from the adrenal gland.

Cortisol: A stress hormone released by the adrenal glands that helps the body prepare for fight or flight by promoting the release of glucose and lipids in the blood for energy metabolism.

Mineralocorticoids: A class of hormones that maintain plasma volume and electrolyte balance, such as aldosterone.

TABLE 3.1 Pathways of Stress Response

Effects	Reaction	Time
The body has several backup dynamics to help ensure physical survival. Here, these dynamics are broken down into categories based on the duration of their metabolic reactions.		
Immediate effects	Epinephrine and norepinephrine from the sympathetic nervous system	2–3 seconds
Intermediate effects	Epinephrine and norepinephrine from the adrenal medulla	20–30 seconds, possibly minutes
Prolonged effects	ACTH, vasopressin, and thyroxine neuroendocrine pathways	Minutes, hours, days, or weeks

Modified from Allen, R. *Human Stress: Its Nature and Control*. Burgess, Minneapolis, 1983.

The inside of the adrenal gland is called the **adrenal medulla**. This portion of the gland secretes catecholamines (epinephrine and norepinephrine), which act in a similar fashion as those secreted at the endings of sympathetic nerves. The adrenal medulla releases 80 percent epinephrine and 20 percent norepinephrine. Under the influences of stress, up to three hundred times the amount of epinephrine can be found in the blood compared to the amount in samples taken at rest.

The Neuroendocrine Pathways

Evolutionary adaptations have provided several backup systems to ensure the survival of the human organism. Not all pathways act at the same speed, yet the ultimate goal is the same: physical survival. First, not only does the hypothalamus initiate activation of the sympathetic nervous system to cause an immediate effect (TABLE 3.1), but the posterior hypothalamus also has a direct neural pathway, called the sympathetic preganglionic neuron, that links it to the adrenal medulla.

Adrenal medulla: The portion of the adrenal gland responsible for secreting epinephrine and norepinephrine.

Intermediate stress effects: The hormonal response triggered by the neural aspects of the adrenal medulla that are released directly into the blood, lasting minutes to hours.

Prolonged effect of stress: Hormonal effects that may take days or perhaps more than a week to be fully realized from the initial stress response.

Next, upon stimulation by the posterior hypothalamus, the adrenal medulla secretes both epinephrine and norepinephrine. Once in the bloodstream, these catecholamines reinforce the efforts of the sympathetic drive, which has already released these same substances through sympathetic neural endings throughout the body. The release of epinephrine and norepinephrine from the adrenal medulla acts as a backup system for these biochemical agents to ensure the most efficient means of physical survival. The hormonal influences brought about by the adrenal medulla are called **intermediate stress effects**. Because their release is via the bloodstream rather than neural endings, travel time is longer (approximately 20 to 30 seconds), and unlike the release of these substances from sympathetic neural endings, the effects of catecholamines from the adrenal medulla can last as long as 2 hours when high levels of secretions are circulating in the bloodstream. These, along with hormones secreted from the adrenal gland, become a "toxic chemical cocktail" if they persist in the body for prolonged periods of time without being flushed out, primarily through exercise.

In addition, there is a third and potentially more potent system joining the efforts of the nervous and endocrine systems to prepare the body for real or perceived danger if the perceived threat continues beyond several minutes. Neural impulses received by the hypothalamus as potential threats create a chain of biochemical messages, which like a line of falling dominos cascade through the endocrine-system glands. Because the half-life of these hormones and the speed of their metabolic reactions vary in length from hours to weeks in some cases, this chain of reactions is referred to as the **prolonged effect of stress**.

BOX 3.5 *Multitasking:* Wired For Stress

The multitasking generation, the age of high technology, certainly has its merits, but less recognizable are its long-range pitfalls. Sociologists grow increasingly alarmed by people of all age groups' obsession with and addiction to smartphones, text messages, email, podcasts, and the Web. Sociologists and psychologists see dangers with a hyperkinetic mind that doesn't know how to unplug, turn off, and relax: Stress! Habitual multitasking may condition the brain to an overexcited state, making it difficult for people to focus even when they want or need to. Add a dearth of patience to the mix with this "Wi-Fi generation," and the stress response is compounded dramatically. As people begin to lose concentration skills, the end result is "chronic mental antsyness" (frustration).

The Myth of Multitasking

Sending a text message while watching (and voting for contestants on) *American Idol* and at the same time doing a Google search for research report content may seem like the height of organizational skills, but don't be fooled. Quantity is not quality. With the use of MRI technology, researchers, including Jordan Grafman, have identified one specific area of the brain's cortex, Brodmann's area 10, as the site specific for alternating attention from one task to another. The prefrontal cortex, which houses Brodmann's area 10, is one of the last regions of the brain to mature and the first to decline as a result of the aging process. As such, youngsters up to age 22 and those over the age of 60 do not multitask well. Research studies reveal that when young adults perform two or more tasks simultaneously, the amount of errors increases dramatically. Although there may be many causes for poor attention span (from the TV remote control to the abundance of toxic food chemicals), the combination of short attention span and the increased use of electronic devices becomes dangerous. The take-home message is that multitasking decreases efficiency.

Although students may excel at locating and manipulating information via the Internet, their reach may be broad but ultimately quite shallow. Moreover, their ability to process the information in a deeper context is considered poor by most educational standards, states Claudia Koonzt of Duke University. "It's like they have too many windows open on their hard drive. In order to have a taste for sifting through different layers of truth, you have to stay with the topic and pursue it deeply rather than go across the surface with your toolbar" (Wallis, 2006). What are the social implications of being wired for stress? Virtual conversations will never replace the nuances of face-to-face expressions and body language that humans have developed over thousands of years of cohabitation and community building. Experts have also noticed a decrease in interaction among family members with a rise in household electronic gadgets, further eroding the family structure. Furthermore, addiction to cell phone use is fast becoming a reason for marriage counseling and breakups (University of Florida, 2007). Studies on the topic of Alzheimer's support the theory that the brain needs stimulation to promote mental acuity. Stress research, however, validates the need for quiet time for the brain. When the brain is constantly stimulated (and overstimulated) these neurological impulses rewire the brain for perpetual stress.

The ACTH Axis

Physiologically speaking, a biochemical pathway is referred to as an axis. In this section, we will discuss the ACTH axis. The other two axes, the **vasopressin axis** and the **thyroxine axis**, are covered in the following sections.

The **ACTH axis**, also known as the hypothalamic-pituitary-adrenal **(HPA) axis** (FIG. 3.6), begins with the release of corticotropin-releasing factor (CRF) from the anterior hypothalamus. This substance activates the pituitary gland to release ACTH, which travels via the bloodstream to in turn activate the **adrenal cortex**. Upon stimulation by ACTH, the adrenal cortex releases a set of corticosteroids (cortisol and aldosterone), which act to increase metabolism and alter body fluids, and thus blood

Vasopressin axis: A chain of physiological events stemming from the release of vasopressin or antidiuretic hormone (ADH).

Thyroxine axis: A chain of physiological events stemming from the release of thyroxine.

ACTH axis: A physiological pathway whereby a message is sent from the hypothalamus to the pituitary, then on to the adrenal gland to release a flood of stress hormones for fight or flight.

HPA axis: The hypothalamic-pituitary-adrenal axis, a term synonymous with the ACTH axis.

Adrenal cortex: The portion of the adrenal gland that produces and secretes a host of corticosteroids (e.g., cortisol and aldosterone).

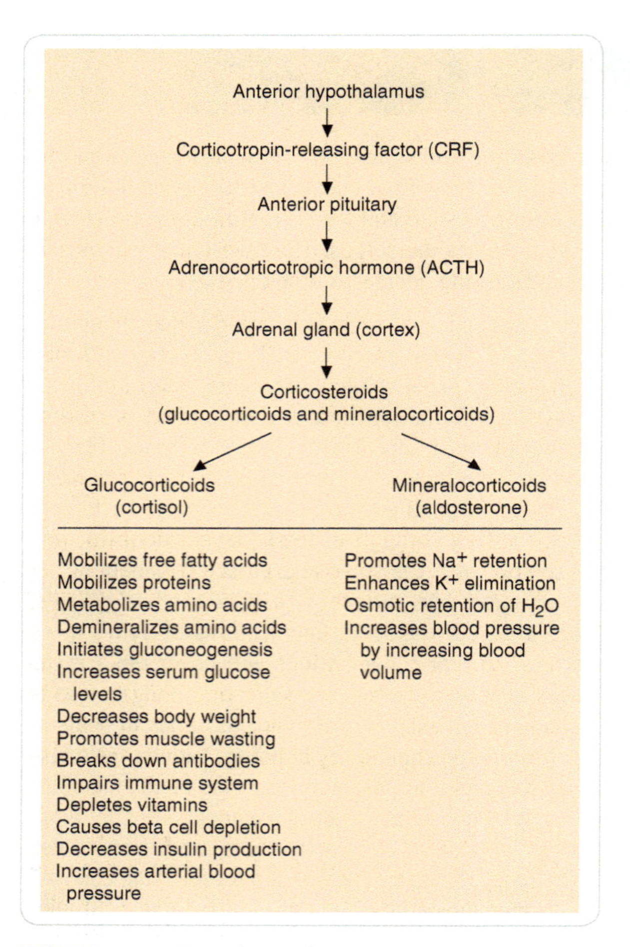

FIGURE 3.6 The ACTH axis.

pressure, respectively. The effects of hormones released by the adrenal cortex are considered to be prolonged because they activate their functions for minutes to hours. Note that increased secretions of cortisol in the blood act primarily to ensure adequate supplies of blood glucose for energy metabolism. However, when increasingly high levels of cortisol are observed because of chronic stress, this hormone compromises the integrity of several physiological systems.

The Vasopressin Axis

Vasopressin or antidiuretic hormone (ADH) is synthesized in the hypothalamus but is released by the pituitary through a special portal system. The primary purpose of vasopressin is to regulate fluid loss through the urinary tract. It does this in a number of ways, including water reabsorption and decreased perspiration. By altering blood volume, however, it also has a pronounced effect on stroke volume, or the amount of blood that is pumped through the left ventricle of the heart with each contraction.

BOX 3.6 Insomnia and Brain Physiology

Brain chemistry is a complicated subject and our understanding of it is embryonic at best, but some facts are clear with regard to how brain physiology works. Not only does an "active" mind release epinephrine and norepinephrine in the brain, compromising the ability to fall sleep, but other neurotransmitters—specifically, melatonin and serotonin—are affected by a host of daily rituals and behaviors, ranging from nutritional habits, caffeine intake, and sunlight exposure to cell phone use. Melatonin is a hormone secreted in the pituitary of the brain. This neurotransmitter is affected by real and artificial light and is thought to be associated with both sleep patterns and skin pigmentation. As daylight decreases, the melatonin level increases, giving rise to the belief that increases in melatonin help promote sleep.

The brain neurotransmitter serotonin is partially affected by light. Decreases in light decrease serotonin levels, a factor associated with seasonal affective disorder (SAD) and depression.

While the use of artificial evening light can alter serotonin levels, it can decrease melatonin levels, thus affecting natural sleep patterns (sleep patterns have changed dramatically since the turn of the twentieth century with the use of electricity). Cell phone use is thought to decrease melatonin with similar results. Increased consumption of carbohydrates (late-night snacks) can increase serotonin levels, which may, in turn, affect melatonin levels. Medications for depression include selective serotonin reuptake inhibitors (SSRIs), which act to increase serotonin levels. This activity may, in fact, act to decrease melatonin levels, thus affecting a full night's sleep.

Consequently, ADH has a pronounced effect on blood pressure. Under normal circumstances, ADH regulates blood pressure by either increasing blood volume (changing the concentration of water in the blood) should it be too low, or decreasing blood volume when it becomes too high. Under the influence of chronic stress, however, many regulatory mechanisms in the body lose their ability to maintain physiological homeostasis. Consequently, the increased secretions of vasopressin produced under duress will increase blood pressure even when someone already has elevated resting values; this is known as hypertension. The purpose of vasopressin as well as aldosterone, epinephrine, and norepinephrine is to increase blood pressure

BOX 3.7 Physiology of Stress: The Take-Home Message

There is no doubt that the details of the physiology of stress can be overwhelming. Here is the take-home message: The stress response involves a cascade of chemicals/hormones in the body, most notably epinephrine and norepinephrine released from the neural endings of the sympathetic nervous system. Additionally, the stress hormone, cortisol (secreted from the adrenal glands), plays a huge role in preparing the body for fight-or-flight. If stress persists, additional hormones are called into play. The strength of this stress hormone cocktail depends on the intensity and duration of the stressor(s), yet the effects can last far longer than the initial exposure/interpretation of the stressor. One notable effect of stress is that repeated stress tends to shrink brain cells. Medical science's love affair with functional magnetic resonance imaging continues to explore the brain under stress.

to ensure that active muscles receive oxygenated blood, but under chronic stress in a resting state this hormonal response—the abundance of stress hormones—is literally overkill, leading to hypertension and ultimately death caused by Coronary Heart Disease (CHD).

The Thyroxine Axis

Stimulation in the hypothalamus triggers the release of thyrotropic hormone–releasing factor (TRF). TRF is transported through a special portal system to the anterior portion of the pituitary, where it stimulates the secretion of thyrotropic hormone (TTH). Once in the bloodstream, TTH follows a path to the thyroid gland, which stimulates the release of two more hormones: thyroxine and triiodothyronine. The purpose of these two hormones is to increase overall metabolism, or basal metabolic rate (BMR). Thyroxine is powerful enough to double one's rate of metabolism. Note that the effects of this pathway are very prolonged. Because the production of thyroxine takes several days, it may be 10 days to 2 weeks before visible signs manifest as significant symptoms through this pathway. This explains why you may come down with a cold or flu a week after a very stressful encounter rather than the day after. The metabolic effects of thyroxine released through this pathway are increased workload on the heart muscle, increased gastrointestinal activity (e.g., gastritis), and, in some cases, a condition called **cerebration** or cerebral excitivity, which is associated with anxiety attacks and/or insomnia.

A Parable of Psychophysiology

A metaphor can be used to illustrate the three pathways discussed earlier (FIG. 3.7). Let us say that your life is in danger because of a classified CIA document you inadvertently stumbled across, and you now pose a threat to

Immediate effects	Intermediate effects	Prolonged effects
Text message or phone call	Email	Overnight delivery
Flushed face Rapid heart rate	Nauseous feeling in stomach Muscle tension	Suppressed immune system

FIGURE 3.7 Like communication networks that send and receive messages, the human body has several complex messenger systems, which not only see that the information gets through but also ensure that the body will survive the perceived threat after the message is received.

national security. You want to deliver a message and a copy of this document to your family, who live a few hundred miles away, to let them know your life is in danger. This message is, of course, very important and you want to make sure your family gets it, so you use a couple of methods to ensure its delivery. First you immediately text message your parents because it is the quickest way to deliver the message, and the message is received instantaneously. This is like the action of the sympathetic nervous system. As a backup, you send an email in case no one responds to the text. This form of communication is fairly quick, taking perhaps minutes, and is equivalent to the preganglionic nerve to the adrenal medulla. And because you also need to send a copy of the document to further explain the contents

Cerebration: A term used to describe the neurological excitability of the brain, associated with anxiety attacks and insomnia.

of your message, you ship a package via overnight delivery. This means of communication allows more comprehensive information to be sent, but it takes much longer. It is like the neuroendocrine pathways. Similarly, our bodies are composed of several communication systems, each with its own time element and function, the overall purpose being to prepare the body for physical survival. As illustrated by this story, there are many backup systems, fast and slow, to get the message through.

In the short term, the combination of these various neural and hormonal pathways serves a very important purpose: physical survival. However, when these same pathways are employed continuously as a result of the influence of chronic stressors, the effects can be devastating to the body. In light of the fact that the body prepares physically for threats, whether they are of a physical, mental, emotional, or spiritual nature, repeated physical arousal suggests that the activation of the stress response is an obsolete mechanism for dealing with stressors that do not pertain to physical survival. The inability of the body to return to homeostasis can have significant effects on the cardiovascular system, the digestive system, the musculoskeletal system, and, research now indicates, the immune system. Organs locked into a pattern of overactive metabolic activity will eventually show signs of dysfunction. For instance, constant pressure and repeated wear and tear on the arteries and blood vessels can cause tissue damage to the inner lining of these organs. Numerous changes can also occur throughout the digestive system, including constipation, gastritis, diarrhea, and hemorrhoids. As was observed by Selye, the inability of the body to return to homeostasis can set the stage for signs and symptoms of disease and illness.

Three Decades of Brain Imaging Research

Prior to the start of each decade, the medical profession selects one area of human physiology to study in-depth. In 1990, the brain was chosen as the target of this research. This area proved so fascinating that many researchers added a second decade to the data collection, despite the fact that the medical community deemed the decade 2000–2010 the bone and joint decade. With the advancement of electromagnetic technology and magnetic resonance imaging (neuroimaging), thousands of studies have been conducted to determine which aspects of the brain are active in a variety of mental states and thought processes (Anderson, 2015). Despite recent news in 2016 that a bug was found in the computer program that analyzes fMRI data, suggesting that many of the findings were invalid, scientists continue to advocate the importance of brain research in unlocking one of the greatest mysteries known to humanity (Anderson, 2015). So enchanted have researchers become with brain physiology, as depicted through MRI technology, a multitude of studies have dominated non-disease-related brain physiology research and most likely will for some time to come. Although MRIs can help determine brain structure and specific physiology, it is the electroencephalagraph (EEG) that is currently needed to best understand brain function. Only recently have the dots been connected to provide a more accurate understanding of this most complex human organ. Bruce McEwen is one researcher working in this area. In his book *The End of Stress as We Know It*, McEwen synthesizes much of this information, including the work of his protégé Robert Sapolsky, author of the acclaimed book *Why Zebras Don't Get Ulcers*. Here are some highlights from McEwen's research:

- The hippocampus and the amygdala together form conscious memories of emotional events.
- The hippocampus is highly sensitive to the stress hormone cortisol, which aids in memory formation of stress.
- The hippocampus region is rich in receptor sites for glucocorticoids.
- The amygdala is responsible for the emotional content of memory, particularly fear.
- Repeated excessive exposure to cortisol accelerates the aging process of the hippocampus and may, in fact, damage or shrink brain cells. Moreover, chronic stress may affect memory and learning processes. (In Vietnam vets with post-traumatic stress disorder [PTSD], this region of the brain was 26 percent smaller than in their peers without PTSD.)
- Research by Sapolsky reveals that damage to brain cells (in animals) caused by chronic stress appears to be irreversible.

McEwen concludes that the human brain is, indeed, wired for stress, or "**allostatic load**" as he calls it.

Allostatic load: A term coined by stress researcher Bruce McEwen to replace the expression "stressed out"; the damage to the body when the allostatic (stress) response functions improperly or for prolonged states, causing physical damage to the body.

Neuroscientists have also discovered that the brain is far more "plastic" than previously thought, giving rise to a new term: *neuroplasticity*. We now know that the brain can generate new connections to various brain cells, recruit various brain tissue for a host of functions, and generate new cell growth (which was previously thought to be impossible) (Powell, 2007).

Based on the success of President Clinton's federally funded Genome DNA Project, President Obama launched the Brain Initiative Project in 2013. The purpose of this initiative is to help scientists explore the dynamics of the brain as a means to create a comprehensive understanding of everything from, the creation of conscious thought and memory to the disease pathology of Alzheimer's, autism, Parkinson's, and several other disorders.

SUMMARY

- *Psychophysiology* is a term to describe the body's physiological reaction to perceived stressors, suggesting that the stress response is a mind-body phenomenon.
- There are three physiological systems that are directly involved in the stress response: the nervous system, the endocrine system, and the immune system.
- The nervous system comprises two parts: the central nervous system (CNS) and the peripheral nervous system (PNS). The CNS includes three levels: the vegetative, the limbic, and the neocortical.
- The limbic system houses the hypothalamus, which controls many functions, including appetite and emotions. The neocortical level processes and decodes all stimuli.
- The most important part of the PNS regarding the stress response is the autonomic nervous system, which activates sympathetic and parasympathetic neural drives. Sympathetic drive causes physical arousal (e.g., increased heart rate) through the secretion of epinephrine and norepinephrine, whereas parasympathetic drive maintains homeostasis through the release of ACh. The two neural drives are mutually exclusive, meaning that you cannot be aroused and relaxed at the same time.
- The endocrine system consists of a series of glands that secrete hormones that travel through the circulatory system and act on target organs. The major stress gland is the adrenal gland.
- The adrenal gland has two parts, each performing different functions. The cortex (outside) secretes cortisol and aldosterone, while the medulla (inside) secretes epinephrine and norepinephrine.
- The nervous system and endocrine system join together to form metabolic pathways or axes. There are three pathways: the ACTH axis, the vasopressin axis, and the thyroxine axis.
- The body has several backup mechanisms to ensure physical survival. These systems are classified as immediate, lasting seconds (sympathetic drive); intermediate, lasting minutes (adrenal medulla); and prolonged, lasting hours if not weeks (neuroendocrine pathways). Each system is involved in several metabolic pathways.
- Stress is considered one of the primary factors associated with insomnia. Good sleep hygiene consists of behaviors that help promote a good night's sleep rather than detract from it, including decreased caffeine consumption, consistent bedtimes, and a host of effective relaxation techniques that enhance sleep quality.
- A decade of brain research reveals that humans are hard-wired for stress through an intricate pattern of neural pathways designed for the fight-or-flight response. Research also suggests that chronic stress appears to atrophy brain tissue, specifically the hippocampus.

STUDY GUIDE QUESTIONS

1. What role does the nervous system play in the stress response?
2. What role does the endocrine system play in the stress response?
3. Name and explain the three pathways (axes) of stress physiology.
4. What role does the amygdala play in the stress response?
5. What are panic attacks?
6. What does new brain imaging tell us about stress physiology?
7. Explain the concept of neuroplasticity.
8. Describe which part of the brain is associated with multitasking.

REFERENCES AND RESOURCES

Allen, R. *Human Stress: Its Nature and Control.* Burgess Press, Minneapolis, MN, 1983.

Allen, R. *Psychophysiology of the Human Stress Response.* University of Maryland, College Park, 1990.

Amen, D. *Change Your Brain, Change Your Life* (Revised Expanded Ed.). Three Rivers Press, New York, 2015.

American Cancer Society. *Making Treatment Decisions: DHEA.* www.cancer.org/docroot/ETO/content/ETO_5_3X_Dhea.asp?sitearea=ETO.

Anderson, S. David Eagleman's New TC Show, "The Brain," Gets Inside Your Head. *Newsweek*, October 15, 2015. http://www.newsweek.com/2015/10/30/david-eaglemans-new-tv-show-brain-gets-inside-your-head-383843.html.

Baker, R. *Understanding Panic Attacks and Overcoming Fear* (3rd ed.). Lion Hudson Books, New York, 2011.

Bar-Tal, Y., Cohen-Mansfield, J., and Golander, H. Which Stress Matters? The Examination of Temporal Aspects of Stress, *Journal of Psychology* 132(5):569–576, 1998.

Bremner, J. D. *Does Stress Damage the Brain? Understanding Trauma-Related Disorders from a Mind-Body Perspective.* W. W. Norton, New York, 2005.

CFIDS Association of America. *Symptoms: Chronic Fatigue Syndrome*. www.cfids.org/about-cfids/symptoms.asp. Accessed February 26, 2008.

Childre, D. L. *Cut-Thru.* Planetary Publications, Boulder Creek, CA, 1996.

Daniel, J., et al. Mental and Endocrine Factors in Repeated Stress in Man, *Studia Psychologica* 15(3):273–281, 1973.

Depression and the Birth and Death of Brain Cells. www.biopsychiatry.com/newbraincell.

Dispenza, J. *Evolve Your Brain: The Science of Changing Your Mind*. Health Communications, Inc., Deerfield Beach, FL, 2007.

Dreinhofer, K. *The Bone and Joint Decade 2000–2010: How Far Have We Come?* www.touchbriefings.com/pdf/2263/Dreinhofer.pdf.

Everly, G. *A Clinical Guide to the Treatment of the Human Stress Response.* 3rd ed. Kluwer Academic Press, New York, 2013.

Everly, G., and Rosenfeld, R. *The Nature and Treatment of the Stress Response.* Plenum Press, New York, 1981.

Greenfield, N. S., and Sternback, R. A. *Handbook of Psychophysiology.* Holt, Rinehart, & Winston, New York, 4th ed. 2017. Cacioppo, J., Tassinary, L., and Berntson, G.

Guyton, A. C., and Hall, J. *Textbook of Medical Physiology,* 13th ed. Saunders, Philadelphia, 2015.

Harris, D. *10% Happier*. Dey Street Books, New York, 2014.

Johnson, S. Emotions and the Brain: Fear, *Discover* 24(3): 32–39, 2003.

Lacey, J. I. Somatic Response Patterning and Stress: Some Revisions of Activating Theory. Reprinted in H. H. Appley, and R. Trumbell, *Psychological Stress: Issues in Research.* Appleton-Century-Crofts, East Norwalk, CT, 1976.

LeDoux, J. *The Emotional Brain.* Simon & Schuster, New York, 1996.

Maas, J. *Power Sleep.* Quill Books, New York, 2001.

Makara, G., Palkovits, M., and Szentagothal, J. The Endocrine Hypothalamus and Hormonal Response to Stress. In H. Selye (ed.), *Selye's Guide to Stress Research,* Van Nostrand Rinehold, New York: 280–337, 1983.

McDonagh, B. *DARE: The New Way to End Anxiety and Stop Panic Attacks*. Beaverton, OR, BMD Publishing, 2015.

McEwen, B. *The End of Stress as We Know It.* Joseph Henry Press, Washington, D.C., 2002.

McEwen, B. S., de Leon, M. J., Lupien, S. J., and Meaney, M. J. Corticosteroids, the Aging Brain and Cognition, *Trends in Endocrinology and Metabolism,* 10:92–96, 1999.

National sleep foundation. www.sleepfoundation.org.

Nemeroff, C. The Neurobiology of Depression, *Scientific American,* June 1998.

Newberg, A., D'Aquili, E., and Rause, V. *Why God Won't Go Away.* Ballantine Books, New York, 2002.

Oatley, K. *Brain Mechanisms and Mind.* Dutton, New York, 1972.

O'Leary, A. Stress, Emotion, and Human Immune Function, *Psychological Bulletin* 108(3):363–382, 1990.

Ornstein, R., and Sobel, D. *The Healing Brain,* 2nd ed. Malor Books, San Francisco, 1999.

Peak Performance Training. New studies of human brains show stress may shrink neurons. www.peakperformancetraining.org/sitefiles/articles/stress.htm.

Pelletier, K. *Mind as Healer, Mind as Slayer.* Dell, New York, 1977.

Pittman, C., and Karle, W. *Rewire Your Anxious Brain*. Oakland, CA, New Harbinger Publications, 2015.

Powell, D., and the Institute of Noetic Sciences. *The 2007 Shift Report: Evidence of a World Transforming*. Institute of Noetic Sciences, Petaluma, CA, 2007:28–36.

Sapolsky, R. Why Stress Is Bad for You, *Science* 273:749–750, 1996.

Sapolsky, R. Stress and Your Shrinking Brain, *Discover,* March, 1999:116–122.

Sapolsky, R. *Why Zebras Don't Get Ulcers.* W. H. Freeman & Company, New York, 3rd ed. 2004.

Schnirring, L. DHEA: Hype, Hope Not Matched by Facts, *Physician and Sports Medicine,* May 17, 1998.

Sherwood, L. *Human Physiology,* 9th ed. Brooks Cole, 2015.

Shreve, J. Beyond the Brain: What's in Your Mind, *National Geographic,* March 2005.

Smith, M., and Segal, J. *Panic Attacks and Panic Disorder*. Healthguide.org. 2016. http://www.helpguide.org/articles/anxiety/panic-attacks-and-panic-disorders.htm.

Stranon, B. *The Primal Teen.* Doubleday Books, New York, 2004.

University of Florida. Addicted to Phones? Cell Phone Use Becoming a Major Problem for Some, Experts Say, *Physorg.com*, January 18, 2007. www.physorg.com/news88356303.html.

Usdin, E., et al. *Catecholamines and Stress.* Pergamon Press, Oxford, 1976.

Vgontazas, A. N., and Kales, A. Sleep and Its Disorders, *Annual Review of Medicine* 50:387–400, 1999.

Wallis, C. The Multi-Tasking Generation. *Time*, March 27, 2006.

William, D. Modernization, Stress and Blood Pressure: New Directions in Research, *Human Biology* 71(4):583–605, 1999.

Zimmer, C. Peering into the Brain, *Newsweek,* June 9, 2003.

CHAPTER 4

Stress and Disease

By comprehending that human beings are energy, one can begin to comprehend new ways of viewing health and illness.

—Richard Gerber, M.D.

An argument started more than 100 years ago about the specific cause of disease, and despite all the recent medical advances, the debate over "nature versus nurture" continues to this day. It was the French chemist Louis Pasteur who postulated that when we make contact with a pathogenic microbe (some virus or bacterium), our immune system is alerted immediately and goes on the defensive. In Pasteur's mind, the state of health or disease was not a measure of the integrity of the immune system, but rather of the strength of the invading microbe. Pasteur's idea took a while to catch on, but once it did, it soon carried considerable weight in the medical community. The acceptance of Pasteur's "germ theory" propelled medical science (with the financial backing of John D. Rockefeller) toward the direction of immunizations, antibiotics, and the pharmaceutical industry as we know it today. But Pasteur also had his critics, not the least of whom was Claude Bernard, a brilliant French physiologist and philosopher who disagreed vehemently with the idea that tiny microbes were the sole reason for imminent illness and death.

Image © Oleinikova Olga/Shutterstock.

Quotation reproduced from Gerber, R. *Vibrational Medicine* (3rd ed.), Bear & Company, Rochester, 2001.

Bernard, who coined the term *homeostasis*, marveled at the complexity of human physiology. He suggested that it wasn't the germs that did the damage, but rather the condition of the body and its state of health that either destroyed the germ or was destroyed by it. Using a metaphor of seeds and soil, he insisted that if the soil is fertile (poor health) enough for a seed (microbe) to germinate, it will. Bernard suggested that good living practices, including one's attitude and sound nutrition, were essential to keep the body at its optimal level of health, thereby creating an infertile and inhospitable place for the seeds of microorganisms to germinate. At the time, Bernard's theory fell on deaf ears. Pasteur remained adamant: Microbes were nondiscriminatory. Their effects would be felt by all those who were exposed to them, regardless of the individuals' state of physical or mental health.

Decades later, Pasteur's germ theory was termed the "theory of specific etiology," according to which every disease is believed to be caused by a specific microorganism. Today, this theory has evolved to suggest that diseases not caused by microorganisms can be reduced to a single genetic flaw in human DNA. As more research findings are revealed through the work of the Human Genome Project, news headlines will continue to promote the link between disease and one's genetic makeup. Despite efforts to shift the paradigm, Descartes's mechanistic philosophy of health is still alive in the Western world!

Etiology, the study of disease, is not an easy science. Some people who are exposed to microbes may carry—and spread—a disease but, in fact, never contract the disease itself. Typhoid Mary is the classic example of this phenomenon, as were people who spread, but never caught, SARS in 2003. In fact, toward the end of his life, Pasteur had a change of mind about his germ theory. On his deathbed, he said, "Bernard is right, [it's not the seed] it's the soil."

At roughly the same time that the germ theory was accepted as fact by Western medicine, another theory was proposed by a Chicago-based physician, Franz Alexander. He observed quite astutely that there appeared to be a profound connection between one's mental/emotional state and one's physical health. He coined the term *organ neurosis*, later called **psychosomatic**, to describe this precarious mind-body relationship. Although the word *psychosomatic* caught on quickly in the American vernacular, 50 years would pass before medical science took Alexander's theory seriously. It would be another two decades before the medical community would acknowledge the highly sophisticated intricacies of mind, body, spirit, and emotions that can produce not just a detrimental effect, but a healing effect as well.

The current focus on the stress-and-disease phenomenon is directed toward the interactions of the immune system, the CNS, and human consciousness. Recently, threads of evidence scattered far and wide throughout the literature of the many allied health disciplines have finally begun to lend credence to the ageless intuition of holism. When looked at from the traditional scientific (biomedical) point of view, however, these traces continue to raise more questions than they answer.

Perhaps because of these complexities, we still can merely speculate about the exact nature of the relationship between stress and disease. All the while, scientists continue to take sides on the nature versus nurture debate. Despite world-class health care, improved living conditions, and abundant food choices, chronic diseases continue to plague the planet. As noted in the acclaimed book *Why Zebras Don't Get Ulcers*, researcher Richard Sapolsky states that there is a colossal link between stress and disease. Current estimates provided by the American Institute of Stress suggest that as many as 80 percent of all doctor's office visits are the result of stress. Moreover, what was once considered to be an association between stress and disease is now understood to be a direct causal link, acne, migraines, and gastrointestinal problems being prime examples (Segerstrom and Miller, 2004). Experts estimate that between 75 and 85 percent of all health-related problems are either precipitated or aggravated by stress. The list of such stress-affected disorders is nearly endless, ranging from herpes and hemorrhoids to the common cold and cancer.

To understand the relationship between stress and disease, you first must recognize that several factors act in unison to create a pathological outcome. These include the cognitive perceptions of threatening stimuli and the consequent activation of the nervous system, the endocrine system, and the immune system. In the past, these three physiological dynamics were studied separately because they were thought to be independent systems. Today they are viewed as one network, and it is this current understanding that has given rise to the new interdisciplinary field of **psychoneuroimmunology** (PNI). As defined by Pelletier (1988), psychoneuroimmunology is "the study of the intricate interaction of consciousness (psycho), brain and central nervous system (neuro), and the body's defense against external infection and internal aberrant cell division (immunology)."

There is a consensus among leaders in the field of psychoneuroimmunology that the expression "mind-body medicine" is rather limited in its scope, leading people such as Joan Borysenko, Deepak Chopra, Andy Weil, Gladys Taylor McGary, James Gordon, Larry Dossey, and others to call the approach to healing "mind-body-spirit healing."

Psychosomatic: A term coined from Franz Alexander's term *organ neurosis*, used to describe a host of physical illnesses or diseases caused by the mind and unresolved emotional issues.

Psychoneuroimmunology: The study of the effects of stress on disease; treats the mind, central nervous system, and immune system as one interrelated unit.

Theoretical Models

There have been several research efforts that seek to explain the relationship between stress and disease. At best, this relationship is still in the speculation stage, with no clear-cut understanding of the complexities involved. After an attempt to synthesize a definitive model, based on his own work as well as on an exhaustive survey of more than 300 research articles, Pelletier admitted that there is still not enough scientific information at the present time to create a substantiated stress and disease model, and certainly not from the current biomedical model. Nevertheless, some of the promising theories described in this section may in time provide medical science with the building blocks to create such a comprehensive model. Once this model is in place, the possibility of preventing and intercepting several disease processes will certainly take precedence over the current medical practice of relieving symptoms and fixing and replacing broken parts. The following are some of the most prominent theories regarding the mind-body-spirit relationship.

The Borysenko Model

In what is currently recognized as the most accurate description of the immune system, former Tufts University immunologist Myrin Borysenko (1987) outlined both a dichotomy of stress-induced dysregulation and a matrix describing the "immune balance" regarding four classifications of disease. The dichotomy broadly divides disease and illness into either **autonomic dysregulation** (overresponsive autonomic nervous system) or **immune dysregulation** (TABLE 4.1).

Borysenko suggests that when the autonomic nervous system releases an abundance of stress hormones, several physiological repercussions can result—among them, migraines, ulcers, and hypertension. The notion that the nervous system is responsible for several symptoms of illness and disease through the release of stress hormones (epinephrine, norepinephrine, cortisol, and aldosterone) was first postulated by Cannon, and then established through the pioneering research of Selye.

TABLE 4.1 Borysenko's Stress and Disease Dichotomy

Autonomic Dysregulation (Overresponsive ANS)	Immune Dysregulation
Migraines	Infection (virus)
Peptic ulcers	Allergies
Irritable bowel syndrome	AIDS
Hypertension	Cancer
Coronary heart disease	Lupus
Asthma	Arthritis

No less important, however, are the repercussions of a dysfunctional immune system, which can precipitate infection, allergies, and perhaps cancer. To understand how the immune system can become dysfunctional or suppressed, let us first take a look at the current perception of this unique physiological system. The purpose of the immune system is to protect the body from pathogens, either externally generated (e.g., bacteria) or internally manufactured (e.g., mutant cells), which impede the proper functioning of the body's regulatory dynamics. Pathogens are composed of certain molecules (antigens) that have the capacity to interact at various receptor sites on several types of immune system cells, which in turn attempt to detoxify them. Metaphorically speaking, the immune system acts like the collective branches of the armed services to ensure national security by protecting the country from both invading forces and internal insurrection. Like all other physiological systems, the immune system begins to develop in the fetus and matures at about the time of birth, when the body becomes vulnerable to external pathogens.

The immune system is a network of several organs. These include bone marrow, which throughout life supplies the lymph tissue with stem cells (the precursors to various lymphoid cells), and eventually become B-lymphocytes (B-cells); the thymus, a gland below the throat that allows stem cells to mature into T-lymphocytes (T-cells); and the lymph nodes, spleen, and gut-associated lymphoid tissue into which T-cells and B-cells migrate and are occasionally housed. Upon completion of their maturation process, both T-cells and B-cells migrate throughout the body, ready to encounter their respective targets known as antigens. Other aspects of the immune system include the tonsils, and unique lymphoid tissue associated with the bronchioles, genitals, and skin. It is interesting to note that only 2 percent of

Autonomic dysregulation: Increased sensitivity to perceived threats resulting from heightened neural (sympathetic) responses speeding up the metabolic rate of one or more organs.

Immune dysregulation: An immune system wherein various functions are suppressed; now believed to be affected by emotional negativity.

lymphocytes are in circulation at any one time. The remaining 98 percent constitute a dynamic defense system, housed and circulated through various organs of the lymphatic system.

The lymphocytes are one of five types of **leukocytes** in the family of cells in the immune system and the major component of the immune system. They are produced in the bone marrow where they eventually migrate to the peripheral organs of the lymphatic system. The other members of the leukocyte family include granulocytes, macrophages (which seem to collaborate with T-cells and B-cells to help identify antigens for destruction), and eosinophils and basophils, which have a lesser role with altered immune function.

T-cells and B-cells may appear morphologically similar, but their function is different. T-lymphocytes are primarily responsible for cell-mediated immunity—that is, the elimination of internally manufactured antigens (e.g., mutinous cells) in organ tissue. It is currently believed that the human body produces one mutant cell approximately every couple of hours. In an action similar to scanning a grocery store product for its bar code, each T-cell travels throughout the body to scan all other cells for a match between their DNA structure and its own. If a cell's structure doesn't match, the T-cell considers it a foreign substance and proceeds to destroy it. Examples are a cancerous cell and transplanted tissue (i.e., organ transplant). In the laboratory where T-cells were observed performing this function, they were called "killer cells" for their search-and-destroy missions. Although the role of T-cells is more global, they have been observed to destroy mutant cells through direct attack in which they release nonspecific substances called cytokines, which assist in the elimination process. B-cells,

Lymphocytes: Immune system cells that are housed throughout the lymphatic system, with 2 percent in circulation at any one time.

Leukocytes: The family of cells that constitute the major component of the immune system.

T-cytotoxic cells: Best known as the cells that attack and destroy tumorous cells by releasing cytokines.

T-helpers: Also known as CD4, these cells help in the production of antibodies released by T-cells.

T-suppressors: Also known as CD8, these cells decrease the production of antibodies, thus keeping a healthy balance of T-cells.

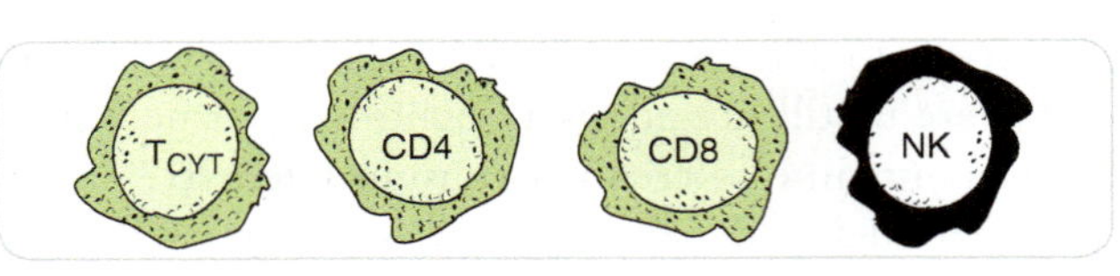

FIGURE 4.1 The family of T-lymphocytes includes three types of cells: T-cytotoxic cells, T-helpers (CD4), and T-suppressors (CD8). The natural killer cells collaborate with the T-cytotoxic cells.

in contrast, are responsible for humoral immunity. This means the antibodies they discharge circulate throughout various body fluids, primarily blood, and combine with foreign antigens to deactivate the agents that make them a threat. Antibodies are a special type of protein, called globulins, found in the plasma and are typically referred to as gamma globulins or immunoglobulins (Ig). The function of B-cells is primarily the elimination of pathogenic microorganisms that contribute to infectious diseases, including viruses and bacteria. Although T-cells and B-cells have their own specific functions, they often work together. In fact, in some cases, B-cells depend on T-cells for their function.

A closer examination of T-cells indicates that there are three subgroups of this crucial leukocyte, plus one additional immune cell (the NK cell) that collaborates with the T-cytotoxic cells to do its function (FIG. 4.1). Each leukocyte cell has a unique molecular configuration and function:

1. **T-cytotoxic cells**: The basic T-cells release cytokines, which then allow the cells to become sensitized to identify endogenous antigens on the cell membrane for destruction. In addition, with the help of macrophages, they attack and destroy tumorous cells.
2. **T-helpers**: Clinically labeled as CD4, these cells appear to increase the production of antibodies released by T-cells. T-helpers and T-suppressors (see Fig. 4.1) are referred to as immunoregulatory cells because they regulate cell-mediated immunity and humoral antibody response.
3. **T-suppressors**: Clinically labeled as CD8, these cells appear to decrease the production of antibodies necessary to assist T-cells in attacking and killing endogenous antigens. A reduction in CD8 is believed to keep cytotoxic T-cells in check so that they do not attack self-proteins and thereby cause degeneration of healthy tissue. A reduction in CD8 is thought to be associated with arthritis

BOX 4.1 The Human Microbiome: A Look at Health Through the Gut

What if I were to tell you that one of the newest theories of disease and illness begins not in the secrets deep inside your DNA, but within the millions upon millions of bacteria that reside in your stomach and small intestine? In what has been called the new "medical landscape of the century," some of the most exciting discoveries in the past decade have been insights into what is going on in our gastrointestinal (GI) tract. The twentieth century may well be known for the emergence of the germ theory of disease, which ushered in the age of antibiotics and vaccinations, and the Genome Project, which sought to link every disease to a defective gene in our DNA, but today a revolution is taking place in medical science about stress and disease right in the gut. While many great things have come about based on the two perspectives of disease—germs and DNA—experts now suggest they have led to a misguided understanding of health. Twenty-first-century medicine may become known for a focus on maintaining healthy gut bacteria to ensure optimal wellness (DeSalle and Perkins, 2015).

Researchers now call the intestinal flora, which is composed of trillions of healthy bacteria, the "microbiome." The premise of the microbiome is that each human being is actually a multispecies superorganism. Each of us hosts a vast and diverse living ecological system. When this ecological system is healthy, so are we. When it is compromised, so are we. Recent evidence suggests that the typical human body hosts over 10,000 microbial species; bacterial cells alone range from 57 to 90 percent of the total number of cells in the human body. The skin, which is the body's largest organ, itself has billions of microbes, many of which are actually essential to our well-being. The twentieth-century approach of wiping out "bugs" via antibiotics has led to a "deforestation" of essential bacteria. The end result sets the stage for many kinds of chronic illness. Maintaining the integrity of the microbiome, however, is far more complicated than eating yogurt or consuming probiotics to reseed the forest of your intestinal flora.

In his book *The Human Superorganism*, Cornell University professor and immunotoxicologist Rodney Dietert explains the delicate balance between the bacteria in our gut and our immune system. When this balance is disrupted the stage is set for a number of noncommunicable diseases, also known as "diseases of civilization." It is now known that 70 percent of our immune system resides in our gut, yet the gut is often ignored in the treatment of many chronic diseases, from asthma, obesity, and arthritis to multiple sclerosis, psoriasis, and attention deficit/hyperactivity disorder (ADHD). Perhaps the biggest take-home message about a compromised microbiome is its association with inflammation. Inflammation (excessive oxidation of tissues) is associated with many chronic diseases, and stress seems to be a major trigger for inflammation (Vida, 2014). Moreover, abysmal eating habits perpetuate a compromised microbiome, leaving one quite vulnerable to chronic disease. Dietert goes so far as to say that we have a whole generation (or more) of kids born with a compromised microbiome, and as such, this qualifies as an epidemic of birth defects.

and lupus. (Borysenko notes that clinical tests show a 2:1 ratio of CD4:CD8 to be normal, whereas a ratio less than this is a signal that this aspect of the immune system is deficient.)

4. **Natural killer (NK) cells**: Unlike cytotoxic T-cells, these immune cells (large lymphocytes) appear to have an innate ability to detect endogenous antigens without the help of any neuropeptides to sensitize them or previous memory experience. NK cells collaborate with cytotoxic T-cells to destroy mutant cells, virus-infected cells, and transplanted grafts. NK cells have a unique role in immune surveillance to detect malignant cell changes. Among immunologists, NK cells are known as "psychosocial friendly cells" because they mirror emotional states (ups and downs) of the mind.

Current research on the relationship between the stress response and immunofunction is now considered definitive by researchers at the Institute for Behavioral Medicine at Ohio State University: Stress increases neuroendocrine hormones, which suppress immune function. In an article reviewing the data over the past two decades, Webster Marketon (2008) states, "Such effects on the immune system have severe consequences on health, which include, but are not limited to, delayed wound healing, impaired responses to vaccination, and development and progression of cancer." Specifically, studies investigating

Natural killer (NK) cells: Large lymphocytes that can detect endogenous antigens, thus helping to destroy mutant cells.

the effect of catecholamines and stress-related hormones have reported questionable integrity of the immune system when excess levels of these substances were found in the blood. Increases in epinephrine and norepinephrine have been observed to promote the release and redistribution of lymphocytes, yet at the same time decrease their efficiency (Calcagni and Elenkov, 2006). Some types of stress (e.g., exercise) cause the release of neuropeptides (endorphins), which not only enhance immunofunction, but also produce an almost euphoric state of mind (the runner's high). Injections of norepinephrine in mice have been shown to enhance NK cell activity. During chronic stress, however, the increase of cortisol and other glucocorticoids has been linked to a marked decrease in T-cells, reducing their ability to locate and destroy mutant cells. The effects of acute and chronic stress on B-cells are still under investigation, but are speculated to be similar to those on T-cells. What all this means is that the integrity of the immune system is thought to be greatly influenced and quite literally compromised by emotional stress.

In Borysenko's model, when the immune system is operating normally, it is said to be "precisely regulated." However, when the immune system is not working as homeostatically intended, the result is immunological overreaction, underreaction, or perhaps both. In any case, disease and/or illness are certain (TABLE 4.2). The causes of overreactions can be exogenous, as in an allergic reaction created by a foreign substance, or endogenous, as when lymphocytes begin to attack and destroy healthy body tissue. Similarly, in an exogenous underreaction, foreign substances outmaneuver and undermine the ability of the B-cells to prevent infection; in endogenous underreactions, antigens are left undisturbed by T-cells, which may then develop into **neoplasms** (cancerous tumors). Similar findings are reported by Biondi (2001).

The concepts of immunity to disease, both exogenous and endogenous, are constantly being rewritten and updated as new studies reveal the nuances and complexities of the lymphatic system and its dynamic interrelationship to all other aspects of human physiology, particularly in light of an increase in lifestyle **autoimmune diseases**

Neoplasms: Another term for cancerous tumors.

Autoimmune diseases: Diseases that occur because of an overactive immune system, which "attacks the body." Examples include lupus and rheumatoid arthritis.

TABLE 4.2 Borysenko's Immune Activity Matrix

	Over-reactions	Under-reactions
Exogenous activity	Allergies	Infections (colds and flu)
		Herpes
Endogenous activity	Arthritis Lupus	Cancer

and the acknowledgment that stress plays a role in this relationship (Kemeny and Gruenewald, 1999; Kiecolt-Glaser et al., 2002).

In Borysenko's opinion, it is psychological stress that throws this precisely regulated mechanism out of balance. Stress is the catalyst that exaggerates the direction in which your immune system is headed, precipitating an over- or underreaction. Note that you can have an allergic reaction (overreaction) and a cold (underreaction) at the same time because they are produced by different dynamics. Borysenko adds that despite the differences among these aspects, the same relaxation techniques work to reinstate precise regulation of the immune system. In other words, regular practice of a relaxation technique, such as meditation or mental imagery, can bring the entire immune system back into homeostatic balance.

Although Borysenko (1991b) believes that "stress alters the vulnerability of the immune system to both exogenous and endogenous antigens," the connection between the mind's ability to perceive situations as stressful and the consequent changes in the integrity of the immune system he left to speculation (FIG. 4.2).

In support of Borysenko's model, ongoing research to understand this link between stress and the immune system suggests that acute psychological stress decreases NK cell activity through a profound effect on cytokine production. Chronic stress is observed to suppress NK cell activity, thereby increasing one's susceptibility to infections and cancer (Herberman, 2002). Moreover, stress-related changes in the immune system have been observed in secondary lymphoid tissue (spleen, lymph nodes) where T-cells are produced. Lymphoid tissues, bathed in a "hormonal milieu," appear to be significantly affected by emotions and thought processing (Rabin, 2002).

FIGURE 4.2 With rapid economic, ecological, and technological changes, the global village appears to have become a more stressful place, which is all the more reason to learn and practice effective stress-management techniques to maintain a sense of balance in one's life despite these winds of change.

New discoveries indicate that the physiological systems are more complex than was once believed. For example, formerly described as specialized lymphocytes, T-helpers and T-suppressors may, in fact, be "double agents" working for the CNS as well.

The Pert Model

Until recently, it was thought that there was no direct link between the nervous system and the immune system; virtually all physiologists believed that these two systems acted independently. But researchers have now isolated neural endings connecting the CNS to the thymus, lymph nodes, spleen, and bone marrow. In addition, the tonsils, adenoids, and some cells of the small intestine have been found to be innervated by sympathetic nerve fibers.

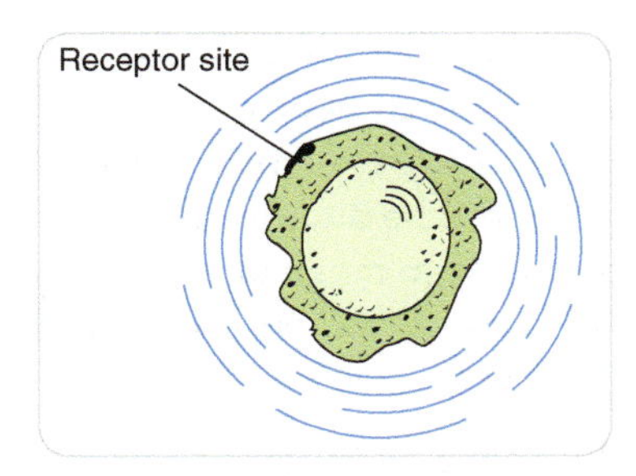

FIGURE 4.3 Pert's early observations were that all known neuropeptides appear to have a single molecular structure. The subtle differences among them may be the rate at which each molecule oscillates.

A second and perhaps more important link indicates that **neuropeptides** (messenger hormones) produced in the brain are able to fit into receptor sites of lymphocytes, much like keys fit into a lock, thus altering their metabolic function. This communication system is altogether different from the efferent/afferent system observed between neuromuscular tissue and the brain. The codes of neuropeptide information are "spoken" through receptor sites of various lymphocyte cells located throughout the body, and their language is apparently influenced by emotional responses.

It was Candace Pert, former Chief of Brain Chemistry at the National Institute for Mental Health, who discovered that immune cells have built-in receptor sites for neuropeptides (1985, 1986, 1987), with similar findings being reported by Edwin Blalock (1985). The identification of neuropeptides themselves is a recent discovery. In trying to uncover the dynamics in the brain associated with chemical addictions, scientists were surprised to find that the brain produces its own (endogenous) opiates, neurotransmitters that have a similar effect to those manufactured externally, such as morphine. The most publicized neuropeptide is beta-endorphin, but so far several hundred neuropeptides have been identified. They are thought to be associated with everything from mood changes to immune regulation. Pert further suggested that there may actually be only one neuropeptide molecule that, like a chameleon, changes its configuration as a result of emotional influences (FIG. 4.3). Pert hypothesized that this spontaneous change may be

Neuropeptides: Unique messenger hormones produced in the brain (and other organs of the body) that fit into the receptor sites of lymphocytes.

accounted for by the wavelike oscillations or vibrations of the electrons in each neuropeptide molecule. Pert's hypothesis parallels work conducted by German physicist Fritz-Albert Popp, who discovered that DNA is capable of sending out a large range of frequencies, with each frequency being associated with a particular metabolic function (McTaggart, 2008).

Because the hypothalamus has the greatest preponderance of neuropeptide receptors, it was first believed that these substances, which are produced by the brain, were involved in the biochemical mediation of emotional responses. Pert discovered, however, that neuropeptides are not produced solely by the brain. Her research revealed that throughout the body immune cells not only have receptors for neuropeptides, but also can manufacture them independently. Furthermore, immune cells seem to have a kind of memory that enables them to adapt to specific emotional responses. Thus neuropeptides are believed to be the means of communication between the brain and T- and B-cells, and it is a bidirectional pathway: Immune cells speak to the brain, and vice versa. Pert's discovery has given credence to the supposition that some emotions may suppress the function of lymphocytes while others may act as immunoenhancers.

Today, the scientific literature is loaded with studies that clearly document the association between the stress response, emotional regulation, and their respective influences on the immune system (Koenig and Cohen, 2002). The following are some of the landmark studies that gave PNI an established foundation of validity in the medical community.

Jermott et al. (1983) looked at the influence of academic stress on the rate of secretory immunoglobulin (S-IgA) in Tufts University dental students. S-IgA is thought to be the first line of defense against upper respiratory diseases. Subjects were administered a personality profile to identify a specific personality trait called power motivation (control), and based on this trait they were divided into two groups. Saliva samples, used to measure S-IgA, were taken five times during the academic year. The results were that mean S-IgA values were significantly reduced during stressful periods, particularly in the students who demonstrated high power motivation.

Immunoenhancement: A term used to describe various stress management techniques that appear to boost the immune system.

Janice Kiecolt-Glaser and her husband, Ron Glaser, both pioneers in the field of PNI, have conducted several landmark studies that linked stress to the suppression of the immune system. Most noteworthy was a classic study that found a decrease in the number of lymphocytes in Ohio State University medical students during their first day of exams, as compared with samples taken prior to and after the exam period (1984). A 1996 paper revealed how stress retards wound healing. Kiecolt-Glaser's research (2003) suggests that chronic stress accelerates the aging process (which entails many diseases) through the overproduction of a specific proinflammatory cytokine.

Studies investigating the relationship between emotional stress and immunosuppression have also been conducted using animals as subjects (Bovbjerg et al., 1984). For example, when rats were subjected to foot shocks they could not control, a significant reduction in immune function (i.e., decreased lymphocyte proliferation) was detected (Laudenslanger et al., 1983). The suppression of the immune system was considered a *conditioned* response. The researchers concluded that a helpless-hopeless attitude, initiated by an inability to control factors of the environment, can pave a path toward illness.

Immunosuppression has also been observed in individuals during bereavement. A study by Bartrop et al. (1977) indicated that people manifested lower lymphocyte proliferation within 8 weeks of the loss of a spouse. Similar findings were observed by Schleifer et al. (1983) in men whose wives had died of breast cancer, with results showing a significant reduction in lymphocyte proliferation. These studies have led some to suggest that humans, like rats, can be conditioned to suppress their immune systems by means of emotions and/or thought processes.

One of the most interesting studies regarding the effects of relaxation and coping techniques on **immunoenhancement** was conducted by Esterling et al. (1994). In this study, the effect of various stress-management skills on NK cell activity was investigated among nursing home patients. Subjects were divided into three groups: (1) those who were taught relaxation techniques, (2) those who were provided with abundant social contact, and (3) those who received no special techniques or contact. Results revealed that after a 1-month period, the NK cell count was significantly higher in those subjects who received stress-management therapy than in the controls. Other studies, inspired by the work of Norman Cousins, have also been conducted to determine the relationship between positive emotions and changes in the immune system.

In her acclaimed book *Molecules of Emotion*, Pert highlights the journey of discovery that brought her to the realization that the body is not a machine. "What is this energy that is referred to by so many alternative healers, who associate it with the release of emotion and the restoration of health? According to Western medical terms, energy is produced strictly by various cellular metabolic processes, and the idea that energy could be connected to emotional release is totally foreign to the scientific mind. . . . It is my belief that this mysterious energy is actually the free flow of information carried by the biochemicals of emotion—the neuropeptides and their receptors." Although the focus of her current research involves peptide T for AIDS treatment, Pert (2004) sees the frontiers of subtle-energy medicine research as the most exciting paradigm of the stress and disease model.

What all these studies seem to indicate is that there is a strong relationship between emotional responses and the biochemical changes they produce, specifically with regard to constituents of the immune system. Whereas before Pert's findings it was believed that cortisol played the crucial role in immunosuppression, it is now thought that structural changes in neuropeptides, influenced by emotional thought, play the most significant role in immunoincompetence. Currently, the search is under way for other neurotransmitters produced and secreted by the brain that may be responsible for producing the emotional thoughts, which in turn synthesize specific neuropeptides to influence the immune system. Pert is of the opinion that this type of search is fruitless. In *Noetic Sciences Review* (1987), she writes, "I think it is possible now to conceive of mind and consciousness as an emanation of emotional information processing, and as such, mind and consciousness would appear to be independent from brain and body." It is this point of view that has led her and others (e.g., Joan Borysenko, Larry Dossey, Deepak Chopra, and Bernie Siegel) to look beyond the physical to the fields of parapsychology and metaphysics for answers to the puzzling relationship between stress and disease. Blazing a trail to this doorstep is cell biologist Bruce Lipton and radiologist Richard Gerber.

The Lipton Model

In tandem with the research of Candace Pert is the work of Bruce Lipton. Lipton is a cell biologist and former faculty member of both the University of Wisconsin's School of Medicine and Stanford University's School of Medicine. He also is the author of the popular book *The Biology of Belief*. For the past three decades, Lipton has researched and explored the nature of human health from the smallest unit: the cell. As one explores the nature of cell physiology, one cannot avoid the structure of the cell nucleus and its contents, specifically the DNA. While Lipton's colleagues were focused on the role of DNA (genetics) in terms of disease causality, he took a different approach: the cell's environment. An outside passion in the field of physics led Lipton to connect dots where others only saw one dot.

Lipton is a proponent of the "epigenetic theory": the study of molecular mechanisms in which environment controls gene activity of the DNA. Lipton goes one step further to suggest that the cell's brain is its cell wall, the cell membrane. The cell membrane holds a complexity of knowledge that allows your body to translate environmental signals into behavior. Understanding that at the molecular level, electromagnetic particles of energy play a significant role in the integrity of the cell's health, Lipton began to explore the significance of electromagnetic properties of the cell membrane.

Lipton's research at Stanford revealed that cells have the ability to promote growth as well as protection of their own integrity. They cannot, however, do both functions at once. The more time that is spent in the protection mode negates time and energy for growth, and thus impedes not only the health of the cell, but the organ it is a part of (and because everything connects energetically, the health of the individual). A state of constant stress can ultimately compromise the health of the cell and hence its vitality. As each cell goes, so goes the organ or system that contains it. Lipton says being scared to death is no mere metaphor. For example, take the effect of the nervous system on the gastrointestinal (GI) tract. Typically, the cells in the lining of your stomach are replaced every 72 hours. This naturally occurring growth process is suspended in the fight-or-flight response of chronic stress with more energy being provided for protection rather than growth. Over time, the functioning of the stomach and small intestine will be impaired significantly.

From cell to physiological systems, Lipton notes that stress hormones greatly affect the vitality of the immune system, so much so that patients undergoing an organ transplant are often given high doses of these hormones (e.g., cortisol) to suppress the immune system so that the new organ won't be rejected.

Over the years, Lipton has observed the relationship of thoughts and beliefs as expressed from both the conscious and unconscious minds. He notes that it is the programmed stress-prone beliefs stored in the unconscious mind that will negatively affect one's health. His research is complemented by studies that reveal that telomeres (a DNA protein) involved with cell division are greatly compromised by chronic psychological stress, hence revealing a credible link between stress and the aging process. Stated simply: Chronic stress shortens the life of cells, specifically immune cells.

Lipton supports the tenet that our learned perceptions have become more powerful than the set programming of our DNA such that our emotions can override our genetically programmed instincts. One needs to look no further than yogis who can control various aspects of human physiology, a feat once thought impossible.

Further research has led Lipton to the connection between one's attitude (belief) and one's health status. He states: "Your beliefs act like filters on a camera lens, changing how you see the world. And your biology adapts to those beliefs" (Lipton, 2008). Lipton calls his work the new biology because he says it goes well beyond the structure of the DNA to the consciousness of each cell and the programming of this consciousness from our unconscious minds. Only when a shift occurs in the belief structure of the subconscious mind will the cell biology itself change.

Lipton also discusses the electromagnetic frequencies of cells and the often unseen electromagnetic spectrum. "Hundreds upon hundreds of scientific studies over the last fifty years have consistently revealed invisible forces of the electromagnetic spectrum profoundly impact every facet of biology regulation" (Lipton, 2008). Lipton is astonished about how these findings are well noted in mainstream medical journals but have yet to be fully incorporated into the medical school curriculum. One person who has made great efforts to change the way medical schools view illness and disease is radiologist Richard Gerber, M.D.

Human energy field: Subtle human anatomy that goes by many names, from the electromagnetic field around an object to a colorful aura. The human energy field is thought to be composed of layers of consciousness that surround and permeate the physical body.

The Gerber Model

Until now, clinical researchers, influenced by the reductionist theory, have designed studies based on the assumption that the mind and the brain are one, in that all thoughts are merely the result of biochemical reactions occurring within the neurons and synapses of the brain's gray matter. Yet, in many clinical circles, human consciousness is referred to as "the ghost in the machine," an intangible entity. In his books *Vibrational Medicine* and *Vibrational Medicine for the 21st Century*, Dr. Richard Gerber reviews hundreds of studies and takes an empirical look at the alternative hypothesis—a holistic or systems-theory approach—that mind as conscious and unconscious thoughts exists as energy that surrounds and permeates the body, influencing a host of corporal biochemical reactions. From this perspective, stress-related symptoms that appear in the physical body are the manifestation of "problems" that have occurred earlier as a result of a disturbance at a "higher energy level."

What at one time sounded like science fiction is now regarded as solid fact as scientists at the vanguard of medicine collaborate with quantum physicists in the search to better understand the energy called consciousness. Paul Rosch, M.D., president of the American Institute of Stress (2003), believes that subtle bioelectric energy modalities will soon replace pharmacological drugs as a means to treat stress-related disease and illness.

Gerber also cites several new studies that have begun to scientifically measure and validate the existence of what is now called the **human energy field.** While these efforts are embryonic at best, Gerber is confident that the end result will be findings that consciousness is indeed composed of subtle energy—a frequency band of oscillations that surrounds and permeates the body—and like Pert suggested, will show that human consciousness is independent yet tightly integrated with the physical body. Gerber describes the human energy field of subtle matter as consisting of several layers of consciousness (FIG. 4.4): the etheric, that closest to the body; the astral, which is associated with emotional thought; the mental, three tiers of consciousness including instinct, intellect, and intuition; and the outermost layer, the causal, which is associated with the soul. Each of these layers of the energy field is associated with a specific vibrational frequency and state of consciousness. Gerber points out that in a state of optimal health all frequencies are in harmony like a finely tuned piano. A disruption in the harmony of frequencies is said to eventually lead to illness and disease. According to this model, a specific thought

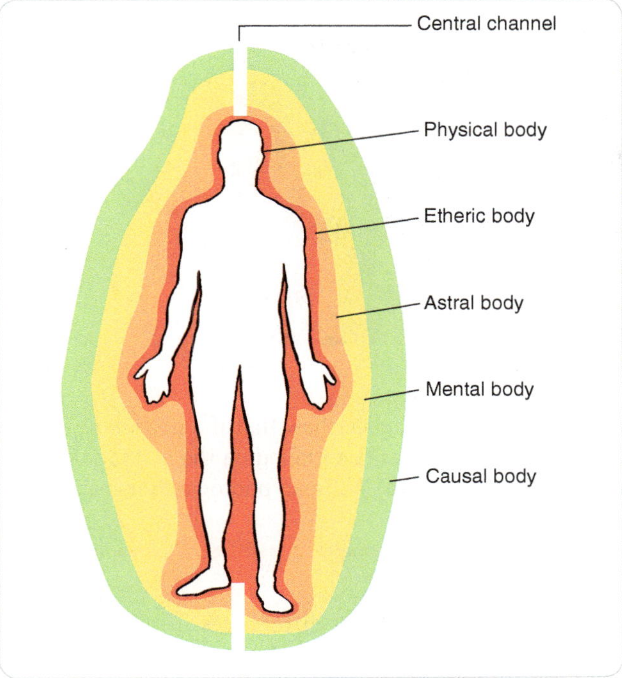

Central channel
Physical body
Etheric body
Astral body
Mental body
Causal body

FIGURE 4.4 The human energy field, also called the electromagnetic field and the auric field, is hypothesized to have many layers, each representing a state of consciousness. Each may also have a subtle vibrational frequency associated with it.

FIGURE 4.5 Each layer of subtle energy around the body vibrates as a specific oscillation. If one layer is "out of tune," like a guitar string, then the entire energy field is affected.

(e.g., "This grade will put me on academic probation") coupled with an emotion (e.g., fear) cascades through the energy levels, resulting in an effect on some aspect of the body (e.g., a suppressed immune system). Based on Einstein's theory of relativity, which asserts, among other things, that matter and energy are interchangeable, Gerber builds a convincing argument that the mind and the brain are two distinct yet tightly intertwined elements of the human condition. In support of the Gerber model is a synthesis of information collected by Lynne McTaggart in her book *The Field*, which cites numerous studies by preeminent scholars in a host of disciplines to substantiate the quantum properties of the human energy field.

Since the beginning of recorded healing powers, shamans and medicine men have alluded to a multilayered body of energy that surrounds the physical body (FIG. 4.5). This energy has gone by several names, including *chi*, *prana*, *breath*, and *spirit*. In academic circles today, this has come to be referred to as **subtle energy**, with the layer closest to the body termed the **etheric energy** level or **bioplasma**. Because subtle energy is composed of matter that appears different (less dense) than that of the physical body, it is often associated in the esoteric literature with the spiritual nature or higher consciousness. Although some people claim to actually see this energy field, which they may describe as an aura, it remains virtually invisible to the naked eye. The human energy field remained undocumented until 1940, when an ingenious photographic technique created by Russian researcher Semyon Kirlian detected traces of this energy field. Using a high-frequency, high-voltage, low-amperage electrical field, electrophotography, or **Kirlian photography** as it is now known, measured the electromagnetic field—the etheric layer—around small living objects. What was revealed through this process appeared very similar to the corona around the sun during an eclipse.

Subtle energy: A series of layers of energy that surround and permeate the body; thought to be associated with layers of consciousness constituting the human energy field.

Etheric energy: The layer of energy closest to the physical body (also known as the etheric body).

Bioplasma: Another term for the etheric layer of energy closest to the physical body.

Kirlian photography: A technique developed by Russian Semyon Kirlian enabling the viewer to see the electromagnetic energy given off by an object such as the leaf of a tree or human hand. This technique is one of several technologies that substantiates the human energy field.

Courtesy of Lyn Gerber.

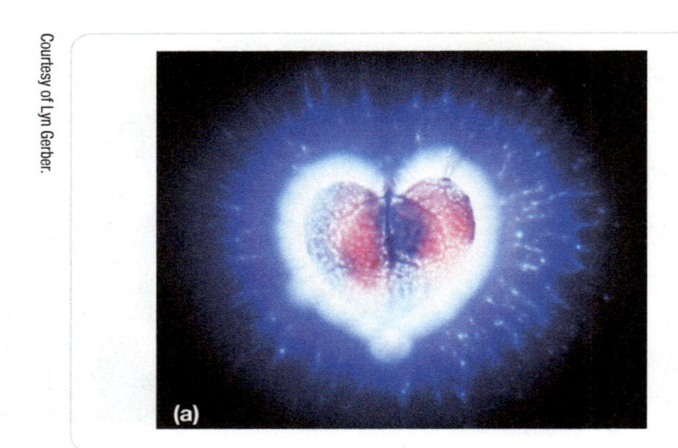

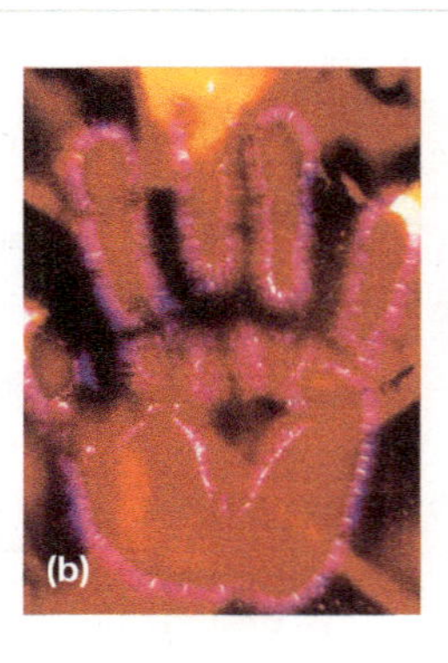

FIGURE 4.6 (a) A Kirlian photograph revealing the aura of an aspen leaf. Some studies show that if a portion of the leaf is torn away, the aura of the complete leaf remains (Gerber, 2001, p. 111). The aura surrounding the leaf is said to consist of tiny light particles observable through the electromagnetic film process. (b) A Kirlian photograph revealing the human energy field (aura) of the hand of renowned healer Olga Worell.

In simple terms, when Kirlian placed a photographic plate between an object—a leaf, say—and a specially designed electrode emitting a specific frequency (Hz), the movement of billions of charged electrons radiating from the object was captured on the film (FIG. 4.6). When the film was processed, brilliant colors and "spark patterns" became evident, creating an electromagnetic image similar to the leaf that was photographed. Surprisingly, if a partial (torn) leaf was photographed, an aura representing the entire leaf still appeared on film. In repeated experiments photographing human hands, Kirlian observed marked differences in the colors and spark patterns between those of healthy people and those diagnosed with cancer.

Subtle anatomy: Also called energy anatomy, subtle anatomy comprises the human energy field (aura), the chakra system, and the meridian system of energetic pathways that supply energy (also known as *chi* or *prana*) to the organs and physiological systems with which they connect.

Chakras: Chakra (pronounced "shock-ra") is a Sanskrit word for spinning wheel. Chakras are part of the subtle anatomy. The seven major chakras align from the crown of the head to the base of the spine and connect to various endocrine glands. Each major chakra is directly associated with various aspects of the mind-body-spirit dynamic. When a specific chakra is closed, distorted, or congested, the perception of stress, disease, or illness may ensue.

Energy psychology: A term used to describe the collaboration of subtle energy (chakras, meridians, and the human energy field) with psychological issues and trauma involving certain aspects of stress.

Among Asian cultures, thoughts and feelings are believed to pass through the many layers of the human energy field through two unique systems constituting what is referred to as our **subtle anatomy**. The first system is a series of energy vortices that align themselves vertically down the front of the body. These "doors" of energy, called **chakras** (Sanskrit for spinning wheel, pronounced "shock-ra"), interface with the physical body at various points corresponding to specific organs of the endocrine and, to a lesser extent, central nervous systems. Invisible to the naked eye, these chakras act as transducers between the various layers of subtle energy.

Currently, there is much interest in the human energy field in consciousness and its relationship to the chakras. Moreover, the study of subtle energy and energy medicine has led to a new field of study called **energy psychology** (Feinstein, 2003), which attempts to unite quantum physics and subtle anatomy with psychology to better understand and treat stress-related diseases at a psychospiritual level. In her collaborative book with Norm Shealy, *The Creation of Health*, author Caroline Myss states that the chakras are the vital link to understanding the dynamics between health and disease. Myss, a clinical intuitive who can see the initial stages of disease in the auric field with a 93 percent accuracy rate, believes that illness does not happen randomly. Rather, she is convinced that the majority of disease and illness results from an overload of unresolved emotional, psychological, and spiritual crises.

Gifted with the ability to see the human energy field and the chakras themselves, Myss has teamed up with several physicians, most notably the founder of the American Holistic Medical Association, Norm Shealy, to explore the mind-body connection with the use of intuitive skills. Myss's work, which substantiates the Gerber model of stress and disease, has proven quite remarkable as the healthcare paradigm slowly shifts from a mechanistic to a holistic approach. Myss is not alone. Physician Christiane Northrup, author of *Women's Bodies, Women's Wisdom* and former president of the American Holistic Medical Association, discusses the relationship between chakras and various disease states. In Northrup's words, "When we have unresolved chronic emotional stress in a particular area of our life, this stress registers in our energy field as a disturbance that can manifest in physical illness." As part of the subtle anatomy, the chakras are a multidimensional network that influences behavior at both the organ and cellular levels. The concept of the chakras may begin to explain why two people with the exact same stressor manifest different symptoms of disease as their thoughts and emotions are processed energetically through the layers of subtle energy and the chakra system.

The following is a synthesis of interpretations from the works of Gerber, Myss, and renowned healer Donna Eden regarding the chakra network system.

First Chakra. The first chakra is commonly known as the root chakra and is located at the base of the spine. The root chakra is associated with issues of safety and security. There is also a relationship with our connectedness to the earth and feelings of groundedness. The root chakra is tied energetically to some organs of the reproductive system, as well as the hip joints, lower back, and pelvic area. Health problems in these areas, including lower-back pain, sciatica, rectal difficulties, and some cancers (e.g., prostate) are thought to correspond to disturbances with the root chakra. The root chakra is also known as the seat of the Kundalini energy, a spiritually based concept yet to be understood in Western culture.

Second Chakra. The second chakra, also known as the sacral chakra, is recognized as being associated with the sex organs, as well as personal power in terms of business and social relationships. The second chakra deals with emotional feelings associated with issues of sexuality and self-worth. When self-worth is viewed through external means such as money, job, or sexuality, this causes an energy distortion in this region. Obsessiveness with material gain is thought to be a means to compensate for low self-worth, and hence a distortion to this chakra. Common symptoms associated with this chakra region may include menstrual difficulties, infertility, vaginal infections, ovarian cysts, impotency, lower-back pain, sexual dysfunction, slipped disks, and bladder and urinary infections.

Third Chakra. Located in the upper stomach region, the third chakra is also known as the solar plexus chakra. Energetically, this chakra feeds into the organs of the gastrointestinal tract, including the abdomen, small intestine, colon, gallbladder, kidneys, liver, pancreas, adrenal glands, and spleen. Not to be confused with self-worth, the region of the third chakra is associated with self-confidence, self-respect, and empowerment. The wisdom of the solar plexus chakra is more commonly known as a gut feeling, an intuitive sense closely tied to our level of personal power, as exemplified in the expression, "This doesn't feel right." Blockages to this chakra are thought to be related to ulcers, cancerous tumors, diabetes, hepatitis, anorexia, bulimia, and all stomach-related problems. Gerber points out that many illnesses related to this chakra region are the result of what he calls "faulty data of old memory tapes" that have been recorded and programmed into the unconscious mind during early portions of the individual's life. Myss adds that the enculturation of fears and issues of unresolved anger are deeply connected to organic dysfunction in this body region.

Fourth Chakra. The fourth chakra is affectionately known as the heart chakra and it is considered to be one of the most important energy centers of the body. The heart chakra represents the ability to express love. Like a symbolic heart placed over the organic heart, feelings of unresolved anger or expressions of conditional love work to congest the heart chakra, which in turn has a corresponding effect on the organic heart.

Anathema to the Western mind so firmly grounded in the mechanistic model of reality, anatomical symbolism may seem to have no place in health and health care. But the ties between a symbolic and organic heart became abundantly clear through the research of cardiologist Dean Ornish. To date, Ornish is the only one known to have scientifically proven the reversal of atherosclerotic plaque. Although diet, exercise, and support groups are factors in Ornish's regime, it is the practice of meditation (what Ornish calls the "open heart meditation" to resolve anger and open the heart chakra) that seems to be the critical factor in the reversal of coronary heart disease.

The heart, however, is not the only organ closely tied to the heart chakra. Other organs include the lungs, breasts, and esophagus. Symptoms of a blocked heart chakra can include heart attacks, enlarged heart, asthma, allergies, lung cancer, bronchial difficulties, circulation problems, and problems associated with the upper back and shoulders. Also, an important association exists between the heart chakra and the thymus gland. The thymus gland, so instrumental in the making of T-cells, shrinks with age. Gerber notes that this may not be so much an age factor, but rather a reflection of the state of the heart chakra.

Fifth Chakra. The fifth chakra lies above and is connected to the throat. Organs associated with the throat chakra are the thyroid, parathyroid glands, mouth, vocal chords, and trachea. As a symbol of communication, the throat chakra represents the development of personal expression, creativity, purpose in life, and willpower. The inability to express oneself in feelings or creativity, or to freely exercise one's will inevitably distorts the flow of energy to the throat chakra, and is thought to result in chronic sore throat problems, temporomandibular joint dysfunction (TMJD), throat and mouth cancers, stiffness in the neck area, thyroid dysfunction, migraines, and cancerous tumors in this region. In *The Creation of Health*, Myss points out that self-expression and creativity are essential to one's health status. She adds that the inability to express one's feelings, whether they be joy, sorrow, anger, or love, is similar to pouring concrete down your throat, thus closing off the energy needed to sustain the health of this region.

Sixth Chakra. The sixth chakra is more commonly known as the brow chakra or the third eye. This chakra is associated with intuition and the ability to access the ageless wisdom or bank of knowledge in the depths of universal consciousness. As energy moves through the dimension of universal wisdom into this chakra it promotes the development of intelligence and reasoning skills. Directly tied to the pituitary and pineal gland, this chakra feeds energy to the brain for information processing. Unlike the solar plexus chakra, which is responsible for a gut level of intuition with personal matters, the wisdom channeled through the brow chakra is more universal in nature with implications for the spiritual aspect of life. Gerber suggests that diseases caused by dysfunction of the brow chakra (e.g., brain tumors, hemorrhages, blood clots, blindness, comas, depression, and schizophrenia) may be caused by an individual's not wanting to see something that is extremely important to his or her soul growth.

Meridian: A river of energy with hundreds of interconnected points throughout the body, used in the practice of acupuncture and shiatsu massage.

FIGURE 4.7 The word *chakra* means spinning wheel. Of the seven major subtle energy chakras, Western culture recognizes only the crown chakra, known in the Judeo-Christian culture as the halo.

Seventh Chakra. If the concept of chakras is foreign to the Western mind, then the seventh chakra may hold promise to bridge East and West. Featured most predominantly in the Judeo-Christian culture through paintings and sculptures as the halo over saintly beings, the seventh chakra, also known as the crown chakra (FIG. 4.7), is associated with matters of the soul and the spiritual quest. When the crown chakra is open and fully functioning, it is known to access the highest level of consciousness. Although no specific disease or illness may be associated with the crown chakra, in truth, every disease has a spiritual significance. And you don't have to be a saint to have a halo—we all have one.

According to Elliot Dacher, M.D., author of *PNI: The New Mind-Body Healing Program*, the insight of chakras can be found in many cultures and disciplines, most notably in the Western culture through the field of psychology with Maslow's hierarchy of needs. Beverly Rubik, president of the Institute of Frontier Sciences in Oakland, California, states that although clinical research findings exist regarding various aspects of subtle anatomy and subtle energies, they remain outside the mainstream of Western medicine because they challenge the dominant biomedical model by defying conventional scientific theory. But she notes that just as Einstein opened the doors of thought that challenged Newtonian physics, the principles of energy and information exchanged through energy will gain validity and acceptance in Western science through the doors of quantum physics.

Similar to the chakras is the **meridian** system: a network of hundreds of interconnected points throughout the

FIGURE 4.8

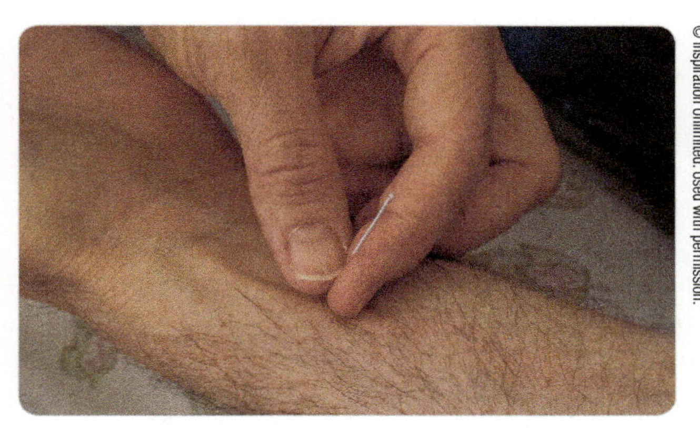

FIGURE 4.9 Acupuncture is an ancient Chinese technique that uses tiny, bulb-shaped needles to unblock congestion at specific energy gates along the paths of subtle energy known as meridians. Classical acupuncture (based on the concept of five elements) treats individuals holistically through the integration of mind, body, and spirit.

body, which allows for the passage of energy between the physical and subtle bodies of the energy field. The meridian system of energy is used in the practice of *shiatsu* massage and Chinese acupuncture.

To most Western physicians, the theoretical concepts behind Chinese acupuncture may seem completely unrelated to the dynamics responsible for the immune system, but to Gerber they are all very much related. If these subtle energy pathways are blocked or congested, the organs they supply may go into a state of dysfunction (FIG. 4.8). Acupuncture is a healing practice that attempts to unblock congested energy pathways, thus allowing a freely flowing current of energy (FIG. 4.9). This healing technique first gained national recognition during President Nixon's trip to China in 1974 (Prensky, 1995). At that time, one of his press corps, James Reston, was stricken with acute appendicitis. Rushed to the nearest hospital, he was successfully treated, without anesthesia, to the amazement of White House officials. Scientists and physicians trained in the Western tradition were quick to ridicule this healing practice, but now studies show that there appears to be a connection, albeit small, between the points designated as meridian gates (acupuncture points) and neuroimmunological crossroads.

The most clinically sound studies to determine the anatomic link between the etheric and physical bodies have been performed by Dr. Kim Han, of Korea, as reported by Rose-Neil in 1967. By injecting a radioactive isotope of phosphorus (P-32) through acupuncture needles at traditional points of insertion, he discovered that traces of the isotope followed a fine ductlike tubule system not related to the circulatory, lymphatic, or nervous systems; rather, they paralleled the acupuncture meridian system. Han's work was validated by Dr. Pierre de Vernejoul in 1985, who used radioactive technetium (^{99m}Tc) to follow the lines of the ancient acupuncture meridians. When samples of the isotope were injected randomly into the skin, no particular pathways were reproduced.

The human energy field has also been studied with regard to the healing power of touch. Several studies by Bernard Grad and Dolores Krieger, involving both plants (to avoid the placebo effect) and people, have demonstrated that "healing thoughts" in the form of energy produce statistically significant changes in chlorophyll and red blood cells, respectively. Similar studies by Drs. Leonard Laskow and Glen Rein have shown that conscious thoughts can decrease the growth rate of cancer cells in the laboratory. This conscious energy transfer is said to show properties similar to those observed with electromagnetic fields. Investigations into the subtle anatomy of the chakras have also been initiated by a handful of other researchers, including Dr. Elmer Green at the Menninger Clinic in Topeka, Kansas; Valerie Hunt at UCLA; Dr. Hiroshi Motoyama at the California Institute for Human Science; and researchers at the renowned HeartMath Institute.

To date, Hunt shows the most promise in detecting electromagnetic frequencies associated with the chakras. Her work began with biofeedback studies of muscle tension, but soon shifted to electrical activity in the seven regions associated with the primary chakras, where she noted a difference in frequency many times higher (1,600 cps) than could possibly be explained by electrochemical tissue of the heart and brain (0–250 cps). So inspired was Green by the concept of the human energy field that he co-created the International Society for the Study of Subtle Energy and Energy Medicine (ISSSEEM), which now publishes its own research journal, *Subtle Energies and Energy Medicine.*

How does the mind-body relationship lose its harmonic equilibrium? Two possibilities have been suggested. The first faults bioecological influences—that is, repeated exposure to those energy frequencies, natural (ultraviolet rays) or human-made (high-tension power lines), with a rhythm greater than 7.8 Hz, which distort some aspect of the human energy field.

To understand this relationship from Gerber's perspective, we need to first understand some additional concepts of the physical world elucidated by Einstein. First, the smallest particle within an atom is composed of energy, and energy and mass are interchangeable; thus, each object gives off a unified rhythm or series of oscillations. These oscillations are depicted in units of measurement called hertz (Hz), or oscillations per second. In turn, objects that oscillate, including the human body, create a magnetic energy field. Through processes known as **sympathetic resonance** and sonic **entrainment**, a vibration can resonate from one object to another, as observed with tuning forks. An object with a lower or weaker frequency of oscillations will alter its own frequency to entrain with (match) that of an object emitting a higher or stronger frequency of oscillations. In humans, the result over time if several organs are influenced to entrain at a higher than normal frequency is a decreased ability to return to homeostasis, resulting in metabolic dysfunction or possibly irregular cell division in those organs.

Sympathetic resonance: A resonating vibration given off by one object that is picked up by another object in close proximity. Tuning forks provide a classic example.

Entrainment: In physics, the mutual phase locking of like oscillations; in human physiology, organs or organisms giving off strong vibrations influencing organs or organisms with weaker vibrations to match the stronger rate of oscillation; thought to conserve energy.

In support of this hypothesis is the work of Dr. Robert Becker. Becker, twice nominated for the Nobel Prize in medicine, researched the relationship between the incidence of cancer and radiation emitted from various electrical sources, including power lines, microwave ovens, electric blankets, and video display terminals (VDTs). He concluded that an unequivocal relationship exists between extremely low frequencies (ELF)—the range in which electrical current oscillates (60 Hz)—and the development of diseases in people who are repeatedly exposed to them. Becker is of the opinion that oscillations of a higher frequency are somehow absorbed through the human energy field (what he calls the human electromagnetic field), resulting in alterations to the genetic makeup of cells at the atomic level.

That the human body had magnetic properties that could be enlisted as a healing mechanism was first suggested by Austrian physician Anton Mesmer in the late 1800s; it was dismissed as nonsense. But in 1992, geobiologist Joseph Kirschvink discovered that human brain cells do, indeed, synthesize a magnetic-like substance called magnetite. Like Becker, Kirschvink speculated that exposure to various electrical impulses can alter the integrity of magnetite and affect the cells' health or rate of activity. Disturbances produced by electrical interference can result in mutations at the cellular level, which may then become cancerous tumors.

Compounding the problem is the fact that T-lymphocytes are also affected by ELFs. Becker cited a study by Dr. Daniel B. Lyle of Pettis Memorial Hospital in Loma Linda, California, in which in vitro T-lymphocytes exposed to a 60-Hz energy field significantly reduced their cytotoxic ability against foreign antigens over a 48-hour period. Becker also suggested that energy currents may affect mood and emotions, which are thought to be associated with the astral and mental layers of the human energy field.

In his ground-breaking book *Cross Currents*, Becker concludes:

> At this time, the scientific evidence is absolutely conclusive: 60-Hz magnetic fields cause human cancer cells to permanently increase their rate of growth by as much as 1600 percent and to develop more malignant characteristics. These results indicate that power frequency fields are cancer promoters. Cancer promoters, however, have major implications for the incidence of cancer because they increase the number of cases of causing agents in our environment,

> ranging from carcinogenic chemicals to cosmic rays. As a result, we are always developing small cancer cells that are recognized by our immune system and destroyed. Any factor that increases the growth rate of these small cancers gives them an advantage over the immune system, and as a result more people develop clinical cancers that require treatment. (Becker, 1990)

Although the hazards of high-tension power lines have fallen off the radar screen of national attention, the dangers of prolific cell phone use have surfaced as a new health care risk as reported in the *Washington Post* and the *International Journal of Radiation Biology and Environmental Health Perspectives.* Several reports highlight incidences of headaches, memory loss, and brain tumors with excessive use resulting from the close proximity of the microwaves (ELFs) to the head. A study conducted at the Cleveland Clinic by Agarwal and colleagues (2008) revealed that cell phone usage is linked to a lower sperm count. Despite the growing popularity of cell phones, the potential dangers of cell phone radiation are now well documented (Davis, 2010; Ketcham, 2010). However, it should be noted that studies regarding the microwave effects of cell phone use are certainly controversial. Excessive exposure to ELFs is considered by many health experts to be harmful. What are your thoughts on cell phone use and its impact on your long-term health status?

Regrettably, Becker's findings have largely been either ignored or denounced by the medical community and federal government. For many reasons, Becker's research, and the research of those who have followed in his footsteps, is still very controversial. For one thing, many people find the idea of electrical pollution hard to believe because it cannot be detected through the five senses. If you find this concept difficult to grasp, think of the classic Memorex TV commercial (now on YouTube) in which the vibrations of Ella Fitzgerald's voice shatter a crystal goblet. Neither a nervous system nor an immune system is necessary to feel the effects of vibrational energy (FIG. 4.10).

Courtesy of Vibe Technologies LLC.

FIGURE 4.10 Scientific studies into the use of healing vibrations are currently under way, exploring technology like the V.I.B.E. machine, created by Gene Koonce. This device creates a slight DC charge of −70 to −90 millivolts to entrain the cells of the body to hold a transmembrane potential and DC difference in potential, thus causing them to function at their optimal level. When a person sits near the V.I.B.E. machine for a specified duration, the body's cells entrain to this vibration of homeostasis.

The second explanation for the loss of mind-body equilibrium is that *self-produced* emotional disturbances congest the energy field at the astral (emotional) layer and precipitate a host of physical maladies. Toxic thoughts that go unresolved, often referred to as emotional baggage, may translate into physical ailments that serve as a reminder of these issues. Gerber believes that, in essence, that which constitutes our human energy field can be thought of as a sixth (and in his opinion underdeveloped) sense. As examples, he suggests that people who have the power of clairvoyance (clear vision) are able to access various levels of the human energy field in themselves and others; out-of-body experiences and near-death experiences may be explained in the same way.

Thoughts, perceptions, and emotions, according to Gerber's theory, originate in the various layers of subtle energy, cascade through the mind-body interface, and are decoded at the molecular level to cause biochemical changes in the body. He states, "Thoughts are particles of energy. [Negative] thoughts are accompanied by emotions which also begin at the energy levels. As these particles of energy filter through from the etheric level to the physical level, the end result is immunoincompetence" (Gerber, 2001).

It is fair to say that human consciousness is the part of psychoneuroimmunology that is the least understood. As specialists examine the mind-body relationship more and more, though, they are beginning to look beyond the conventional scientific wisdom of a mind within a body and consider the alternative idea, a body within a mind. Gerber's theory may test the limits of your credibility. However, given his careful documentation and the support of a growing body of empirical research from members of ISSSEEM, the HeartMath Institute, and the Institute of Noetic Sciences, the possibility of this phenomenon is gaining ground every day. Gerber reminds us that Nobel laureates Lister and Pasteur, who were once mocked for their theories of "invisible bacteria" as causes of infectious disease, were vindicated after years of research. Ironically, practitioners in Western medicine are quick to use electromagnetic resonance imaging to diagnose disease, but are still reluctant to use energy medicine (e.g., acupuncture, homeopathy, Reiki, Healing Touch) as a bona fide treatment despite the fact that the National Institutes of Health's Center for Complementary and Alternative Medicine has identified subtle energy as one of five modality areas. Ultimately, what Gerber is saying is that the medical community is beginning to experience a paradigm shift in its approach to health, and this change is being met with much resistance.

The Pelletier Premodel

As mentioned earlier, Pelletier is yet to be convinced that sufficient medical evidence has been collected to substantiate a definitive stress-disease model. Nevertheless, his comprehensive research article entitled "Psychoneuroimmunology Toward a Mind-Body Model" and other research (e.g., Achterberg et al., 2005; Schlitz and Amorok, 2005) bring to the attention of the allied health professions some valid points he believes must be considered and understood before such a comprehensive model can be constructed. In the years since Pelletier's article was first published, significant medical advances have been made, and the National Institutes of Health's Center for Complementary and Alternative Medicine now allocates funding for areas of research involving prayer and energy medicine. Despite these efforts, many pieces of the stress and disease puzzle remain missing, suggesting that a complete model has yet to be fully realized.

Spontaneous remission: The sudden (sometimes gradual) disappearance of a nonmedically treated disease, most often observed with cancerous tumors, but other diseases as well.

Some intriguing findings in the medical literature approach the fringes of parapsychology and metaphysics, areas that Pelletier hints should be taken a little more seriously and investigated empirically to develop a comprehensive stress-disease model. The following highlight some of these findings:

1. *Multiple personality disorder:* Braun (1983) cites people diagnosed as having multiple personality disorder (MPD) whose different personalities manifest different illnesses. For instance, a patient may be a diabetic under the influence of one personality, yet show no signs of this disease in the presence of another. Similarly, one personality may require prescription glasses or have asthma or severe allergies, whereas the remaining personalities show no traces of these symptoms. These disease states disappear within the individual when another personality becomes dominant. In most cases of MPD, the patient experienced some incredibly traumatic event as a child. Stress is thought to be strongly associated with the etiology of disease, yet its appearance and disappearance from personality to personality have medical experts baffled.
2. *Spontaneous remission:* Perhaps even more baffling to the medical community is the notion of **spontaneous remission**—the sudden disappearance of diseased tissue—most often observed with cancerous tumors but acknowledged with other diseases as well. What makes these reports so remarkable is that many people who were spontaneously cured were originally diagnosed as terminally ill. There are now even several documented cases of HIV remission (Health News, 2005). Typically, the first reaction of members of the medical community is denial, with the standard explanation that the patient was misdiagnosed. But a closer look into the matter reveals that in documented cases, some people who were given weeks to live seemed to go through an "about-face attitude" resulting in a "spontaneous cure." These people end up living years, if not decades, beyond their estimated time of departure.

Stress with a Human Face

Spontaneous remission is still considered to be an anomaly in Western medicine. What should be a celebration when malignant tumors disappear is instead looked upon as a peculiarity—another unexplained ghost in the machine. But Jim Gill will tell you, it's no ghost. Rather, he says, it's a dynamic alchemy of divinity and humanity—one he now welcomes with open arms.

On September 1, 1994, Jim was diagnosed with oat cell cancer, one of the deadliest forms of cancer. Test results revealed two large tumors in his chest, one of which was wrapped around his vena cava, disrupting the flow of blood back to his heart. So discouraged were his team of physicians with the test results that they gave him at most 2 weeks to live with no treatment, and as long as 4 months with treatment consisting of radiation and chemotherapy. "Basically, they told me I wouldn't see Christmas," he said. Although Jim was scheduled for the usual routine of chemotherapy, the prognosis looked anything but promising. Knowing the odds were against him, Jim decided to call in reinforcements. He contacted Mary Linda Landauer, a therapist who was trained in mind-body-spirit healing, who taught him meditation, visualization, and guided mental imagery. She also encouraged him to explore all possible options of healing, with the most important being the power of faith. And that he did! Jim quit working for 7 months and, as he said, "I became the captain of my ship."

Courtesy of Nancy and Jim Gill.

Jim's curiosity led him to several modalities of healing, including a trip to Tijuana, Mexico, where he stayed at a medical facility for 4 weeks to boost his immune system. His healing regime included diet supplements and herbs, but he takes delight in describing his spiritual awakening as well. When he returned to the Arthur James Cancer Center in Columbus, Ohio, one tumor had completely disappeared; the other, originally the size of a baseball, was now the size of a walnut. Fifteen years later, Jim is the picture of health.

"The medical experts were baffled, but I wasn't. Ever since then I get four to five phone calls a week from people with cancer. Most are looking for the magical silver bullet. But let me tell you something. It wasn't Mexico, or the herbs or the chemo that did it," Jim explains. "It was my reconnection to spirituality that did it. Although it was a lot of work, so many positive things have come out of that darkness. I wouldn't have traded this growth experience for anything!"

The Institute of Noetic Sciences began to document cases of spontaneous remission in the mid-1980s. It found more than 3,000 cases of spontaneous remission in the medical literature, 15 percent of which occurred with no clinical intervention (e.g., radiation or chemotherapy).

In a review of these findings, Jaylene Kent et al. (1989) noted several cases that today are still unexplained. For instance, they examined the results of the International Medical Commission of Lourdes (CMIL), a body of medical professionals that investigates the clinical cases of people who visit the shrine of St. Bernadette at Lourdes, France. Of 38 cases of "cures" examined by the commission since 1954, 19 were found to be medically and scientifically inexplicable. Kent and her colleagues are quick to point out that evidence of spontaneous remission is rare, yet its existence cannot be ignored. To date, however, it *has* been ignored, in part because the findings are "anecdotal" and cannot be replicated in controlled laboratory studies.

3. *Hypnosis:* When the powers of the unconscious mind are accessed through hypnosis, documented physiological changes have been observed that also prove baffling. Hypnosis can create a state of increased suggestibility that appears able to influence the biochemical mechanisms responsible for healing. According to Pelletier, the following illnesses have been shown to be cured by hypnosis: warts, asthma, hay fever, contact dermatitis, and some animal allergies. Case studies of ichthyosis, a congenital skin disease, have also been successfully treated with hypnosis (Dossey, 1999). Pelletier notes

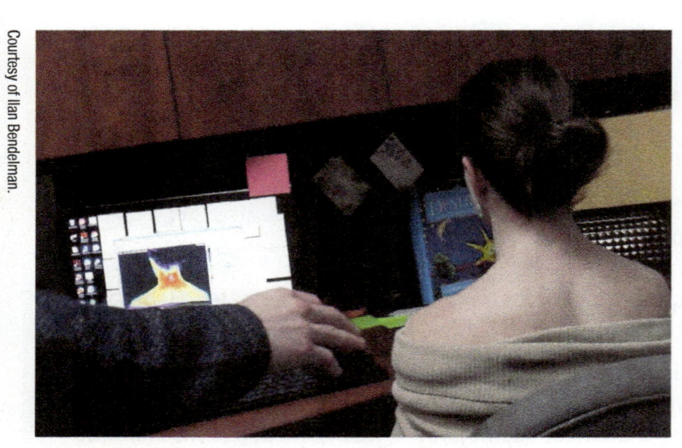

Courtesy of Ilan Bendelman.

FIGURE 4.11 Canadian energy healer Ilan Bendelman demonstrates his energy healing technique at the Psy-Tek Subtle Energy Laboratory in Encinitas, California, in which he is able to sense the human energy field and recalibrates frequencies (e.g., thoughts and emotions) that are no longer conducive to/compatible with one's health, or do not resonate a positive frequency.

that although hypnosis can produce a very relaxed state in which the stress hormone ACTH may be suppressed, enhancement of immune responses alone cannot account for these hormonal changes.

4. *Placebos and nocebos:* **Placebos** fall within the realm of faith healing, where a person so strongly believes that the medication he or she received will cure the illness that a healing effect occurs even when what was ingested is no "real" medication at all. The fact that a person suffering from an illness can be cured by taking a sugar pill may sound ludicrous, but indeed this is often the case. In fact, the Food and Drug Administration (FDA) insists that new medicines must produce a cure rate of greater than 35 percent—the demarcation of the placebo effect—in clinical studies before they can be approved. But some placebos have a cure rate of 70 percent (Brody, 2000). In his book *Love, Medicine, and Miracles*, Dr. Bernie Siegel cites several examples of patients who were healed by their "faith" in medicine even when it wasn't really "medicine," particularly when their attending physicians were very supportive. This type of faith healing is an aspect of clinical medicine not fully understood. What was once thought of as a fluke in modern medicine, however, is now considered a part of the mystery of the stress-disease phenomenon.

   Nocebos is a name given to explain the phenomenon when a medication that has been proven to be extremely effective is given to a patient who is told that it is experimental and most likely it won't work. In many cases, the result is that the medication does nothing despite its proven effectiveness.

5. *Cell memory:* With the development of medical technology that has made organ transplants possible, a critical mass of case histories has revealed that cells of various organ tissues hold an energetic memory pattern that transfers to the next recipient. In the book *The Heart's Code*, author Paul Pearsall cites several case studies where people with transplanted organs began to have memories of events in which they took no part (yet the organ donor did). One remarkable story is that of Claire Sylvia, who, upon having a heart transplant, began to have dreams of a young blond-haired man named Tim, wearing a motorcycle jacket. Although a vegetarian and a connoisseur of wine, Claire had cravings for KFC and beer—the last food Tim had before he died in a motorcycle accident. These and other stories like them suggest that cells retain some level of consciousness that is then passed on to the recipient of the organ. Similarly, some people, who, while in therapy, recount memories of childhood physical abuse, begin to manifest bruises in the places where they were beaten decades earlier.

6. *Subtle energy:* Another area of scientific investigation that merits attention is the concept of subtle energy. Pelletier (1988, 2000) states, "Mind-body interaction clearly involves subtle energy or subtle information exchange. . . . Given that mind-body interactions involve an exchange of subtle energy, principles of physics may be appropriately applied to issues of health and disease." Pelletier advocates the use of magnetic resonance imaging (MRI) and the superconducting quantum interference device (SQUID), which are based on the concept of subtle energy, for clinical diagnosis of disease and illness. He also suggests that researchers in the

Placebos: A nonmedicine (e.g., sugar pill) that can prove to be as effective as the medicine it is supposed to represent. Healing occurs as a matter of belief.

Nocebos: A bona fide, effective medicine that does *not* work because the patient doesn't believe that it will.

field of psychoneuroimmunology try to understand and apply the principles of quantum theory and astrophysics.

7. *Immunoenhancement:* Pelletier points out that if a suppressed immune system can, by way of conscious thought, influence the progression of tumors and other disease processes, psychological factors (e.g., mental imagery, meditation, and cognitive restructuring) may also be able to *enhance* the immune system to create an environment conducive to spontaneous remission and other healing effects. Pelletier cites two studies opening the door to this possibility. In addition to the study by Kiecolt-Glaser et al. (1999) with nursing home residents discussed earlier, he points to the findings of McClelland and Kirshnit (1989) in which subjects watched an inspirational movie about Mother Teresa. Salivary IgA samples were collected before and after viewing the film, and it was observed that values increased afterward, regardless of the subject's opinions of Mother Teresa's work.

In his review of the medical literature, Pelletier has found that most of the evidence collected so far has been anecdotal, meaning that, in his opinion, controlled studies cannot yet prove that positive emotions can enhance immune function. But he suggests that this is a prime area for research. In particular, Pelletier raises the following questions:

1. Is immunoenhancement merely a return to existing baseline levels of the constituents of this precisely regulated system?
2. Are some constituents of the immune system suppressed (e.g., T8) to create an *illusion* that the entire system is enhanced?
3. Could stressors produce a rebound effect, causing elements of the immune system to increase above baseline levels once the stressor is removed?
4. Can the immunological responses actually be increased above baseline?

These are questions he feels need to be answered to better understand what immunoenhancement really is. Pelletier's scientifically trained, analytical side is skeptical about the probability of the healing powers of the mind, but his intuitive side allows for the possibility of immunoenhancement. He writes, "Speculations concerning the ultimate role of beliefs, positive emotions, and spiritual values in organizing and transcending biological determinism might seem like philosophical speculation if the answers to these questions were not so critical to our survival as a species balanced between health and illness, life and death."

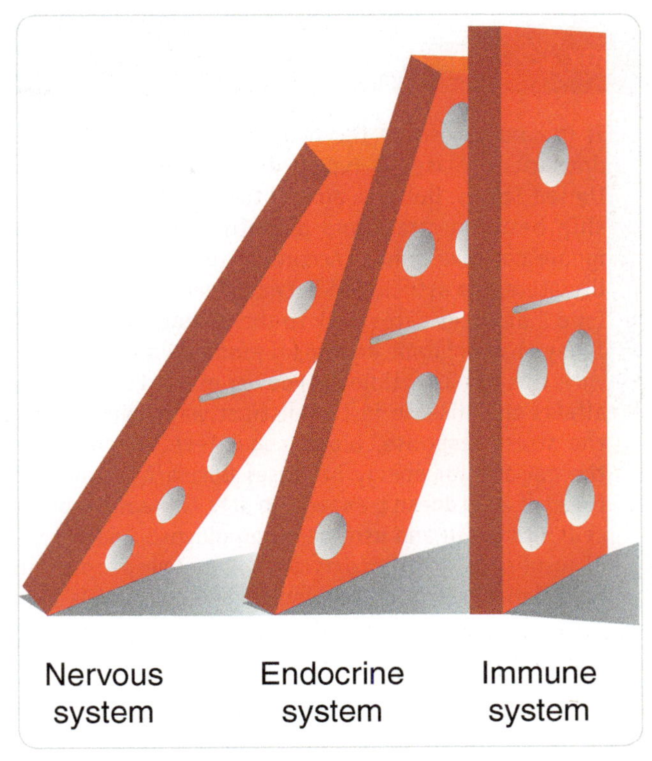

FIGURE 4.12 The balance between the nervous system, endocrine system, and immune system is quite delicate when repeatedly affected by chronic stress.

Pelletier does not specifically use the word *spirituality* with regard to stress and disease, but we can infer that he believes spiritual well-being has been largely ignored by clinical medicine, which leaves the stress-disease model incomplete. He suggests that the only logical approach to understanding the stress-disease/mind-body phenomenon is to take the whole systems approach, in which the individual is greater than the sum of its physiological parts. Until a viable model explaining the relationship between stress and disease is complete, we must work with the information we have. And what is known through the current medical model is that physical symptoms arising from stress can wreak havoc on physical health in specific regions of the body. Two decades later, Pelletier has not changed the premise of his stress and disease premodel. However, his interest has taken him further into the exploration of mind-body healing—specifically, in the realm of complementary medicine (Pelletier, 2000a).

BOX 4.2 Stress and Type 2 Diabetes

It is hard to escape the headline news regarding the dramatic increases in type 2 diabetes, not only in the United States, but also around the world. The relationship between stress and diabetes is one to neither ignore nor take lightly. According to European medical literature, the association between emotional stress and type 2 diabetes dates back to the seventeenth century. Today, many chronic emotional problems are associated with this disease etiology (Pouwer et al., 2010). Stress affects this disease in two distinct ways. First, during the stress response, blood sugar levels increase, as the demand for energy increases during fight or flight (even if one doesn't engage in it). The ability of the cells to take in and use the blood glucose (via the role of insulin) is greatly compromised among people with type 2 diabetes, thus keeping blood sugar levels high. Secondly, emotional problems associated with chronic stress serve as a distraction to self-care behaviors (e.g., poor monitoring of sugar levels, no time for exercise, poor eating habits, more alcohol consumption, etc.). As a result, blood sugar levels remain elevated, paving the way for serious health complications (e.g., poor circulation, macular degeneration, etc.). The American Diabetes Association recommends effective stress management behaviors for all people with type 2 diabetes, including a combination of effective coping skills (e.g., cognitive restructuring, creative problem solving, even hobbies) and effective relaxation techniques (e.g., breathing exercises, progressive muscular relaxation, meditation, healthy nutrition, and physical exercise). Learning to relax is an essential skill for everyone with type 2 diabetes.

DNA, Telomeres, Stress, and Aging

At the end of each DNA strand is a region of repetitive sequences, called a telomere, that serves to protect the end of the chromosome from deterioration. Simply stated, telomeres are associated with DNA replication and become shorter each time the process is repeated. The enzyme telomerase is used to protect the telomeres by ensuring their stability. If the telomeres shorten without restoration, then cell replication becomes compromised. When cell replication is compromised, the health of the tissue is compromised, as seen in the aging process. In 2009, the Nobel Prize in Physiology or Medicine was awarded to researchers whose work substantiated the importance of telomeres and how they are influenced by stress and aging. Research now substantiates the fact that oxidative stress (the presence of free radicals) shortens telomeres. This shortening affects health in a number of ways, including compromising the cell division process and the integrity of our DNA. Speculation is that chronic stress may have the same effect. Physical exercise is suggested as a means to enhance the integrity of telomeres. Could other relaxation techniques lead you to the fountain of youth? Perhaps! While more research is needed, all evidence points in this direction. Stress not only kills, it speeds up the aging process.

Target Organs and Their Disorders

Looking back at Borysenko's model, we can begin to see how disease and illness can arise from either an overresponsive autonomic nervous system (elevated stress hormones) or a dysfunctional (suppressed) immune system. The importance of understanding how these physiological systems work, as well as the pathways leading to disease, is considered by Borysenko, Pert, Gerber, and Pelletier to be the first step in the healing process. Borysenko, Gerber, and Pelletier also advocate the use of relaxation techniques, including meditation and mental imagery, as supplemental aids in any recovery process. In fact, some healing methods now take a multimodal approach, combining standard Western medical practices with healing methods that employ the powers of the mind. Although this approach is now entering the mainstream of the American healthcare system, many physicians still remain "doubting Thomases," in part because they have received no formal training in these areas; others perceive the multimodal approach as a threat. Although there has been no predictive correlation between a specific stressor (e.g., divorce) and a physical outcome (e.g., ulcers), several studies have shown relationships between the inability to express emotions, the personalities most closely associated

BOX 4.3 Lyme Disease and Stress

It may have started out as a tick bite. There was no telltale "bulls-eye marking," as described in the medical literature, but then again, new research about the epidemic of Lyme disease reveals that this diagnostic sign only occurs 20 percent of the time. Molly isn't even sure when she first contracted Lyme disease, but it may have been during her college years. Nearly everyone in her extended family in western Pennsylvania has it. Her symptoms began years ago with a condition called "restless leg syndrome" characterized by spasmatic muscle tremors in the legs (and arms). What began as an occasional tremor late at night exploded into a full-blown, debilitating disease during the course of her husband's illness and his subsequent death a few years later. Looking back, Molly can identify the perfect storm of stress, from the caretaking of her young husband coupled with coastal property flooding and several other monumental stressors, all of which lowered her resistance and set the stage for her own chronic health issues. Stress, it turns out, is the catalyst for chronic Lyme disease, because when the immune system is suppressed from a repeated flood of cortisol, the bacteria that cause Lyme disease are given the opportunity to take over.

It wasn't until a few months ago that Molly was correctly diagnosed with Lyme disease (many tests are false negatives, which only compounds the difficulty of diagnosis and treatment). By all accounts, Lyme is an insidious disease that seems to be related to (or perhaps the cause of) chronic fatigue syndrome, multiple sclerosis, fibromyalgia, and even Alzheimer's/dementia, as recently noted with news headlines of beloved singer/songwriter Kris Kristofferson (Libov, 2016). Experts call Lyme disease the "great mimicker" because it mimics the symptoms of so many other diseases. Unfortunately, most physicians are not educated about what experts now call an epidemic, with some suggesting that perhaps as many as 50 percent of Americans have Lyme disease. Dr. Zubcevik, a Harvard Medical School professor and co-director of the Dean Center for Tick Borne Illness, states that a compromised immune system sets the stage for chronic Lyme disease to reveal associated symptoms, and she states that many people younger than age 50 and everyone older than age 50 has a compromised immune system (Stringfellow, 2016).

Like several diseases that are named from their place of origin, the name for the disease comes from the town of Lyme, Connecticut, where, decades ago, several people were first diagnosed with identical chronic health problems. The source of the disease is the bacteria *Borrelia burgdorferi*, which is carried by a tiny deer tick. New research from New York, Europe, and Australia, where the disease also exists, suggests that mosquitos, fleas, and mice can also carry the bacteria that cause Lyme disease. Infection with these bacteria can cause serious problems with the nervous, cardiovascular, and digestive systems. Because of its molecular make-up, Lyme is now considered to be a sexually transmitted disease, further increasing the number of people carrying it, often unknowingly (Howenstine, 2004).

Headaches and general fatigue are some of the first symptoms, but left untreated the acute problems become chronic to the point where they kidnap one's life. Sixty-nine percent of people with Lyme go untreated, and as many as 20 percent of patients suffer long-term symptoms.

Antibiotics are the first course of treatment when the disease is detected. Long-term antibiotic use is one form of treatment for chronic Lyme, yet this method can create its own series of health problems in the gut. Current research suggests that there are 10 different strains of the Lyme disease in the United States. In addition, antibiotics (e.g., doxycycline) only stop the bacteria from replicating, it doesn't kill them, hence complicating the healing process (Buhner, 2015).

Lyme disease is also a very political disease, as well documented in the acclaimed film *Under Our Skin*. Many insurance companies and pharmaceutical companies—who stand to profit by maintaining the status quo—claim that there is no such thing as chronic Lyme disease. Their efforts have led to many physicians losing their licenses for treating chronic Lyme disease (Wilson, 2009). The state of Connecticut has now passed legislation protecting all physicians who treat this disease.

The newest treatment for chronic Lyme disease is low-dose immunotherapy (LDI), a type of homeopathy, and it has been met with great success by some people. Additional therapies include relaxation techniques to help boost the immune system to keep Lyme disease in check (Vincent and Elder, 2016).

with this characteristic, and the incidence of some illness and disease. For instance, the expression of hostility is a behavioral trait of the Type A personality and is commonly associated with coronary heart disease.

For some unexplained reason, during various stages of acute and chronic stress, certain regions of the body seem more susceptible to excessive metabolic activity than others. The organs that are singled out or targeted by increased metabolic activity are called **target organs**. Any organ can be a target organ: hair, skin, blood vessels, joints, muscles, stomach, colon, and so on. In some people one organ may be singled out, while in others several organs may be targeted. Genetics, emotions, personality, and environmental factors have all been speculated as possible explanations for target organs, without conclusive evidence to support any of them. In fact, it is likely that they may all contribute to the disease process. The following are some of the more common disorders and their respective target organs, which are now known to be influenced by the stress response. Using Borysenko's model, they have been divided into two categories: nervous system–related disorders and immune system–related disorders.

Nervous System–Related Disorders

In the event of perceived stress, organs that are innervated by neural tissue or acted upon by the excessive secretion of stress hormones increase their metabolic rates. When denied the ability to rest, organs may begin to dysfunction, much like a car engine that overheats on a very hot day. Several states of disease and illness first appear as stress-related symptoms that, if undetected or untreated, may result in serious health problems. The following are descriptions of the more common ones.

1. *Bronchial asthma:* Bronchial asthma is an illness in which a pronounced secretion of bronchial fluids causes a swelling of the smooth-muscle tissue of the large air passageways (bronchi). The constriction of these passages produces a choking effect, where the individual feels as if he or she cannot breathe. Asthmatic attacks can be severe enough to send someone to the hospital and, in some cases, are even fatal. Several studies have linked the onset of asthmatic attacks with anxiety; others have linked it with an overprotective childhood (Hatfield, 2007). Currently, drugs (e.g., prednisone) are the first method of treatment. However, relaxation techniques, including mental imagery, autogenic training, and meditation, may be just as effective in both delaying the onset and reducing the severity of these attacks.
2. *Tension headaches:* Tension headaches are produced by sympathetic-mediated contractions of muscles of the forehead, eyes, neck, and jaw. Tension usually builds as the parasympathetic inhibition of muscular contraction gives way to sympathetic drive, increasing the state of muscular contraction. Increased pain results from increased contraction of these muscles. Lower-back pain can also result from the same process. Although pain relievers such as aspirin are the most common source of relief, tension headaches have also been shown to dissipate with the use of meditation, mental imagery, and biofeedback.
3. *Migraine headaches:* Unlike a tension headache, which is produced by nervous tension in the facial muscles, a migraine headache is a vascular headache. The word *migraine* literally means "half a skull," and usually when a migraine occurs, the sensation of pain occupies either the right or left side of the head but not both. Migraines are thought to be the result of a sympathetic response to the baroreceptors of the carotid artery, which undergo a rapid constriction (prodrome) followed by a rapid dilation. During the dilation phase, blood quickly moves in from the periphery to flood the cerebral vasculature. The change in vascular pressure combined with humoral secretions is considered the cause of the intense pain so often associated with migraines. Symptoms can include a flash of light followed by intense throbbing, dizziness, and nausea. It is interesting to note that migraines do not occur in the midst of a stressor, but rather hours later. Migraines are thought to be related to the inability to express anger and frustration. Although several medications are prescribed for migraines, current research indicates that biofeedback and mental imagery can be equally effective, with fewer side effects.
4. *Temporomandibular joint dysfunction:* Excessive contraction of the jaw muscles can lead to a phenomenon called temporomandibular joint

Target organs: Any organ or tissue receiving excess neural or hormonal stimulation that increases metabolic function or abnormal cell growth; results in eventual dysfunction of the organ.

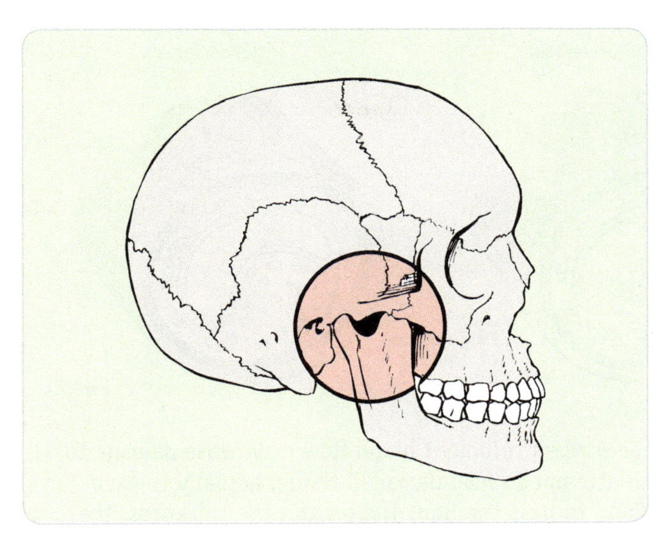

FIGURE 4.13 There are many forms of TMJD, including clicking of the jaw and grinding one's teeth during sleep. Experts suggest that 20 percent of the American population has some form of TMJD.

dysfunction, or TMJD (FIG. 4.13). In many cases, people are unaware that they have this illness because the behavioral damage occurs during sleep. But when they make a trip to the dentist, they find that they are showing signs of clenching and grinding their teeth (bruxism). Other symptoms include muscle pain and clicking or popping sounds when chewing, as well as tension headaches and earaches. Like migraines, TMJD is often associated with the inability to express feelings of anger. However, other behaviors are also associated with this symptom, including excessive gum chewing, resting one's chin on a hand, and even nail biting. Severe cases require that a mouth brace be worn at night. Relaxation techniques, including biofeedback and progressive muscular relaxation, have been shown to be effective in decreasing the muscular tension associated with TMJD.

5. *Irritable bowel syndrome:* IBS is characterized by repeated bouts of abdominal pain or tenderness, cramps, diarrhea, nausea, constipation, and excessive flatulence. It is often considered a result of excessive sympathetic neural stimulation to one or more areas of the gastrointestinal (GI) tract. Although symptoms may vary from person to person, this stress-related disorder is most commonly associated with anxiety and depression. One reason IBS is considered so closely related to stress is that the hypothalamus, which controls appetite regulation (hunger and satiety), is closely associated with emotional regulation as well. Various diets and medications may be prescribed, depending on the nature of the symptoms. Several recent studies have employed various types of relaxation and cognitive skills, including thermal biofeedback, progressive muscular relaxation, mental imagery, cognitive reappraisal, and behavior-modification techniques to reduce existing levels of anxiety. All had promising results.

6. *Coronary heart disease:* There are two major links between the stress response and the development of coronary heart disease, which the American Heart Association now estimates kills one person every 32 seconds. The first link is elevated blood pressure, or hypertension. In an effort to shunt blood from the body's core to the peripheral muscles in the event of physical movement during the fight-or-flight response, several stress-related hormones are released into the bloodstream. Sympathetic arousal releases epinephrine and norepinephrine from neural endings as well as from the adrenal medulla. These agents increase heart rate and myocardial contractility and cause the heart to pump a greater supply of oxygenated blood to the body's muscles for energy production. These catecholamines are also responsible for constricting blood vessels of the gastrointestinal tract while at the same time dilating vessels to the body's periphery, causing an overall change in total peripheral resistance. Aldosterone, secreted from the adrenal cortex, increases blood volume by increasing water retention. Vasopressin, or ADH, also acts to increase blood volume. The net effect of these stress hormones is to "jack up" blood pressure far above resting levels so as to transport blood to areas where it is needed. Ironically, stress provokes the same physiological response, even when there is no conscious attempt to physically move.

When pressure is increased in a closed system, the risk of damage to vascular tissue caused by increased turbulence is significantly increased. This damage to the vessel walls appears as small microtears, particularly in the intima lining of the coronary heart vessels, which supply the heart muscle (myocardium) itself with oxygen. As a way of healing these tears, several constituents floating in the blood bind with the damaged vascular cell

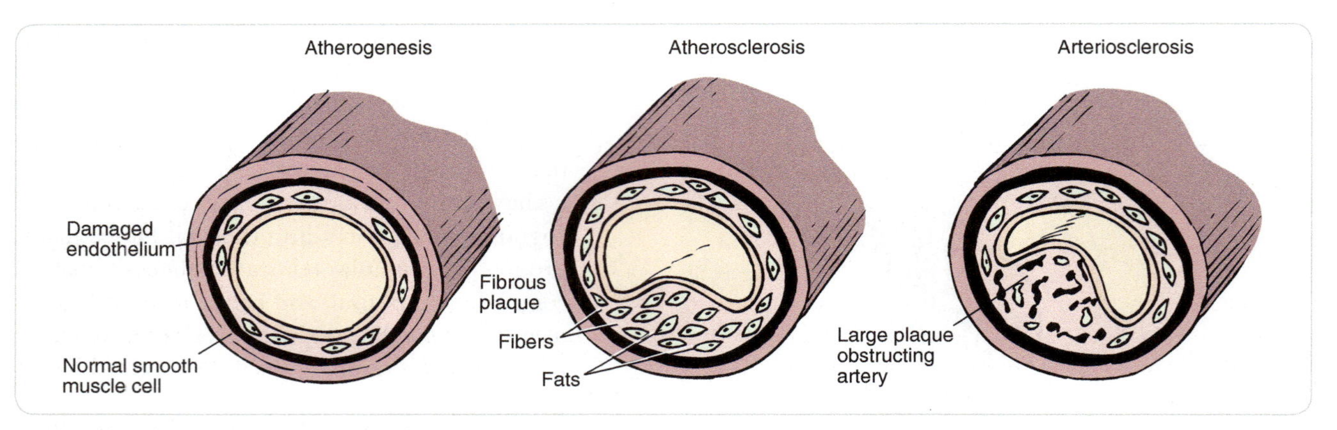

FIGURE 4.14 Coronary heart disease can start as early as age 5 when turbulent blood flow may cause damage to the inner lining of the artery wall. Cholesterol deposits, which attempt to heal damaged tissue, actually thicken the passage, thus decreasing the diameter of the vessel for blood to pass through. The greater the thickness, the greater the chance for an occlusion to that vessel—and an ensuing heart attack.

tissue. Paradoxically, the primary "healing" agent is a sticky substance found floating in the blood serum called cholesterol.

The second link between coronary heart disease and the stress response is the release of cortisol from the adrenal medulla. One of the many functions this stress hormone performs is to increase the level of free fatty acids carried by lipoproteins from the adipose (fat) tissue sites into the blood, to be used by the working muscles for energy production. An abundance of cholesterol in the blood makes it readily available for use in the attempt to repair damaged vascular cell tissue. However, what may seem like a protective mechanism actually becomes a major hindrance to the efficiency of the heart muscle, causing coronary heart disease.

The three stages of coronary heart disease are atherogenesis, atherosclerosis, and arteriosclerosis (FIG. 4.14). With **atherogenesis**, the initial stage, a fatty streak appears on the inner lining of the artery wall. Some evidence suggests that this can occur as early as age 5. As this fatty streak continues to circumnavigate the perimeter of the artery as well as travel its length, it creates a buildup of plaque, which narrows the inside of the artery. The stage at which the passage narrows because of thickening of plaque is referred to as **atherosclerosis**. As this fatty plaque accumulates, it attracts other constituents in the blood, including calcium, causing increased resistance to blood flow and increased blood pressure. With age, plaque hardens, making the artery walls like lead pipes that are no longer able to constrict or dilate. This compounds the effect of high blood pressure, which is one reason resting blood pressure increases with age. At the third stage, **arteriosclerosis**, the arteries themselves become hard, and possibly occluded from the flow of blood. If blood flow is impeded, the heart muscle may show signs of oxygen deprivation (ischemia), resulting in either angina (chest pain) or death of myocardial cell tissue. The end result is a heart attack, or myocardial infarction (MI). The degree of coronary artery blockage determines the severity of the heart attack, with the most extreme result being death. Similar etiology may occur with tears in the carotid arteries (located on either side of the vocal cords) that supply oxygenated blood to the brain. Strokes, like coronary heart disease, are

Atherogenesis: The first stage of coronary heart disease, wherein a fat streak appears on the inner lining of artery walls.

Atherosclerosis: The second stage of coronary heart disease, wherein artery walls slowly become occluded by cholesterol-plaque buildup.

Arteriosclerosis: The third and final stage of coronary heart disease, wherein the arteries become hardened by cholesterol buildup, calcium deposits, and loss of elasticity.

BOX 4.4 Stress and Inflammation

Researchers in the field of PNI have discovered that chronic stress is associated with the body's inability to regulate the inflammatory response. This inability, due, in part, to the impact cortisol has on the immune system, appears to be a strong factor in the stress and chronic disease equation. Researcher Sheldon Cohen at Carnegie Mellon University found that people with high levels of inflammation (chronic inflammation) were more susceptible to colds and flu (Cohen et al., 2012). Further research from the Oral Biology lab at The Ohio State University reveals that chronic stress, due to its impact on the sympathetic nervous system, appears to change the gene activity of immune cells before they enter the bloodstream (Huffington Post, 2013). Inflammation, now confirmed to be a result of stress, is associated with many chronic diseases and the acceleration of the aging process and is tied to both the nervous and the immune systems.

the result of blocked arteries creating an inadequate oxygenated blood supply, in this case to the brain.

The abyss between the emotions and physiology narrowed in 2005, when Western researchers discovered that emotional stress can, indeed, produce symptoms of a heart attack. Although the research team headed by Ilan Wittstein concluded that the mechanism underlying reversible left ventricular dysfunction precipitated by emotional stress remains unknown, it was suggested that stress hormones might temporarily overwhelm heart cells. Nicknamed the **broken heart syndrome**, the cause might best be described as "adrenaline poisoning."

Immune System–Related Disorders

As mentioned previously, emotional stress appears both to alter the molecular structure of biochemical agents or neuropeptides and to suppress the number and functions of various key leukocytes. Stress hormones (cortisol) may also decrease the effectiveness of leukocytes. With this process under way, protective mechanisms are less efficient and the body becomes more vulnerable to exogenous and endogenous antigens. As previously discussed, diseases that are the result of immune dysfunction can be classified as (1) **exogenous-underreactive**, (2) **exogenous-overreactive**, (3) **endogenous-overreactive**, and (4) **endogenous-underreactive**. The following are examples of some diseases in each of these categories:

1. *The common cold and influenza (exogenous underreaction):* In 1991, a study (Cohen, Tyrrell, and Smith) published by the prestigious *New England Journal of Medicine* supported the hypothesis that colds are unequivocally related to undue stress. The results made headlines across the country. From Borysenko's model of the immune system, we can see that as the number of B-lymphocytes decreases, the body becomes more vulnerable to the influences of the viruses that produce the common cold. Colds and influenza fall into the category of exogenous underreaction in Borysenko's immune activity matrix because there are insufficient B-lymphocytes to combat the exogenous antigen.
2. *Allergies (exogenous overreaction)* (FIG. 4.15): An allergic reaction is initiated when a foreign substance, or antigen (e.g., pollen, bee venom, dust spores), enters the body. In response to this intrusion, granulocytes secrete antibodies called histamines. When histamines encounter the antigens they form inactive complexes, in essence neutralizing their toxic effect. In an overreactive immune response to exogenous antigens, the excess of histamines causes swelling of mucous membrane tissue, in the case of inhaled antigens, or of skin tissue, in the

Broken heart syndrome: A name given to the condition where symptoms of a heart attack occur as a result of emotional stress; when stress hormones temporarily overwhelm heart tissue cells.

Exogenous-underreactive: An underreactive immune system affected by external pathogens (e.g., colds and flu).

Exogenous-overreactive: An overreactive immune system affected by external pathogens (e.g., allergies).

Endogenous-overreactive: An overreactive immune system affected by internal pathogens (e.g., rheumatoid arthritis and ulcers).

Endogenous-underreactive: An underreactive immune system affected by internal pathogens (e.g., cancer).

FIGURE 4.15 The list of allergy-producing substances is nearly endless. Pollen and dust are two of the most common ones.

case of infection. Some studies have shown that the introduction of foreign antigens isn't necessary to trigger an allergic reaction. Borysenko suggests that B-lymphocytes have the capacity of memory that may induce the production of histamines and other antibodies (immunoglobulins) without direct contact with an antigen. In some people, allergic reactions can occur just by thinking about the stimulus that provoked a previous attack. Several studies have also shown that allergic reactions are more prevalent and severe in subjects prone to anxiety (Lehrer et al., 1993). Over-the-counter medications containing antihistamines and allergy shots are the most common approaches to dealing with allergies. New data suggest that relaxation techniques also minimize the effects of external antigens (Wright, 2003).

3. *Rheumatoid arthritis and lupus (endogenous overreaction):* Tissue swelling may also occur from inflammation produced by an overreactive immune system responding to cells perceived to be (endogenous) antigens. In this case, constituents of the immune system begin to attack apparently healthy tissue, mistaking it for a foreign substance. Rheumatoid arthritis, a joint and connective tissue disease, occurs when synovial membrane tissue swells, causing the joint to become inflamed. Over time, synovial fluid may enter cartilage and bone tissue, causing further deterioration of a joint. Severe cases of rheumatoid arthritis are most evident in deformed finger joints. A substance identified as rheumatoid factor, a protein found in the blood, is thought to be associated with this disease. There is speculation that rheumatoid arthritis has a genetic link. It also has an association with stress, because it has been noted that the severity of arthritic pain is often related to episodes of stress, particularly suppressed anger. The treatment for this disease varies from pain relievers (e.g., aspirin) to steroid injections (e.g., cortisone), depending on the severity of pain and rate of joint deterioration. Relaxation techniques are now being recommended as a complementary treatment to help reduce symptoms. Similarly, lupus is an autoimmune disease in which the body's tissues are attacked by its own immune system, leading to chronic inflammation anywhere in the body. Primarily, inflammation affects the skin, heart, lungs, kidneys, and joints.

4. *Ulcers and colitis (endogenous overreaction):* Ulcers are often described as a hole in the stomach, and this depiction is not far from the truth. The series of events that lead to the destruction of this organ tissue begins with an excessive sympathetic neural drive. Increased secretions of norepinephrine are thought to cause a constriction of the vasculature in the lining of the stomach. This in turn is believed to decrease mucous secretions produced by the inner lining of the stomach wall. The purpose of mucus is to protect against the strong digestive enzymes that break down foodstuffs in the stomach. If the balance of mucosal fluid and digestive enzymes (hydrochloric acid) is thrown off, the inner lining becomes susceptible to these enzymes. The stomach may actually begin to digest itself, producing a hole in the stomach wall. Ulcers were one of the first diseases associated with undue stress; Selye noted this in his earliest studies with rats. Similarly, physicians immediately noticed an association between anxiety and the symptoms of ulcers in their patients, most notably sharp pains in the stomach.

The colon, situated below the stomach along the gastrointestinal tract, is also prone to ulceration, with a similar etiology producing colitis, or inflammation of the inner lining of the colon. Stress in the form of anxiety is thought to be strongly associated with colitis as well. Relaxation techniques are usually recommended, in conjunction with a special diet, to minimize the symptoms of this disease. Some techniques, including mental imagery, have even helped to heal ulcerations in the stomach wall.

For years, if not decades, it was thought that stress was the primary reason for ulcers. But in 1981, Barry Marshall, M.D., of Perth, Australia, proved that more than 75 percent of ulcers are caused by a bacterium known as *Helicobacter*, a carcinogen (Ubell, 1995). Clinical studies showed that these bacteria can settle in the lining of the stomach, creating an open wound that stomach acids then worsen, resulting in moderate to severe ulceration. Previously, it was thought that microbes such as *Helicobacter* could not survive in an acid-rich environment, but Marshall discovered this not to be the case. Treatment with antibiotics is now shown to be highly effective for a large percentage of people who have ulcers, yet two questions remain: What makes some people more vulnerable to the *Helicobacter* bacterium than others? and Why are antibiotics effective in only 75 percent of the cases of people with ulcers?

5. *Cancer (endogenous underreaction)*: Cancer has proved to be one of the most perplexing diseases of our time, affecting one out of every four Americans according to the American Cancer Society (ACS). To date, there is still no cure short of prevention and early detection. The ACS defines cancer as "a large group of diseases all characterized by uncontrolled growth and spread of abnormal cells." In other words, there are many types of cancers and the specific etiologies are still not completely understood. There are also many theories that attempt to explain the development of cancer. The two most prominent theories include the following: the first, falling back on the germ theory, suggests that all cancers are the result of an invading microbe or pathogen. The second theory suggests that there is a gene (called an **oncogene**) somewhere in the DNA structure that produces an abnormal or mutant cell (McClean, 1997). There is even a medical journal dedicated to this vein of research called *Oncogene*. Whether this gene can be inherited or is somehow externally triggered is yet to be determined; there are arguments both ways. The production of an abnormal cell in the body by itself is not uncommon. Some research suggests that the body produces about six mutant cells per day. In a precisely regulated immune system, T-cells and NK cells keep such endogenous antigens in check.

When a cell does mutate (that is, its genetic structure deviates from that of normal cells), it is regarded as an endogenous antigen and becomes subject to destruction by the cytotoxic T-lymphocytes, or T-cells. T-lymphocytes have a commando mission to search for and destroy malignant cells. If for some reason their ability is suppressed, the likelihood of a cancerous tumor is increased. Although the life span of a mutated cell is markedly shorter than that of normal cells (this process is called *relative inviability*), if undetected, it proliferates much more quickly than a normal cell, producing a tumor. Because of their structural inability to manufacture various enzymes necessary to perform normal cellular functions, cancerous tumors rob healthy cells of their nutrients. Unlike normal organ tissue, cancer cells are not self-contained and thus are able to detach from their original site and move to other areas throughout the body. This spread of cancerous tumors is referred to as metastasis, and at this advanced stage prognosis for recovery is not good.

Explanations for the manifestation of oncogenes are still speculative. Research has shown that external factors called carcinogens (e.g., ultraviolet rays, benzopyrene in cigarettes, asbestos) produce tumorous growths in both laboratory rats and humans. Medical researchers are still looking for endogenous factors that may also play a role in this disease process. At the same time, attention has been given to personality characteristics, and some traits have been found to be common among those who develop cancer. Although it is hard to put one-quarter of the American population into the same personality category, some studies show that the incidence of cancer appears higher among people who have a hard time expressing their emotions, have low self-esteem, and experience feelings of rejection (Brodie, 2008). By no coincidence, these same traits are said to characterize the codependent or addictive personality.

Oncogene: A gene in the DNA double-helix strand thought to be responsible for producing a mutant (cancerous) cell.

The treatments for cancer include drugs, radiation, and surgery. However, thanks to the work of O. Carl Simonton, Elisabeth Kübler-Ross, Bernie Siegel, Joan Borysenko, and Jeanne Achterberg, coping skills involving cognitive restructuring, art therapy, and relaxation techniques including mental imagery and meditation are being used as complementary healing methods. Although these methods are not a cure for cancer in themselves, in some cases they seem to have a pronounced effect when used in combination with traditional medicine.

Much attention is currently being given to the relationship between stress and disease in America. As lifestyles appear to become more stressful, the incidence of several illnesses that appear to be closely linked with stress is also increasing. Although stress may not seem like a direct cause of disease and illness, the association between them is too significant to be considered a mere coincidence. With the continued work of people like Borysenko, Pert, Gerber, Pelletier, and many others, some answers may be uncovered shortly.

SUMMARY

- There has been an intuitive association between stress and disease for centuries, but the link has come to be accepted scientifically only in the last decade or so. Scientists from several disciplines have come together to form a whole new field of study called psychoneuroimmunology.
- Recently, the immune system has been discovered to be greatly affected by prolonged bouts of stress.
- Pelletier states that there are still not enough data to substantiate a definitive stress-disease model that would help us to understand the relationship between the two. The focus of the stress-disease model appears to be divided between two areas: genetic predisposition, and energy medicine and subtle energy anatomy.
- Borysenko's model outlines both a dichotomy of autonomic dysregulation and immune dysregulation, and an immune activity matrix, which classifies diseases in one of four categories: (1) exogenous overreaction, (2) endogenous overreaction, (3) exogenous underreaction, and (4) endogenous underreaction.
- Pert's model cites research findings linking the nervous system with the immune system. Various cell tissues in the immune system can synthesize neuropeptides just as the brain can. Pert believes that all neuropeptides are really one molecule that undergoes a change at the atomic level brought about by various emotional states or energy thought forms.
- Lipton suggests that it is the cell membrane that is the brain of each cell. As a gatekeeper, it not only guards what goes in and out but does so by environmental programming, including the programming from our subconscious mind.
- Gerber's model states that the mind consists of energy (bioplasma) surrounding and permeating the body. Disease, then, is disturbance in the human energy field, which cascades through the levels of the subtle energy to the body via chakras and meridians.
- Pelletier's premodel states that a number of issues must be addressed and understood before a stress-disease model can be developed. These issues include disease states in people with dissociative identity disorders, spontaneous remissions, hypnosis, placebos, subtle energy, and immunoenhancement.
- Based on Borysenko's model, stress-related diseases were placed into one of two categories: those related to an overresponsive autonomic nervous system (e.g., migraines, ulcers, and coronary heart disease) and those associated with a dysfunctional immune system (e.g., colds and cancer).
- Research shows that several relaxation techniques are effective as complementary strategies in decreasing the symptoms of stress-related illness.

STUDY GUIDE QUESTIONS

1. Describe Borysenko's (immune system) stress and disease model.
2. What is the microbiome?
3. Describe Pert's (brain neurophysiology) stress and disease model.
4. Describe Lipton's (epigenetics) stress and new biology model.
5. Describe Gerber's (energy system) stress and disease model.
6. Describe Pelletier's stress and disease premodel.
7. List five diseases that occur when the nervous system is affected by stress.
8. List five diseases that occur when the immune system is affected by stress.
9. How does stress affect Lyme disease?
10. How does stress affect DNA strands?
11. How does stress affect inflammation?

REFERENCES AND RESOURCES

Achterberg, J. Imagery and Medicine: Psychophysiological Speculations, *Journal of Mental Imagery* 8(4):1–14, 1984.

Achterberg, J., et al. Evidence for Correlations Between Distant Intentionality and Brain Functions of Recipients, *Journal of Alternative and Complementary Medicine* 11(6):956–971, 2005.

Ader, R. Developmental Psychoneuroimmunology, *Developmental Psychobiology* 10:251–267, 1983.

Agarwal, A., Deepinder, F., et al. Effect of Cell Phone Usage on Semen Analysis in Men Attending Infertility Clinic: An Observational Study, *Fertility and Sterility* 89(1):124–128, 2008.

American Cancer Society. *Homepage*. www.cancer.org/docroot/home/index.asp.

American Diabetes Association. How Stress Affects Diabetes. December 6, 2013. http://www.diabetes.org/living-with-diabetes/complications/mental-health/stress.html.

American Diabetes Association. Living with Diabetes: Stress. www.diabetes.org/living-with-diabetes/complications/stress.html.

American Heart Association. *1991 Heart and Stroke Facts*, National Center, Dallas, TX, 1991.

American Heart Association. *Homepage*. www.Heart.org

American Psychological Association. Stress Affects Immunity in Ways Related to Stress Type and Duration, as Shown by Nearly 300 Studies. July 4, 2004. http://www.apa.org/news/press/releases/2004/07/stress-immune.aspx.

American Psychological Association. Stress Affects Immunity in Ways Related to Stress Type and Duration, as Shown by Nearly 300 Studies, *APA Online*, July 4, 2004. www.apa.org/releases/stress_immune.html.

Arntz, W., Chasse, B., and Vincente, M. *What the Bleep Do We Know!?* Health Communications, Inc. Deerfield Beach, FL, 2007.

Austin, J. A., et al. Complementary and Alternative Medicine Use Among Elderly Persons: One Year Analysis of a Blue Shield Medicare Supplement, *Journal of Gerontology* 55(1):M4–9, 2000.

Barrows, K., and Jacobs, B. Mind-Body Medicine, *Complementary and Alternative Medicine* 86(1):11–31, 2002.

Bartrop, R. W., et al. Depressed Lymphocyte Function after Bereavement, *Lancet* 1:834–836, 1977.

Becker, W. *Cross Currents*. Tarcher Press, Los Angeles, 1990.

BioInitiative 2012. A Rationale for Biologically Based Exposure Standards for Low-Intensity Electromagnetic Radiation. *Cell Phone Radiation Study Confirms Cancer Risk*. May 31, 2016. http://www.bioinitiative.org/cell-phone-radiation-study-confirms-cancer-risk/.

BioInitiative Report: A Rationale for a Biologically Based Public Exposure Standard for Electromagnetic Fields (ELF and RF). *Serious Public Health Concerns Raised Over Exposure to Electromagnetic Fields (EMF) from Powerlines and Cell Phones.* www.bioinitiative.org/press_release/index.htm.

Biondi, M. Effects of Stress on Immune Functions: An Overview. In R. Ader, D. L. Felten, and N. Cohen (eds.), *Psychoneuroimmunology*, 3rd ed., Academic Press Inc., San Diego, CA, 2001.

Blalock, J. E., Harbour-McMenamin, D., and Smith, E. Peptide Hormones Shared by the Neuroendocrine and Immunologic Systems, *Journal of Immunology* 135(2): 858s–861s, 1985.

Blanchard, E. B., et al. Biofeedback and Relaxation Treatments for Headaches in the Elderly: A Caution and a Challenge, *Biofeedback and Self-Regulation* 10(1):69–73, 1985.

Borysenko, M. Personal communication, December 10, 1991a.

Borysenko, M. Psychoneuroimmunology, *Annals of Behavioral Medicine* 9:3–10, 1987.

Borysenko, M. *Stress and the Immune System*, paper presented at the Sheraton Hotel, Washington, DC, October 25–26, 1991b.

Bovbjerg, D., Ader, R., and Cohen, N. Acquisition and Extinction of Conditioned Suppression of Graft-vs.-Host Responses in the Rat, *Journal of Immunology*, 132:111–113, 1984.

Braun, B. Psychophysiological Phenomena in Multiple Personality and Hypnosis, *American Journal of Clinical Hypnosis* 26(2):124–137, 1983.

Brennen, B. A. *Hands of Light: A Guide to Healing Through the Human Energy Field*. Bantam, New York, 1987.

Brodie, W. D. *The Cancer Personality*. Puna Wai Ora Mind–Body Center. 2008. www.alternative-cancer-care.com/The_Cancer_Personality.html.

Brody, H. (with Daralyn Brody). *The Placebo Response*. Cliff Street Books, New York, 2000.

Brotman, D., Golden, S., and Wittstein, I. The Cardiovascular Toll of Stress, *Lancet* 370:1089–1100, 2007.

Buhner, S. H. *Healing Lyme*. Raven Press, Silver City, NM, 2015.

Calcagni E., and Elenkov, I. Stress System Activity, Innate and T Helper Cytokines, and Susceptibility to Immune-Related Disease, *Annals of the New York Academy of Sciences* 1069:62–76, 2006.

Cawthon, R. M., Kin, J., Dhahhar, F. S., Adler, N. E., and Morrow, J. D. U.S. Study Suggests Link Between Psychological Stress, Aging, *U.S. Department of State*, November 30, 2004.

Clark, W. *The Experimental Foundations of Modern Immunology*, 4th ed. Wiley, New York, 1991.

Cohen, S., et al. Chronic Stress, Glucocorticoid Receptor Resistance, Inflammation, and Disease Risk. *Proceedings of the National Academy of Science USA*, 109(16):5995–5999, April 2, 2012.

Cohen, S., and Herbert, T. B. Health Psychology: Psychological Factors and Physical Disease from the Perspective of Human Psychoneuroimmunology, *Annual Review of Psychology* 47:113–142, 1996.

Cohen, S., Tyrrell, D., and Smith, A. P. Psychological Stress and Susceptibility to the Common Cold, *New England Journal of Medicine*, 325:606–612, 1991.

Cohen, S., and Williamson, G. M. Stress and Infectious Disease in Humans, *Psychological Bulletin* 109:5–24, 1991.

Collinge, W. *Subtle Energy: Awakening to the Unseen Forces in Our Lives*. Warner Books, New York, 1998.

Dacher, E. A Challenge to Healers: An Integrated Healing Model, Fifth Annual ISSSEEM Conference, Boulder, CO, June 26, 1995.

Dacher, E. *PNI: The New Mind-Body Healing Program.* Marlowe & Company, New York, 1992.

Davis, D. *Disconnect: The Truth About Cell Phone Radiation* Dutton. New York, 2010.

DeSalle, R., and Perkins, S. *Welcome to the Microbiome*. Yale University Press, New Haven, CT, 2015.

de Vernejoul, P., et al. Etude des Meridiens, D'Accupuncture par les Traceurs Radioactifs, *Bulletin de l'Acádemie Nationale de Médecine* 169(Oct):1071–1075, 1985.

Dietert, R. *The Human Superorganism*. Dutton, New York, 2016.

Dossey, L. *Reinventing Medicine*. Harper-San Francisco, San Francisco, 1999.

Dowdell, K., and Whitacre, C. Regulation of Inflammatory Autoimmune Diseases. In D. S. McEwen (ed.), *Coping with Environment: Neural and Endocrine Mechanism*, Oxford University Press, New York, 2000.

Eden, D. *Energy Medicine*. Tarcher/Putnam Books, New York, 2008.

Emoto, M. *The Message from Water*. Hado Books, Japan, 2004.

Eskola, S., Ylipaavalniemi, P., and Turtola, L. TMJ-Dysfunction Symptoms Among Finnish University Students, *Journal of American College Health* 33(4):172–174, 1985.

Esterling, B. A., Kiecolt-Glaser, J. K., Bodnar, J. C., and Glaser, R. Chronic Stress, Social Support, and Persistent Alterations in the Natural Killer Cell Response to Cytokines in Older Adults, *Health Psychology* 13:291–299, 1994.

Feinstein, D. Subtle Energy: Psychology's Missing Link, *Noetic Science Review* 64:18–23, 35, 2003.

Ferguson, M. Electronic Evidence of Aura, *Chakras* in UCLA Study, *Brain/Mind Bulletin* 3(9), 1978.

Gerber, R. Personal communication, November 25, 1991.

Gerber, R. *Vibrational Medicine*, 3rd ed. Inner Traditions, Rochester, VT, 2001.

Gerber, R. *Vibrational Medicine for the 21st Century*. Eagle Brook, New York, 2000.

Glasser, R., and Kiecolt-Glaser, J. (eds.), *Handbook of Human Stress and Immunity*. Academic Press, San Diego, CA, 1994.

Glasser, R., and Kiecolt-Glaser, J. Stress-Associated Immune Modulation, *American Journal of Medicine* 105(3A): 35s–42s, 1998.

Gordon, J. *Manifesto for a New Medicine*. Addison-Wesley, Reading, MA, 1996.

Grad, B. Healing by the Laying on of Hands: A Review of Experiments. In D. Sobel (ed.), *Ways of Health: Holistic Approaches to Ancient and Contemporary Medicine*. Harcourt Brace Jovanovich, New York, 1979.

Green, E. Presidential Address, Second International ISSSEEM Annual Conference, Boulder, CO, June 26–28, 1992.

Greenberg, J. *Comprehensive Stress Management*, 13th ed. McGraw-Hill, New York, 2012.

Harman, W., and Clarke, J. *New Metaphysical Foundations of Modern Science*. Institute of Noetic Sciences, Sausalito, CA, 1994.

Hatfield, H. Stress and Asthma, *WebMD*, March 1, 2007. www.webmd.com/asthma/features/asthma-and-anxiety.

Health News. *First Case of HIV Cure Reported*, Daily News Central, November 13, 2005.

Henri-Benitez, M., et al. Autogenic Psychotherapy for Bronchial Asthma, *Psychology Psychosomatica* 11(6):11–16, 1990.

Herberman, R. Stress, Natural Killer Cells and Cancer. In H. Koenig and H. Cohen (eds.), *The Link Between Religion and Health. Psychoneuroimmunology and the Faith Factor*. Oxford Press, New York, 2002.

Hirshberg, C., and Barasch, M. *Remarkable Recovery*. Riverhead Books, New York, 1995.

Horrigan, B., and Ornish, D. Healing the Heart, Reversing the Disease, *Alternative Therapies* 1(5):84–92, 1995.

Horrigan, B., and Pert, C. Neuropeptides, AIDS, and the Science of Mind-Body Healing, *Alternative Therapies* 1(3):70–76, 1995.

Howenstine, J. New Ideas about the Cause, Spread and Therapy of Lyme Disease. Townsend Letter for Doctors and Patients, July 2004. http://www.samento.com.ec/sciencelib/4lyme/Townsendhowens.html.

Huffington Post. Chronic Stress Changes Immune Cell Genes, Leading to Inflammation Study. November 7, 2013. http://www.huffingtonpost.com/2013/11/07/chronic-stress-health-inflammation-genes_n_4226420.html.

Hunt, V. *Infinite Mind: Science of the Human Vibrations of Consciousness*. Malibu Publishing, Malibu, CA, 1996.

Hunt, V., et al. A Study of Structural Integration from Neuromuscular, Energy Field, and Emotional Approaches, paper presented at the University of California at Los Angeles, 1977.

Iliades, C. How Stress Affects Type 2 Diabetes. Everyday Health. www.everydayhealth.com/health-report/type-2-diabetes-lifestyle/stress-management-helps-type-2-diabetes.aspx.

Jermott, J. B. Psychoneuroimmunology: The New Frontier, *American Behavioral Scientist* 28(4):497–509, 1985.

Jermott, J. B., et al. Academic Stress: Power Motivation and Decrease in Saliva Immunoglobulin-A Secretion Rate, *Lancet* 1:1400–1402, 1983.

Johnston, V. *Why We Feel: Science of Human Emotions*. Perseus Books, New York, 1999.

Justice, B. *A Different Kind of Health: Finding Well-being Despite Illness*. Peak Press, Houston, TX, 1998.

Kemeny, M. E., and Gruenewald, T. L. Psychoneuroimmunology Update. *Seminars in Gastrointestinal Disease* 10:20–29, 1999.

Kent, J., et al. Unexpected Recoveries: Spontaneous Remission and Immune Functioning, *Advances* 6(2):66–73, 1989.

Kerns Geer, K. Is Stress the Source of Your Blood Sugar Swing? August 8, 2015. http://www.everydayhealth.com/hs/type-2-diabetes-management/stress-blood-sugar-swing/.

Ketcham, C. Warning: Your Cell Phone May Be Dangerous to Your Health. *Gentleman's Quarterly*, February 2010.

Kiecolt-Glaser, J. K. Slowing of Wound Healing by Psychological Stress, *Lancet* 346(8984):1194–1196, 1996.

Kiecolt-Glaser, J. K. Stress, Personal Relationships and Immune Function: Health Implications, *Brain, Behavior, and Immunity*. 13:61–72, 1999.

Kiecolt-Glaser, J., et al. Chronic Stress and Age-Related Increases in the Proinflammatory Cytokine IL-6. www.pnas.org/cgi/doi/10.1073/pnas.1531903100.

Kiecolt-Glaser, J., et al. Marital Stress: Immunological, Neuroendocrine, and Autonomic Correlates. *Annals of the New York Academy of Sciences* 840:656–663, 1998.

Kiecolt-Glaser, J., et al. Psychosocial Modifiers of Immunocompetence in Medical Students, *Psychosomatic Medicine* 46(1):7–14, 1984.

Kiecolt-Glaser, J., and Glaser, R. Chronic Stress and Mortality among Older Adults. *Journal of American Medical Association* 282(23), 2215–2219, 1999.

Kiecolt-Glaser, J. K., McGuire, L., Robles, T. F., and Glaser, R. Psychoneuroimmunology: Psychological Influences on Immune Function and Health. *Journal of Consulting and Clinical Psychology* 70:537–547, 2002.

Kiecolt-Glaser J. K., Preacher, K. J., MacCallum, R. C., Atkinson, C., Malarkey, W. B., and Glaser, R. Chronic Stress and Age-Related Increases in the Proinflammatory Cytokine IL-6. *Proceedings of the National Academy of Sciences* (US), 22; 100(15):9090–9095, 2003.

Kirlian, S., and Kirlian, V. Photography and Visual Observations by Means of High-Frequency Currents, *Journal of Scientific and Applied Photography* 6:145–148, 1961.

Kirschvink, J., et al. Magnetite in Human Tissues: A Mechanism for the Biological Effects of Weak ELF Magnetic Fields, *Bioelectronics Supplement* 1:101–114, 1992.

Koenig, H., and Cohen, H. (eds.). *The Link Between Religion and Health: Psychoneuroimmunology and the Faith Factor.* Oxford Press, New York, 2002.

Kopp, M. S., and Rethelyi, J. Where Psychology Meets Physiology: Chronic Stress and Premature Mortality—The Central-Eastern Health Paradox, *Brain Research Bulletin* 62:351–367, 2004.

Krieger, D. Healing by the Laying on of Hands as a Facilitator of Bioenergetic Change: The Response of In-Vivo Hemoglobin, *International Journal of Psychoenergetic Systems* 1:121, 1976.

Krieger, D. The Response of In-Vivo Human Hemoglobin to an Active Healing Therapy by Direct Laying on of Hands, *Human Dimensions* 1 (Autumn):12–15, 1972.

Krieger, D. Therapeutic Touch: The Imprimatur of Nursing, *American Journal of Nursing* 75:784–787, 1975.

Laskow, L. *Healing with Love*. HarperCollins, San Francisco, CA, 2008.

Laudenslanger, M. L., et al. Coping and Immunosuppression: Inescapable Shock Suppresses Lymphocyte Proliferation, *Science* 221:568–570, 1983.

Learner, M. *Choices in Healing*. MIT Press, Cambridge, MA, 1996.

Lehrer, P. M., Isenberg, S., and Hochron, S. M. Asthma and Emotion: A Review, *Journal of Asthma* 30:5–21, 1993.

Levenson, J. L., and Bemis, C. The Role of Psychological Factors in Cancer Onset and Progression, *Psychosomatics* 32(2):124–132, 1991.

Libov, C. Kris Kristofferson Has Lyme Disease, Not Alzheimer's. Newsmax Health, June 9, 2016. http://www.newsmax.com/Health/Headline/Kris-Kristofferson-Lyme-Disease/2016/06/09/id/733155/.

Lipton, B. *The Biology of Belief.* Sounds True CD set, 2006.

Lipton, B. *The Biology of Belief: Unleashing the Power of Consciousness, Matter, and Miracles*. Hay House, 2016.

Lipton, B. *The New Biology: Where Mind and Matter Meet*. DVD, Jean Meyers Productions, 2001.

Lipton, B. Epigenetics; The New Science of Human Empowerment. The Institute of Noetic Sciences 15th Conference. Indian Wells, CA, July 20, 2013

Lipton, B. *The Honeymoon Effect*. Hayhouse Books. Carlsbad, CA, 2013.

Lipton, B. Personal conversation, September 17, 2007.

McClean, P. *How Oncogenes Cause Cancer*. 1997. www.ndsu.edu/instruct/mcclean/plsc431/cellcycle/cellcycl5.htm.

McClelland, D. C., and Kirshnit, C. The Effect of Motivation Arousal Through Films on Salivary Immunoglobulin A, *Psychology and Health* 2:31–52, 1989.

McEwen, B. *The End of Stress as We Know It*. Joseph Henry Press, Washington, DC, 2002.

McTaggart, L. *The Field: The Quest for the Secret Force of the Universe*, 2nd ed. HarperCollins, New York, 2008.

Miller, G. E., Cohen, S., and Ritchey, K. Chronic Psychological Stress and the Regulation of Pro Inflammatory Cytokines: A Glucocorticoid-Resistance Model, *Health Psychology* 21(6):531–541, 2002.

Miller, R. Bridging the Gap: An Interview with Valerie Hunt, *Science of Mind*, October 12, 1983.

Mitchell, M. C., and Drossman, D. A. Irritable Bowel Syndrome: Understanding and Treating a Biopsychosocial Disorder, *Annals of Behavioral Medicine* 9(3):13–18, 1987.

Moran, M. Psychological Factors Affecting Pulmonary and Rheumatological Diseases: A Review, *Psychosomatics* 32(1):14–23, 1991.

Moriyama, Y., Kishimoto, A., and Mastushita, T. The Relationship Between Stress and the Onset of Gastrointestinal Diseases: Questionnaire Survey of Patients with Gastric Cancer and Gastric Ulcers, *Kyushu Neuropsychiatry* 34(3–4):282–288, 1988.

Motoyama, H., and Brown, R. *Science and the Evolution of Consciousness*. Autumn Press, Brookline, MA, 1978.

Motz, J. *Hands of Life*. 2nd ed. Bantam Books, New York, 2000.

Myss, C. *Anatomy of the Spirit*. Harmony Books, New York, 1996.

Nature Communications. Oncogene. www.nature.com/onc/index.html.

Nordqvist, C. Cell Phone Usage Linked to Lower Sperm Count, *Medical News Today*, October 23, 2006. www.medicalnewstoday.com/articles/54866.php.

Northrup, C. *Women's Bodies, Women's Wisdom*. Bantam Books, New York, 2010.

O'Leary, A. Stress, Emotion, and Human Immune Function, *Psychological Bulletin* 108(3):363–382, 1990.

Ornish, D. *Dr. Dean Ornish's Program for Reversing Heart Disease*. Random House, New York, 1990.

Pare, W. P. Stress Ulcer Susceptibility and Depression in Wistar Kyoto (WKY) Rats, *Physiology and Behavior* 46(6):993–998, 1989.

Pearsall, P. *The Heart's Code*. Broadway Books, New York, 1998.

Pelletier, K. *The Best Alternative Medicine: What Works? What Does Not?* Simon & Schuster, New York, 2000a.

Pelletier, K. Between Mind and Body, Stress, Emotions and Health. In D. Goleman (ed.), *Mind Body Medicine*, Consumer Reports Books, Yonkers, NY, 1993.

Pelletier, K. Life with a New Roommate: Alternative Medicine Moves in with Conventional Medicine. *Healthcare Forum Journal*, November/December: 35–37, 41, 1998.

Pelletier, K. *Mind as Healer, Mind as Slayer*. Dell, New York, 1977.

Pelletier, K. Personal communication, September 20, 2000b.

Pelletier, K. *Toward a Science of Consciousness*. Celestial Arts, Berkeley, CA, 1985.

Pelletier, K., and Herzing, D. Psychoneuroimmunology: Toward a Mind-Body Model, *Advances* 5(1):27–56, 1988.

Pert, C. B. *Everything You Need to Know to Feel Go(o)d*. Hay House Books, Carlsbad, CA, 2007.

Pert, C. B. *Molecules of Emotion: Why You Feel the Way You Feel*. Scribner, New York, 1997.

Pert, C. B. Neuropeptides: The Emotions and Bodymind, *Noetic Sciences Review* 2:13–18, 1987.

Pert, C. B. Personal communication, December 18, 1991.

Pert, C. B. Personal communication (phone), July 30, 2003.

Pert, C. B. Personal communication (phone), August 18, 2004.

Pert, C. B. The Wisdom of the Receptors: Neuropeptides, The Emotions, and Bodymind, *Advances* 3(3):8–16, 1986.

Pert, C. B., et al. Neuropeptides and Their Receptors: A Psychosomatic Network, *Journal of Immunology* 135 (2 suppl.):820s–826s, 1985.

Pert, C. B., Dreher, H., and Ruff, M. The Psychosomatic Network: Foundations of Mind-Body Medicine, *Alternative Therapies in Health and Medicine* 4(4):30–40, 1998.

Pfaffenrath, V., Wermuth, A., and Pollmann, W. Tension Headache: A Review, *Fortschritte der Neurologie Psychiatrie* 56(12):407–422, 1988.

Pouwer, F., Kupper, N., and Adriaanse, M. Does Emotional Stress Cause Type II Diabetes Mellitus? *Discovery Magazine*. February 11, 2010. www.discoverymedicine.com/Frans-Pouwer/2010/02/11/does-emotional-stress-cause-type-2-diabetes-mellitus-a-review-from-the-european-depression-in-diabetes-edid-research-consortium/.

Powell, D., and the Institute of Noetic Sciences. *The 2007 Shift Report: Evidence of a World Transforming*. Institute of Noetic Sciences, Petaluma, CA, 2007.

Prensky, W. L. Reston Helped Open a Door to Acupuncture, Letter to the Editor, *The New York Times*, December 9, 1995. http://query.nytimes.com/gst/fullpage.html?res=9E0DE5DE1739F937A25751C1A963958260.

Rabin, B. Understanding How Stress Affects the Physical Body. In H. Koenig and H. Cohen (eds.), *The Link Between Religion and Health. Psychoneuroimmunology and the Faith Factor,* Oxford Press, New York, 2002.

Rabin, B., et al. Bidirectional Interaction Between the Central Nervous System and the Immune System, *Critical Reviews in Immunology* 9:279–312, 1989.

Radin, D. *The Conscious Universe*. HarperSanFrancisco, NewYork, 2009.

Rayhorn, N. Understanding Inflammatory Bowel Disease, *Nursing* 29:57–68, 1999.

Rein, G. As reported in *Vibrational Medicine for the 21st Century* by Richard Gerber. Eagle Brook, New York, 2000:375.

Rosch, P. Personal communication, American Institute of Stress, August 11, 2003.

Rose-Neil, S. The Work of Professor Kim Bong Han, *Acupuncturist* 1:15, 1967.

Roundtree, R., with Carol Coleman. *Immunotics*. Putnam Books, New York, 2000.

Rubik, B. Energy Medicine and the Unifying Concept of Information, *Alternative Therapies* 1(1):34–39, 1995.

Rubik, B. Personal communication, July 30, 2003.

Saibil, F. *Crohn's Disease and Ulcerative Colitis*. Firefly Books, New York, 3rd ed. 2011.

Sapolsky, R. *Why Zebras Don't Get Ulcers* (4th ed). Holt Paperback Books, New York, 2009.

Schleifer, S., et al. Suppression of Lymphocyte Stimulation Following Bereavement, *JAMA* 250(3):374–377, 1983.

Schlitz, M., and Amorok, T. *Consciousness and Healing*. Elsevier Press, St. Louis, MO, 2005.

Schwartz, J. Cell Phones May Have Cancer Link, *Washington Post*, Saturday, May 22, 1999.

Seaward, B. L. Alternative Medicine Complements Standard, *Health Progress* 75(7):52–57, 1994.

Segerstrom, S. C., and Miller, G. E. Psychological Stress and the Human Immune System: A Meta-Analytical Study of 30 Years of Inquiry, *Psychological Bulletin* 130(4):601–630, 2004.

Shavit, Y., et al. Stress, Opioid Peptides, the Immune System and Cancer, *Journal of Immunology* 135:834–837, 1994.

Shealy, C. N., and Myss, C. *The Creation of Health*. Stillpoint Press, Walpole, NH, 1998.

Siegel, B. *Love, Medicine, and Miracles*. Perennial Library, New York, 1986.

Smith, E. M., Harbour-McMenamin, D., and Blalock, J. E. Lymphocyte Production of Endorphins and Endorphin-Mediated Immunoregulatory Activity, *Journal of Immunology* 135:779s–782s, 1985.

Smith, M., et. al., Outcomes of Touch Therapies During Bone Marrow Transplant, *Alternative Therapies* 9(1):40–49, 2003.

Spiegel, D. Healing Words: Emotional Expression and Disease Outcome, *JAMA* 281(14):1328, 1999.

Sternberg E. *The Balance Within: The Science Connecting Health & Emotions*. W. H. Freeman, New York, 2000.

Straley, C. Is Stress Hurting Your Skin? *Parents Magazine*, November: 1999:193.

Stringfellow, B. Visiting Physician Sheds New Light on Lyme Disease. *Martha's Vineyard Times*, July 13, 2016.

Talbot, M. *The Holographic Universe*. HarperCollins, New York, Reprinted 2011.

Tasner, M. *TMJ*, *Medical Self-Care*, November/December: 47–50, 1986.

Tecoma, E., and Huey, L. Psychic Distress and the Immune Response, *Life Sciences* 36(19):1799–1812, 1985.

Temoshok, L. Personality, Coping Style, Emotion, and Cancer: Towards an Integrative Model, *Cancer Surveys* 6:545–567, 1987.

Trieschmann, R. Spirituality and Energy Medicine, *Journal of Rehabilitation* 67(1):26–38, 2001.

Tucker, L., Cole, G., and Freidman, G. Stress and Serum Cholesterol: A Study of 7000 Adult Males, *Health Values* 11:34–39, 1987.

Ubell, E. Soon, We Won't Have to Worry About Ulcers, *Parade Magazine*, April 2: 18–19, 1995.

University of Maryland Medical Center. *Acupuncture*. www.umm.edu/altmed/articles/acupuncture-000345.htm.

Vida, C., Gonzalez, E. M., and De la Fuenta, M. Increase of Oxidation and Inflammation in Nervous and Immune Systems with Aging and Anxiety. *Current Pharmaceutical Design*, 20(29):4656–4678, 2014.

Vincent, T., and Elder, A. Low Dose Immunotherapy (LDI) and Lyme Disease. Personal communication. June 10, 2016.

Webster Marketon, J. I., and Glaser, R. Stress hormones and immune function. *Cell Immunology*. Mar–Apr;252(1–2):16–26, 2008.

Wilson, *A. Under Our Skin: The Untold Story of Lyme Disease*. Documentary Film, July 19, 2009. http://underourskin.com/film/.

Wittstein, L. Neurohumoral Features of Myocardial Stunning Due to Sudden Emotional Stress, *New England Journal of Medicine* 352(6):539–548, 2005.

Wright, R. J. Alternative Modalities for Asthma that Reduce Stress and Modify Mood States: Evidence for Underlying Psychobiological Mechanisms, *Annals of Allergy, Asthma, and Immunology* 92:1–6, 2003.

Wright, R. J., and Cohen, S. Stress and Allergy. May 19, 2005. http://www.thedoctorwillseeyounow.com/content/stress/art2431.html.

Wright, R. J., and Cohen, S. News: Stress and Allergy. www.thedoctorwillseeyounow.com/news/behavior/0505/allergies.shtml.

Young, E. I *Contain Multitudes: The Microbes Within Us and a Grander View of Life*. Ecco/Harper Collins Books, New York, 2016.

PART TWO

The Mind and Soul

To thine own self be true.

—William Shakespeare

CHAPTER 5

Toward a Psychology of Stress

Modern man is sick because he is not whole.

—Carl Gustav Jung

For centuries, scientists have debated the relationship between the mind and the brain. Is the mind a function of the brain, a series of biochemical reactions, or is the mind a complex dynamic of consciousness, a separate entity unto itself that uses the brain as its primary organ of choice? This question has polarized researchers to believe either that all thoughts and feelings can be explained as neurochemical messages transmitted from brain cell to brain cell or that the mind exists separately from the brain yet somehow is housed and fused with it. This one question, perhaps more than any other, initiated the discipline of psychology at the turn of the twentieth century. As the mind-body connection is more closely examined with regard to the stress response, it becomes increasingly clear that the mind is a very complex phenomenon, and not merely a by-product of neurochemical interactions. The interactions of thoughts, emotions, behaviors, and personality traits—the mind is held accountable for all of them and a bit more (Baruss, 2017). In this chapter, we will look at how the mind perceives stress so that the "antiquated" stress response can be updated or recircuited, highlighting some specific aspects of the psychology of stress.

Since the advent of the discipline of psychology, many notable figures have made significant contributions to the understanding of the mind—specifically, those regarding personality, emotions, perceptions, and a whole realm of human behaviors. From these individuals have come a host of theories attempting to interpret the complexities of emotional well-being on which stress has so great an influence. These theories have been inspired by such questions as, Why does the mind perceive some events as threatening? and What cognitive dynamics are used to deal with psychological stress? The list of those people who have contributed to the body of knowledge of human consciousness would comprise a book itself, not the least of which includes Albert Ellis (Rational Emotive Behavior Therapy), Richard Lazarus (Daily Hassles), and countless others. Although no one theorist seems to explain the psychological aspects of stress in its totality, together the following theories at least begin to address several significant issues involved. The following psychiatrists, psychologists, and therapists offer a glimpse of some of the greatest insights into the mind's role in the psychology of stress.

Freud and the Egg

Because of his profound influence on the field of psychology (perhaps more than any other individual), the work of Sigmund Freud (FIG. 5.1) is chosen by many scholars as the reference point from which all other psychological theories emanate. Most recognized for his concepts of conscious and unconscious thought and their associations to sexual drive, Freud established the groundwork for understanding human behavior. Specifically, he made tangible the abstract concepts of emotional thought processes and the constructs of personality. From Freud's perspective, humans operate from an instinctual nature, or those biological and physiological impulses he referred to as the id. These impulses aim to satisfy the body's immediate needs. In Freud's opinion, there is a constant **instinctual tension** between body and mind as the mind attempts to cater to these impulses in socially acceptable ways. This internal tension can be decreased, but because of the power of human instincts, it is never fully extinguished. Consequently, Freud believed that humans have some degree of *innate* stress.

Freud developed a wonderful metaphor to illustrate the intangible complexities of the human psyche. He compared the mind's innermost thoughts, memories, and feelings, components that make up one's identity, to an egg (FIG. 5.2). Like the contents of an egg, the human psyche is extremely delicate and fragile. And like an egg it is enclosed and protected by a sturdy yet quite vulnerable shell. According to Freud, the primary purpose of the **ego** is to seek pleasure and to avoid pain with regard to our biological impulses (a function now thought to be similar to that of the hypothalamus). That is, the ego is primarily responsible for controlling the flood of impulses from the id. The ego is also vulnerable to perceptions of outside stimuli, which constantly threaten the stability of the contents within. This, too, he observed, produces tension.

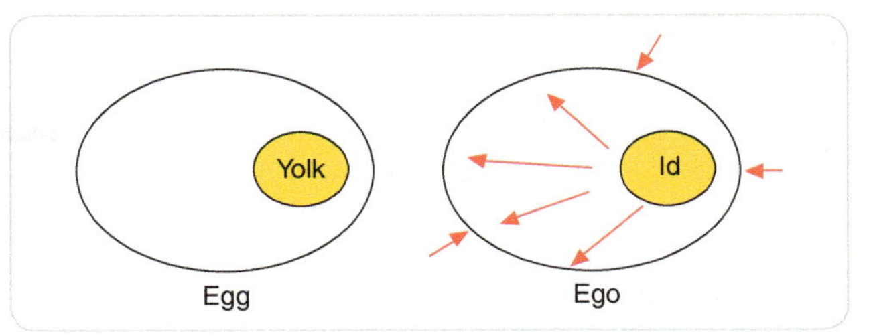

FIGURE 5.2 Freud compared the abstract human psyche to an egg. Instinctual tension is always present, Freud believed, because the id constantly releases impulses. These, along with external stimuli, threaten the integrity of the ego, which must protect itself with what Freud termed defense mechanisms.

The metaphor of the egg and Freud's theory of the function of the ego have been useful to comprehend the environmental balance of the mind, specifically in terms of cognitive stress-management strategies. Understanding that stress or anxiety is aroused simultaneously by internal impulses and perceived outside stimulation (threats) means that the protection of identity (ego) is critical to survival. As if a missile were headed for the

FIGURE 5.1 Sigmund Freud.

Instinctual tension: A Freudian term used to highlight the tension between the mind's impulses and the body's response, suggesting that stress is humanly inherent.

Ego: A term coined by Freud naming the part of the psyche that not only triggers the stress response when threatened, but also defends against all enemies, including thoughts and feelings generated from within.

White House, anxiety triggers the mind's alarm system, signifying imminent danger to the existence of the ego. Defense systems are immediately activated. Should these defenses fail to function properly, panic and disaster ensue. Through his work with mentally and physically ill patients, Freud observed enough stress-related behaviors to credit excessive anxiety (unknown fears that penetrate the ego's shell and produce pain) and inadequate defenses with the primary roles in the development of neurotic and psychotic behavior.

According to Freud, the mind's defense system consists of a host of thought processes, or **defense mechanisms,** to aid in the protection of the ego's fragile contents. They act to shield the contents from harm by minimizing the impact of perceived threats. From his perspective, defense mechanisms are a collection of coping strategies to deal with stress. Because of both constant inner tension produced by instinctual impulses and stressfully perceived external stimuli, Freud believed that defense mechanisms must always be in operation to some extent. Thus, he was convinced that all behavior is defensive in nature. Freud theorized that all defense mechanisms share two characteristics: (1) they are denials or distortions of reality, and (2) they operate unconsciously. Furthermore, an individual rarely uses just one defense mechanism. Rather, each person employs a variety of ego-protecting mechanisms overall, and usually several at the same time. Freud postulated a number of defense mechanisms, including denial, repression, projection, rationalization, reaction formation, regression, displacement, sublimation, and humor. The following are most commonly used in the defense of stress-produced anxiety:

Defense mechanisms: Described by Sigmund Freud; unconscious thinking patterns of the ego to either decrease pain or increase pleasure.

Denial: One of the primary defense mechanisms noted by Freud in which one disbelieves what occurred when personally threatened.

Repression: The involuntary removal of thoughts, memories, and feelings from the conscious mind so they are less threatening to the ego.

Projection: The act of attributing one's thoughts and feelings to other people so that they are less threatening to the ego.

Rationalization: The reinterpretation of the current reality to match one's liking: a reinterpretation of the truth.

1. ***Denial:*** When people are confronted with circumstances they find to be a threat, they often deny association or involvement with any aspect of the situation. Young children are often caught in the act of lying (denial) when they are accused of eating cookies right before dinner or making a mess in the bathroom. Examples in adulthood include denying a drinking or gambling problem. Any stimulus perceived to be a threat to the integrity of one's identity can push the button to deny involvement or knowledge. At a conscious level, the person truly believes he or she is innocent and sees nothing wrong with the behavior.
2. ***Repression:*** Repression is the involuntary removal of thoughts, memories, or feelings from the conscious mind. It differs from suppression, wherein painful experiences are intentionally forgotten, in that the conscious mind is unaware of this process. Freud referred to repression as an unconscious denial of something that brings emotional discomfort or pain. Examples are memories of unpleasant family holidays, child abuse, or embarrassing moments you cannot seem to recall even when friends and family tell you in fine detail what you did.
3. ***Projection:*** Projection is a process in which an individual defends the ego by attributing unacceptable feelings, impulses, and behaviors to other people—or objects such as dogs, tennis racquets, swim goggles, or the weather. In this way, when an impulse or emotion is manifested, it is now less threatening because its source appears to be generated externally rather than from within. Ownership of painful feelings is minimized. According to Freud, projection is most prevalent in response to feelings of sexual desire, insecurities, and aggression. An example of projection is oversleeping, getting a late start for work, getting caught in traffic, and then blaming every dumb driver for your lateness.
4. ***Rationalization:*** Rationalization is the reinterpretation of the reality of one's behavior or circumstances. It's a manipulation of the truth. Rationalization can be described as a filtered lens that makes emotional pain more acceptable, even appealing, to one's emotional vision. Actions or thoughts that are perceived to be threatening are quickly reinterpreted in terms of another, more acceptable, rational explanation. For example, someone who has been fired from a job he loved might rationalize this outcome by saying, "It was

an awful job and I'm glad to be done with it." Another example would be when your boyfriend breaks up with you and you tell friends you wanted to break it off because the relationship was too great a time commitment.

5. ***Displacement:*** When something that causes pain to the ego is inaccessible or otherwise cannot be responded to directly, the painful feelings can be transferred to an unrelated person or object. This is what Freud called displacement. Displacement involves transferring emotional pain and its related behavior from an unacceptable object (e.g., an authority figure) to a nonthreatening object (usually children and pets). For example, your boss is a jerk and you would love to choke him, but instead you go home and shoo away the cat who begs for attention. Even though feelings of anger and aggression are most commonly cited as those that are displaced, it is also possible to displace feelings and behaviors associated with joy and love to those you perceive to be most receptive to them, rather than those you believe would not respond favorably.
6. ***Humor:*** Later in his career, Freud began to study the psychology of humor and jokes. Reviewing the works of several humorists, he was at first perplexed at the phenomenon but soon saw it as a device for the body to release sexually repressed thoughts through laughter. This is the rationale he proposed to explain the popularity of "dirty" jokes. Humor, remarked Freud, is a unique defense mechanism unlike the others. It simultaneously decreases pain and increases pleasure, making it the most advanced of all the defense mechanisms.

These are but six of the many defense mechanisms Freud believed are most commonly used in response to anger and fear. Each mechanism, used to protect our identity, is a camouflage of reality (FIG. 5.3). The ego perceives uncamouflaged threatening stimuli as attacks on the existence of our innermost feelings, perceptions, values, beliefs, and attitudes, so protection is often necessary, especially for children in the early stages of growth and development. However, overprotection of the ego can ultimately be as dangerous to the maturation process as lack of adequate protection. Overprotection usually results in the inhibition of emotional growth and maturation of the individual's mental and emotional boundaries, a situation analogous to a houseplant rootbound by too small a pot. When anxiety or a perceived threat enters the walls of the ego, emotional pain results. With a less defensive attitude, however, this pain can enable the individual to expand his or her self-awareness and personal growth. In this case, the result is an expansion of the ego. Each time this "space" grows, therein lies an opportunity to expand one's capabilities and enhance one's human potential. It may not seem that stress always involves the ego, but in truth, it really does. Our ego is *our identity*, and whether it is fear or anger that triggers the stress response, things that cause stress typically attack the integrity of our identity and perceptions of self-worth. Freud's coping mechanisms are the front-line defense. The degree to which defense mechanisms are innate or learned behavior has yet to be decided. Perhaps because Freud understood anxiety to be an inseparable part of the individual, he left no substantial advice on minimizing it, short of psychoanalysis. Despite varying opinions of his work, Freud's theories of personality have become so well acknowledged, if not respected, it is not uncommon to find strong parallels in the concepts of other theorists.

FIGURE 5.3

Displacement: The transference of emotional pain (usually anger) from a threatening source (one's boss) to a nonthreatening source (one's cat).

Humor: The defense mechanism noted by Freud that both decreases pain and increases pleasure.

Jung and the Iceberg

The theories of Freud inspired many physicians to investigate the new clinical field of the psyche and human behavior. One such physician was Carl Gustav Jung (FIG. 5.4) of Switzerland, who was hand-picked by Freud to be his "heir apparent" and champion his theories. During the close collaboration of the two, Jung began to voice disagreement with some of Freud's theoretical concepts. As a result, their professional (as well as personal) relationship quickly eroded. Although Jung and Freud parted company in their opinions of the mysteries of the mind, Jung has become respected as the second greatest influence on modern psychological thought. His theories involving introverts and extroverts, personality types (inspiring the Myers-Briggs Type Inventory), midlife crisis, synchronicity, anima-animus, archetypes, the shadow, and the spiritual nature of humankind sowed many seeds in the human potential movement, and his following continues to grow both within and outside the field of psychology.

FIGURE 5.4 Carl Gustav Jung.

Unlike Freud, who postulated that humans act by instincts, biological forces, and childhood experiences, Jung theorized human personality as a process of self-discovery and realization, a concept he referred to as **individuation**. Individuation involves not only the culmination of childhood experiences, but also a spiritual life force that shapes one's being and life direction. Jung was convinced that self-awareness and a quest for a greater understanding of the self enhance the process of individuation, helping one navigate through the difficult passages of life. This ability to soul-search, to wrestle with personal issues, and to further the understanding of one's life purpose, he believed, augmented psychological health. On the other hand, reluctance, avoidance, and indolence contribute to self-ignorance and perpetuate the stress associated with underutilized inner resources. Jung also disagreed with Freud's notion that human behavior is driven primarily by sexual impulses. And although Freud placed less importance on aspects of the unconscious mind, Jung focused his life's work on this construct, particularly in his empirical research on dreams as a means to enhance the individuation process.

Individuation: A term coined by Carl Jung to describe self-realization, a process leading to wholeness.

Personal unconscious: A repository of personal thoughts, perceptions, feelings, and memories.

Jung likened the human mind to an iceberg (FIG. 5.5). Metaphorically speaking, the conscious mind is represented by the tip above the water, while the unconscious, the greatest percentage of the mind, lies below the water. The conscious mind, with its limited awareness, focuses on specific thoughts, which compete for attention (e.g., What should I have for dinner tonight? How will I be able to afford a new car? What time is it? Will he ask me to the formal?). The unconscious mind is the receptacle for ideas, images, and concepts the conscious mind has no room to hold, as well as repressed thoughts, memories, and a host of undiscovered thoughts of enlightenment. Jung divided the unconscious mind into two levels. The first layer, the level he referred to as the **personal unconscious**, is the repository of the thoughts, perceptions, feelings, and memories of the individual—everything dropped from the attention of the conscious mind. However obscure these ideas, feelings, and perceptions may be, they do not cease to exist, and in fact continue to influence conscious thought and behaviors. The second level Jung called

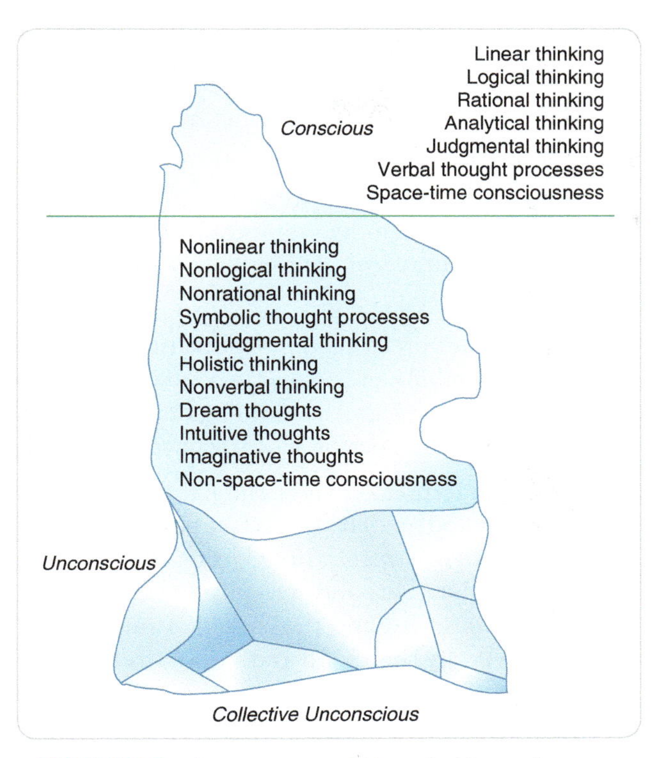

FIGURE 5.5 Jung compared the mind to an iceberg. That which is above the water represents the conscious mind, while that below represents all unconscious thought processes. Despite the fact that the unconscious mind may appear dormant at the conscious level, Jung theorized that it is perpetually active.

the **collective unconscious**, a profound and potentially inexhaustible reservoir of human thoughts and ideas integrated with ancient wisdom, which he claimed is essentially passed down from generation to generation, not unlike physical characteristics genetically passed down through generations of humanity. Jung believed that although this level was more difficult to access, the resources in this reservoir were invaluable in aiding the self-discovery process.

Jung believed that the passage of thoughts from the conscious to the unconscious mind is quite easy when compared to the difficult migration of intuitive or suppressed thoughts and dream images trying to surface to conscious attention. From Jung's viewpoint, consciousness naturally rejects anything unknown and unfamiliar. Consequently, the threshold of consciousness, like the membrane of a cell, acts as a barrier, censoring material from the unconscious mind that seems irrelevant, incoherent, inane, or ego-bruising.

From the analysis and interpretation of his own dreams as well as thousands of dreams of his patients, Jung discovered that the conscious and unconscious minds speak two different languages. The conscious mind communicates through very linear, rational, analytical, and verbal processes. Conversely, the processes of the unconscious mind are nonlinear, irrational, intuitive, and non-time-oriented processes represented through dreams in symbols and vivid colors. (It is interesting to note that Nobel Prize–winning research by Roger Sperry et al. has documented a similar division of cognitive functions in the left brain and right brain, respectively.) If you reflect on some of your own dreams, you may recall images that seem absurd—flying, swimming in red air, a herd of elk grazing in the attic, or a conversation with a college buddy and a high school sweetheart who in real life are thousands of miles apart and have never even met.

In Jung's view, daily stress is compounded by internal tension between the seemingly incompatible thought processes of the two minds. Although we are not typically aware of our unconscious minds' activities during the waking hours of the day (unlike the dream state during sleep), the unconscious mind is constantly open to sensory stimulation and countless thought processes, whereas the conscious mind only functions this way while we are awake. Moreover, the unconscious mind acts as a navigator for the driver of the conscious mind. Yet in many cases, the two are worlds apart in the front seat of the same car, with the conscious mind in a dominant role, charting its own course. In the dream state, however, the unconscious mind both navigates and drives, working to resolve issues raised in the course of the day. Confusion arises when the unconscious presents resolutions in dream symbols that the conscious mind passes off as ludicrous or unimportant. To the conscious mind, dreams hold little significance if there is no overt understanding, yet in Jung's opinion they continually offer impeccable insight into the problem-solving process.

To understand the concept of the unconscious better, imagine that while driving in a foreign country you become lost and stop to ask directions from people who speak no English. You do not speak a word of their native tongue either. They try to warn you that the road you are

Collective unconscious: A term coined by psychologist Carl Jung; the deepest level of unconsciousness, which connects all people together as one; divine consciousness.

on is unsafe, but even their pantomimes are unclear. You proceed and encounter the same situation with more natives a mile down the road. Baffled and discouraged, you shake your head, ignoring the warnings and continuing to drive on into potential danger.

Similarly, Jung proposed that internal tension develops at the interface of the conscious and unconscious minds because of the inability of these two entities to communicate effectively. In an attempt to minimize this tension, Jung explained that the conscious mind acts as a censoring mechanism that limits access to unconscious thought processes trying to bubble up from below. This explains why many people initially cannot recall their dreams or make sense of them if they do remember them. Although the censoring process may seem effective in the short term, the inability to decipher the language of the unconscious perpetuates internal stress in the long run.

New languages may be difficult to master at first, but with practice comes fluency. According to Jung, the conscious mind can be trained to interpret the dream symbols created by the unconscious mind by manipulating and playing with these images. Based on five decades of dream analysis, Jung made the following observations about dreams:

1. Dreams should be treated as fact, not as fabrications of the mind.
2. Dreams have a definite and purposeful idea or theme expressed in unique symbols.
3. Dreams make sense when time is devoted to understanding their meaning.
4. Recurring dreams may represent a traumatic life event, be an attempt to compensate for a personal defect in attitude, or signal an event of importance in the future.
5. Dream interpretation is individualistic in that no dream symbol can be separated from the person who dreams it (e.g., the meaning of a plane crash is specific to the person who dreamed it).
6. Dream interpretation is essential to the resolution of stress and anxiety. In his last published book, *Man and His Symbols*, Jung wrote, "For the sake of mental stability and even physiological health, the unconscious and the conscious minds must be integrally connected and thus move in parallel lines."

> **Psychic equilibrium:** A term coined by Carl Jung to describe the balance of thought (and subsequent health-wholeness) between the conscious and unconscious minds, by having the conscious mind become multilingual to the many languages of the unconscious mind (e.g., dream interpretation).

Jung's concept of individuation emphasized the importance of self-reflection: quality time spent in solitude dedicated to expanding one's conscious awareness as well as learning the language and wisdom of the unconscious mind. His travels to Asia, during which he studied the concepts behind meditation, reinforced his belief that self-reflection was essential to mental health. Jung was convinced that when you take the time to examine the depths of your own mind, a unity of conscious and unconscious thought processes occurs, which helps you to resolve personal issues and leads to a greater sense of inner peace. This unity he called **psychic equilibrium**.

FIGURE 5.6 Dreams offer a source of insight and information that we often don't get any other way. For this reason it is important to pay attention to our dreams.

Stress with a Human Face

Pattie is a middle-school teacher who is currently working on her master's degree in psychology at the University of Northern Colorado. One day, after hearing a lecture on dreams and dream therapy, she became very intrigued with the notion of accessing the wisdom of the unconscious mind through dream interpretation. It didn't take long for her to decide the focus of her term paper for this course. It would be on the study of dreams and dream therapy.

Like most people, Pattie confides that she doesn't remember her dreams, yet knowing that all people have dreams, she was curious to learn more about herself and what wisdom would be revealed to her by making a more concerted effort to remember her dreams. The research paper became a catalyst for self-exploration.

Based on information she researched, Pattie knew that it was possible to train the conscious mind to remember dreams and uncode the language of dream symbols. She bought a notebook specifically to record her dreams and made a habit of practicing a relaxation technique before she went to bed, a technique she noted as an important step in the dream therapy process. Just as one would learn any skill, the first few attempts to record dreams were fruitless, but Pattie persisted.

One night, after listening to a relaxation tape, Pattie fell asleep. When she awoke, she recalled having a dream so vivid, so real, that she remembered the entire dream sequence. Taking pen in hand, Pattie recorded the dream in her notebook.

"I dreamt I was in my classroom and a student came by and popped her head in the door and smiled. She was much older than my typical students and, although I didn't recognize her, I knew her. In analyzing the dream, I came to understand that she was actually a composite of several former students, and her appearance in my door was a message. She had come back to tell me that my teaching had had a positive influence on her life, and her smile to me was an acknowledgment of her gratitude. I interpreted her visit as a vote of confidence in my teaching skills and the dream served as a reminder that my job is worthwhile, and my work is having a positive impact on my students.

"Through my research I really learned how valuable dream therapy is to people with post-traumatic stress disorder (PTSD), and through my own experience I learned how valuable dream interpretation is. It has had a positive impact on my life."

In describing her dream experience, she added, "I would like to pass along a quote from Carl Jung: 'No dream symbol can be separated from the individual who dreams it, and there is no definite or straightforward interpretation of any dream.' "

To assist his patients toward the goal of psychic balance, Jung employed what he called **active imagination**. This is a process where, in a conscious yet relaxed state, an individual uses creativity to manipulate dream fragments and complete the dream experience. This technique is most useful with recurring dreams, where the dreamer gives a desired ending to the neglected issues represented in these unfinished stories. Active imagination has been adapted to many coping and relaxation techniques alike, including mental imagery, journal writing, and art therapy. Jung was of the firm opinion that sickness, both mental and physical, was the result of the inability to bridge the gap between conscious and unconscious minds as a way to share knowledge to resolve inner tensions. In fact, he was once quoted as saying, "Modern man is sick because he is not whole," with wholeness being a peaceful union of the conscious and unconscious minds.

Jung suggested that each individual become introspective and dive below the waters of the conscious mind to gain insight into the causes of specific anxiety and stress. Once this awareness is gained, the source of anxiety can be confronted and handled at the conscious level, where it can lead to resolution and strength of the spirit. Throughout his life, Jung was devoted to the development of human potential, which begins with self-awareness. Many of Jung's followers have augmented and developed his concepts for application to psychotherapy, specifically

Active imagination: A term coined by Carl Jung describing a mental imagery process where, in a lucid dream state or relaxed state, you consciously imagine (and resolve) the end of a recurring dream. Active imagination is a form of visualization.

dream therapy. All in all, Jung's theories are quite profound, and they invite us to continue the exploration of the mysteries of the mind.

With the groundwork established by Freud and Jung, other theories were added throughout the twentieth and twenty-first centuries to the collective body of psychological knowledge. With each new insight we gain a stronger grasp of the psyche, particularly the influence that stress has on it. The following theories only begin to touch on aspects of emotions, behavior, and personality. Yet when combined with those of Freud and Jung, they give a wider perspective on the factors associated with the psychology of stress.

Elisabeth Kübler-Ross: The Death of Unmet Expectations

When the Social Readjustment Rating Scale was designed, it became obvious to its creators that the death of a spouse is the most stressful event a person can experience. The death and dying process, be it your own or that of someone you are close to, is very traumatic. Similarly, the death (grieving) of any unmet expectation is stressful and hence relates to this theory. One person who brought the issue of death to the forefront of human consciousness is Elisabeth Kübler-Ross (FIG. 5.7). A Swiss psychiatrist, Kübler-Ross stepped onto the global stage in 1969 with her pioneering work studying and counseling terminally ill cancer patients. Through her work she taught the world about the emotions and mental processes associated with death. Her work was inspired by her experiences as a teenager assisting in first-aid stations in Poland and Russia after World War II with survivors of Nazi concentration camps. From the carnage of the war and the concentration camps, Kübler-Ross realized that humankind had a great need to understand and cope with the problems of death and dying. She soon learned that the fear of death is universal, and that the death and dying process brings with it an abundance of emotional baggage. Not only grief, but guilt, shame, fear, and anger are all associated with the death experience.

FIGURE 5.7 Elisabeth Kübler-Ross.

Relocating to the United States after earning her degree in psychiatry, she was asked to join a group of physicians conducting a research seminar involving interviews and counseling sessions with terminally ill cancer patients. In the course of this work, she noted similarities in the patterns of emotional behaviors among the patients, which led her to outline a process of mental preparation for death applicable to everyone. In her most acclaimed book, *On Death and Dying*, Kübler-Ross refers to these stages as the psychological **stages of grieving**. Although these stages were observed among dying cancer patients, the same stages apply to any type of loss, including the death of unmet expectations. The following is a description of the five stages with examples she observed among her cancer patients. Also included are examples of how each stage applies to the death of an unmet expectation—a more common stressor—the discovery that one's wallet has been stolen.

Stages of grieving: A process outlined by Elisabeth Kübler-Ross regarding the mental preparation for death, including denial, anger, bargaining, depression, and acceptance.

1. *Denial:* The refusal to accept the truth of a situation—a rejection of the truth. Kübler-Ross observed denial in her patients who, upon learning of their diagnosis, were often heard to exclaim, "I don't have cancer. This isn't happening to me.

It cannot happen to me. I'm too young to die. I won't let it happen." Denial is also described as shock. In the case of a stolen wallet, the comparable reaction would be observed, "My wallet must be at home. I couldn't have misplaced it. Perhaps it's in my other pants (purse)."

2. *Anger:* The anger stage is a fit of rage that may include yelling, pounding, crying, and/or deep frustration manifested in a physical and emotional way. In this stage, anger is the physical expression of hostile feelings. Kübler-Ross typically saw anger directed not only at clinicians and family members but also toward a "higher power," even in those people who claimed not to believe in one. Similarly, a stolen wallet can provoke an outward expression of anger, where everyone becomes a suspect in its disappearance.
3. *Bargaining:* Kübler-Ross described this phase as a very brief but important one. Bargaining is an agreement between the conscious mind and the soul involving an exchange of offerings—primarily, a negotiation for more time to live. With cancer patients it may be expressed as, "If you let me live, I'll never smoke again." In the case of the stolen wallet, the negotiations would be something along the lines of, "Go ahead and take the money—but please don't use my credit cards."
4. *Depression:* Kübler-Ross divides the depression stage into two categories: reactive depression, when a patient grieves for a specific anatomical loss resulting from surgery (as with breast or bone cancer), and preparatory loss, feelings of impending losses related to the cancer, including personal freedom, time, family, and perhaps one's own life. Preparatory-loss depression is best described as a quiet or passive mood of uneasiness while feeling overwhelmed with thoughts and responsibilities at the same time. With depression there is very little, if any, perceived hope. In the case of the wallet, not only is there depression over the missing article, but also a feeling of being overwhelmed by having to arrange the replacement of its contents.
5. *Acceptance:* If and when a person has moved through the previous stages of the grieving process, then and only then can he or she arrive at the final stage, acceptance. Acceptance is an approval of existing conditions, a receptivity to things that cannot be changed. Acceptance is *not* giving in or giving up. It is *not* a surrender to the circumstance. Rather, it is acknowledgment of the particular situation in which you find yourself. Acceptance allows you to move on with your life. With acceptance comes hope. For those cancer patients who arrive at this stage, their frame of mind can be described as, "Okay. So this is the way it is. I'm going to keep living my life as best I can. I'm going to put up a good fight." In the case of the stolen wallet, "So I lost my wallet. I'll get a new license, credit cards, ATM card, and a new wallet." In the acceptance stage there is no trace of anger or pity. Kübler-Ross indicates that this stage is very difficult to arrive at; in fact, many people never reach this stage in the course of their grieving. A significant component of the stage of acceptance is **adaptation**—consciously adapting to the new situation with thoughts and actions.

Kübler-Ross states that these stages are experienced by virtually every terminally ill patient. By no coincidence, these same stages are observed, to a greater or lesser degree, among people who go through other losses, including relationships (the end of a romantic relationship, divorce, or separation), identity (unemployment, retirement, new location, or new job), possessions (a lost/stolen wallet, damaged car, or fire-damaged house), as well as less tangible items (a failed exam, poor athletic performance). Actually, it could be the loss of anything significant. This mental-preparation-for-death process happens hundreds of times in one's lifetime. As Kübler-Ross explains, the stress associated with the mental stages is a catalyst to provide a greater mental awareness of several or all unresolved emotions. As an individual passes from one stage to the next, he or she enters a deeper level of mental awareness. In later years, Kübler-Ross amended her original theory to suggest that, in some cases, one of the first four stages may be skipped. She has devoted her whole life to assisting people so that they may complete the final stage peacefully.

To paraphrase Kübler-Ross, acceptance is your ability to acknowledge the emotional chains that bind you to your primary cause of stress, and acceptance allows you to free yourself from their bondage. Complete, unconditional acceptance, a full resolution without any resentment, animosity, or pity associated with these emotional potholes,

Adaptation: A behavior and attitude considered the epitome of the acceptance stage of grieving, where a person adapts to the new situation and no longer views him- or herself as a victim.

leads to what Kübler-Ross calls essential inner peace. The process of acceptance, resolving pent-up feelings or frustrations, is not an easy one. In fact, it can be quite emotionally painful. In her work, she observed some people with a stubborn streak who would rather leave matters unresolved than face the fear of this process. Others were unsure how best to resolve these emotions and eventually became hostage to them.

Typically, individuals repress or rationalize painful feelings that are perceived to be a threat to their inner self. As Kübler-Ross notes, the defense mechanisms of the ego serve, function, and manipulate well on a short-term basis but cause utter chaos in the long run. Through repression and rationalization, unresolved feelings, like phases of the moon, come full circle and ultimately resurface to haunt the conscious mind. To leave these emotional debts unresolved is what she refers to as the unfinished business of the soul. Kübler-Ross suggests that the process of addressing and completing unresolved feelings should not be delayed; rather, it should take top priority on a daily basis. The best way to initiate this resolution process, she says, is to grant yourself some quality "alone-time" to learn to recognize unresolved feelings between yourself and others, and perhaps most importantly within yourself, and then attempt to resolve them. There may be several strategies for resolution, including accepting a situation that is unchangeable and continuing to live with this fact. In any case, without a doubt, unconditional acceptance promotes inner peace.

Viktor Frankl: A Search for Life's Meaning

Stressors come in all shapes and sizes. Little problems, like small potholes on a dirt road, are easily avoided, but major stressors obstruct your progress in the journey of life and can stop you dead in your tracks. Whatever the events in your life you perceive as stressful, few, if any, can match the intensity of the suffering experienced by psychiatrist Viktor Frankl (FIG. 5.8) as a Nazi concentration camp prisoner and survivor. Frankl's experiences prior to and during his 3 years in Auschwitz led him to the development of a form of psychoanalysis he refers to as **logotherapy**, an existential analysis simply defined as a search for the meaning of life.

Logotherapy: A term coined by psychiatrist Viktor Frankl describing the search for meaning in one's life.

FIGURE 5.8 Viktor Frankl.

In his most acclaimed book, *Man's Search for Meaning*, Frankl illustrates the depth of human suffering in the Nazi concentration camps. From this basis of personal experience and observation, he augmented his understanding of the human quest for the meaning of existence. Having been stripped of every possible possession including clothes, jewelry, and even hair, camp prisoners were left with what Frankl calls the last human freedom: "the ability to choose one's attitude in a given set of circumstances." Of the prisoners who were fortunate enough to avoid the gas chambers and crematoriums, Frankl noted that it was largely the ability to choose one's attitude that ultimately distinguished those who lived from those who later perished from disease and illness in the concentration camps. Those who found and held onto a reason to live were able to survive the ghastly conditions, while those who saw no substantial meaning for living became physically and spiritually weak and succumbed to death.

Many of Frankl's psychological theories center on the concept of human pain and the meaning of suffering. Unequivocally, suffering is a direct consequence of profound stress. One does not have to experience the horrors of Auschwitz to feel suffering. Any experience that promotes feelings of emotional trauma, according to Frankl, contains the essence of a purposeful meaning.

The death of a child, severe illness, major debt, retirement, a change of jobs—these are all candidates for inducing personal suffering. Frankl was convinced that suffering is as much a part of life as happiness and love, and that like love, suffering has a purpose in the larger scheme of things. From his own observations, Frankl realized that suffering is a universal experience. Therefore, he reasoned, it must have some significant value to the advancement of one's human potential or spiritual evolution. In *Man's Search for Meaning* he writes, "If there's meaning in life then there must be meaning in suffering. Suffering is an ineradicable part of life, and death. Without suffering and death, human life would not be complete." Frankl did not advocate avoiding suffering, but rather suggested that the cause of emotional pain be examined to try to make some rational sense out of it—to find a meaningful purpose in suffering. This search for meaning is not a defense mechanism, a rationalization of pain, but the search for a truthful understanding. In fact, writes Frankl, meaning is not a fabrication of the mind, but a truth uncovered by the soul.

A tool to augment the search for meaning, as defined by Frankl, is **tragic optimism.** Tragic optimism he defined as the ability to turn suffering into a meaningful experience, and to learn from this experience with a positive perspective on life's events. The history of humanity is filled with inspiring examples of people who completed their grieving by finding meaning in their stressful suffering. One such person was Candy Lightner, who after losing her young daughter to the recklessness of a drunk driver, assembled her creative energies and formed the national organization Mothers Against Drunk Driving (MADD). Another example is Bethany Hamilton, who in 2003 overcame the emotional anguish of losing her left arm in a shark attack while surfing. She continues to compete and win professional surf competitions. In fact, many contemporary heroes and role models are individuals who overcame obstacles of biblical proportions, and soon became the epitome of human potential in action for others to emulate.

Finding meaning in a painful experience is not easy. Frankl notes that many people in contemporary society look upon victimization as more prestigious than personal achievement. Quite often people tend to wallow in self-pity beyond the point where it serves any beneficial purpose. So how does one begin a quest for the meaning of one's own life? Frankl suggests that the best time for this to occur is when you feel mental anguish or emotional suffering of any kind. When these conditions surface, you must journey into the garden of your soul and examine your conscious mind. A mental examination quite often leads to questioning your ideals and values, and testing your will to fulfill or abandon them. Frankl notes that the will to find meaning in most people is *supported* by something or someone, not based on faith alone. It is also important to note that each person must find his or her own unique meaning, not a universal one, and that one cannot be borrowed or adopted from others. In fact, as people age there will be many different meanings to be searched for and recognized in their lifetimes. And suffering awaits in between the periods of life's meanings.

Frankl was convinced that, to an extent, stress plays an important role in mental health. Like Freud and Jung, Frankl believed that internal tension is inevitable among humans, but he held that mental health is dependent on the tension that exists between past accomplishments and future endeavors. A sense of boredom is what he called an existential vacuum, a state of tension where the current meaning to life is as yet undiscovered. In his experience, this reason outnumbered all other reasons combined for bringing people to psychotherapy and counseling. Frankl coined the term **noo-dynamics** to describe a process to resolve this existential vacuum by using the tension of boredom to search for life's meaning. Whereas Freud placed emphasis on childhood experiences, Frankl was concerned with the present and future as if to say, "So, what happened, happened. What are you going to do with your life now? Where are you headed from here? What new contribution can you make to humanity?" In logotherapy, Frankl advocates the concept of goal-setting to aid in the search for personal meaning in one's life. Setting and accomplishing goals involve creativity, to visualize where you are going, and stamina, the energy to get you there. The fundamental purpose of personal goals, Frankl states, is to enhance one's human potential. Furthermore, pleasure should be a consequence of meaning, not a purpose in and of itself. Frankl also suggests that a quest for true meaning has a spiritual quality to it. (*Logos* in Greek translates not only as "meaning" but also as "spirit.") In this case, however, the term *spirituality*

Tragic optimism: A term coined by psychiatrist Viktor Frankl to explain the mindset of someone who can find value and meaning in the worst situation.

Noo-dynamics: A term coined by Viktor Frankl describing a state of tension, a spiritual dynamic, that motivates one to find meaning in life. The absence of noo-dynamics is an existential vacuum.

has less of a formal religious connotation; rather, it refers to the human dimension of inner balance between faith in self-reliance and individual will. Spiritual health is imperative in the search for one's own meaning in life and in dealing with the suffering brought about by various life experiences, regardless of their cause. In his autobiography, Frankl spoke of those who, in the midst of a crisis, lost their belief in the future, in themselves, and their spiritual hold. Without spiritual health they were subject to mental and physical deterioration and eventual premature death.

Although Frankl's theories may seem rather abstract, the fundamental messages are clear: (1) one must continually search from within for life's meaning to achieve inner peace, and (2) in the absence of everything but one's body, mind, and soul, one has the ability to choose one's attitudes; in so doing one either perpetuates or resolves each circumstance. He writes, "We had to learn from ourselves and we had to teach despairing men that it did not matter what we expected from life, but rather what life expected from us."

FIGURE 5.9 Learning to live in the present moment.

Wayne Dyer: Guilt and Worry

Relaxation is said to be achieved when the present moment is fully experienced and appreciated; this belief has been passed down for more than 2,000 years by wise people of all cultures (FIG. 5.9). Yet for many people, the present moment is a scary and insecure place to be. Feelings of discomfort, boredom, and inadequacy arise. In the earliest years, all a child knows is the present moment. But as the child matures into adulthood, the ability to enjoy the present moment seems to become ever more elusive. Instead, the mind becomes willingly preoccupied (often paralyzed) with either past or future events. The fact that many people spend their conscious thought processes in either the past or the future has not gone unnoticed. Psychotherapist Wayne Dyer (FIG. 5.10) observed this phenomenon in virtually all his clients. His most present works integrate the mind and the soul, but his earliest work is as solid today as it was decades ago.

In his best-selling book *Your Erroneous Zones*, Dyer states that to be occupied with the past or future can diminish, even extinguish, our appreciation of the present moment, thus robbing us of the ability to relax and be at peace with ourselves. The zones Dyer describes highlight certain stress-prone emotional responses—those unhealthy defensive processes learned very early in life as cognitive survival skills. In his theory of unproductive emotions and their related behaviors, Dyer states that one of two

FIGURE 5.10 Wayne Dyer.

emotions, guilt or worry, is associated with virtually every stressor perceived by people in America. Guilt is an expression of self-anger; worry, a manifestation of fear. When these emotional responses are triggered, they tend to immobilize rational thought processes, resulting in clouded thinking, delayed reactions, and poor decision making. Dyer goes as far as to say that guilt and worry are in fact the most ineffective coping techniques for stress management because they perpetuate the avoidance of stress-related issues needing resolution.

FIGURE 5.11 Freud's analysis of guilt.

The Sin of Guilt

Dyer defines guilt as the conscious preoccupation with undesirable past thoughts and behaviors. Guilt feelings surface in our internal but conscious dialogue in the form of "should haves." Guilt feelings can easily be produced by thinking about something you said or did just as easily as by something you didn't say or do but feel you should have. Dyer is of the opinion that guilt contains a perplexing element of cultural respect, like that recorded by those who fled religious persecution in Europe to become this nation's earliest settlers. Three hundred years later, guilt, he observes, is still a socially acceptable way to express the responsibility of caring. Yet true, productive caring, Dyer believes, should never be confused with this immobilizing emotion. When guilt is the overriding emotion, all thoughts and behaviors are influenced by it. Guilt is so powerful an emotion that it can have a paralyzing effect on all other thoughts and feelings and prevent a positive behavior or action from taking place. According to Dyer, guilt experienced to any extent can result in mild to severe depression. He states that, for the most part, guilt is fruitless because no amount of it can change the past. Although guilt appears to be a "natural" human emotion, Dyer is convinced that it serves no functional purpose beyond fostering recognition of important lessons to be learned and issues to be resolved. If and when these lessons are learned, guilt disappears.

From observations he made counseling his clients, Dyer created a dichotomy of guilt. **Leftover guilt** he describes as remnant thought patterns originating in early childhood, primarily through parental disciplinary tactics as, for example, shame imposed by an authority figure for naughty or unapproved behaviors. What worked as an inspirational force during childhood (approval seeking to avoid guilt), however, produces significant stress when carried into adulthood, yet the same unhealthy behaviors are usually continued. By contrast, **self-imposed guilt** is described as the guilt placed on oneself when an adult moral or ethical behavior, based on the constructs of one's personal value system, has been violated. Examples are missing church on Sunday or saying yes to something because it seemed like the right thing to say, then later regretting having agreed to it because you were never committed to it. Dyer notes that guilt is also used as a conventional tool for manipulating other people's thoughts, feelings, and actions, a behavior that inappropriately transfers stress to others. He advocates avoiding using guilt and shame on others, and most important, avoiding using it on yourself.

The Art of Worrying

While guilt, like Dickens's Ghost of Christmas Past, is associated with keeping the mind hostage with thoughts and behaviors from the past, worry infiltrates the mind to immobilize thought processes regarding events yet to

Leftover guilt: A term coined by psychologist Wayne Dyer explaining the ill effects of unresolved guilt left over from an early childhood experience.

Self-imposed guilt: A term coined by psychologist Wayne Dyer to describe the guilt one places on oneself when a personal value has been compromised or violated.

come. Dyer defines worry as the immobilization of thinking in the present moment as a result of preoccupation with things that may, or may not, occur in the future. Like guilt, Dyer notes that worry is looked on by many as an act of compassion. In reality, it too immobilizes cognition, clouds rational thought processes, and cultivates stress. The practice of worrying, like guilt, can lead to severe depression. Corrie ten Boom, a Dutch Christian who helped Jews escape from the Nazis during the Holocaust, said that "Worry does not empty tomorrow of its sorrow, it empties today of its strength." The bottom line is that worry is a misuse of your imagination.

Dyer believes it is essential for everyone to distinguish the difference between worrying about the future and planning for the future. Worrying paralyzes and overrides present-moment thought processes and dilutes self-control. Then the imagination goes wild, creating a series of worst-case scenarios, all of which can seem very real and threatening. Dyer is convinced that worrying tends to produce a rebound effect, first resulting in a less effective means to deal with a given situation, which then produces more worry. Ironically, Dyer notes that people typically worry about matters over which they have no control. In addition, many seemingly insurmountable worries are later regarded as quite trivial (the making-a-mountain-out-of-a-molehill syndrome). Unfortunately, the knowledge of hindsight is ignored when worrying thoughts surface again. Unlike the worrying process, the constructive thought process of planning contributes to a more effective and productive future, minimizing potential stressors. Planning for the future, for example, by setting goals, making a strategy, and evaluating progress, provides a sense of empowerment.

To illustrate this difference, consider a person who worries about finding a job after graduation: He sits and stews about not finding a job and the hazards of being unemployed. Conversely, planning involves drafting a résumé, making phone calls, writing cover letters, networking, following up with contacts, and making appointments. Although planning a strategy of options for future events does not guarantee a "smooth ride," it does provide a base of security, whereas worrying leaves one in the driver's seat with no keys, gas, or tires.

> **Love:** The emotion studied and advocated by Leo Buscaglia as being the cornerstone to self-esteem and ultimately altruism.

As mentioned earlier, Dyer suggests that American culture breeds the emotion of worry by equating it with caring and love. He discovered that many of his clients emphatically prove their love by demonstrating the worry process. Several other psychotherapists note a similarity between this characteristic and the stress-prone codependent personality.

What the emotions of guilt and worry share is the *distraction* of one's present mental processes. Both guilt and worry are what Dyer calls negative or nonproductive emotional states of cognition, and he confirms that these emotions are a waste of energy. As a therapist, Dyer counsels that the first step to removing these two erroneous zones is the awareness that they are used as ineffective coping techniques. When the practice of employing guilt or worry enters your awareness as a result of perceived stress, Dyer suggests removing guilt or worry by reframing your perception either to find the lessons to be learned from the past or to start planning strategically for future events that are occupying your attention. Like other leading psychologists, Dyer advocates acceptance of past events as an important stress-management strategy to enable you to move on with your life. Dyer is in the company of several prominent psychologists and scholars who concur with his theories of guilt and worry, two emotions responsible for more visits to psychologists' offices than all others combined.

Since his first book, *Your Erroneous Zones*, Dyer has written several other best-selling books that focus on the theme of moving from a motivation of fear to a motivation of love. In his book *Your Sacred Self*, Dyer continues the theme of erroneous zones, with guilt and worry both manifestations of fear. Ultimately, Dyer says, the ego is the cause of these two "erroneous zones," and the sooner the ego is tamed, the sooner we move to a place of love.

Leo Buscaglia: The Lessons of Self-Love

Of all the psychological theories developed over the past century, most, if not all, have been influenced by anxiety as the primary force of human motivation. This narrow focus has eclipsed several equally motivating emotions, particularly love. Until the start of the twenty-first century, science had remained reticent on this subject. To paraphrase the words of psychologist Abraham Maslow, "It's amazing how little time the empirical sciences have to offer on the subject of love." One might assume that the concept of **love** has been perceived to be either unimportant or too complex an emotion to adequately define and study. Both assumptions hold elements of truth. In the past, love was left to poets, philosophers, actors, and songwriters to be explored, explained, and elaborated; psychology maintained a hands-off approach. Although this approach continues today, love as a viable motivational force and healing tool has recently moved out of the anthologies of poetry and Hollywood cinema and into classrooms, corporate boardrooms, and operating rooms. Upon taking a closer look at the theory and application of this enigmatic emotion, love is now recognized as a powerful inner resource much too important to ignore (Johnson, 2003). In simple terms, love is the epitome of eustress; its absence, distress. In recognition of the importance of love and health, the Institute for Research on Unlimited Love was created in 2000 as a joint collaboration between the Fetzer Institute and Sir John Templeton so that the merits of love, expressed as altruism, could be studied.

One man to bring the theoretical concept of love into the respectable forum of academia was Dr. Leo Buscaglia (FIG. 5.12). Buscaglia developed an experimental undergraduate course at the University of Southern California in the late 1960s called the "love class." Through his investigations, he brought forth some simple yet profound concepts of this elusive emotion, with many implications for both eustress and distress. Furthermore, he gave credibility to a component of emotional well-being that had been long overlooked.

FIGURE 5.12 Leo Buscaglia.

Buscaglia is quick to admit that love is very difficult to define. First and foremost, he states, "Love is a response to a learned group of stimuli and behaviors." An infant learns to love primarily through contact with his or her parents in the home environment. Love—specifically, self-love—is not innate, but taught. Yet, unlike many other subjects, it is taught neither in school nor in church. Buscaglia notes that as children we are taught to control our emotions (e.g., don't cry, stop laughing, wipe that smile off your face). As a result, the ability to express our emotions fully is denied, including the emotion of love. The emotional pain of rejection, or denied love, only compounds this inability. That is, ego defenses strengthen to prevent or minimize recurrences. As a child matures to adulthood, love often diminishes to the point of dormancy. Sadly enough, Buscaglia indicates, most of us never really learn to love at all. This, he believes, can have dangerous repercussions later in the growth process, when one forms lifelong relationships. And this may be the reason, he explains, why the divorce rate is hovering around 50 percent.

One reason why love is so hard to define, Buscaglia admits, is that so many people equate it with related concepts: sex, romance, attraction, needs, security, and attention. Love is also perceived to comprise a wide spectrum of feelings, including ecstasy, joy, irrationality, dissatisfaction, jealousy, and pain. In Buscaglia's opinion, however, there may be many degrees of love, from joy to grace, but there is only one love, that which leads to the positive growth process of self-discovery. Love is love, he proclaims. In his best-seller, *Love*, he writes, "for love and the self are one, and the discovery of either is the realization of both." Love brings with it change, and change requires adaptation, which like other types of stress can produce either pleasure or pain. Despite fairy-tale endings in which love conquers all with relative ease, Buscaglia repeatedly states that love takes much work, continuous work. There is much responsibility with love. Left unattended and unnurtured, it will evaporate and disappear. Buscaglia also compares love to knowledge, which you must have before you can teach it. Likewise, you must feel and experience love before you can share it. There are no exceptions.

In Buscaglia's words, "To love others, you must first love yourself," and this is no small feat. As youngsters, we experience some degree of love from our parents, yet self-love is rarely taught and thus remains a foreign concept to many people. In fact, self-love is misrepresented as egotistical selfishness and is strongly discouraged. Humbleness *is* advocated, but often at the risk of sacrificing self-love. The Christian ethic commands that you "love your neighbor as yourself"; however, Buscaglia observes that this equation is rarely balanced. Through his research, Buscaglia has found that most people are deficient in their capacity to love themselves unconditionally, and that they are restrained from expressing self-love by their low self-esteem. Moreover, he cites several deterrents to self-love. The greatest of these are the conditions we place on ourselves for self-acceptance, primarily physical appearance and capabilities—in short, everything that prevents perfection. A recurring pattern of "not completely liking myself because . . ." creates a negative-feedback system that perpetuates a lifetime of unhappiness. This phenomenon is more descriptively referred to as chronic stress, and it is associated with low **self-esteem**.

Buscaglia offers an alternative to this self-defeating attitude. He suggests that you take an honest look at yourself from within. Be prepared to openly accept all that there is to see, for better or worse, and exclude nothing. From this honest look, begin to accept yourself as you really are. This means accepting all those qualities you cannot change (e.g., height, eye color, parents) while pushing the limits of those qualities that allow room for growth (e.g., creativity, humor, intellect, love). Then, take the initiative to enhance those qualities that will help you reach your highest potential. In addition, Buscaglia emphasizes the need for each individual to focus on his or her individuality rather than aiming for conformity by comparing oneself to others. He coined the term the **X-factor** to symbolize a prized quality that makes each person special and unique. People need to focus on this quality to move toward unconditional self-acceptance and unconditional self-love.

In Buscaglia's quest for love, he has searched for every color of love's rainbow to comprehend and share his understanding of this often misused, misunderstood, and misacknowledged emotion. His attempts to understand the fundamental concepts of love have taken him to the shores of nearly every continent. Unlike the approach of Western culture, which is geared toward the achievement of happiness through external pleasures, Buscaglia has turned toward the East, adopting a philosophy that supports unconditional self-love. The philosophy of many Eastern cultures is one in which the individual focuses inward to understand him- or herself; the continuous journey toward self-understanding yields inner peace. Inner peace, in turn, creates universal harmony. Harmony, in turn, promotes happiness. And happiness nurtures love. Buscaglia illustrates this concept with the Hindu greeting *namaste*, which literally translated means, "I honor the place in you where, if you are at peace with yourself, and I am at peace with myself, then there is only one of us."

Buscaglia argues that for love to be an inner resource it cannot lay dormant. It must be acted out and acted on continually. And for love to exist there must be a will or desire to love. The will to love is an attitude of choice. Poets, film directors, and songwriters often make love seem too dynamic, distant, or elusive, sometimes even unattractive. But love of the self begins and grows with positive feelings toward the self, which each person is capable of creating. Buscaglia's message of self-love is directly tied to self-esteem, for we value only those things we love and feel positively about. When we do not love ourselves completely, or place conditions on our self-love, our self-esteem is compromised and thus deflated. And low self-esteem makes us vulnerable to, and almost defenseless against, the perceptions of stress.

From all his research, Buscaglia has developed six hypotheses regarding love as a motivating influence:

1. One cannot give what one does not possess. To give love you must possess love.
2. One cannot teach what one does not understand. To teach love you must comprehend love.
3. One cannot know what one does not study. To study love you must live in love.
4. One cannot appreciate what one does not recognize. To recognize love you must be receptive to love.
5. One cannot admit what one does not yield to. To yield to love you must be vulnerable to love.
6. One cannot live what one does not dedicate oneself to. To dedicate yourself to love you must be forever growing in love.

Self-esteem: The sense of underpinning self-values, self-acceptance, and self-love; thought to be a powerful buffer against perceived threats.

X-factor: A term coined by psychologist Leo Buscaglia to describe that special quality that makes each one of us unique. By focusing on our X-factor and not our faults and foibles, we enhance our self-esteem.

Buscaglia's attempt to validate love as a crucial component of human motivation has been met with both enthusiasm and apathy. His work is accepted by many professionals who implement his concepts in counseling and therapy with their clients, but for the most part, the topic today remains ignored by researchers. Be that as it may, the focus on love in psychology is slowly gaining momentum as the field of psychospirituality begins to unfold.

Abraham Maslow: The Art of Self-Actualization

Perhaps the most optimistic of all psychologists who have made contributions to modern psychology is Dr. Abraham Maslow (FIG. 5.13). While his predecessors and contemporaries studied mentally ill, emotionally disturbed, and maladjusted individuals to form the basis of their theories of human behavior, Maslow chose to study examples of men and women who epitomized the height of human potential, individuals exhibiting the unique combination of creativity, love, self-reliance, confidence, and independence. Despite the atrocities of World War II, Maslow was convinced of the existence of a brighter side of human nature, and he became committed to the development of a theoretical construct to support this hypothesis of a humanistic approach to psychology. Maslow's faith in humankind led him to believe that by understanding individuals with positive personality characteristics and admirable traits, he could devise a framework to serve as a model for others to follow in their pursuit of self-improvement. Unlike other psychologists, who attempted to describe how personality and behavior are affected by stress, Maslow placed emphasis on personality traits, those reflections of inner resources that seem to help people cope with stress and achieve psychological health. In other words, certain personality traits he observed in this special collection of people combine to act as a buffer in personal confrontations with stress.

FIGURE 5.13 Abraham Maslow.

Maslow's concept of behavior and personality is referred to as the **theory of motivation** for the nature of the characteristics he studied. This theory suggests that human beings operate on a **hierarchy of needs** that influence behavior. When the needs at one level are met, then needs at higher levels can be addressed in a linear, stair-step approach. In this hierarchy, the more advanced needs will not appear until lower needs have been acknowledged and addressed. In addition, when lower needs, such as hunger, reappear, all higher needs momentarily vanish.

This hierarchy of needs consists of six tiers or levels (similar in many ways to the chakras). Once described in terms of climbing a ladder, it is now usually illustrated as a series of steps (FIG. 5.14). The first tier comprises the most basic physiological needs to ensure survival of the human organism. These include food, sleep, and sex (and, in some cases, the need for drugs or alcohol when chemical dependency is involved). The second tier, safety needs, also contributes to survival and includes those factors that provide security, order, and stability, including clothing, money, and housing. Maslow called these first two tiers lower, or deficit, needs, while the remaining levels of the hierarchy he referred to as growth needs. Affection and strong bonding relationships constitute the third stage, belongingness and love needs. The fourth tier he called personal esteem needs, or the need and

Theory of motivation: Maslow's theory associated with personality and behavior, based on his theory of the hierarchy of needs.

Hierarchy of needs: Maslow's concept of a stair-step approach of consciousness (thoughts and behaviors), ranging from physiological needs to self-transcendence.

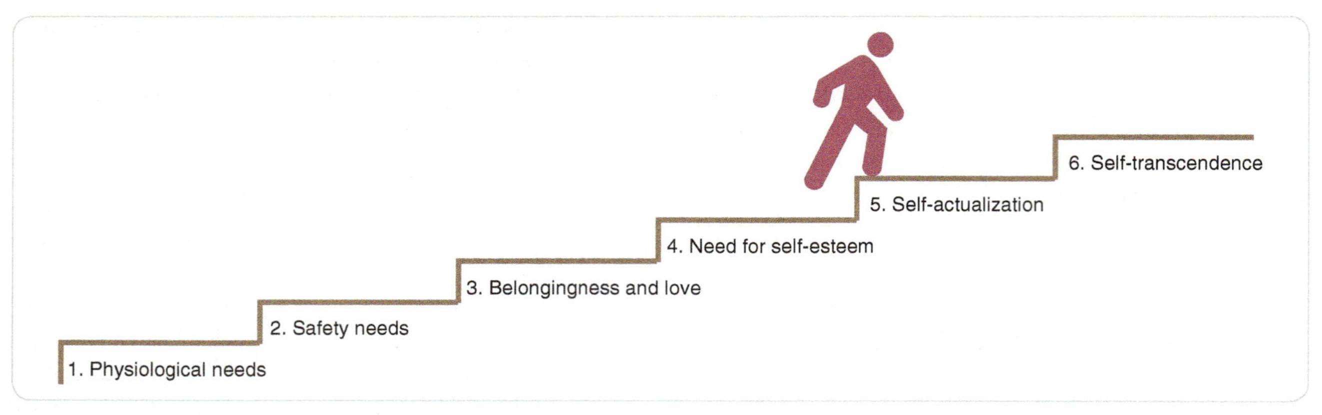

FIGURE 5.14 Maslow's hierarchy of needs. Note the similarity in the levels of self-actualization to the chakra system.

desire to seek or prove self-worth. The fifth level Maslow called the need for **self-actualization**, a stage of personal fulfillment in which ego boundaries and attachments are virtually eliminated, and a feeling of oneness with the universe is experienced, thus allowing one to maximize one's human potential. Ideally, self-actualization is the fulfillment of one's highest human potential and capabilities. Maslow writes in *Religions, Values, and Peak Experiences*, "Self-actualization is the point where one is ultimately at peace with oneself." In later years, Maslow added a sixth stage, which he referred to as the highest stage: **self-transcendence**, where one offers oneself to the service of others or dedicates oneself to a bigger cause for pure altruistic purposes.

According to Maslow, to progress from one level to the next, each area or need must be fulfilled and satisfied. What is important to note is that there is often fluctuation between levels when needs in the lower levels reappear. Even a person who has reached the level of self-actualization does not stay there indefinitely. What makes the level of self-actualization so challenging to attain is the requirement that one lower the walls of the ego and explore the unknown with anticipation, not fear. In fact, Maslow states that the need to know (curiosity), and a desire to take risks and actively pursue an understanding of oneself are essential to reaching self-actualization.

Self-actualization: The fifth level of Maslow's hierarchy of needs where one experiences a sense of personal fulfillment.

Self-transcendence: The sixth and highest stage of Maslow's hierarchy of needs, where one offers oneself altruistically to the service of others. Mother Teresa, Jane Goodall, Jimmy Carter, and Desmond Tutu serve as examples of this stage.

In his quest to understand this highest level of needs, self-actualization, Maslow studied the lives of thousands of people, including students, acquaintances, public figures (Albert Einstein, Eleanor Roosevelt, and Albert Schweitzer), and historical figures (Thomas Jefferson, Jane Addams, and Abraham Lincoln), finding a number he considered both healthy and prime examples of quality human beings. From his research, cited in *Motivation and Personality*, Maslow noticed many characteristics common to people he identified as being self-actualized. It is this collection of characteristics that appears to contribute to the resilient nature of people who possess psychological health. To the untrained eye, these people appear to have no stress in their lives, but upon closer scrutiny of the makeup of their personalities, they do in fact have stress but know how to deal with it effectively. According to Maslow, self-actualized people display the following characteristics (or coping techniques):

1. *A highly efficient perception of reality:* Self-actualizers are individuals who are able to maintain a clear and objective perspective on themselves and others. Their perceptions are not clouded or disturbed by egotistical influences; rather, they are unbiased by prejudice and supposition. Maslow found that these people had a strong sense of qualitative judgment.

2. *Acceptance:* People in this class of individuals are aware of not only their strengths, but their weaknesses as well. Like everyone else, they have faults

and imperfections. But they harbor no guilt, animosity, or shame about the failings or shortcomings in themselves or others. These people accept their shortcomings and do not victimize themselves with their less-than-desirable traits. They work to move beyond them.

3. *Naturalness and spontaneity:* Self-actualizers are themselves, and they feel very comfortable with themselves. They display no false facade, nor are they rigid in their mannerisms. They are open, frank, and present natural, unfiltered behavior in most, if not all, situations and circumstances. Most important, they go with the flow and are unthreatened and unfrightened by the unknown. They can think on their feet and react favorably to changes in a spontaneous fashion. They are not easily stressed when plans or circumstances change abruptly.
4. *Problem centering:* People who exhibit the traits of self-actualizers have a strong sense of commitment and dedication to their jobs and other responsibilities. They see themselves as part of the whole, not the whole. When problems arise, these people do not get bogged down in petty personal issues. They confront issues, not people. Because of this strong sense of commitment and purpose in life, self-actualizers work very hard, yet they derive much pleasure from their work. Maslow was once quoted as saying, "If the only tool you have is a hammer, you tend to see every problem as a nail." Self-actualizers have many tools for problem solving.
5. *Solitude and independence:* Self-actualized people can find as much pleasure in being by themselves as in the company of friends, without feeling lonely. They like their moments of privacy and make time for them. Solitude is considered a blessing, often a time to recharge. Satisfaction is derived from within, as opposed to being dependent on others. Alone-time is often a time of reflection and a time to draw on inner strengths. There is a strong element of autonomy and free-spiritness.
6. *A continual freshness of appreciation:* Grasshoppers, falling leaves, the Big Dipper—these people "stop and smell the roses" along the way. Not only do self-actualizers continually find unexpected wonder and awe in the simplest of surroundings, but like children they typically face daily living with freshness and a bigger-than-life attitude. These people know how to live in the present moment, minimizing feelings of guilt and worry. Rarely do they take anything for granted, and they count their blessings regularly.
7. *Creativity:* Self-actualizers are highly creative individuals who bring imagination, inventiveness, originality, and energy to the thought process. They are able to conceive an idea, visualize it, and then implement it. They are inquisitive and open to new possibilities in their thinking. They are not afraid to fail because they know that failure leads to success. In his book *The Farther Reaches of Human Nature,* Maslow writes, "My feeling is that the concept of creativeness and the concept of the healthy, self-actualized, fully human person seem to be coming closer and closer together, and may perhaps turn out to be the same thing."
8. *Interpersonal relationships:* To be self-actualized does not mean one has hundreds of friends. Rather, the circle of friends is small, but those in this circle are very similar in interests and compatible. Self-actualizers develop closeness to individuals who stimulate them and who contribute to their own growth and human potential. Relationships are selective and based on the ability to inspire rather than influence.
9. *Human kinship:* Self-actualizers appear compelled to assist in social and moral causes, and they are willing to help all levels of humanity. According to Maslow, they take on a brother or sister role toward other people. Above all, these people have a genuinely unselfish desire to help the human race.
10. *A democratic character:* People who display this characteristic find they have something to learn from everyone. They do not come across as condescending or "uppity." These people have the ability to relate to people from all walks of life.
11. *Strong sense of ethical values:* Maslow found that people he considered self-actualized consistently demonstrated knowledge of right and wrong in their own terms. "These people," wrote Maslow, in the book *Motivation and Personality*, "rarely show the confusion and inconsistency, or the conflict that are so common in the average person's ethical dealings."
12. *Resistance to enculturalization:* Self-actualizers are their own people. They are not likely to conform to or follow trends of fashion or politics. Although

they may greatly appreciate aspects of other cultures, they do not adopt them as their own. They are directed more by their own nature rather than by the influences of cultural tides.

13. *A sense of humor:* Self-actualizers possess the ability to appreciate the flood of incongruities and ironies in life as well as laugh at their own foibles and mistakes. A light and happy heart is a common trait; these people do not employ sarcasm or hostility in their repertoire of humor. There is a strong spontaneous and playful nature to their sense of mirth.
14. *Mystical or peak sensations:* A peak experience is considered by Maslow to be the climax of self-actualization. A peak experience is any experience of real excellence, real perfection, or of moving toward a perfect justice or perfect values. He found that people who described a peak experience often analogized it to spiritual orgasm. A **mystical (peak) sensation** is a very spiritual moment when you feel one with the world and very much at peace with yourself.

If all of this sounds like the Wonderful World of Disney, it is, because there are very few people who completely fit this description. Maslow estimated from his research that approximately 1 percent of the human population has ever reached this level with any great frequency. And even then, people who do fulfill this need don't tend to stay at this level for their entire lives. Most of the people he classified as self-actualizers were over 30 years old. Teenagers, he found, were too busy polishing their identity to reach this level in high school, or even college. What Maslow came to realize is that individuals are not born self-actualizers. Instead, they must evolve through a multitude of human experiences, smooth the rough edges, and polish the surface of their personal existence. Those who succeed have developed a remarkable human potential and, in the process, a healthy example for others to follow. Yet, to be sure, people who show the traits of self-actualization don't *always* exhibit these characteristics. Maslow noted that, on occasion, they get angry, bored, depressed, selfish, and perhaps, on occasion, even rude. They, too, have ups and downs, and must address the other needs of their existence as well. Overall, though, it is their desire to be all they can be that puts them in this select group of individuals. Self-actualizers are not angels, messiahs, or prophets. They have imperfections and flaws like the rest of Earth's inhabitants. But unlike other people, they don't dwell on them. Basically, self-actualizers are people with a strong positive outlook on themselves and life in general. They hold a tremendous amount of faith in themselves and their work. They live life with a passion, not a grudge. They know themselves inside and out, and without a doubt, they are their own best friends.

Mystical (peak) sensation: A euphoric experience during which one feels a divine or spiritual connection with all life.

Meta-disease: A concept by Maslow that depicts origins of physical disease as being based in unresolved emotional issues.

It is interesting to note that Maslow often talked about the relationship between emotional states and disease. In a presentation to a group of people at the Esalen retreat center in California, he spoke of the concept of **meta-disease**, where disease and illness are the results of unresolved emotional states of consciousness.

The exciting aspect of Maslow's theory of self-actualization is that we all have this potential. We all have the ability to access our inner resources, and we are all capable of becoming self-actualized. Unfortunately, Maslow states, we limit our capabilities, and these limits stifle our evolution to self-actualization. We place barriers (defense mechanisms) around ourselves for emotional protection. But the barriers around emotional security often cause us to stagnate and eventually inhibit the growth of this remarkable human potential. Self-actualizers have learned to collapse the barriers, lower the walls of the ego, and welcome the opportunity for growth. In a society where stress is becoming more and more apparent, Maslow's theory is an illuminating torch in the field of psychology, so much so that several psychologists have taken his lead and advocated his "hardy" characteristics as being among those conferring the ability to resist the effects of stress.

Martin Seligman: Optimism and the Art of Being Happy

For the past several decades, the field of psychology has been greatly influenced (some say co-opted) by the pharmaceutical industry, with a proliferation of medications for depression, anxiety, bipolar disorder, and so on. At the same time, however, several people championed a different perspective of psychology. In the wake of Maslow's theory of self-actualization and human potentials, comes

Courtesy of Martin Seligman.

FIGURE 5.15 Martin Seligman.

Martin Seligman, Ph.D. (FIG. 5.15), a renowned psychologist, who, like Maslow, opted to look at the brighter side of human potential rather than its darker side. Seligman first gained notoriety for his work on the topic of learned helplessness and the traits associated with the helpless-hopeless personality. It was this work that created the platform for his landmark theories of **positive psychology** and launched two best-selling books, *Learned Optimism* and *Authentic Happiness*. Seligman was so well respected by his colleagues for his work that he was elected president of the American Psychological Association (APA) by the widest margin in its history. It was in this position as president of the APA where he began to shift the focus of the field of psychology to include positive aspects of the human psyche. In doing so, many colleges across the country now offer courses and degree programs in this specialty.

Seligman writes in his book *Authentic Happiness*, "For the last half century, psychology has been consumed with a single topic only—mental illness." He explains further that psychosis and neurosis are rooted in rotten-to-the-core religious dogma and that over the years the field of psychology, so greatly influenced by pharmacology, became derailed in its efforts to nurture people's highest potential. By focusing on the negative aspects of human psychology, little if any limelight has been placed on those aspects that make life worth living. In an effort to move beyond a theory of happiness to a documented science that supports this theory, or what Aristotle called the "Good Life," Seligman set out to prove that positive thoughts and emotions are an inherent part of the human condition and a birthright for everyone. Moreover, it is these traits we need to cultivate, nurture, and enhance during times of stress.

According to Seligman, the field of positive psychology is based on three aspects: (1) the study of positive emotions (e.g., happiness, joy, trust, gratitude, forgiveness); (2) positive personality traits (what Seligman calls strengths and virtues); and (3) the study of positive institutions (e.g., democracy, strong families, free inquiry). Seligman believes that the time has finally arrived for a science and paradigm that seeks to understand positive emotions, build strength and nurture the virtues for optimal living, and provide a workable structure to help people achieve a balanced life. Positive psychology reveals the pathway to live in what he calls "the upper reaches of your set-point of happiness." The events of September 11, 2001, only reinforced his belief that the suffering during troubled times does not trump the understanding and building of happiness. In the preface to his book *Authentic Happiness*, Seligman shares what Hans Selye discovered in the last decade of his life: "Experiences that induce positive emotion cause negative emotions to dissipate rapidly."

One concept that Seligman expounds upon is the "happiness thermostat," an abstract emotional control made tangible through real thoughts, perceptions, memories, and personal experiences. This thermostat is one that can be programmed through our thoughts and intentions. It also can be programmed through our inherent strengths and virtues, which include wisdom and knowledge, courage, love and humanity, justice, temperance, and spirituality and transcendence.

As president of the APA, and well beyond his term in this position, Seligman has devoted much time to shifting the paradigm of Western psychology from a disease-based model to a more holistic model that includes the

Positive psychology: A field of modern psychology that focuses on three aspects: (1) positive emotions, (2) positive personality traits, and (3) positive institutions.

prevention of mental illness and a greater understanding and application of authentic happiness. Seligman's talk on positive psychology isn't just fluff. He backs up his words with research, whether it's the landmark happiness and longevity study on 180 Catholic nuns, or countless research studies on optimism. His work has also inspired others (Emmons, 2007) to explore the topic of gratitude as a pathway toward authentic happiness. Suggesting that his happiness theory has fallen short of positive psychology's potential, Seligman has revised his theory to include five measurable constructs that he describes in his new book, *Flourish*: positive emotions, engagement, relationships, a purposeful life meaning, and achievements/accomplishments. Augmenting the base of the human potential movement, Seligman now dedicates his life work to teaching others how to amplify their strengths and virtues; human assets in times of strife pay an immeasurable dividend, allowing people to enjoy the good times even more. In the words of Benjamin Franklin, whom Seligman quotes often: "The constitution only gives you the right to pursue happiness. Ultimately, you have to catch it yourself."

A Tibetan Perspective of Mind and Stress

Long before Freud coined the terms *ego* and *id*, millennia before Jung realized the importance of synchronicity, and eons before anyone ever dreamed of drugs like Prozac and Ritalin, the concept of mind (and the stress associated with it) was examined by a young man who tried to understand the nature of human existence, particularly human suffering. Today that man is referred to as the Buddha (the enlightened one), and his introspection of the human mind is studied extensively throughout the world. It is believed that the philosophy of Buddhism arrived in Tibet more than one thousand years ago. When Tibet was invaded by China in 1959, however, not only did its citizens flee to all corners of the world, but they took with them the ancient wisdom of inner peace they had practiced for hundreds of years and have now begun to share it with the world.

Desires: In the Buddhist perspective of stress, desires are conditions and expectations that are associated with goals. Desires with attachments cause stress.

Self, the (two versions, Tibetan psychology): The *Self* is the higher self or the true self; the *self* is identified as the false self or the ego-driven self.

In the past decade, many Tibetan lamas, including the Dalai Lama, have spoken and written extensively on the topic of stress as viewed through the perspective of the mind. Based on the concept of the four noble truths, suffering (stress) is believed to be a consequence of **desires** with strong attachments. In the words of the Dalai Lama, "I think there are two kinds of desire. Certain desires are positive, a desire for happiness. It's absolutely right. The desire for peace. The desire for a more harmonious world, a friendlier world. But at some point, desires can become unreasonable." Expectations, conditions, and fears associated with desires become negative, as a result of the ploys of the ego. Initially, these teachers didn't make reference to the ego. Instead, this concept was referred to as the **self** (lowercase). Over the years, however, Western vernacular has been adopted to share this message in a context that can be more easily understood.

In the acclaimed book *The Art of Happiness*, the Dalai Lama writes, "Hatred, jealousy, anger, and so on are harmful. We consider them negative states of mind because they destroy our mental happiness."

Sakyong Mipham is a Tibetan lama who was raised in India and educated in the United States. In his book *Turning the Mind into an Ally*, Mipham describes the nature and complexities of the mind and the training it takes to find a place of balance (mental stability). Laziness, procrastination, and desire are the strengths of the ego, which Mipham suggests needs taming so that the smaller mind can connect with the higher mind to reach one's full potential. Meditation is advocated as a means to "domesticate the ego" and cultivate the mind's potential.

A tamed mind, detachment from desire, and a connection to the higher mind (higher self) set the stage for healing and inner peace. Tulku Thondup is a Tibetan rimpoche (teacher) who describes stress as the mind's grasping for things that it cannot own, but merely enjoy. With a dualistic perspective, the mind creates judgments and anxiety as one differentiates between oneself and others—good from bad, rich from poor, and so on. As the mind clears itself from the limitations of ownership (attachment) and sees the oneness of everything, however, inner conflict ceases. Happiness begins, and the true nature of the collective mind is revealed.

Some Theoretical Common Ground

From these theories, we can see that the mind creates several strategies to deal with stressful stimuli. Many of these strategies fall in the realm of defenses used to protect the mind from the threat of painful or dangerous events in our lives. Whether these defenses are as specific as those described by Freud and Jung, or more general, like those described by Kübler-Ross, Frankl, Dyer, and Buscaglia, they appear to be a very real, if primitive, part of the coping process to deal with stress. When one looks at these theories, it becomes evident that self-awareness is a critical process to move beyond defensive action and into the realm of resolution (FIG. 5.16). In fact, the premise of psychotherapy is to put the client back on track through the process of self-awareness, as painful as it may be. Moving from a stance of defensive thoughts and actions toward more positive coping styles based on the strength of our inner resources is thought to be the most effective strategy to deal with stress. It is these inner resources that Maslow began to identify with his theory of self-actualization. His theory indicates that we all have the potential to move beyond the primitive defense mechanisms outlined by Freud, which stunt our human potential.

FIGURE 5.16 Stress awareness chart. Select a problem you are confronted with and ask yourself the questions suggested by each theorist.

SUMMARY

- Many theories attempt to explain the psychological nature of stress or, more specifically, how humans attempt to deal with the problems they face. These theories are based on the many aspects of psychology, including personality, emotional responses, perceptions, and a wide range of human behaviors.
- Freud believed that humans maintain a level of (instinctual) tension that arises from both internal sources (instinctual impulses) and external sources that attack our ego or identity. The ego copes with stress through the use of a host of defense mechanisms, including denial, repression, projection, rationalization, displacement, and humor.
- Jung suggested that there is a certain level of innate tension, psychic tension, which exists because of the language barrier between the conscious and unconscious minds. This tension can be reduced through the process of individuation, a continual soul searching that builds a bridge of understanding between the conscious and unconscious minds. Jung advocated self-awareness through dream analysis because he believed that the unconscious mind works to resolve issues and problems, but the conscious mind, which does not understand the language of symbols presented in dreams, tends to ignore them.
- Stress can also be aroused through the death of unmet expectations, which produces a series of mental processes described by Kübler-Ross. These are denial, anger, bargaining, depression, and acceptance. Resolution of emotional baggage leads one to the final stage, acceptance, which in turn enhances inner peace.
- Viktor Frankl's logotherapy was founded on the belief that for life to be complete there must be suffering, but that there must also be a search for the meaning of the suffering to resolve the issues of emotional stress.
- Stressors fall into two categories, according to psychologist Wayne Dyer: guilt and worry, which are two emotional states that immobilize the thought processes, distract one from the present moment, and thus make one unable to conquer stress and attain inner peace.
- Self-love is the critical inner resource described by Leo Buscaglia to cope with life's hardships. Self-love is unattainable, however, without unconditional acceptance of who you are (self-acceptance). To share love, you must first possess love.
- People who are able to achieve self-acceptance and self-love are what Abraham Maslow called self-actualized people. They are well centered, balanced, and enjoy an unparalleled appreciation of life, proving self-acceptance and self-love to be sound tools to deal effectively with stress. This chapter listed fourteen characteristics Maslow found to be common among self-actualized people. These characteristics seem to allow them to interpret situations in a nonstressful manner and buffer themselves against undue stress.
- Authentic happiness is not a gift but a birthright for all humans. Increasing one's level of happiness to balance the scale of emotions is not only possible but encouraged in this stress-filled world, according to Martin Seligman.
- Eastern philosophy (Tibetan Buddhism) explains stress as the tension between the self (ego) and the greater mind (higher self), with desired expectations and outcomes pointed to as the specific cause of this tension.
- Common themes among the theories are the concepts of self-awareness and self-acceptance, two inner resources that become the most important coping skills to manage personal stress effectively.

STUDY GUIDE QUESTIONS

1. According to Freud, what does the mind do to defend against stress?
2. According to Jung, what should the mind do to resolve stress?
3. According to Kübler-Ross, what process does the mind use to cope with stress?
4. According to Frankl, what aspect needs to be addressed in coping with stress?

5. According to Dyer, which two aspects perpetuate emotional stress?
6. According to Buscaglia, what is essential to cope with and resolve personal stress?
7. According to Maslow, what inner resources can be used to cope with stress?
8. According to Seligman, what aspect constitutes positive psychology?
9. What can be learned from the Tibetan culture about the mind and stress?
10. What do the views espoused by these theorists have in common?

REFERENCES AND RESOURCES

Baruss, I., and Mossbridge, J. *Transcendent Mind: Rethinking the Science of Consciousness*. American Psychological Association, Washington, D.C., 2017.

Briggs Myers, I. *Gifts Differing*. Consulting Psychologists Press, Palo Alto, CA, Reprint 1995.

Buscaglia, L. *Born for Love: Reflections on Loving*. Fawcett Columbine, New York, 1994.

Buscaglia, L. *Living, Loving, and Learning*. Fawcett Books, New York, 1982.

Buscaglia, L. *Love*. Fawcett Crest, New York, 1996.

Campbell, J. (ed.). *The Portable Jung*. Viking Press, New York, 1976.

Dalai Lama, H. H., and Cutler, H. *The Art of Happiness*. Riverhead Books, New York, 10th ANP ed. 2009.

Dyer, W. *Pulling Your Own Strings*. HarperCollins, New York, Reprint 2001.

Dyer, W. *Wisdom of the Ages*. Harper, New York, 1998.

Dyer, W. *Your Erroneous Zones*. 1st Harper Perennial, New York, 2001.

Dyer, W. *Your Sacred Self Make the Decision to Be Free*. HarperPaperback Books, New York, 2001.

Emmons, R. *Thanks: How the Science of Gratitude Can Make You Happier*. Houghton Mifflin, New York, 2007.

Ewen, R. *An Introduction to Theories of Personality*. Lawrence Erlbaum Associates. Mahwah, NJ, 8th ed., 2010.

Feinstein, D. Subtle Energy, Psychology's Missing Link, *Noetic Sciences Review* 64:18–23, 35, 2003.

Fetzer Institute, Scientific Research on Altruistic Love and Compassionate Love. www.fetzer.org/Programs/programs_altrusic_comp_love.htm. www.unlimitedloveinstitute.org/grant/request_proposal.html.

Frankl, V. *The Doctor and the Soul*. Knopf, New York, 1986.

Frankl, V. *Man's Search for Meaning,* Beacon Press, New York, 2006.

Freud, S. *Jokes and Their Relation to the Unconscious*. Norton, New York, 1960.

Freud, S. *Standard Edition of the Complete Psychological Works of Sigmund Freud*. Hogarth Press, London, 1986.

Gedo, J. The Enduring Scientific Contributions of Sigmund Freud, *Perspectives in Biology and Medicine* 45(2):200–212, 2002.

Hall, C. *A Primer of Freudian Psychology*. Mentor Books, Harper & Row, New York, 1999.

Johnson, S. *Research on Altruism and Love*. Temple Foundation, 2003.

Jung, C. G. *Man and His Symbols*. Anchor Press, New York, 1964.

Jung, C. G. *Memories, Dreams, Reflections*. Vintage Books, New York, 1963.

Jung, C. G. *Modern Man in Search of a Soul*. Harvest Books, New York, 1933.

Jung, C. G. *The Undiscovered Self*. Mentor Books, New York, 1958.

Kübler-Ross, E. Death Does Not Exist. In E. Brown et al., eds. *The Holistic Health Handbook*, And/Or Press, Berkeley, CA, 1981.

Kübler-Ross, E. *Death, the Final Stage of Growth*. Simon & Schuster, New York, 1988.

Kübler-Ross, E. *On Death and Dying*. Touchstone, New York, 1997.

Kübler-Ross, E. *On Life after Death*. Scribner Arts, Berkeley, CA, 2014.

Kübler-Ross, E. Personal communication. Scottsdale, AZ, January 14, 2000.

Kübler-Ross, E. *The Wheel of Life: A Memoir of Living and Dying*. Scribner, New York, 1997.

Kübler-Ross, E., and Kessler, D. *Life Lessons*. Scribner, New York, 2nd ed. 2014.

Maslow, A. H. *The Farther Reaches of Human Nature*. Penguin Books, New York, 1976.

Maslow, A. H. *Motivation and Personality,* 3rd ed. Harper & Row, New York, 1997.

Maslow, A. H. *Religions, Values, and Peak Experiences*. Penguin Books, New York, 1976.

Maslow, A. *Self-Actualization,* Esalen Lecture Series, Big Sur Tapes, Tiburon, CA, 1966 and 1972.

Maslow, A. H. Self-Actualization and Beyond. In J. F. T. Bugental (ed.), *Challenges of Humanistic Psychology*. McGraw-Hill, New York, 1967.

Maslow, A. H. *Toward a Psychology of Being,* 3rd ed. Van Nostrand Reinhold, New York, 1999.

Mipham, S. *Turning the Mind into an Ally*. Riverhead Books, New York, 2003.

Positive Psychology Center. www.ppc.sas.upenn.edu.

Restak, R. *The Brain: The Last Frontier*. Grand Central Press, New York, 2004.

Schultz, D. *Theories of Personality,* 7th ed. Wadsworth, Belmont, CA, 2013.

Scully, M. Victor Frankl at Ninety: An Interview. www.firsthings.com/ftissues/ft9504/scully.html.

Scully, M. Victor Frankl at Ninety: An Interview. *First Things*, April 1995. https://www.firstthings.com/article/1995/04/004-viktor-frankl-at-ninety-an-interview.

Seligman, M. *Authentic Happiness: Using the New Positive Psychology to Realize Your Potential for Lasting Fulfillment*. Free Press, New York, 2002.

Seligman, M. *Flourish: A Visionary New Understanding of Happiness and Well-Being*. Atria Books, New York, 2012.

Seligman, M. *Learned Optimism*. Pocket Books, New York, 2006.

Seligman, M. *Optimism and Positive Psychology*. National Wellness Institute Conference, Stevens Point, WI, 1999.

Seligman, M. *The Optimistic Child*. Mariner Books, New York, 2007.

Seligman, M. *What You Can Change and What You Can't: The Complete Guide to Successful Self-Improvement*. Vintage Books, New York, 2007.

Sperry, R. The Great Cerebral Commissure, *Scientific American* 174:42, 1964.

Thondup, T. *The Healing Power of Mind.* Shambhala Books, Boston, 1996.

Ursin, H., Baade, E., and Levine, S. *Psychobiology of Stress.* Academic Press, London, 1978.

CHAPTER 6

The Stress Emotions: Anger, Fear, and Joy

"As I walked out the door toward the gate that would lead to my freedom, I knew if I didn't leave my bitterness and hatred behind, I'd still be in prison."

—Nelson Mandela

Sandy Hook Elementary School, Virginia Tech, Ft. Hood, the Aurora, Colorado, movie theater, and Columbine High School are more than locations on a map. These places, and several others like them, have become synonymous with episodes of uncontrolled rage, senseless violence, and carnage. Though we may never know the full rationale behind these acts of violence, experts remind us that as stress continues to escalate on the national stage, this renowned list of locations across the country will likely grow to include many others.

Human nature may be slow to change, but the horror of senseless violence is never diminished. Sadly, with memories of the Great Depression and the hardship of two World Wars retreating into the background, there is a cost to forgetting the past. Sociologists have observed that the Western lifestyle has become a little too comfortable for the "Millennials." In this age of abundance, the "Entitlement Generation" has arrived for whom expectations are high, and unmet expectations generate a wellspring of unbridled stress emotions: anger and fear.

Emotional well-being, as defined in the wellness paradigm, is the ability to feel and express the entire range of human emotions and to control them, not be controlled by them. This sounds like a tall order, yet it is not impossible. It takes some unlearning, relearning, and implementation. At an early age, we are socialized to behave in a certain way. We are told to calm down, chill out, never talk back, not cry, and wipe that smile off our face. The implied message that we receive is that it is not socially acceptable to exhibit various emotions. Consequently, as adults we carry a lot of unresolved emotional baggage with us. Many health-related problems are thought to

Courtesy of Sabrina Neu.

FIGURE 6.1 Stressful situations can promote feelings of either anger or fear, or in some cases both.

be directly tied to our inability to recognize and appropriately express our emotions. There are two primary emotions especially associated with the stress response: anger, which produces the urge to fight, and fear, which promotes the urge to run and hide (FIG. 6.1). Each of these emotions has many shades and layers, which often overlap each other and allow them to coexist in the same situation. This chapter will look at both anger and fear, the dangers that await those who do not recognize these emotions consciously, the problems associated with mismanaging or being controlled by these emotions, their relationship to depression, and some helpful strategies to gain control of them.

The Anatomy of Anger

As the story goes, Cain killed his brother Abel in a fit of jealous rage. Since this early case of blatant, hostile aggression, the expression of anger has haunted men and women alike as perhaps the most uncomfortable of all human emotions. It is uncomfortable because the feelings are powerfully real, yet at the same time the hazards of expressing them can be very serious. Anger is equally uncomfortable, perhaps, because mixed messages abound as religious dogma and society's ethic advocate turning the other cheek in the face of aggression, while recent voices in the field of psychology advocate the benefits of ventilating it. Only in the past two decades have researchers begun to uncover the importance of this dark and powerful emotion and its potential relationship to coronary heart disease, as well as other serious maladies. And only recently have new behaviors been suggested as effective ways to creatively ventilate anger and thus bring about a clear resolution of frustrations to promote inner peace. This is a good thing because anger has escalated to become a national issue, including the likes of road rage, air rage, phone rage, desk rage, and sports rage.

In its most basic form, anger is a survival emotion common to all animals. Darwin referred to this as the **rage reflex**. He believed that this aggressive nature was essential to the survival of all species. While animals act instinctually to defend and protect themselves, their territory, or their young, humans have engineered the ability to combine conscious thought with the rage reflex to produce a hybrid of anger unparalleled in the animal kingdom. In that sense, human anger is a unique phenomenon. Humans are the only species that can process anger into delayed revenge and behave aggressively for seemingly inexplicable reasons. Freud, in his study of the human psyche, wrote off the rage reflex as an immutable instinct. Although he and his protégés studied acts of human aggression, Freud focused most of his attention on anxiety, an emotional state he believed could be more greatly influenced by psychotherapy. For the better part of a century, caused in large part by Freud's influence, anger was considered to be uncontrollable by conscious thought. Hence, little research was conducted in this area. Even today, in the *Diagnostic and Statistical Manual of Mental Disorders* (DSM-5), the diagnostic bible for psychiatrists and psychologists, there are few diagnoses specifically addressing anger or aggression.

In the last two decades, researchers have uncovered some myths and simple truths about this baffling emotion. One of the first myths to be revealed is that although anger is apparently a universal emotion, aggressive behavior is not instinctual in nature; that is, it is not a part of the genetic makeup of humans. For example, the Semai people of Malaysia are reported to show no aggressive behavior toward one another, rather, they display passive behavioral responses thought to be a result of resolving issues through informal group dream analysis. From this and other research reports the so-called **Seville Statement** was drafted in Seville, Spain, in 1986 by twenty prominent researchers from twelve

Rage reflex: A concept coined by Darwin that reflects the aggressive (fight) nature of all animals as a means of survival.

Seville Statement: A statement drafted in Seville, Spain, endorsing the belief that aggression is neither genetically nor biologically determined in human beings.

countries, and endorsed by the American Psychological Association. This document proclaimed that aggression is neither genetically nor biologically determined in humans. A second myth about anger regards a theory presented by Dollard et al. in 1939, which stated that aggression is a direct result of frustration. Contrary to this hypothesis, two cultures in the South Pacific—the Kwoma of Papua New Guinea and the Balinese of Bali—demonstrate withdrawal, avoidance, and fasting, not aggression, in the face of frustration. These findings reveal that aggressive behavior is only one of several possible responses to feelings of frustration.

About thirty years ago, *Psychology Today* published an article on anger, titled "The Hostile Heart," citing that the average person experiences approximately 15 situations each day that provoke an anger response. All of these episodes were found to be based on violations of unmet expectations, such as long lines at the checkout stand, car problems, a game of phone tag, or a rude driver on the way to work. Although data on the number of anger episodes per day have not been measured since, experts suggest that the number is closer to 20 to 25 per day, given the rapid acceleration of the pace of life for members of what some call the "entitlement generation" who complain repeatedly about unmet expectations (Svitil, 2006). When one considers the many emotions related to anger, including rage, hostility, frustration, jealousy, prejudice, resentment, guilt, impatience, and even fear, it becomes clear that this number of anger episodes per day is not high. It was also revealed that the expression of anger is influenced by the source of provocation, with a predominantly passive style toward figures of higher authority, and a more active style with people of equal or lower status.

Perhaps it's no coinsidence that one of the most popular video games today is Angry Birds. Typically, the manifestation of the anger response reveals the dark underside of civilization rather than the height of human achievement. Newspaper headlines and newscast sound bites are repeatedly filled with stories pointing a finger at the dangers of uncontrolled aggression. Yet despite its negative reputation, anger has a place in human interactions. First and foremost, anger is a form of communication. It reveals information about one's values and personal constructs of importance. Like other species of animals, humans communicate territorial boundaries through the expression of anger. But with humans, these territorial boundaries represent the ownership of the ideas, perceptions, values, and beliefs that constitute one's identity or ego, as well as the ownership of material possessions. In addition, the expression of anger is used to assert authority as well as to strengthen or terminate relationships. Anger also provides an incredible source of energy and physical strength that remains unparalleled when compared to the influences of other emotions. The hormonal and other metabolic processes that occur during feelings of aggression have spared several lives in the face of death, and reportedly even fueled the performance of many athletes to Olympic medals (in which case it is called "controlled aggression").

Jane Middelton-Moz is a nationally recognized therapist and author of the book *Boiling Point*. She explains that anger is a force to be reckoned with in the American culture. Road rage, sky rage (disgruntled airline passengers), and teenagers who shoot teenagers are just the tip of the iceberg of the anger phenomenon. It is her contention that the primary reason for the heightened level of anger is the loss of connection, a result of technology, poor community relations, and the illusion of the American dream.

Raising Cain is an expression to connote making trouble, but it's also the title of a book that explores the emotional life of boys. Authors Kindlon and Thompson suggest that because of social pressures, boys are not encouraged to get in touch with their emotions. Episodes of violence, which typically involve men (and sadly young boys and teenagers, too), are traced back to a series of episodes where boys learn to mask and hide their true feelings. Although boys may transfer their aggression in sports activities, not all boys take up sports. In their research, Kindlon and Thompson have found that a growing number of boys are hurt, sad, afraid, angry, and silent—not because of protective mothers, male programming, or testosterone, but rather because of the emotional miseducation of boys. Like many others, Kindlon and Thompson are advocates of **emotional literacy**, a term used to describe the awareness of emotional well-being: the ability to feel and safely express the entire range of human emotions and to control them, rather than be controlled by them.

Gender Differences

In her landmark book *The Dance of Anger*, Harriet Lerner discusses the gender differences and inequities between male and female anger styles (FIG. 6.2).

Emotional literacy: A term used in reference to one's ability to express oneself in an emotionally healthy way. Someone who routinely goes ballistic would be said to lack emotional literacy.

FIGURE 6.2 Anger knows no gender difference, yet women have been socialized not to display anger because it contradicts the image of femininity.

From her research, Lerner concluded that social mores allow men to express their anger openly and freely in public, and even encourage them to express aggression in some sports (e.g., ice hockey and football). Women, on the other hand, have been denied the same opportunity. The inability of women to express their feelings of anger has fueled much personal frustration and depression over the decades, if not centuries. According to social mores, women are supposed to be pleasant and happy, not angry, aggressive, or violent. When "temperament" is displayed by a woman, it is perceived by men (and some women) to be unfeminine, unladylike, sexually unattractive, and symbolic of evil. As a result of such cultural influences, women are less likely to express their anger. The ramifications can be dangerous to their health. In addition to the more obvious anger-related symptoms (e.g., ulcers, migraines), a study by Greer and Morris (1975) found that breast cancer is related to unresolved anger. Similar findings were cited by Mate (2011). In other surveys and questionnaires designed to study the phenomenon, virtually all women said that they feel uncomfortable, and even guilty and afraid, when anger feelings surface. Lerner also points out that even when men are cursed for their bad behavior with names such as "son of a bitch" or "bastard," it is the female gender that ultimately takes the blame, as these names indicate. Observations made by psychologist Mary Kay Biaggio (1988) indicate that men feel more comfortable with aggressiveness and tend to project their feelings onto the person who provoked them. Women, she noted, are more likely to feel shame, or direct their anger inward, which often manifests itself in physiological symptoms.

Lerner states that the greatest problem for many women is to recognize feelings of anger because these feelings are often ignored, avoided, or suppressed. Until anger can be recognized and validated, she adds, it cannot be expressed correctly.

Is there an advantage to feeling angry? Deborah Cox and colleagues (2003) think so, when one approaches anger consciously rather than irrationally. Cox picked up where Lerner's *The Dance of Anger* ends by starting the Women's Anger Project with a mission to study women's anger. She and her colleagues studied and interviewed more than one thousand women from a broad range of populations to better understand the baggage associated with unresolved anger. The conclusion: Ingrained thoughts and behavior patterns associated with dysfunctional anger must be unlearned and the energies of this emotion must be reharnessed for self-improvement. In their acclaimed book *The Anger Advantage*, Cox, Bruckner, and Stabb write, "When women attempt to get around their anger without fully acknowledging it, they lose a lot of valuable information and experiences that keep them from evolving into their full selves. When we attend to our anger, give it a place of respect in our consciousness, allow it to take shape and become spoken aloud, we increase the odds of our learning from it, growing through it, making important things happen in our lives because of it."

A significant finding by Kessler and McLeod presented in 1984 revealed not only that men and women respond to the same types of stressors differently, but also that the two genders have different stressors. It was observed that women, for example, carry an additional burden of responsibilities—and stress—in their roles as mothers and wives. The Framingham study investigated various aspects of anger in both women and men. Using a specially designed questionnaire, the Framingham Anger Scales Inventory, researchers measured anger-in (anger withheld and internalized), anger-out (the physical expression of anger toward others), anger discussed (confiding to a friend about anger), and anger-related symptoms (physical symptoms possibly brought on by anger episodes). The results were that women scored higher than men in both anger-in and anger-related symptoms.

In a similar study conducted in 1991, Thomas and Donnellan observed that the manifestation of anger-related symptoms in middle-aged women was strongly associated with a high number of daily hassles and a less-than-adequate social support system. Paradoxically, they also reported that, like women who suppress their feelings of hostility, women who habitually expressed their anger did not escape anger-related physical symptoms, specifically breast cancer. Several other empirical studies designed to uncover variations in the expression of anger between men and women show no overt differences, yet there is still a consensus that differences exist as a result of strong cultural influences. Whatever is the case, the topic of inequities in anger expression between men and women is now gaining attention as a major focus with regard to women's health issues. Just how these emotions influence the body's physiological systems and pave the path toward dysfunction is also under clinical investigation.

Physiological Responses

As might be expected, sensory stimuli that are interpreted as aggressive threats produce physiological arousal, or the stress response. Research into the physiology of anger first suggested that it triggered the release of norepinephrine because large amounts were once found in the blood during moments of intense aggression. More recent studies, however, show that norepinephrine in urine and blood samples appears in conjunction with several emotional states, not solely anger. Past attention was also focused on the role of the hypothalamus, which was thought to control emotional responses. But again, recent studies have revealed that the hypothalamus is not solely responsible for the feelings and responses associated with anger; indeed, there are several interactions involved between the hypothalamus and the higher cognitive centers of the brain.

Early studies by Albert Ax in 1953 showed that although most of the physical responses to anger and fear are similar, some are different—specifically, peripheral vasodilation. Anger produces a flushed face—a greater percentage of blood flow to the skin of the face and neck. Fear produces the opposite effect, causing the face to become pale. Studies designed to investigate the relationship between stress and disease—more specifically, emotional response and manifestations of the stress response—found that migraine headaches, ulcers, colitis, arthritis, and hypertension were a few of the ailments significantly associated with anger. But the most startling finding, presented by Friedman (1988) and Rosenman (1985), was that hostility was directly linked to the development of coronary heart disease, making this the most prominent disease-related behavioral trait.

Even though perceptions that arouse sensations of anger may bend the limits of reality, the feelings produced by those perceptions are very real. The current focus of anger research and therapy suggests that anger is within the normal range of human emotions and that feelings of anger should be recognized and validated as legitimate. Along with this validation, however, comes the responsibility to diffuse anger sensations in a healthy fashion. Problems arise when feelings of anger are either suppressed or expressed violently. Anger is considered by many psychologists to be healthy only when expressed or ventilated correctly. Yet it is now documented to be unhealthy, perhaps fatal, when improperly expressed. Herein lies the myth of anger ventilation.

The Myth of Catharsis

In perhaps the most comprehensive review of the subject of anger, social psychologist Carol Tavris described the difference between effective and noneffective catharsis, dispelling yet another myth about anger. To ventilate anger randomly is no longer thought to be therapeutic. The term **catharsis**, used by Freud to mean "purification," is a concept to describe the emptying of emotional reservoirs, such as by crying, laughing, yelling, and, in some cases, exercise. Citing several studies in which subjects were encouraged to ventilate anger as a therapeutic catharsis, Tavris concluded that randomly released feelings of anger and ventilated frustrations did not produce a healthy catharsis. To the contrary, not only did the random release of pent-up emotions not relieve feelings of aggression, but it also validated them, in effect reinforcing anger and causing even greater emotional arousal. In a study by Ebbesen, Duncan, and Konecni (1975), 100 aerospace engineers were interviewed after losing their jobs prior to the end of their 3-year contract. Their responses were compared to those of engineers who left voluntarily with no apparent grievances. Results showed that both responses to questionnaires and the chance to ventilate during interviews by those who were laid off proved to be an ineffective catharsis, resulting in greater hostility toward management (FIG. 6.3). To the surprise of many psychologists, these and similar findings by psychologist Edward Murray (1985) indicate that random, hostile expression of anger is not a suitable means of achieving emotional composure, despite popular belief to this effect.

As someone who has spent a great deal of time studying the connections among anger, Type A behavior, and health, Dr. Redford Williams cautions against feelings of unresolved anger. Williams predicts that at least

Catharsis: Emotional release through crying, yelling, laughing, and the like.

FIGURE 6.3 Recognizing one's anger is the first step toward resolving it.

20 percent of the American population has levels of hostile anger that can produce serious health problems, with another 10 to 20 percent teetering on the edge of anger-health-related issues. In his book *Anger Kills*, Williams underscores the significance of the connection between unreconciled anger and a plethora of symptoms associated with it, from ulcers to coronary heart disease. Williams notes that hostile people, as a rule, tend to be loners or lack a strong social support network, thus making their plight even more difficult. Many thoughts and feelings can surface as sarcasm, cynicism, and pessimism, and the use of these behaviors is a sure sign of unresolved issues. One way Williams recommends to deal with anger is to first make yourself aware of your thoughts, feelings, and behaviors through journaling, including the time and date of the anger episode, the thought, feeling, action, and involvement, so that patterns of behavior can be tracked and modified.

Taking note of the strong association between anger and heart disease, Joseph Sundram and colleagues at the Institute of HeartMath in Boulder Creek, California, have designed several studies to develop an understanding of the effect on the heart of the connection between stress and disease. Their findings, many of which can be found in the book *Cut-Thru* by Doc Lew Childre, speak to the importance of love, compassion, and empathy as the most effective means to defuse the anger response and reverse the physiological parameters maladapted by a closed heart.

To generate a healthy catharsis of anger, certain criteria must be met. In her book *Anger—The Misunderstood Emotion*, Tavris made the following recommendations regarding effective catharsis, all of which should be used simultaneously to resolve anger conflicts:

1. *The expression of anger must be cast in the direction of the provocation.* Tavris observed that for anger feelings to be resolved, they must be vented directly at the person or object that is perceived to violate personal space, values, or identity, not randomly. The ventilation of anger at third parties or at unrelated inanimate objects provides temporary relief but no lasting resolution.
2. *The expression of anger must restore a sense of self-control.* For anger to feel resolved, there must be a sense of justice, a vindication of the personal violation you felt, whether this means just explaining your side of the story or seeing that someone is tried in a court of law for his or her misconduct. Self-esteem must be reinstated, but not at the expense of the person you feel did you an injustice. In other words, revenge is not a viable option in anger resolution.
3. *The expression of anger must change the behavior of the provoker or provide insight to create personal resolution.* When feelings of anger are verbalized, drawn, or written out in a journal, new insights are often revealed, which can explain and give a wider perspective on the problem. Conversation with friends who act as sounding boards is also beneficial when this means of communication invites objective viewpoints. The most beneficial conversations, however, are with the person(s) with whom you share a grievance and ultimately influence toward a common understanding. In the words of Tavris, "such repeated expressions, without illumination, are not cathartic." Insight provides understanding, and understanding cultivates forgiveness (resolution).
4. *Anger must be expressed in understandable language.* When animals communicate anger there is no doubt about it; their language is direct. Humans, however, can be less than direct in their expressions of anger.

Frustrations can be candy-coated and passed over, exaggerated, or masked in deceptive retaliation, none of which is beneficial. The ventilation of anger verbally causes an immediate defensive reaction in those who are nearby. For this reason, anger must be communicated clearly but diplomatically. Psychologists suggest the use of "I" statements (e.g., I am angry because I . . .) rather than "you" statements (e.g., You really made me mad when you . . .), which are less effective in bringing about resolution. In situations where verbal communication is not possible (as with a deceased parent), some type of communication (e.g., an unsent letter) is advocated.

5. *The expression of anger must not provoke retaliation.* For a catharsis to be beneficial, it must put an end to feelings of anger on all sides. Retaliation to one or more outbursts of anger will result in ongoing battles that only perpetuate the anger cycle, making the problem(s) more difficult to resolve.

A review of the literature regarding the expression of anger shows that holding anger in is not the answer, yet neither is yelling to the wind. The expression of anger, like love, requires direct and diplomatic contact, two elements that seem rather distant if not absent when most people get angry. Rarely is anger managed correctly.

Anger Mismanagement Styles

What has become obvious from research on anger is that those who mismanage their feelings of aggression far outnumber those who express it effectively. In his acclaimed book, *Make Anger Your Ally*, describing the expression of anger, Neil Warren categorizes people into four classic anger-mismanagement types based on the behaviors they typically employ: somatizers, self-punishers, exploders, and underhanders. As you read through these four styles, see if you can recognize yourself doing these behaviors.

1. **Somatizers**: Somatizers, as the name implies (*soma* = body), present a passive behavior style that takes its toll on the body. Somatizers are individuals who choose not to express their feelings of anger overtly, but rather suppress them for fear of rejection or loss of approval by those who have caused a grievance. This management style promotes the role of martyr for those who choose it. Somatizers can also be distinguished from those employing other mismanagement styles by the fact that their suppressed anger may soon manifest as physical symptoms such as migraine headaches, ulcers, colitis, arthritis, and temporomandibular joint dysfunction (TMJD).
2. **Self-punishers**: A second passive mismanaged-anger style involves those who channel their anger into guilt. These people often get angry with themselves for getting angry at others. As a result, they deny themselves the proper outlet or catharsis of their anger. Instead, they punish themselves with control measures that, in effect, lower self-esteem. For example, overeating or deliberate starvation, excessive drinking, and sleeping and shopping can all deflate self-esteem and are displayed by self-punishers. Sadly, self-mutilation and cutting are examples of this style.
3. **Exploders**: Exploders represent the stereotype of uncontrolled aggression. These people express their anger in a hostile manner, either verbally or physically, and like a volcano they erupt, spreading their hot lava in a path of destruction toward anyone around them. These people make headline news, as was evidenced by the Virginia Tech massacre in the spring of 2007. Exploders hold in their feelings of anger and then often erupt at people or objects that have nothing to do with the cause of their frustration. Explosive behavior is sometimes displaced onto others, as when feelings of anger toward the provoker are suppressed, then released onto innocent bystanders such as employees, spouses, and children. In many cases, explosive anger is used as a form of intimidation (e.g., swearing, yelling) to maintain control over a situation or other people's emotions. Road rage is explosive behavior. It is this behavior that is considered by psychologists to be indicative of Type A personality, and the factor most closely associated with coronary heart disease.

Somatizers: People exhibiting an anger style by suppressing rather than expressing feelings of anger. *Soma* means body, and when anger is suppressed, unresolved anger issues appear as symptoms of disease and illness.

Self-punishers: People exhibiting a mismanaged-anger style by denying a proper outlet of anger, replacing it with guilt. Self-punishers punish themselves by excessive eating, exercise, sleeping, cutting, or even shopping.

Exploders: People exhibiting a mismanaged-anger style by exploding and intimidating others as a means to control them.

Stress with a Human Face

Courtesy of Brian Dalrymple.

Brian had just completed his sophomore year and, like every other college student, he was looking forward to summer vacation. The Boston waterfront is the place to be on hot summer nights, and there were many that year. But this particular summer was hot in another way, too, the likes of which Brian had never experienced. Things just seemed to get out of control. First, his summer job working construction fell through. Second, and more important, his father, to whom he was very close, was diagnosed with terminal cancer. He was given 2 months to live, a prognosis that turned out to be right on the button. Brian got angry that his summer plans, and for that matter his life plans, didn't go as expected.

To Brian, this just wasn't how it was supposed to turn out. The whole dynamics of his life changed, and there was resentment in every corner of his heart. When I saw Brian the first day of school I barely recognized him, for he seemed to have doubled his body weight in muscle mass, and his typical smile was absent. Right away he told me how difficult it can be to lose a father and become the head of a household while still a teenager. Brian was in a lot of pain. After a few minutes I thought I would change the subject and inquire about his new and improved physique. But Brian didn't want to change the subject.

"Well," he said, "I started lifting weights to take out my aggression. I'd go down to the gym every night and try to release it somehow."

"It must have worked," I replied, "Just look at you." "Yeah!" he answered. "I was really pissed." Then he paused for a moment and added, "You know, it didn't solve my problems, but it did help me work through them."

Brian had directed his feelings of anger in a way that literally augmented his strength to deal with the situation in which he found himself.

4. **Underhanders**: Like the exploder, the underhander exhibits an active style of mismanaged anger that inflicts mild abuse on individuals in his or her proximity. What separates underhanded behavior from the explosive style is that underhanders usually target their aggression toward the cause of the threat, but indirectly—in what they perceive to be socially acceptable ways (**passive-aggressive** behavior). Underhanders seek revenge for injustices to their egos and try to sabotage their "enemy" with little acts of aggression that are somewhat socially acceptable. Underhanded behavior is the most common style at the worksite. Examples include Facebook jabs, walking into a staff meeting late, and making sarcastic comments (verbal sabotage) that demonstrate the need to gain control of the aggressor. Underhanders see themselves as life's victims, and although their anger is often directed at the proper cause, resolution is rarely accomplished.

Warren points out that we each tend to employ all of these mismanagement styles at some time, depending on the situation and people involved. One style, however, becomes the dominant behavior in our personality and is used most extensively in daily interactions. It should be pointed out that none of these four behavior patterns is healthy; that is, to switch from being a somatizer to an exploder is not recommended. Warren suggests that we begin to recognize our feelings of anger, and then channel them into more creative outlets.

Underhanders: People exhibiting a mismanaged-anger style by seeking revenge and retaliation. This passive-aggressive anger style is a means to control others, but in a very subtle way.

Passive-aggressive: A mismanaged-anger style (see Underhanders) in which people seek revenge, while at the same time fronting a smile.

Creative Anger Strategies

Human anger is thought to consist of conscious thought, physiological changes, and some form of consequent behavior. Therefore, the most successful strategies to deal with anger involve cognitive coping strategies, relaxation techniques, and behavior modification to deal with these three components. Anger *should* be dealt with and reconciled. But there are both effective and noneffective ways to deal with the various shades of this emotion. The best approach is to learn a variety of ways so that one or more are available when various situations trigger the anger response in you. Based on the works of Tavris (1989), Weisinger (1985), Fleeman (2003), and Cox, Bruckner, and Stabb (2003), and in the spirit of twelve-step self-help programs to modify behaviors, the following suggestions are provided to help you learn to manage your anger more creatively:

1. *Know your anger style.* Is your anger style predominantly passive or active? Are you the type of person who holds anger in, or are you the kind of person who explodes? Are you a somatizer, exploder, self-punisher, or underhander? Become aware of what your current style of anger is. Take mental notes of what ticks you off and how you react when you get angry.
2. *Learn to monitor your anger.* Keep track of your anger in a journal, or even on a calendar. Write down the times that you get angry and what precipitates it. Are there predictable trends to your anger feelings? Ask yourself why. After several entries, look for patterns of circumstances or behaviors that lead to the "critical mass" or "boiling point" of your anger.
3. *Learn to deescalate your anger.* Rather than show an immediate response, count to ten, take a walk around the block, get a drink of water, try some deep breaths, use some mental imagery to relax—but calm down. Research shows that the anger response is initially quick, then followed by a long simmering process. Give yourself 10 to 20 seconds to diffuse, to collect and regroup your mental faculties. A great way to begin to deescalate your anger is to take a deep breath (and continue abdominal breathing for several cycles). No rational conversation can take place while you are shouting in anger. So, take a "time-out" by removing yourself from the scene momentarily to cool off. Time-outs are very helpful to validate your feelings, and at the same time get a full perspective on the circumstances. Remember, though, that a time-out must be immediately followed by a "time-in."
4. *Learn to out-think your anger.* What are some ways to resolve this feeling in a constructive way so that you and everyone involved feel better? Anger carries with it much energy. How can you best utilize this energy? Learn to construct rather than destruct.
5. *Get comfortable with all your feelings, and learn to express them constructively.* People who are most vulnerable to stress-related disease and illness are those who are unable to express their feelings openly and directly. In other words, don't ignore, avoid, or repress your feelings. Anger, especially, is like acid; it needs to be neutralized. And it is neutralized by creative (constructive) expression.
6. *Plan ahead.* Some situations can be foreseen as potential anger provocations. Identify what these situations are, and then create viable options to minimize your exposure to them. Interactions with people (e.g., family get-togethers, traffic, long lines at the post office) are especially likely to trigger anger. Try to plan your time wisely and work around situations you think will light your fuse.
7. *Develop a support system.* Find a few close friends you can confide in or vent your frustrations to. Don't force a person to become an ally; rather, allow him or her to listen and perhaps offer an insight or objective perspective your anger blinds you to. By expressing yourself to others, you can begin to process bits of information, and a clearer understanding of the situation will usually surface.
8. *Develop realistic expectations of yourself and others.* Many moments of anger surface because the expectations we place on ourselves are too high. Anger also arises when we place high expectations on others and these are not met. Learn to reappraise your expectations and validate your feelings before your top blows off. Learning to assess a situation by fine-tuning your perceptions is essential to minimizing anger episodes.
9. *Learn problem-solving techniques.* Don't paint yourself into a corner. Implement alternatives to situations by creating viable options for yourself. To do this you must be willing to trust your imagination and creativity. You must also take risks with the options you have created and trust the choices you have made. But remember that problem-solving techniques do not include retaliation.
10. *Stay in shape.* Staying in shape means balancing your mental, emotional, physical, and spiritual components of well-being. Studies show that people who are in good physical shape bounce back from anger episodes more quickly than those who are not. Exercise has been proven to be beneficial as

one step in the catharsis process, to validate feelings of anger. Eat well, exercise on a regular basis, give yourself alone-time or solitude, and learn to laugh more. Laughter is a great form of stress reduction, and it gives you a better perspective on the situation at hand. Remember, though, that although laughter is the best form of medicine, anger vented in sarcasm is neither creative nor healthy for anyone.

11. *Turn complaints into requests.* Pessimists tend to complain, whine, and moan. Anyone can complain. Complaining is a sign of victimization. When frustrated with a co-worker or family member, rework the problem into a request for change with the person(s) involved. Seek opportunities rather than problems. Take a more optimistic outlook on how you perceive situations. This will most likely aid in the request process.
12. *Forgiveness: Make past anger pass.* Learn to resolve issues that have caused pain, frustration, or stress. Resolution involves an internal dialogue to work things out within, and an external dialogue to work things out with others, done of course in a diplomatic way. Most important, learn to forgive both yourself and others. Forgiveness is an essential part of anger management. Set a "statute of limitations" on your anger, and hold to it.

There are some who say that anger and fear are two very different sides of the same coin. There are others who believe that anger is really just another shade of fear, inspired by that which generates a sense of uneasiness inside of us. Whether they are two entirely different emotions, or derived from the same source but expressed differently, they are both very real. Left unresolved, they perpetuate stress.

The Anatomy of Fear

Like anger, fear is an element of survival. In its most primitive form, fear stimulates a physical response to flee and hide from threats that are intimidating, overwhelming, and sometimes fatal. In some cases, it produces a period of inactivity known as "freezing"—or

"I spend a lot of time at the airport, trying to lose my emotional baggage."

FIGURE 6.4

the "deer in the headlights" moment. Often described as a state of anxiety, fear comes in many shades, including embarrassment, prejudice, anxiety, despair, worry, arrogance, doubt, intimidation, and paranoia, to name a few. This aspect of human behavior spurred extensive inquiry long before Freud recognized it as a purpose for therapy. Perceptions of what is intimidating or fatal are extremely individual to the person who experiences them. A large black dog, for example, can be perceived as either friendly or dangerous. Freud's theories substantiated the need to deal with human fears, and his work has paved the way for a host of anxiety-reduction therapies (FIG. 6.4). According to Freud, anxiety is an unknown fear, meaning that the individual is unaware of his or her reason for feeling anxious. More recently, many psychologists and other health professionals have used the terms *fear* and *anxiety* interchangeably, which is how they are used in this chapter as well. Like anger, chronic anxiety produces physiological adaptations created by the stress response, with a strong involvement of the immune system. Repeated episodes of fear are thought to be associated with colds, flus, warts, impotence, and, according to some research, cancer.

The current school of thought suggests that fears are not instinctual. Rather, they are a learned response from one or more exposures to an event (e.g., a third-degree burn, the death of a loved one, a poor exam grade, being jilted) that resulted in some amount of physical or emotional pain. Exposures can be either direct, as in getting stung by a wasp, or indirect, by learning through another's experiences, as in listening to horror stories or even watching TV. These exposures create a **conditioned response**, ranging from caution and apprehension to

Conditioned response: A response learned over time to a particular (negative) situation, such as displaying caution or apprehension about something perceived as stressful.

paralysis in the presence of the event that initiated it. After one or more experiences, fear can be manufactured and replicated by the imagination, and it can seem as real as any face-to-face confrontation. For this reason, anxiety is categorized as either **rational** (useful) or **irrational** (useless). Useful fears are stimulated by real events that are life-threatening and require a response to survive or avoid the threat. Conversely, irrational or useless fears are imagined, exaggerated, or distorted threats that override cognitive processes in the higher brain centers, resulting in some degree of mental, emotional, physical, or spiritual paralysis. Useless fears are illusions created by the ego. Over time, irrational fears can produce a dangerous habit of negative self-talk that feeds upon itself, creating a whirlpool of negativity that is hard to escape from. Illusory fear is the target of therapy and treatment in stress management.

In his groundbreaking books *Emotional Intelligence* and *Destructive Emotions*, author Daniel Goleman synthesizes a plethora of research and information about the emotional aspect of the human condition. As Goleman explains, whereas mental intelligence (as measured in IQ) is praised and rewarded, our emotional intelligence, the ability to feel and express the full range of human emotions, suggests a higher level of intellect than that measured by mere brain power alone. Emotions offer a different, if not superior, level of intelligence, and our ability to use our emotional skills to our greatest advantage will separate those who live a healthy life from those who are prone to disease.

As one of the basic human emotions, fear tends to dominate the emotional palette; Goleman refers to this as "emotional hijacking." Neuroscientists now indicate that one portion of the brain, the amygdala, is responsible for registering and acknowledging any fear-based stimulus. In a complicated network, neural transmissions quickly travel from one or more sensory ports (e.g., eyes) to the thalamus and on to a specific area of the cerebral cortex. Yet another impulse goes from the thalamus directly to the amygdala, which itself can arouse the stress response before the cortex can even decipher the cause of fear.

Whereas with anger there is a rush of adrenaline and with it a surge of energy, fear is a very draining emotion. The urge to hide serves as a metaphor for pulling in one's energy rather than radiating it, for whatever purpose. Worries that become chronic in nature tend to become self-defeating, says Goleman. In other words, problems, issues, and concerns do not get resolved through worry or fear. Rather, they are perpetuated by the emotional energy put into them. And Goleman is one of many people who are convinced of the stress and disease connection. He is convinced that learning to identify, empathize, and resolve our feelings (e.g., anger, anxiety, depression, pessimism, and loneliness) is in itself a necessary form of disease prevention.

In an age of terrorism, is there a good side to fear? Gavin De Becker thinks so. In fact, he calls fear "a gift." Fear, he suggests, is part of the survival dynamic, a necessary aspect of life in times of true danger. The problem arises when people get stuck in the fear mode or what he calls **unwarranted fear**. De Becker, one of the country's leading authorities on fear and violence, states that real fear is a momentary signal from the brain based on a combination of sensory information and intuition (a gut feeling) for the sole purpose of physical survival. Any sensation of fear that lasts longer than the initial signal can cause serious problems. Perpetual fear, a condition that affects millions of Americans, deafens the signal of real fear when real danger is imminent. Given the potential for terrorism in today's world and the fear associated with it, De Becker is concerned about a blanket of unwarranted fear covering the country.

Although anger is a problem in our society, so is fear, and much of our nation's fear is fueled by the media. In the Academy Award–winning documentary *Bowling for Columbine*, director Michael Moore concludes that changes approved by the Federal Communications Commission shifted the focus of news and entertainment entirely to viewer ratings. Fear brings big advertising dollars, and the reverberations of fear-based programming are reflected throughout society on a daily basis, as perhaps you've noticed.

Basic Human Fears

Virtually anything can trigger fear. However, events or situations that elicit anxiety tend to fall into one of six categories: (1) failure, (2) rejection, (3) the unknown,

Rational: A term to mean useful, as in rational fear of poisonous snakes.

Irrational: An overwhelming feeling of anxiety based on a false perception.

Unwarranted fear: Similar to an irrational fear, an instance when anxiety overcomes one's thoughts based on a nonphysical threat to one's existence.

(4) death, (5) isolation, and (6) loss of self-dominance. The complexity of anxiety, as Freud and his followers discovered, lies in the fact that many of these basic fears tend to overlap and intertwine, making the origin of some stressors difficult to isolate. But if attention is paid to identifying stressors that trigger anxiety, one basic fear will usually become evident. That is, typically one basic fear tends to dominate our perceptions of specific threats. The six categories of fears are all associated with the inability to access and utilize inner resources, resulting in low self-esteem. The following provides a description and some examples of each category:

1. **Fear of failure**: Fear of failure is associated with low self-esteem or the potential loss of self-esteem. People are more apprehensive about and less likely to try new ventures or repeat their efforts at a previously defeating task when their self-value is low. Fear of failure is a conditioned response from a past experience wherein one's performance did not meet one's own expectations. When people perceive that they have failed at something, their confidence, and thus their self-value and self-acceptance, decrease. This can become a cyclical process, paving the way for repeated failures. A bad experience in the past inhibits a person from attempting an identical or similar task again. Examples include public speaking, using a computer, taking an exam, even marriage. Maslow called this the **Jonah complex**, and it means that one is afraid to maximize one's potential. Fear of failure sets the stage for the self-fulfilling prophecy: If a person thinks he or she will not succeed at a given task, chances are he or she will not. If for some reason someone does succeed, chance and fate are given credit, not his or her own resources and talents. Failure is often associated with lack of achievement, when in reality it is caused by lack of effort—not giving something your all when called upon to do so. The flip side of fear of failure is fear of success. This occurs when people achieve success and then become frightened of "defending the title," fearing they cannot match their previous success.
2. **Fear of rejection**: Fear of rejection is also associated with low self-worth, but this fear involves your perception of how others perceive and accept you, whereas fear of failure is based solely on self-acceptance. The seeds of this fear are sown early in life, when a child seeks the approval and love of parents and figures of authority. At a young age, however, children cannot distinguish between disapproval for acts for which they are responsible (e.g., breaking a lamp) and nonrelated incidents (a parent's bad day at the office); rejection appears identical in both cases. As one matures, fear of rejection manifests itself during daily interactions with family, friends, bosses, co-workers, and acquaintances in one's environment. Circumstances in which fear of rejection may surface include negotiating a raise, asking a woman or man for a date, applying for a job, pursuing an intimate relationship, exchanging presents, submitting manuscripts to publishers, and remarrying into families with stepparents and/or stepchildren. Fear of rejection also goes by other names, including fear of intimacy and fear of commitment. Rejection becomes anxiety only when lack of approval or acceptance supports one's inner feelings of low self-esteem. Dyer associated fear of rejection with feelings of guilt and worry.
3. **Fear of the unknown**: There is great comfort in the familiar, and there can be tremendous apprehension of and intimidation by the unknown. This is one reason why many battered women stay in bad relationships and why many people stay in jobs they hate. It may seem paradoxical, but there is some degree of comfort and security even with the undesirable, while there appears to be intolerable tension with the unknown. Jung called this **misoneism**, the fear or hatred of anything new. At its worst, fear of the unknown is paralyzing. With all other basic fears, there are "known quantities" to work with and manipulate; this fear produces shades of panic caused by a lack of information. Other fears give you a visible "enemy"; fear of the unknown makes you feel defenseless. When details and sources are unavailable, security of

Fear of failure: Anxious feelings of not meeting your own expectations.

Jonah complex: A term coined by Abraham Maslow to illustrate the fear of not maximizing one's potential.

Fear of rejection: Anxious feelings of not meeting the expectations of others.

Fear of the unknown: Anxious feelings about uncertainty and future events.

Misoneism: A term coined by Carl Jung to explain the fear or hatred of anything new (fear of the unknown).

the ego begins to evaporate. Examples of this fear include vacationing in new corners of the globe, graduating from college, getting married, becoming pregnant, or getting lost while driving. In the case of a battered wife, fear of the unknown entails how to survive financially without the support of a husband. Fear of the unknown is a black hole in the wall of the ego. It may appear difficult to create a comfortable strategy for dealing with situations unknown, but it is not impossible. Methods include gaining information about the situation, and employing the inner resources of faith and self-reliance.

4. **Fear of death**: Fear of death falls into the domain of useful fears when danger is present and survival is jeopardized. But this fear becomes a useless fear when the danger is exaggerated or "fabricated out of whole cloth." The fear of death includes many phobias where death seems imminent, such as acrophobia (heights), claustrophobia (small spaces), and hydrophobia (water). In a more general sense, this fear is coupled with fear of the unknown when one contemplates the existence of an afterlife and reaches no comfortable answers. The conscious mind can't fathom life without itself, and the thought of nonexistence is less than comforting. Psychologists indicate that many people who demonstrate fear of death are excessively cautious, typically have many unresolved issues in their lives, and have many personal regrets. They may also acquire many possessions as a base of security, and feel naked without them. This fear inhibits the ability to take calculated risks. Kübler-Ross felt that fear of death was universal, but also conquerable.

5. **Fear of isolation**: Fear of isolation is the fear of being left alone, and may very well be the first fear developed in life. From the moment we enter this world, we are nurtured in the company of caregivers who address all our needs. In a baby, the absence of this nurturing presence elicits crying. Later, in adulthood, lack of quality social contact through support systems results in anxiety and depression. Just as people need quality alone-time for self-reflection, they also require human interaction and support to feel connected to other members of their community. Buscaglia notes that the absence of love does not produce fear of rejection so much as it cultivates fear of loneliness. Moreover, Harold Benjamin, founder of the Wellness Community, in his book *From Victim to Victor*, states that this fear and fear of the loss of self-dominance are the two significant fears of cancer patients.

6. **Fear of the loss of self-dominance**: This fear is exhibited when one feels the loss of control over major events and circumstances in one's life. In other words, this is a fear of loss of personal freedom. This is a predominant fear of people with substance addictions, battered wives and children, nursing home patients, and even the nation's homeless. It also surfaces when individuals contract prolonged illnesses such as cancer or AIDS. This fear is also prevalent in people whose personality type is described as learned helpless-hopeless, people who feel they have little control of their lives.

Fear, Vulnerability, and Shame

Fear takes many forms, but what is the foundation of fear? If you were to ask Professor Brené Brown, Ph.D., at the University of Houston, you would hear the word "shame." Dr. Brown has spent years doing research on the topics of vulnerability, fear, shame, empathy, and courage, but she gained national recognition when her TED Talk, "The Power of Vulnerability," went viral, with over 26 million views (and counting). In her book *Daring Greatly*, Brown explains that fear has deep roots in feelings of shame (the fear of disconnection) with thoughts, feelings, and actions. From her observations in the corporate world, where shame (the absence of connection) is as prevalent as at home and the early school years, she describes stress as the following: the fear of staying relevant in a rapidly changing world and the desire for clarity of purpose. She states, "When shame becomes a management style, engagement dies. When failure is not an option, we can forget about learning, creativity, and innovation." The opposite of shame is the alchemy of whole-heartedness and vulnerability, where self-worth and the courage to be imperfect allows complete authenticity, and fear does not exist. When vulnerability and shame are numbed, so is the ability to experience joy, happiness, and purpose in life (Brown, 2010, 2012).

Fear of death: Anxious feelings about death and the dying process.

Fear of isolation: Anxious feelings of being left alone.

Fear of the loss of self-dominance: Anxious feelings of losing control of your life.

Strategies to Overcome Fear

Because of the complexity of anxiety, several types of therapies exist to help people overcome specific fears and phobias. Although no therapy holds dominance over another, what they all have in common is the premise that the fear must be confronted at some level. Using a pure psychoanalytical approach (Freud's approach), attention is focused on uncovering childhood experiences (e.g., child molestation) that have been suppressed or repressed in the unconscious mind and are thought to be the cause of the anxiety. The length of this type of therapy is dependent on the type and severity of the anxiety. A second option is called **behavioral therapy**, based on the work of behavioral psychologist John B. Watson, where an individual engages in coping (cognitive reappraisal) and relaxation (mental imagery) techniques to desensitize himself or herself to the stressor(s) (Wolpe, 1988). Additional work by Joseph Wolpe (1992) helped clients to create a mindset that would be conducive to modifying behaviors. In **systematic desensitization** and **exposure desensitization**, clients are repeatedly exposed to their stressors, first at small and tolerable levels, and then with a systematic progression toward face-to-face confrontation with the stressor. In essence, people are taught to overcome their fears by piecemeal steps in which they always feel in control of their tolerance level.

Lufthansa Airlines offered a very successful program based on this technique for potential passengers who have a fear of flying. Such people take a course in airflight anxiety reduction, which includes visiting an airport terminal and waiting for a plane; boarding a mock plane, sitting for a short duration, and deplaning without flying; and then progressing to very short flights (Kindelbacher, 2007). Another type of behavior therapy is assertiveness training, the goal being to increase self-esteem. The greatest success with these therapies comes from awareness of the fear(s) and the stressors that produce them, proficiency in applicable coping and relaxation techniques, and the ability to confront stressors peacefully, emerging the victor, not the victim.

The HeartMath Institute provides a series of instructional biofeedback training programs in which clients are taught to control and reframe not only their thoughts, but also their emotions (both anger and anxiety), which often govern their thought processes. Based on years of well-documented research, an interactive PC software package, titled EmWave PC Stress Relief System, guides the user through a series of activities that, in essence, opens the heart to resolve anxiety- and anger-related issues that affect the mind, body, and spirit (www.HeartMath.org).

Here is a closing thought on fear from the celebrated Sufi poet Hafiz: "Fear is the cheapest room in the house. I would much prefer to see you living under better conditions."

Behavioral therapy: A therapy based on the work of John B. Watson, in which coping and relaxation techniques are used to desensitize oneself to stress.

Systematic desensitization: A process of learning to destress from something in small, manageable stages.

Exposure desensitization: A process of learning to destress from something by brief, yet safe, encounters with the stressor.

Depression: A state of mind where thoughts are clouded by feelings of despair. Physiologists suggest that depression is caused by a chemical imbalance; psychologists suggest that depression is the result of unresolved stress emotions (anger turned inward).

Depression: A By-Product of Anger or Fear?

It would be erroneous to assume that anger and fear are the only two emotions associated with stress. There are, in fact, many others, but they all appear to be linked, either directly or indirectly, to anger and/or fear. One emotion that surfaces as a result of unresolved stress is depression.

Overwhelming sadness. The blues. Eternal darkness. Shuffling underwater. Prolonged grieving. Deep heaviness. Melancholy. Just like anger and fear, **depression** goes by several names and descriptions. With estimates from the Centers for Disease Control and Prevention that more than one-quarter of the American public is on medication for depression, this topic certainly merits more attention than a passing comment. Depression is the silent face of stress. And depending on who you talk to, there seem to be many causes of mood swings, from high-carbohydrate diets and traumatic childbirth to hormonal imbalances and poor brain chemistry. What is often overlooked are stressful events that precede each bout of depression.

Although it's true that no one word seems to adequately describe this emotional state, many of the following symptoms are common to those who share this feeling:

- Persistent sadness or empty moods
- A loss of interest or pleasure in activities
- Lethargic moods with decreased productivity

- Loss of appetite and weight loss or overeating and weight gain
- Difficulty concentrating, remembering, or making decisions
- Pervading hopelessness in personal and professional lives
- Alcohol and drug use to cope with problems
- Thoughts of death and suicide to "resolve" issues

Depression is a lot more than just brain chemistry. And although Prozac, Paxil, and Zoloft may work to alleviate the imbalance in serotonin, norepinephrine, and dopamine levels in the brain, in the words of author Susan Skog, "a chemical cure cannot heal emotional wounds." For many people, pharmacological aids have worked wonders; however, given the complexity of depression, the best approach is a holistic one.

Those who have studied this emotion describe depression as "anger turned inward." Experts now agree that unresolved anger issues, however long they have been lingering in the psyche, are essential to resolve for the clouds of depression to lift and clear.

Although it is common to feel down in the dumps at times, to be locked into this emotion for prolonged periods, to the exclusion of all others, is neither normal nor healthy. Some type of intervention is needed to reestablish a balance between the positive and negative feelings generated by daily life so as to regain emotional well-being. Psychotherapeutic intervention to treat depression includes many coping and relaxation techniques. For example, several studies have shown that physical exercise results in a less depressed state of mind. In a literature review on the topic of exercise and depression, authors Gill, Womack, and Sanfranek (2010) reported that, indeed, exercise decreases patient-perceived symptoms of depression, with a combination of high-frequency, light-resistance exercise and aerobic exercise offering the best results. T'ai Chi and yoga were also noted to decrease symptoms of depression. In an article titled "Exercise Against Depression" (1998), authors Artal and Sherman state that exercise plays a significant role in the treatment of depression. Similar results have been observed following the use of St. John's wort, nutrition therapy (decreasing simple sugars), music therapy, art therapy, and humor therapy. These same techniques are equally effective for individuals who find themselves occasionally "under the weather" after a stressful day, and may in fact help move them toward a peaceful resolution of their stress.

Joy, Eustress, and the Art of Happiness

Fear and anger may be the most recognized, if not most common, stress emotions, but let us not forget that there is another emotion associated with stress: joy and happiness, also known in stress circles as eustress. The emerging field of positive psychology has placed joy and happiness as a big X on the psychological treasure map. The search for happiness has begun in earnest in all corners of the globe. A quick look at the titles in the self-help section of any bookstore or on Amazon.com, from authors including the Dalai Lama, Harvard professors, and HBO comedians, reveals that the pursuit of happiness is a hot commodity in the age of twenty-first-century stress.

Simply stated, joy is the antithesis of distress. Although some researchers in the field of positive psychology insist that joy is the anticipation of an event, spiritual luminaries suggest that happiness is a state of living in the present moment. Happiness, however, isn't just a psychological issue. It appears to be a leading economic indicator as well, which may explain why experts in the field of economics also contribute significant amounts of research to the happiness data collection. Interestingly, the Asian country of Bhutan measures its country's growth not just in GDP (gross domestic product) but GDH (gross domestic happiness). Other countries, such as England and France, are considering similar measures. There is even a world database of happiness in Rotterdam, the Netherlands (http://worlddatabaseofhappiness.eur.nl/).

Is happiness a function of nature or nurture? Experts suggest that it's a combination of both, but that each of us has the ability to nurture the nature of our happiness, hence bringing a sense of emotional balance to our lives (FIG. 6.5).

What do scientific studies tell us about happiness? Researchers have looked at all kinds of indices, such as stress hormones, neuropeptides, cardiac activity, facial coding (smiles per day), creative pursuits, nutritional diets, and spending habits. The following are some conclusions from the current research on joy and happiness, known in research circles as "subjective social well-being."

- Until people's basic needs are met (food, clothing, shelter, income), happiness is elusive (Graham, 2010).
- There is a strong correlation between happiness and trust. If trust is lacking, happiness is non-existent. Trust is a prerequisite for happiness (Robinson, 2008).

FIGURE 6.5 The search for happiness and joy begins inside, cultivating and focusing on pleasant thoughts and perceptions. Creating a pleasurable environment and surrounding yourself with happy people and friends also helps to cultivate feelings of eustress.

- Serotonin, a neurotransmitter, seems to be a chemical by-product of feeling happy. (A lack of serotonin is associated with depression, hence the name the "happiness hormone" given to serotonin.) Carbohydrates may increase serotonin levels, but carbohydrates do not necessarily make one happy (Sommers, 1999).
- Having choices (freedom) makes people happy to a point, after which too many choices make people feel overwhelmed and eventually stressed (Nauert, 2006).
- Money does not equate with happiness, but poverty can promote stress (Deaton, 2008).
- There is a strong correlation between happiness and the ability to be creative, according to findings by Harvard researcher Teresa Amabile (2005).
- Fulfilling relationships are the cornerstone to lifelong happiness (Buettner, 2010).
- The happiest people aren't always found living on tropical islands. Eric Weiner, the author of the best-seller *The Geography of Bliss*, states that people in Iceland, Denmark, Sweden, Holland, and Switzerland rank as some of the happiest people on the planet (the people of Moldova ranked last).
- There may be a genetic component to happiness, yet one's environment can either increase or decrease one's general disposition. Cultural distractions and ego (i.e., technology, emails, text messages, Facebook posts) where one can easily compare his or her life with others may reduce happiness (Kluger, 2013).

Happiness may be many things to many people, and there may be many things that cause one to be happy, including wealth, a quality standard of living, and great relationships, but research suggests that trust, more than income, fame, or even health, is the biggest factor in determining happiness (Weiner, 2008). Happiness has proven to be quite popular as a field of study, though rather than referring to happiness the scientific term is "psychological wealth." According to many sources, creativity is also a significant factor of happiness; when people are busy creating art, apps, gardens, music, film, or any other creative work, the act of creation promotes true happiness. Conversely, one of the greatest sources of unhappiness is isolation (a common occurrence in the cyber-filled world we live in).

Health is also an essential criteria for happiness, and we now have data to prove it. In 1938, researchers at Harvard University designed and ran a longitudinal health study, which continues to this day. It has become known as the Harvard Happiness Study. Initially, 724 men were enrolled in the study, including Harvard students and various people from the Boston area. Initial data were drawn from personal interviews, medical records, and conversations with wives. About 60 of the initial participants are still alive. In a popular TED Talk, researcher Robert Waldinger explains that the study's findings, although not necessarily groundbreaking, nevertheless prove quite validating with regard to happiness and longevity and health. Simply stated: Happiness is love and love reveals itself in social connections, whereas isolation becomes toxic and kills.

In the continual debate between nature and nurture on the human condition, research indicates that both play a vital role in one's state of happiness, yet a third factor—consciousness—also plays a pivotal role (Nichols, 2014). In what is now being referred to as "happiness baselines," current research suggests that the alchemy of happiness is composed of three aspects: genetics, circumstances, and one's choices. Genetics (nature) is responsible for 50 percent of one's happiness. Circumstances (nurture) are associated with 10 percent, and the remaining 40 percent is greatly influenced by the choices we make and the actual practice of being happy (Nichols, 2014). This suggests that happiness, as a perception, is greatly influenced by our choice of thoughts. Ryan Howell, an assistant professor at the San Francisco State University, advocates the philosophy of Aristotle, noting that there are two kinds of happiness.

The first is commonly referred to as "Hedonistic happiness" (short-term happiness based on short-term pleasures). The second type of happiness is referred to as "eudemonic happiness," and is derived from working toward a greater life purpose (Chopra, 2014; Nichols, 2014).

Finally, March 20 is International Happiness Day, but don't relegate it to one day, try to celebrate good stress every day.

First and foremost, happiness is a perception—a thought combined with an emotion generated from within. Money, cars, clothing, food, or vacations in Tahiti may seem to promote happiness, but the real measure of happiness is your attitude—your ability to appreciate these things. In the words of Abraham Lincoln, "People are about as happy as they make their minds up to be."

SUMMARY

- Anger and fear are two sides of the same coin. Both emotions are triggered by stimuli perceived to be a threat at a physical, mental, emotional, or spiritual level, or perhaps a combination of these.
- Feelings of anger initiate the fight response to defend oneself and the components that constitute one's identity.
- Fear triggers the flight response, which makes one want to run and hide.
- Both anger and fear are thought to be survival emotions, yet when conscious thoughts are combined with these innate reflexes, feelings are magnified rather than resolved, leading to an unbroken cycle of stress.
- Social factors may play a significant role in the different anger-management styles of men and women. Women are often flooded with feelings of guilt after tempers flare; men demonstrate anger in more overt ways.
- There are several myths regarding the emotion of anger, the most common being that any type of ventilation producing a catharsis is healthy. However, research reveals that undirected ventilation only validates and perpetuates feelings of anger.
- People who do not ventilate anger correctly are categorized as one of four mismanaged-anger types: somatizer, self-punisher, exploder, or underhander.
- Current stress-management programs are introducing courses in creative anger management to change anger-generated thoughts and feelings into constructive energies that work toward peaceful resolution.
- Fear is based on an actual or vicarious exposure to physical or emotional pain. Those fears that enable a person to avoid life-threatening situations are called useful fears, while those that are exaggerated and immobilize the individual are deemed useless fears. It is the latter, irrational fears that are targeted for change.
- Fear is now recognized as a gut feeling that occurs seconds before physical danger. Anything after that is unwarranted fear.
- Basic human fears include failure, rejection, the unknown, death, isolation, and loss of self-control. Most anxieties can be placed in one of these categories.
- The most effective way to dissolve fear is to confront it. One way to do so is through a technique called systematic desensitization, where the stressor is confronted piecemeal to build a psychological immunity to it.
- The road to resolution for both anger and fear is not difficult, yet it is often avoided, resulting in mismanaged styles of anger and fear and consequent physical ailments.
- Left unresolved, both anger and fear can sow the seeds of depression, an emotional state that may require therapy.
- Several strategies, involving both coping and relaxation techniques, are recommended to express anger and fear in a healthy fashion and to control these emotions for optimal well-being.
- Joy and happiness are the eustress emotions. The field of positive psychology has illuminated these two emotions as vital aspects of life, necessary for emotional balance.

STUDY GUIDE QUESTIONS

1. Describe the emotion of anger (the fight response).
2. In what ways is anger mismanaged?
3. What are ways to help cope with, manage, and resolve anger feelings?
4. Describe the emotion of fear (the flight response).
5. In what ways does fear become manifested as stress?
6. Describe one or more ways to cope with, manage, and resolve fear or anxiety.
7. Explain eustress as a means to achieve emotional balance.
8. Describe the two kinds of happiness.

REFERENCES AND RESOURCES

Agentur Texter-Millott. *Seminars for Relaxed Flying*. www.flugangst.de/en/prim00/00.php3.

Amabile,T., et al. Affect and Creativity at Work, *Administrative Science Quarterly* 50:367–403, 2005.

Amen, D. G., and Routh, L. *Healing Anxiety and Depression*. Putnam, New York, 2003.

Archer, J. *The Behavioral Biology of Aggression*. Cambridge University Press, Cambridge, 2009.

Artal, M., and Sherman, C. Exercise Against Depression, *Physician and Sports Medicine* October: 55–60, 1998.

Ax, A. F. The Physiological Differences Between Fear and Anger in Humans, *Psychosomatic Medicine* 15:433–442, 1953.

Baumeister, R., Smart, L., and Boden, J. Relation of Threatened Egotism to Violence and Aggression: *The Dark Side of Self-Esteem, Psychological Review* 103(1):5–33, 1996.

Benjamin, H. *From Victim to Victor*. Dell Publishing, New York, 1989.

Biaggio, M. *Sex Differences in Anger: Are They Real?* Paper presented to the American Psychological Association, Atlanta, Georgia, 1988.

Bramson, R. *Coping with Difficult People*. Dell, New York, 1988.

Breakey, P. The Entitlement Generation Expects All. *DailyStar*, July 2, 2005. www.thedailystar.com/news/stories/2005/07/02/gen1.html.

Britten, R. *Fearless Living*. Perigee Books, Berkeley, CA, 2002.

Brown, B. *Daring Greatly*. Avery Books, New York, 2012.

Brown, B. The Power of Vulnerability. TED Talk, June 2010. https://www.ted.com/talks/brene_brown_on_vulnerability?language=en.

Buettner, D. *Thrive: Finding Happiness the Blue Zone Way*. National Geographic Society, Washington, DC, 2010.

Buscaglia, L. *Love*. First Ballantine Books, New York, 1996.

Childre, D., and Rozman, D. *Transforming Anger*. New Harbinger Publications, Oakland, CA, 2003.

Childre, D. L. *Cut-Thru*. Planetary Publishing, Boulder Creek, CA, 1996.

Chopra, D. Two Kinds of Happiness (One Is Bad for You). October 3, 2014. https://www.linkedin.com/pulse/20141003223344-75054000-two-kinds-of-happiness-one-is-bad-for-you.

Cox, D., Bruckner, K., and Stabb, S. *The Anger Advantage*. Broadway Books, New York, 2003.

Dalai Lama. *The Art of Happiness*, 10th anniversary ed. Riverhead Press, New York, 2009.

Dalai Lama. *Healing Anger—The Power of Patience from a Buddhist Perspective*. Snow Lion Publishers, New York, 1997.

Deaton, A. Income, Health, and Well-Being Around the World: Evidence from the Gallup World Poll, *Journal of Economic Perspectives* 22:2, 2008.

De Becker, G. *The Gift of Fear*. Dell Books, New York, 1999.

Dentan, R. K. *The Semai—A Nonviolent People of Malaysia*. Thompson Custom Publishing, New York, 2002.

Dollard, J. R., et al. *Frustration and Aggression*. Praeger, Westport, CT, 1980.

DuPont, R. *Phobia*. Brunner/Mazel, New York, 1982.

Ebbesen, E., Duncan, B., and Konecni, V. Effects of Content of Verbal Aggression on Future Verbal Aggression: A Field Experiment, *Journal of Experimental Social Psychology* 11: 192–204, 1975.

Engel, B. *Honor Your Anger*. John Wiley & Sons, New York, 2004.

Esler, G. *United States of Anger: The People and the American Dream*. Penguin Books, New York, 1997.

Fleeman, W. *Pathways to Peace: Anger Management Workbook*. Hunter House, Alameda, CA, 2003.

Friedman, M. *Overcoming the Fear of Success*. Warner Books, New York, 1988.

Gilbert, D. *Stumbling on Happiness*. Vintage Press, New York, 2007.

Gill, A., Womack, R., and Safranek, S. Clinical Inquiries: Does Exercise Alleviate Symptoms of Depression? *Journal of Family Practice* 59(9):530–531, 2010.

Glassner, B. *The Culture of Fear: Why Americans Are Afraid of the Wrong Things*. Basic Books, New York, 2009.

Goldstein, A. *Agress-less: How to Turn Anger and Aggression into Positive Action*. Prentice-Hall, New York, 1982.

Goleman, D. *Destructive Emotions: A Scientific Dialogue with the Dalai Lama*. Bantam Books, New York, 2003.

Goleman, D. *Emotional Intelligence: Why It Can Matter More Than I.Q.* Bantam Books, New York, 1997.

Goodwin, D. *Anxiety*. Oxford University Press, New York, 1986.

Graham, C. *Happiness Around the World: The Paradox of Happy Peasants and Miserable Millionaires*. Oxford University Press, Oxford, England, 2010.

Greer, S., and Morris, T. Psychological Attributes of Women Who Develop Breast Cancer: A Controlled Study, *Journal of Psychosomatic Research* 19:147–153, 1975.

Handly, R., and Neff, P. *Beyond Fear*. Fawcett Crest, New York, 1991.

Harbin, T. J. *Beyond Anger: A Guide for Men: How to Free Yourself from the Grip of Anger and Get More Out of Life*. Marlow & Company, New York, 2000.

Haynes, S., et al. The Relationship of Psychosocial Factors to Coronary Heart Disease in the Framingham Study, I. Methods and Risk Factors, *American Journal of Epidemiology* 107:362–383, 1978.

Howell, R. T. Train Your Brain to Spend Smarter. Beyond the Purchase, August 1, 2014. www.beyondthepurchase.org/blog/.

Institute of HeartMath. *Homepage*. www.heartmath.org. Accessed February 26, 2008.

Jung, C. G. *Man and His Symbols*. Dell Press, New York, 1968.

Kessler, R., and McLeod, J. Sex Differences in Vulnerability to Understand Life Events, *American Sociological Review* 46:443–452, 1984.

Kindelbacher, B. Personal conversation, November 10, 2012.

Kindlon, D., and Thompson, M. *Raising Cain: Protecting the Emotional Life of Boys*. Ballantine Books, New York, 2000.

Kluger. J. The Happiness of Pursuit. *Time*. 24-32. July 8, 2013.

Kübler-Ross, E. *Death: The Final Stage of Growth*. Touchstone Books, New York, 1988.

Lazarus, R. *Stress and Emotions*. Springer, New York, 1999.

Lerner, H. G. *The Dance of Anger*. 1st Perennial Currents, New York, 2005.

Lyon, L. Taking a Bite Out of Anger, *U.S. News and World Report*, December 17, 2007:66.

Martinsen, E. W. Benefits of Exercise for the Treatment of Depression, *Sports Medicine* 9(6):219–231, 1985.

Maslow, A. H. *The Farther Reaches of Human Nature*. Arkana, New York, 1993.

Mate, G. *When the Body Says No: Understanding the Stress– Disease Connection*. John Wiley & Sons, New York, 2011.

McEwen, B. *The End of Stress as We Know It*. Dana Press, Washington, DC, 2002.

McKay, M., Rogers, P., and McKay, J. *When Anger Hurts: Quieting the Storm Within*. New Harbinger Publications, Oakland, CA, 2003.

Middelton-Moz, J. *Boiling Point: The High Cost of Healthy Anger to Individuals and Society*. Health Communications, Deerfield Beach, FL, 1999.

Middelton-Moz, J. *Boiling Point: The Workbook*. Health Communications, Deerfield Beach, FL, 2000.

Mogg, G. *Creative Anger Management*. American University, Washington, DC, 1992.

Moore, M. *Bowling for Columbine*. Michael Moore Productions, 2002.

Murray, E. Coping and Anger. In T. Field, P. McCabe, and N. Schneiderman (eds.), *Stress and Coping*, Erlbaum, Hillsdale, NJ, 1985.

Naiman, L. Happiness, *Creativity at Work Newsletter*, May 2007. www.creativityatwork.com/blog/2007/05/28/creativity-at-work-newsletter-happiness/.

Nauert, R. Does Freedom of Choice Ensure Happiness? *PsychCentral*, July 18, 2006. http://psychcentral.com/news/2006/07/18/does-freedom-of-choice-ensure-happiness/101.html.

Neale, R. E. *The Art of Dying*. Harper & Row, New York, 1977.

Nichols, W. *Blue Mind*. Bantam Books, New York, 2014.

Nuckols, C., and Chickering, B. *Healing an Angry Heart: Finding Solace in a Hostile World*. Health Communications, Deerfield Beach, FL, 1998.

Prinzivalli, S. How Not to Be Offended. The Unbounded Spirit, 2016. http://theunboundedspirit.com/how-not-to-be-offended/.

Reed, G. L., and Enright, R. D. The Effects of Forgiveness Therapy on Depression, Anxiety and Posttraumatic Stress for Women After Spousal Emotional Abuse, *Journal of Consulting and Clinical Psychology* 74(5): 920–929, 2006.

Reich, J. The Epidemiology of Anxiety, *Journal of Nervous and Mental Disease* 174(3):129–136, 1986.

Robinson, J. Happiness Flows from Trust, *National Post*, October 24, 2008. www.nationalpost.com/story.html?id=906300.

Rosenman, R. H. Health Consequences of Anger and Implications for Treatment. In M. A. Chesney and R. H. Rosenman (eds.), *Anger and Hostility in Cardiovascular and Behavioral Disorders*, Hemisphere, Washington, DC, 1985.

Santella, A. All the Rage. *Utne Reader*, November 2007: 36–41.

Schimelpfening, N. Depressed Women at Greater Risk for Breast Cancer. http://depression.about.com/health/depression/library/weekly/aa100300.htm.

Schwartz, G. E., Weinberger, D. A., and Singer, J. A. Cardiovascular Differentiation of Happy, Sad, Anger, and Fear Following Imagery and Exercise, *Psychosomatic Medicine* 43:343–364, 1981.

Segal, J. *Living without Fear*. Ballantine Books, New York, 1989.

Serotonin—The Molecule of Happiness, *HubPages*. http://hubpages.com/hub/Serotonin-The-Molecule-of-Happiness.

Shekelle, R., et al. Hostility and Risk of CHD, and Mortality, *Psychosomatic Medicine* 45:109–114, 1983.

Skog, S. *Depression: What Your Body's Trying to Tell You*. Avon, Whole Care Books, New York, 1999.

Snyder, C. R., and Heinze, L. S. Forgiveness as a Mediator of the Relationship Between PTSD and Hostility in Survivors of Childhood Abuse. *Cognition and Emotion*, 19(3):413–431, 2005.

Sommers, E. *Food and Mood*. Henry Holt, New York, 1999.

Sundram, J. *Re-engineering the Human System: The Physiology of Conscious Evolution*. Institute of Noetic Sciences, 5th Annual Conference, Boca Raton, FL, July 18–21, 1996.

Sussman, V. To Win, First You Must Lose, *U.S. News and World Report*, January 15, 1990.

Svitil, K. *Psychology Today: Calming the Anger Storm*. Alpha/Penguin Books, New York, 2006.

Tavris, C. *Anger–The Misunderstood Emotion*. Touchstone, New York, 1989.

Thomas, S., and Jefferson, C. *Use Your Anger: A Woman's Guide to Empowerment*. Pocket, New York, 1996.

Thomas, S. P., and Donnellan, M. M. Correlates of Anger Symptoms in Women in Middle Adulthood, *American Journal of Health Promotion* 5(4):266–272, 1991.

Warren, N. *Make Anger Your Ally: Harnessing Our Most Baffling Emotion*. Living Books, New York, 1999.

Weiner, E. *The Geography of Bliss*. 12 Books, New York, 2008.

Weisinger, H. *Weisinger's Anger Work-Out Book*. William Morrow, New York, 1985.

Williams, R., and Williams, V. *Anger Kills*. Harper-Perennial, New York, 1994.

Williams, R. B., et al. Type A Behavior, Hostility, and Coronary Atherosclerosis, *Psychosomatic Medicine* 42: 539–549, 1980.

Witvliet, C. Surprised by Happiness, *Huffington Post*, November 25, 2010. www.huffingtonpost.com/charlotte-vanoyen-witvliet-phd/surprised-by-happiness-wh_b_787126.html.

Wolpe, J. *The Practice of Behavior Therapy*. 4th ed., Allyn: Bacon, New York, 1992.

Wolpe, J., and Wolpe, D. *Life without Fear*. New Harbinger Publications, Oakland, CA, 1988.

Wood, C. The Hostile Heart, *Psychology Today* 20:9, 1986.

World Database of Happiness. http://worlddatabaseofhappiness.eur.nl/.

Worthington, E. L., Jr., and Scherer, M. Forgiveness Is an Emotion-Focused Coping Strategy That Can Reduce Health Risks and Promote Health Resilience: Theory, Review and Hypotheses. *Psychology and Health* 19(3): 385–405, 2004.

Zane, M., and Milt, H. *Your Phobia*. American Psychiatric Press, Washington, DC, 1984.

CHAPTER 7

Stress-Prone and Stress-Resistant Personality Traits

Happiness is a decision. . . . Optimism is a cure for many things.

—Michael J. Fox

In the summer of 1966, at the age of 55, Nien Cheng (FIG. 7.1) was placed under house arrest in her private home in Shanghai. It was the dawn of the Cultural Revolution in Mao Tse-Tung's communist China. Thousands of innocent people found themselves incarcerated, political prisoners accused of being enemies of the state. Educated in London, employed by Shell Oil as a management advisor, and widow of a former official of Chiang Kai-shek, Nien Cheng quickly became the target of several communist indictments. She was soon moved from house arrest to solitary confinement, in a cell no bigger than a walk-in closet, at the Number 1 Detention House for political prisoners. Convinced she had committed no crime, she defended her innocence despite hunger, disease, intimidation, terror, and humiliation. Many innocent prisoners perished from the torture of the communist Red Guards, yet Nien Cheng was determined not merely to survive but to prove her innocence. Upon her release in 1972, after six and a half years in solitary confinement, she was declared a victim of false arrest. At this time, she frantically sought the whereabouts of her only daughter. What she discovered about the fate of Meiping Cheng made it impossible for her to remain in her homeland. In 1980, Nien Cheng emigrated to North America, whereupon she wrote of how she prevailed over this tumultuous experience in her stirring autobiography, *Life and Death in Shanghai*. As a guest speaker in my Strategies for Stress Reduction class, Mrs. Cheng was asked what it was that allowed her to survive such a harrowing ordeal. Gracefully, she answered, "I saw my stay at the detention house as a challenge, and with the grace of God, I was committed to proving my innocence." She left no doubt that she demonstrated a special personality in surviving her ordeal.

Until her death in 2009 at age 94, Nien Cheng practiced T'ai Chi ch'uan daily and stayed current with world events. In my last conversation with her, in which she reflected back on that time in prison as well as present-day events, she said, "Patience is an important aspect of survival, as is faith. The pace of the world has become quite fast today.

FIGURE 7.1 Mrs. Nien Cheng was falsely imprisoned at age 56 for six and a half years during the rule of Mao Tse-Tung. She credited her survival to many factors, including commitment to her innocence and patience, which helped her cope with a grueling ordeal.

Please tell your students how important it is to employ these inner resources."

Many words can be used to describe the likes of Nien Cheng and others who express the epitome of the triumph of the human spirit—Nelson Mandela, Rosa Parks, and the scores of unsung heroes, who grace the Facebook feeds, have overcome great adversity to declare victory and move on with their lives. That word is resiliency. Resiliency is the new catchphrase in corporate stress management circles. It is also the new buzzword in military training, where soldiers and military officers are being taught skills to cope with stress both on the battlefield and in the transition back to civilian life. The most common definition of resiliency is to bounce back from crisis. The people we call heroes share a common personality trait: resiliency. For some it's innate, for most it's learned.

Although almost everyone has a concept of what personality is, scholars in the field of psychology have yet to agree on a definition of the term. The word originally derives from the Latin word *persona*, meaning mask, as in the masks used by actors in ancient Greek plays. In more contemporary times, personality has come to mean a conglomeration of several characteristics—behaviors, expressions, moods, and feelings—that are perceived by others. The complexity of one's personality is thought to be shaped by genetic factors, family dynamics, social influences, and a wealth of personal experiences. Just as there are many definitions, so there are also many theories of personality that attempt to explain the differences in the psychological make-up from one person to another. The basis of many of these theories centers on whether these traits and behaviors are primarily innate or learned—the nature versus nurture question. No clear-cut answers have emerged, and whether personality can actually be changed is still being argued. The research findings are fascinating but quite inconclusive. Can you change your personality? Like the ability to improve your IQ, the answer seems to be yes! Pessimists can become optimists. Curmudgeons can learn to laugh regularly. Introverts can abandon shyness. Addicts can remain drug free. Currently, a growing body of opinions suggests that the most likely components of one's personality to be alterable are behaviors and traits associated with these behaviors. By changing various personality traits, one can change one's personality. It is this consensus that has led to the formation of, and emphasis on, behavior modification, counseling, and classes in health promotion programming, including stress management.

The story of Nien Cheng is a remarkable testimony to the strength of the human spirit. It is this characteristic, as well as many others, that psychologists and psychiatrists have attempted to study to determine which personality types are prone to suffering the effects of stress, and which seem to be immune or resistant to it. Although the search has not been easy, researchers have identified specific personality traits and behaviors, classified as personality types, that have begun to shed some light on the relationship between personality and disease. They include Type A behavior, codependent personality, helpless-hopeless personality, hardy personality, survivor personality, and sensation seeker or Type R personality. As people strive to learn more about themselves, these labels have now become household words in North America. What follows is a look at these personality types and the factors that separate stress-prone from stress-resistant traits and behaviors.

Type A Behavior

In the late 1950s, coronary heart disease emerged as the number one killer in the country, claiming the lives of many men and women, including several politicians, physicians, and executives of the nation's leading corporations. Unlike infectious diseases initiated by viruses and bacteria, this disease was attributed to factors associated with specific lifestyle behaviors and, therefore, was recognized as being potentially preventable. During the Eisenhower and Kennedy administrations this "epidemic" was given national attention, and federal funds were appropriated for research to understand the nature of this disease. Like detectives at the scene of a murder, federally funded researchers searched for potential clues that might lead to the development of this killer disease. Studies conducted at Harvard University and the Framingham Study in Massachusetts revealed several factors that were believed to place an individual at risk for coronary heart disease, including cigarette smoking, hypertension, elevated levels of cholesterol and triglycerides, inactivity, diabetes, obesity, and family history of heart disease. Surprisingly, data also revealed that several heart attack victims had few, if any, of these risk factors. So the search went on.

Although assumptions had previously been made about the seemingly obvious relationship between emotional responses and health status, it was the initial work of cardiologists Meyer Friedman and Ray Rosenman whose research in 1964 added one more significant risk factor to the list: **Type A personality**, or a rushed or hurried lifestyle. As the story goes, they stumbled upon this insight while having their office furniture reupholstered, during which they discovered that their patients literally sat on the edge of the chairs while waiting to be seen. This tip led them to look at the psychological profiles of their patients, as well as the usual physical assessments. From their research, they developed an assessment tool to diagnose Type A behavior, called the Structured Interview. This interview process between the trained physician and patient was designed to measure the intensity, frequency, and duration of several criteria associated with Type A behavior. Later, a second assessment questionnaire, based on Friedman and Rosenman's work, was developed by psychologist David Jenkins and called the Jenkins Activity Questionnaire (JAQ). Because of its simplicity—individuals can fill it out on their own—the JAQ has been used more often than the Structured Interview to assess Type A behavior.

Type A personality: This personality, once associated with time urgency, is now associated with unresolved anger issues.

Time urgency: A characteristic or behavior of someone who displays Type A personality, someone who is constantly time conscious.

Polyphasia: A trait of thinking or doing many activities at once, also known as multitasking. This is also a trait of the Type A personality.

Initially, Friedman and Rosenman referred to Type A behavior as the "hurried sickness." In several research studies, the behavioral traits of "tense" individuals were compared to others who were regarded as "laid back" and called Type B individuals. Striking evidence was observed by Rosenman et al. (1964) in the landmark Western Collaborative Groups Study, which examined more than 3,500 subjects over an 8-year period. Results revealed that Type A behavior was a greater predictor of heart disease than all other risk factors combined. Physiologically speaking, research shows that Type A individuals are more prone to sympathetic arousal (i.e., increased secretion of catecholamines), hypertension, and elevated levels of cholesterol and triglycerides, placing these people at greater risk for several stress-related disorders, but especially coronary heart disease (Rice, 1992). Based on years of research by Rosenman, Friedman, and others, the following personality traits may identify Type A behavior. As you will see, many of these traits are interrelated. Friedman and Rosenman felt that it took only one of these traits to be classified as Type A, though in truth Type A's have been found to share many of these characteristics.

1. *Time urgency (impatience):* Type A people were found to be preoccupied, if not obsessed, with the passage of time and appeared very impatient. Typically these individuals hate to wait in lines, honk at the car in front when the light turns green, and show incredible impatience with others who are too slow with tasks that threaten their own work schedule or personal responsibilities. Type A's feel uncomfortable or guilty about relaxing when there is no set agenda. They rarely take vacations. Everything in the course of a working day—eating, walking, talking—is done with speed. Time itself becomes a major stressor in **time urgency**.
2. *Polyphasia:* **Polyphasia** is engaging in more than one thought or activity at one time. Today, it's called

multitasking. It can lead to sensory overload as the mind juggles thoughts competing for attention. An example of polyphasia is the following: driving to work, talking on a cell phone, putting on make-up or shaving, and listening to the radio, all at the same time. Polyphasia is related to the sense of time urgency in that these people feel that they must do many things at once because their time is so limited.

3. *Ultra-competitiveness:* Type A's are very self-conscious in that they compare themselves with others of similar social status. This trait is exhibited by working extra hours, working on several projects at one time, and vying for top recognition at work. All colleagues or peers at the same status level are perceived as personal threats. Type A's may also appear to be egocentric, perceiving that they are more important than others with regard to their work. Moreover, Type A's are found to be more concerned with quantity of work than quality of work, despite what they may say. The ultra-competitiveness may carry over into non-work-related events, such as sporting activities. This manifests itself when Type A's are in the presence of other people who exhibit a similar competitive drive.
4. *Rapid speech patterns:* Type A people are found to raise their voices in normal conversations, and use explosive words to influence, control, or intimidate others. During conversations, Type A's often finish sentences for people who take their time expressing or articulating their thoughts.
5. *Manipulative control:* Manipulative control is a trait symbolic of a person who is very ego driven. This behavior results from a desire to influence, and even intimidate, co-workers, family members, and acquaintances. Control is achieved through either direct intimidation or circuitously, in a passive-aggressive way. As one might expect, this attitude of dominant control is maintained to promote feelings of one-upmanship. Type A's assert control when they feel threatened.
6. *Hyperaggressiveness and free-floating hostility:* Type A's have a need to dominate other people. They not only strive for high goals, but walk over people to get to the top, showing little or no compassion. These people are very aggressive and may even come across as abrasive. Type A's are also noted to have what is now called free-floating hostility, which is permanently in-dwelling anger that erupts at trivial occurrences like traffic lights, long lines at the supermarket, or broken photocopy machines. At closer range, Type A's seem to have an inability to express anger in a creative fashion. In many cases, they momentarily suppress feelings of anger and then later explode. Hostility of this nature is also observed to be unfocused, free-floating, and often unresolved. Type A's typically display annoyance with circumstances that would seem barely noticeable to Type B's.

One factor that all these traits share is low self-esteem, here meaning the perception of self-worth based on both how one perceives oneself and how one perceives others' perceptions of oneself. People classified as Type A are also preoccupied with how they are perceived by others regarding material possessions and social status. (The issue of self-esteem will be explained in more detail at the end of this chapter.)

Hostility: The Lethal Trait of Type A's

Originally, time urgency was considered the most critical factor associated with Type A and heart disease, and it was this trait that was thought to be directly related to hypertension. Upon closer examination, several people classified as Type A exhibited neither hypertension nor coronary heart disease, leaving doubt as to whether this criterion merited further research. Investigations by Rosenman (1990) and others suggest that the most important, even dangerous, component of Type A behavior is hostile aggression. Work in this area now supports the idea that this factor alone is more responsible for the strong correlation to coronary heart disease than are all the other traits classified as Type A behavior.

With the suspicion that hostile aggression was the most important predictor of CHD, new ways to assess aggressive behavior were considered. To date, the most popular method is the Cook-Medley Hostility Index, also referred to as the Ho Scale (Cook and Medley, 1954). This index was developed from questions on the Minnesota Multiphasic Personality Inventory (MMPI) to measure hostility. Using this and other assessment tools (e.g., Potential for Hostility Scale, or PoHo),

Multitasking: Acting on many responsibilities at one time (driving and talking on a cell phone) to save time, yet potentially compromising the integrity of both outcomes.

several studies have begun to show a strong correlation between hostility and the development of CHD. In one study by Williams et al. (1980), for example, it was found that hostility was correlated with coronary blockage, suggesting that hostile aggression could be used as a predictor for CHD. Studies by Barefoot et al. (1983, 1987) also indicated a strong correlation between hostility and increased risk of heart disease. Using the Ho Scale, Barefoot and colleagues studied a group of physicians over a 25-year period. Those who scored high on the aggression index showed a fourfold greater incidence of CHD than those who scored low.

Hostility is an expression of anger, and anger can surface in many ways, including cynicism, sarcasm, intimidation, and various other aggressive behaviors. It should be noted that impatience is also a form of anger, and although it may not seem as potent as hostility, Friedman and Rosenman were not far off when they cited time-consciousness as the cornerstone of the Type A personality and its relationship to CHD. It may be that impatience festers into what they referred to as free-floating hostility, which in turn snowballs into mismanaged anger. Whatever the case, hostility and aggression are thought to be the most important factors with regard to heart disease, rather than the collection of Type A behaviors as a whole.

Behavior Modification for Type A Behavior

Since the identification of the Type A personality, much research has been conducted to determine if its traits and behaviors can be changed or modified to reduce the risk of coronary heart disease. Friedman et al. (1984), for example, placed more than 500 post–heart attack patients in an education/behavior modification program, including 29 counseling sessions, for a 3-year period. Those who participated in this program showed a 44 percent decrease in Type A behaviors as measured by questionnaires and personal interviews. Many individuals also reduced the incidence of recurring heart attacks. The findings of this and other studies have led many health specialists to develop intervention programs that can alter negative health behaviors and improve health status. The same study also indicated that although the totality of personality will not change, components of it can be favorably influenced and altered to improve one's health status. Currently, behavior modification programs focus on the creative release of anger. It is the findings of Friedman and associates that led to current behavior modification programs in anger management.

Social Influences on Type A Behavior

Several researchers have speculated on the origins of Type A behavior, and the nature (genetics) versus nurture (environment) issue surfaces again. It is well accepted that children model their behavior on that of parents and other figures of authority, including aggressive behaviors. But researchers seem to agree that Type A behavior is a product of broader social and cultural factors as well, including the corporate culture, which breeds employee burnout through long hours, 24/7 accessibility, multitasking, and guilt associated with taking vacation time. Many of the behaviors associated with Type A are often rewarded in our society as positive attributes leading toward success in one's career. Based on the work of Friedman and Rosenman, Schafer (1992) lists these as the following:

1. *Material wealth:* Part of the American dream is to have the freedom to own a house, car, and a number of consumer goods. In a free-market economy, people seem caught up in the accumulation of material goods. This fact became most evident in the 1980s, when sociologists noted a veritable obsession with material possessions.
2. *Immediate gratification:* The ability to drive up to a window and receive service immediately, whether for food, liquor, money, or videos, has had a big impact on our expectations for virtually all goods and services. In general, the pace of life has quickened in tandem with the pace of technology. In keeping pace with technological advancements, people have come to expect immediacy in everything.
3. *Competitiveness:* Competition for grades, salary increases, and sales are just three examples of the ways people feel pressured to become successful and get ahead. There is constant pressure to keep up with the Joneses. Friedman and Rosenman referred to this as "the excess of the competitive spirit," where more never seems to be enough.
4. *People as numbers:* Bureaucratic policies and procedures often make one feel like a number rather than a person. To be identified by your Social Security number for class registration, auto insurance, or taxes decreases the personal aspect of human interaction. This lack of personal attention is thought to contribute to an overall sense of alienation from oneself and others.
5. *Secularization:* As people become less and less involved with spiritual issues and growth, a vacuum

is created, leading to a decline in self-reliance, self-esteem, and social connectedness.

6. *Atrophy of the body and right brain:* Reliance on technology to carry out functions humans used to do can make us physically sedentary. Moreover, there is a general consensus that our society encourages left-brain thinking processes, such as analysis and judgment skills, over right-brain thinking processes, which in excess can lead to increased tension and frustration.
7. *Television watching:* Studies show that the average person watches between 20 and 40 hours of television per week. Many of the qualities and behaviors observed in Type A's are the same ones depicted in television programming. The rise in violent crimes, for example, is thought to be significantly correlated to the preponderance of violence seen on TV. The sheer number of violent acts on television programs implies condoning of this behavior.

It should come as no surprise that the behavioral traits associated with Type A personality precipitate the stress response. When left unmanaged, these create a vicious cycle of perceived stress-related problems spiraling into physiological responses. The pressures of time, threats of competition, and unresolved anger generate a modus operandi of perpetual stress.

Did Someone Say Type D Personality?

Research is now shifting its focus from Type A (aggression) to what some call Type D (depression) and others call "psychocardiology" or "behavioral cardiology": the relationship between emotional stress (specifically, anxiety and depression) and cardiac function. The idea that personality traits associated with anxiety and depression affect the course of heart disease is now supported by clinical data. It is now noted that the words *anger* and *angina* share a common root.

Dr. Johan Denollet, intrigued by the personality differences among heart attack patients, devised a 14-question survey (DS-14) to help determine a person's cardiovascular health based on a proclivity to depression, what he calls negative affectivity (BOX 7.1). Questions attempt to identify personality traits such as worry, irritability, gloom, social inhibition, and depression (e.g., "I am often down in the dumps"). With an estimated one-quarter of the American population on antidepressants, the Type D personality is taking on greater relevance in the medical community with regard to many chronic illnesses.

Given the connection between anger and depression (anger turned inward), perhaps Type A and Type D personalities share some common ground: Stress! The association between stress and heart disease appears so strong that *Newsweek* magazine dedicated nearly a whole issue to the topic in the fall of 2005 with a feature article by renowned cardiologist Dr. Dean Ornish, the first person to prove the reversal of plaque buildup in the arteries. Ornish states that love, expressed through compassion, is often the missing component in people prone to heart disease. Love and compassion, it should be noted, are not traits commonly expressed in either the Type A or Type D personalities.

Codependent Personality Traits

The concept of **codependency** was introduced by psychologists in the 1980s to describe individuals who, in simple terms, are dependent on making other people dependent on them as a means of self-validation. In layman's terms, this label has been used to describe people who "love (conditionally) too much." Codependency is also referred to as an addictive personality because the behaviors associated with it are similar to those observed with other process addictions ("addictions" to behaviors rather than substances). The term *codependency* was first coined by a handful of counselors and therapists who were themselves recovering from chemical and process addictions. It evolved primarily from the study of individuals participating in alcohol rehabilitation programs. Originally, these programs focused solely on the addict. Over time, however, it was found to be imperative to include the spouses and children for greater success of the recovery process of the addict. When family members were introduced into the therapy process, it was learned that many of these individuals "enabled" the alcoholic to continue his or her addictive habits by covering up for

Codependency: A stress-prone personality with many traits and behaviors that seem to increase the likelihood of perceived stress and the inability to cope effectively with it; addictive in nature; based on the need to make others dependent to receive self-validation.

BOX 7.1 Type D Personality Inventory

The following questionnaire is adapted from Johan Denollet's Type D (Depression) Personality Questionnaire, which connects the dots between personality (negativity and social inhibition) to the predictability of coronary heart disease. Please read each question and answer as you are (not how you wish to be), circling the most appropriate answer. Then check your answers with the key below.

	Never	Somewhat	Maybe	Often	Always
1. More often than not, I feel "blue" or unhappy.	0	1	2	3	4
2. I tend to make mountains out of molehills.	0	1	2	3	4
3. I am shy and reserved with people I meet.	0	1	2	3	4
4. I tend to get overwhelmed with responsibilities.	0	1	2	3	4
5. I am not a very sociable person.	0	1	2	3	4
6. I tend to get frustrated easily.	0	1	2	3	4
7. I find social interactions rather awkward.	0	1	2	3	4
8. I tend to be a loner.	0	1	2	3	4
9. The word "moody" describes me well.	0	1	2	3	4
10. In the company of others, I tend to be reserved.	0	1	2	3	4
11. It's a bother to maintain relationships.	0	1	2	3	4
12. I tend to worry a lot about most things.	0	1	2	3	4
13. No one can relate to me and my problems.	0	1	2	3	4
14. I would best describe my tendencies as pessimistic.	0	1	2	3	4

Negativity Index:
Add scores for questions 1, 2, 4, 6, 9, 12, 14 ______

Social Inhibition Index:
Add scores for questions 3, 5, 7, 8, 10, 11, 13 ______

Scores of 10 or higher for both Negativity and Social Inhibition suggest one is very likely classified as a Type D and possibly prone to coronary heart health issues.

Data from Denollet, J. Standard Assessment of Negative Affectivity, Social Inhibition, and Type D Personality. *Psychosomatic Medicine*, 67(6), 2005.

them, allegedly out of concern, loyalty, and love, but in fact to act out their need to be needed. Thus, these individuals were labeled **enablers**, and strangely enough, it was observed that many of their own personality traits and related behaviors were of an addictive nature as well.

Enablers: A term coined in the alcohol recovery movement, referring to a person who enables a spouse, parent, or child to continue either a substance or process addiction.

Further studies on this group of people, many of whom were adult children of alcoholics (ACOA), led researchers to redefine the parameters of the enabler personality type and the traits associated with it.

Codependency, as defined by Melodie Beattie in her book *Codependent No More* (a book that continues to sell millions of copies each year), is "an addiction to another person(s) and their problems or to a relationship and its problems." This personality first became evident among children of alcoholics, but now, three criteria have been established as precursors to the development of this personality: having alcoholic parents or guardians, having divorced parents, or having emotionally repressive parents. A fourth criterion suggests that codependent traits are simply a product of American social mores. Regardless of one's background, codependent traits and their related behaviors are thought to develop early in childhood, in a lifestyle or environment that is chaotic, unpredictable, or threatening. Children are believed to unknowingly adopt various codependent behaviors as **survival skills** in their developmental years, usually to win approval and love from the parents and elders who most influence their lives, as well as to cope with family stress on a day-to-day basis. In many cases, these children assume adult responsibilities long before they reach high school. As they mature, they carry these survival skills—many inappropriate—into adult relationships as excess baggage. Nevertheless, these skills remain the first line of defense in their attempt to deal effectively with others and themselves, yet the nature of these characteristics only perpetuates the stress cycle of threatening perceptions and consequent physical arousal.

Psychologist Ann Wilson Schaef (1986) describes codependency as a **process addiction** because each behavior is like a "fix" to acquire self-validation. But like the effects of a chemical addiction, the "high" is only short-lived so these behaviors are continually repeated. New process addictions include constant checking of email and voice mail and constant cell phone use. The traits associated with this personality type are many and have been criticized by some (Katz and Lieu, 1991) as being so widespread that they include nearly everyone living in the United States. Perhaps because the identification of this personality style emerged from psychotherapy and not clinical medicine, it has not been researched to the same extent as Type A personality. Regardless, there are several key traits that stand out as indicative of individuals who validate their own existence through the approval and manipulation of others. It should be pointed out, first, that codependent people are extremely nice and very well liked because they like to please others. (Many gravitate to the health-care industry; Schaef points out that many nurses are first-born children of alcoholics.) Either individually or collectively, the traits associated with codependency are not considered bad; in fact, many of them are looked on as being quite admirable. However, it is the habitual exhibition of these traits, in an obsessive-compulsive manner, that defines the codependent personality. These traits include the following:

1. *Ardent approval seekers:* Codependent people know how to say the right things, wear the right clothes, and do the right things to draw other people to them and to avoid rocking the boat. Often they ask for an opinion or feedback on their performance and appearance, looking for approval from others.
2. *Perfectionists:* These people are extremely well organized and are in the habit of going beyond a quality job every time. They do, however, get caught up in details, spending extra time on every project or activity to make everything just right. They get very stressed (either annoyed or worried) when things aren't perfect.
3. *Super-overachievers:* This trait means being involved in an abundance of activities and obligations—school, sports, social functions—and receiving stupendous recognition for all of these (FIG. 7.2). These people do it all, and they do it all extremely well.
4. *Crisis managers:* Perhaps because of the environment in which they were raised, codependents thrive on crisis. They constantly try to make order out of chaos and, for the most part, are successful at it. They rush to take control in time of crisis and show that they can be counted on to be there and steer the ship back to a safe harbor.
5. *Devoted loyalists:* Codependents are extremely loyal to friends and family, despite their addictions and abusive behavior. It has been suggested that extreme loyalty may be shown for fear of rejection and abandonment.
6. *Self-sacrificing martyrs:* People who express this personality put everyone else first, before their own needs, to the point of sacrificing their own time, values, property, and even life goals.
7. *Manipulators:* Unlike Type A's, who use intimidation and dominance to manipulate others, codependents manipulate others through acts of generosity and "favors." They feel that the ability to express their own emotions and control their own lives is nowhere

Survival skills: A term associated with codependency in which certain behaviors are adopted in adolescence to "survive" demanding, alcoholic, or abusive parents.

Process addiction: The addiction to a behavioral process such as shopping, intercourse, gambling, television watching, cutting, and codependent behaviors.

FIGURE 7.2 People with a codependent personality are typically super-overachievers. They take on many responsibilities and do them all extremely well.

as easy as doing these for other people. Control and manipulation are performed in a humbling fashion. Codependents adopt what Schaef calls the **illusion of control**, wherein they try to control others and their environment to compensate for the fact that they cannot maintain self-control (e.g., of emotions or perceptions).

8. *Victims:* In tandem with repeated acts of martyrdom, these people perceive that they never receive enough gratitude or credit for self-sacrifice. These people find it impossible to say no but feel taken advantage of after the fact when feeling used sets in. Both crisis management and simple charitable tasks are unconsciously described by the codependent individual as "I've been wronged."
9. *Feelings of inadequacy:* Simply stated, codependents have a black cloud of inferiority over their heads, despite the fact that they are overachievers. (Remember, every action is a "fix" of self-validation.) They feel that the quality and quantity of work done are never to their satisfaction, that more is always expected of them. By being dependent on others for approval, they forfeit self-reliance, the ability to turn inward for strength, faith, and confidence. Self-reliance is the ability to be inspired from within, not motivated solely by external factors. And feelings of inadequacy dissolve self-reliance.
10. *Reactionaries:* Codependent individuals tend to overreact rather than respond to situations. At a young age, these **reactionaries**' expressions of concern and worry were perceived as expressions of love. But worrying is an immobilizing emotion that inhibits the ability to respond adequately to a given situation. When small problems arise, overreacting makes them appear catastrophic, which in turn makes them all the more important to address.

Illusion of control: A term used in association with codependent behavior, thinking that one can control (manipulate) things/others that one really cannot.

Reactionaries: A term associated with the codependent personality illustrating a behavior of reacting, rather than responding, to stress.

Schaef elaborates on several behaviors that appear to be hallmarks of the codependent personality in her book *Co-dependence: Misunderstood, Mistreated.* The manifestation of codependent traits includes the following behaviors:

1. *External referencing:* This is a process whereby an individual gains feelings of importance from external sources. Codependents often doubt their own intrinsic value, so the greatest percentage of their self-validation is derived externally. An example of this behavior is trying to live up to other people's expectations.
2. *Lack of emotional boundaries:* This means that an individual takes on other people's emotional feelings—sadness, happiness, fear, or whatever people around them are feeling or thinking. Codependents often cannot delineate where their feelings end and where the feelings of others begin.
3. *Impression management:* Codependents are always trying to be good people, and they believe they can control the perceptions of others by their good deeds. Their main goal in life is to try and figure out what others want and then deliver it to them. They develop amazing abilities to learn about

the likes and dislikes of other people. They truly believe that if they can just become what others want, they will be safe and accepted. When things go unexpectedly wrong, they often use the words, "I'm sorry," to win sympathy and approval.

4. *Mistrust of one's own perceptions:* Codependents tend to ignore their own perceptions of situations unless or until they are verified externally by others. Even though they might have a very clear impression of a person or a situation, they often dismiss it as being crazy or mistaken. They have learned not to trust their own intuition.

5. *Martyr syndrome:* There is a difference between helping people in need and living their lives for them. Codependents will help anyone (most often their immediate families), and they help them with everything. They say yes because they don't know how to say no. They are afraid that saying no will mean permanent rejection. Martyrs actually perpetuate chaotic situations by accepting responsibility for spouses, parents, and other family members to keep the household together, rather than blowing the whistle on inappropriate behavior.

6. *Lack of spiritual health:* Codependents adopt a mode of dishonest behavior (lying) to survive. The habit of lying begins as white lies to appease people. In this process, they also lie to themselves, hiding their own feelings. In the opinion of Schaef, "Lying does not keep with our deepest spiritual self. Lying to ourselves is always destructive to the self, and it is always destructive to others." According to Schaef, this is a form of spiritual destruction. The mental, emotional, and often physical imbalances spill over into a spiritual imbalance as well.

Estimates by Larsen (1983), Wegscheider-Cruse (1984, 2008), and Schaef (1987) suggest that the codependent personality is so prevalent in the United States that it has become "the American personality," with over 96 percent of Americans exhibiting traits of codependency (and leading to what Schaef calls "an addictive society" as a whole). This number is quite likely inflated, but according to data provided by the National Association for Children of Alcoholics (NACoA) for 2007, one out of every eight Americans (approximately 12.5 percent) is an alcoholic. Also, data show that 76 million Americans (approximately one out of every four children) are directly affected by the behavior of an alcoholic—this does not include other family members or co-workers. A spokesperson for the NACoA stated that the terms *enabling* and *codependency* are the primary focus of intervention. (Some estimates are that each alcoholic negatively affects between 10 and 12 people, thus surpassing the country's population.) In many families where one or both parents are alcoholics, children often assume the role of an adult, handling many parental responsibilities. These children learn to react to family crises by taking charge in hopes of winning love and approval. Like Type A behavior, codependency is not gender specific, and both personality types include the inability to recognize and express emotions. But unlike Type A individuals, who operate on the energy of misdirected and unresolved anger, codependents are motivated by fear—most notably, fear of rejection, fear of the unknown, and fear of failure. The codependent personality has many similarities to what medical researchers have identified as the cancer-prone personality (Type C personality), which is described as a people-pleasing and emotionally repressed personality.

Helpless-Hopeless Personality

The **helpless-hopeless personality**, while less defined by various traits than the Type A or codependent personality, nevertheless is a stress-prone personality based on low self-esteem. Seligman (1975) was the first to study this personality and to derive the theory of what he called learned helplessness. Seligman described people with this personality as those who have encountered repeated bouts of failure, to the point where they give up on themselves in situations where they clearly have control. That is, repeated failure becomes a learned response. Seligman noted that the signatures of learned helplessness are (1) poor self-motivation, where no attempt is made at self-improvement; (2) cognitive distortion, where perceptions of failure repeatedly eclipse prospects of success; and (3) emotional dysfunction, where repeated failures result in chronic depression. Dr. Arthur Schmale (Locke and Colligan, 1986) also has studied individuals whom he classifies as the helpless-hopeless personality. These individuals, he found, perceive that their problems are beyond the range of their own resources and ultimately give up. Schmale defines the helpless-hopeless personality as "Feelings

Helpless-hopeless personality: Describes a person who has given up on life, or aspects of it, as a result of repeated failure.

of frustration, despair, or futility perceived as coming from a loss of satisfaction for which the individual himself assumed complete and final responsibility by a sense of frustration that one has failed miserably at accomplishing anything in life." In a study reported by Locke and Colligan (1986), Schmale and Iker surveyed the personalities of 51 women using psychological tests and personal interviews to detect an intrinsic state of hopelessness. Based on the analysis of these tests and interviews, eighteen women were predicted to contract cancer, and these predictions held true.

Perhaps the characteristic that best identifies the helpless-hopeless personality is referred to as an external **locus of control**. This concept was developed by psychologist Julian Rotter in the early 1960s. Rotter theorized that behavior is normally influenced by both internal and external sources. A preponderance of external factors reinforcing behavior constitutes what Rotter defined as an external locus of control. Examples of external factors might include other people, luck, the weather, chance, or even astrological influences. Conversely, people who demonstrate an internal locus of control feel responsible for their own actions as derived by the internal resources of self-confidence, faith, intuition, and willpower.

Rotter observed that those individuals identified as having an internal locus of control were, on the whole, healthier and more productive individuals. They were observed to be information seekers and goal directed, and to obtain a sense of mastery to cope with problems. Individuals who were identified as having an external locus of control often showed signs of apathy and complacency. The helpless-hopeless personality is the epitome of an external locus of control. Such attitudes and behaviors appear to have been learned early in life, when failure with tasks was a common occurrence. The lack of success, coupled with less-than-desirable environmental factors, shapes the individual's personality to feel helpless in stressful situations and give up productive attempts to overcome the circumstances perceived as stressful. Rotter believed that although many features of personality were fixed entities, locus of control was not an absolute; it could be changed to the advantage of the individual. This is the premise of many drug- and alcohol-treatment programs, wherein patients are taught to capitalize on aspects of their lives they do in fact have control over so as to beat the chemical dependency.

Locus of control: A sense of who or what is in control of one's life; people with an internal locus of control take responsibility for their actions; those with an external locus of control place responsibility on external factors like luck or the weather; the latter is associated with the helpless-hopeless personality, a stress-prone personality.

Extreme examples of individuals with the helpless-hopeless personality type include alcoholics, drug addicts, abused children, abused wives, some elderly, and some of the nation's homeless. Although these examples may seem distant from the average person, everyone experiences moments of hopelessness. However, repeated bouts of failure at any time in one's life could allow shades of this personality to manifest. Because of the failure-control issues involved, the helpless-hopeless personality is considered synonymous with an ongoing stress response.

Resiliency: The Hardy Personality

Using the framework of the mechanistic medical model, many researchers in the 1960s and 1970s were trying to find a relationship between personality traits and the leading killers in the country, coronary heart disease and cancer. Growing evidence suggested a link between mind (negative thoughts) and body (physical symptoms), and this in turn spurred the pessimistic suggestion that the greater the stress level, the greater the chance of disease and illness.

But one group of researchers, headed by Dr. Suzanne Kobasa and Salvatore Maddi, became interested in individuals who despite stressful circumstances appeared *resistant* to the psychophysiological effects of stress. Kobasa et al. (1979, 1981, 1982, 1983) studied several hundred AT&T employees during the period of federal deregulation when scores of executives were laid off or transferred to other positions. In this study, more than 700 executives were given a version of the Holmes and Rahe stress inventory and a checklist of physical symptoms and illnesses. Although hundreds of executives showed physical symptoms of stress, under the same circumstances several did not. When this smaller group of individuals was studied further, it became quite obvious that what distinguished them from those who succumbed to the stress were specific personality traits enabling them to cope with their perceptions of stress. Kobasa et al. found

BOX 7.2 Hardy Personality Profile: Test Your Hardiness

This questionnaire is adapted from the work of Suzanne Kobasa, co-creator of the hardy personality. This inventory is based on 12 questions. In the words of Kobasa, "Evaluating hardiness requires more than a quick test, but this survey will give you an idea of your degree of hardiness." Using a scale of 0–3, estimate your answer for each question. Please answer how you are, not how you would like to be. Then score your answers for Control, Commitment, and Challenge.

0 = strongly disagree, 1 = mildly disagree, 2 = mildly agree, 3 = strongly agree

_______ 1. My best efforts at work/school make a difference.

_______ 2. Trusting to fate/universe is sometimes all I can do in a relationship.

_______ 3. I often wake up each day eager to start, work on, or complete a project.

_______ 4. Viewing myself as a free person tends to promote stress and frustration.

_______ 5. I would be willing to sacrifice financial security in my work if something really challenging came along.

_______ 6. I get stressed when my plans go awry and my schedule is disrupted.

_______ 7. Anybody, from any social demographic, can have an influence on politics.

_______ 8. Without the right breaks, it is difficult to be successful in my field.

_______ 9. I know what I am doing and why I am doing it at work/school.

_______ 10. Becoming close to people makes me feel a sense of obligation to them.

_______ 11. I relish the chance to encounter new situations as an important part of life.

_______ 12. I really don't mind when I have lots of free time with nothing to do.

Score: To estimate your level of hardiness, calculate the scores for each component (by adding and subtracting where indicated). A total score of 10–18 indicates a hardy personality, 0–9 suggests moderate hardiness, and a score less than 0 indicates low hardiness.

Control Score = _______	Commitment Score = _______	Challenge Score = _______
1 _____ + 7 _____	3 _____ + 9 _____	5 _____ + 11 _____
subtract	subtract	subtract
2 _____ + 8 _____	4 _____ + 10 _____	6 _____ + 12 _____
		Total Hardiness Score _______

three specific personality traits that collectively acted as a buffer to stress and contributed to what Kobasa called the **hardy personality** (BOX 7.2):

1. *Commitment:* The dedication to oneself, one's work, and one's family that gives the individual a sense of belonging. Commitment involves an investment of one's values and life purpose to the growth of one's human potential and is a direct reflection of one's willpower.
2. *Control:* In this case, control means a sense of personal control, a sense of causing the events in one's life rather than a feeling of helplessness. Self-control, or empowerment, helps one overcome

Hardy personality: A term coined by Maddi and Kobasa; personality characteristics that, in combination, seem to buffer against stress: control, commitment, and challenge.

factors and elements in one's environment so that one does not feel victimized.

3. *Challenge:* The ability to see change and even problems as opportunities for growth, rather than threats to one's existence. Challenge, in Kobasa's mind, symbolized a hunger of the heart that serves as an inspiration. Challenge can also be viewed as a sense of adventure.

The results of this and similar studies with lawyers, housewives, and other groups revealed that the traits of the hardy personality were not limited to white, upper-middle-class, executive males employed by AT&T, but were found in people from both genders and all races and religions. In addition, Kobasa concluded the following:

- A hardy personality may override a genetic disposition to illness.
- A person can exhibit several Type A traits without risk of heart disease.
- Inner resources are more important than strong family support during high-pressure jobs.
- Some people observed as hardy showed signs of Type A personality minus feelings of hostility. These people enjoyed life so much they would often hurry with some tasks to enjoy others.

Kobasa and a colleague, Sal Maddi (1982, 1999, 2002), are of the opinion that although the hardy personality appears to be innate, the traits of commitment, control, and challenge can be learned as well. In a study to determine the efficacy of teaching hardiness skills to Illinois Bell executives over an 8-week period, sixteen executives experiencing stress-related health problems were divided into two groups: a treatment group to learn hardiness skills, and a control group. The skills taught to the treatment group were (1) **focusing**, or recognizing the body signals of stress (e.g., muscle tension); (2) **reconstruction**, reinterpretation of a stressor, and viable options to resolve it; and (3) **compensation**, turning control of personal talents into abilities that accent strengths rather than foster helplessness. After exposure to the new behavior skills, the treatment group scored higher on the hardiness scale, and even demonstrated a decrease in resting blood pressure, while the control group showed no change. The research findings of Kobasa et al., which closely parallel the theories of Abraham Maslow and his concept of self-actualization, led them to believe that commitment, control, and challenge were necessary traits to maintain a buffer against the effects of stress, and that a hardy personality contributed to overall good health. Today, Maddi continues his research of the hardy personality at the University of California at Irvine where he calls hardiness a type of "existential courage" (Maddi, 2004). His research adds to the body of knowledge in the discipline of positive psychology. Maddi's faculty Web site states that he is especially interested in stress management and creativity. Through deepening the attitudes of commitment, control, and challenge and marking hardiness, persons can simultaneously develop, reach their highest potentials, and cope with any stress encountered on the way.

Focusing: The ability to recognize the body signals of oncoming stress (e.g., muscle tension, increased breathing, sweating).

Reconstruction: The reinterpretation (from negative to neutral or positive) of a stressor (also known as reframing).

Compensation: The ability to cultivate and utilize one's strengths in times of need, rather than claim victimization.

Reivich (2003) and Al Siebert (2005) have taken the premise of the hardy personality and renamed it for the twenty-first century. Each calls it "resiliency." Resiliency can best be defined as the ability to pick yourself up after being knocked down in the face of adversity from life-changing events (BOX 7.3).

Survivor Personality Traits

Aron Ralston is a survivor—perhaps the epitome of it. While rock climbing in the southwest corner of Utah's desert in spring 2003, Ralston got caught. An 800-pound boulder wedged itself over his right arm, pinning him against the side of a mountain. Unable to free himself, Ralston did the unthinkable. After days of deliberating about his situation, he pulled out his pocket knife and proceeded to amputate his own arm. Once liberated from the boulder, he was still a long way from safety. He rappelled 80 feet down the rock face and then hiked several miles in the direction of his car to reach help. Although Ralston's story, portrayed by Academy Award–nominated actor James Franco in the biopic *127 Hours*, is unfathomable, he stands in good company among those who survive, even thrive, in the face of unbeatable odds

BOX 7.3 Resiliency 101

The newest buzzword in stress management is the term "resiliency," a twenty-first-century makeover of the hardy personality. More than just the ability to bounce back from personal setbacks, resiliency is the ability to overcome the tremendous stress of trauma, loss, and tragedy. In the words of philosopher Friedrich Nietzsche, "That which doesn't kill us, makes us stronger." Moreover, the traits of resiliency are now considered to be those that enrich our lives—an attitude of *can do*. The alchemy of resiliency includes optimism, courage, flexibility, humor, compassion, and the ability to adapt to change (rather than be a victim of circumstance). Al Siebert, author of *The Resiliency Advantage* and *The Survivor Personality*, explains that resilient people have the ability to create good luck out of circumstances that many others see as bad luck. Others describe resiliency as our capacity to not only deal with discomfort and adversity, but also thrive in the face of chaos. Professional dancer Adrianne Haslet-Davis is one such example. Nearing the finish line at the 2013 Boston Marathon, she was thrown off her feet during the second bomb explosion. Her husband (an Air Force captain who served in Afghanistan) quickly put a tourniquet on her leg. She was rushed to the hospital, where doctors did all they could to save her foot, but to no avail. She ended up losing her foot and lower leg. This event has not deterred her from her passions. Adrianne is committed to continuing her career as a dancer and vows to complete her next Boston Marathon, even if she has to crawl across the finish line.

For some people resiliency comes naturally, yet many believe that it is a life skill that can be learned and practiced by everyone. Resiliency training is available for people from all walks of life, including returning soldiers from Iraq and Afghanistan, first responders (police and EMTs), corporate executives, and Olympic athletes. Courses in resiliency, from those taught at the Mayo Clinic to nearly all branches of the U.S. military, include some or all of these aspects to strengthen the resolve of those moving through life's transitions:

1. *Positivity:* Carrying a positive attitude about life and your role in it
2. *Creative problem-solving:* Focusing on the solution to a problem rather than the problem itself
3. *Compassion and gratitude:* Being grateful for what you have rather than what you don't have; seeing yourself as a victor, not a victim; and honoring the connectedness of life through service to others
4. *Self-care:* Honoring yourself to engage in personal wellness activities
5. *Humor:* Having the ability to laugh at yourself without sacrificing self-esteem
6. *Purpose in life:* Being able to cultivate a meaningful purpose in one's life through change

The topic of resiliency is being studied from a great many perspectives, including brain activity scans (fMRIs) during the practice of resiliency skills to the inclusion of mindfulness meditation as a resiliency-based activity. These and other topics were the subject of discussion at the 2013 Harvard Medical Schools conference on resiliency, under the direction of Herbert Benson, M.D.

In a quiet corner of the second floor of the Claude Moore Nursing Education Building at the University of Virginia is the Resiliency Room. This room is used for yoga classes, mindfulness meditation, and personal solitude for students and faculty alike. As professionals on the front lines of health care who help others cope with the spectrum of issues from disease to death, resiliency is considered a necessary skill in nursing. Students, faculty, and staff are all encouraged to make good and frequent use of the room. The University of Virginia is not alone with this strategy. *Fortune* 500 corporations and the U.S. Army are exploring ways to create resiliency centers for their employees as the rapid pace of life quickens.

(and making a mockery of all reality TV shows). Moreover, anyone who has heard the story of Ernest Shackleton and the crew of the *Endurance*, for example, knows the story of incredible and grueling survival in the world's most inhospitable climate, Antarctica.

Al Siebert, the author of *The Survivor Personality*, has studied the likes of Ralston and Shackleton—that is, people who have kept a cool head in the face of danger and come out alive from their ordeal. Siebert defines this type of personality as someone who responds rather than reacts to danger. The traits of a **survivor personality** include acceptance (of the situation), optimism, and creative problem solving. Beyond the classic will to survive, this personality type integrates the right-brain abilities of intuition, acceptance, and faith with the left-brain skills of judgment and organization. Siebert suggests that the survivor personality has mastered an integrative problem-solving ability with the use of **biphasic** (left and right brain) **personality traits**: proud yet humble, selfish yet altruistic, rebellious yet cooperative, spiritual yet irreverent. Perhaps the most important trait is mental flexibility, according to both Siebert and Peter Suedfeld (Jenkins, 2003). Beyond the will to survive, the foremost character trait of a survivor is intellectual flexibility. As the expression goes, there are three ways to cope in times of crisis: leave the environment, change the environment, or change your attitude. The survivor personality isn't determined by genetic make-up. Instead, those who study the survivor personality agree that these traits can be learned and practiced by anyone, whether it's Nien Cheng, Aron Ralston, or someone with a flat tire on a highway in the middle of nowhere.

FIGURE 7.3 Calculated risk taking is what separates sensation seekers from those who choose to sit on the sidelines watching the world go by. To accomplish a goal under these conditions is thought to augment self-esteem, which in turn enables one to deal more effectively with stress.

Sensation Seekers

If you are familiar with extreme sports, the X Games, or even the reality shows that depict extreme survival challenges, then no doubt you are familiar with whom psychologists refer to as **sensation seekers** or Type R (risk taker) personalities, a term coined by Zuckerman (1971) to describe people whose personalities appear to be dominated by an adventurous spirit (FIG. 7.3). For these people, adrenaline is their drug of choice. Studies by both Zuckerman (1971) and Johnson, Sarason, and Siegel (1979) found that people who are inclined toward "extreme" activities providing intense sensation, like rock climbing, skydiving, windsurfing, hang gliding, and exotic travel, are better able to cope with life events than those who are more inclined to avoid taking risks. It is hypothesized that in their intentional exposure to "approachable stress," or sensation activities, they calculate the risks involved. This prepares them for unexpected stressful events, which they also approach in a calculated manner. In other words, sensation seekers think through their strategies rather than reacting impetuously. They are spontaneous, yet calculating. An additional hypothesis suggests that the inner resources required to perform sensation activities (e.g., confidence, self-efficacy, courage, optimism, and creativity) are the same qualities used as coping skills to deal effectively with stress. These hypotheses do not imply that sensation seekers do not have stress; rather, they try to meet it head on and aim to overcome it. Examples might include athletes who participate in extreme sports.

In a questionnaire designed to assess this characteristic, Zuckerman focused on four specific traits—adventure seeking, experience seeking, disinhibition, and susceptibility to boredom—to define the parameters of sensation seeking. Results suggested that individuals who had a low stimulation threshold are more vulnerable to stressful life events. Perhaps for that very reason, many outdoor education programs, including Outward Bound, Project

Survivor personality: The traits that comprise a unique winning attitude to overcome adversity and challenges, no matter what the odds may be, so that one comes out the victor, not the victim.

Biphasic: Survivor personality traits; the ability to use both right-brain and left-brain thinking processes to successfully deal with a problem or stressors.

Personality traits: Thoughts and behaviors that combine to form or color one's personality; in this case, cognitive traits associated with survival.

Sensation seeker: Also known as Type R personality, these courageous people confront stress by calculating their risks in extreme situations and then proceeding with gusto.

Adventure, and National Outdoor Leadership School (NOLS), use the concept and application of calculated risk taking in their activities to build "survival skills" that will carry over into the everyday lives of adolescents and corporate executives alike.

Self-Esteem: The Bottom-Line Defense

There are many traits common to all individuals, which makes distinguishing among personality types and their related behaviors difficult at times. Level of **self-esteem**, however, appears to be a critical factor in how people respond to stress, regardless of personality type. Low self-esteem is the common denominator in stress-prone personalities, as can be seen in Type A, codependent, and helpless-hopeless types. High self-esteem is a prerequisite for creating stress-resistant personalities because it is directly linked to the accessibility of one's internal resources. Self-esteem is often described as self-value, self-respect, even self-love. It is reflected in the things we say, in the clothes we wear, and perhaps most evidently in our behaviors. Self-esteem has also been described as the harmony or discrepancy between actual self-image and ideal self-image, where high self-esteem is harmony between the actual and ideal, and low self-esteem is the distance between the two.

When we place little or no value on our self, we become quite vulnerable to the perceptions of stress. Conversely, with high self-esteem, problems and worries tend to roll off one's back and might even go unnoticed. Self-esteem is continually fed by the thoughts, feelings, actions, and even memories that contribute to our identity. Self-esteem, however, is a variable entity; it rises and falls, like ambient temperature, over the course of a day. But these variations remain within a specific range where the core of one's self-value resides. Individuals with stress-resistant personalities typically have a high level of self-esteem. For this reason, it is the construction and maintenance of high self-esteem that is the goal of many behavior modification programs involving recovering addicts, battered wives and children, and juvenile delinquents.

In his classic book *The Six Pillars of Self-Esteem*, Nathaniel Branden calls self-esteem the immune system of the consciousness. The author of several books on the topic of self-esteem, Branden highlights what he calls the six pillars (practices) of self-esteem, the internal resources that guide us on the human journey:

- *The practice of living consciously:* Living in the present moment, rather than confining yourself to past or future events, and being mindful of each activity you are engaged in.
- *The practice of self-acceptance:* The refusal to be in an adversarial relationship with yourself.
- *The practice of self-responsibility:* Choosing to acknowledge responsibility for one's feelings, such as saying, "I am responsible for my own happiness," rather than surrendering your feelings to the whims of those you are in a relationship with.
- *The practice of self-assertiveness:* Honoring one's wants, needs, and values, and seeking appropriate ways in which to satisfy these.
- *The practice of living purposefully:* Getting out of the thought processes of hoping and wishing, and instead doing what you need to do to make your goals happen.
- *The practice of personal integrity:* Working to achieve congruence between your values and actions.

Researchers are now placing a greater focus on ways to raise self-esteem as the primary goal in stress management therapy programs. As might be expected, prevention is more effective than rehabilitation, and for this reason, a special task force was created in California to incorporate self-esteem lesson plans into classroom curricula at the primary- and secondary-education levels. It is too early to know any results from this curriculum change, but it is hoped that, by giving attention to this crucial element of human potential, significantly fewer problems with **substance addiction**, divorce, and homelessness will result in the coming decades. According to child psychologists Harris Clemes et al. (1990), the seeds for self-esteem are planted early in childhood and comprise four basic elements: connectedness, uniqueness, power, and models. All four of these factors need to be present, and cultivated continuously, to ensure a high sense of self-esteem. And these four characteristics are essential for self-esteem not only in early childhood development, but also in all

Self-esteem: The sense of underpinning self-values, self-acceptance, and self-love; thought to be a powerful buffer against perceived threats.

Substance addiction: The addiction to a host of substances, from nicotine and caffeine to alcohol and various drugs.

developmental stages throughout one's life. They are defined as follows:

1. *Connectedness:* A feeling of satisfaction that associations and relationships are significant, nurturing, and affirmed by others.
2. *Uniqueness:* A feeling that the individual possesses qualities that make him or her special and different, and that these qualities are respected and admired by others as well as oneself.
3. *Power:* A sense that one can access inner resources as well as use these resources and capabilities to influence circumstances in one's life, and not give one's power away to other people or things.
4. *Models:* A mentoring process by which reference points are established to guide the individual on his or her life journey by sharing goals, values, ideals, and personal standards.

Individuals with low self-esteem often feel powerless, are easily influenced by others, express a narrow range of emotions, become easily defensive and frustrated, and tend to blame others for their own weaknesses (FIG. 7.4). Individuals with high self-esteem promote their independence, assume given responsibilities, approach new challenges with enthusiasm, exhibit a broad range of emotions, are proud of accomplishments, and tolerate frustration well. Because high self-esteem is central to the stress-resistant personality, much attention is now placed on ways to increase self-esteem in people of all ages. Among the many ways to raise and maintain self-esteem, Clemes gives the following suggestions:

1. Disarm the negative critic. Challenge the voice inside that feeds the conscious mind with put-downs and negative comments. A critic taking only one side is unbalanced and dangerous to your self-esteem.
2. Give yourself positive reinforcements and affirmations to remind yourself of your good qualities. Write these down, and look at the list when you're feeling down.
3. Avoid "should haves," where you place a guilt trip on yourself for unmet expectations. Learn from the past, but don't dwell on it. Look for new opportunities for growth.
4. Focus on who you really are, your own identity, and your role models or mentors (BOX 7.4).
5. Avoid comparisons with others. Respect your own uniqueness, and learn to cultivate it.
6. Diversify your interests. Don't put all your eggs in one basket. Diversify so that if one aspect of your life becomes impaired, other areas can compensate to keep you afloat. (For instance, if you see yourself solely as a student and you do badly on an exam, this will pull down your self-esteem like a rock.)
7. Improve your connectedness. Widen your network of friends, and find special places in your environment that recharge your energy and strengthen your social bonds.
8. Avoid self-victimization. Martyrs may be admired, but begging for pity and sympathy gets old and the effects are short-lived.
9. Reassert yourself and your value before and during a stressful event.

Is there a difference between self-esteem and self-image? Yes! Self-image, how you perceive yourself, and self-esteem, how you value yourself, are related, yet two different concepts. Self-image is recognized as being a by-product of one's level of self-esteem. This difference between self-esteem and self-image became quite clear in the early 1960s through the work of Maxwell Maltz, author of the book *Psycho-Cybernetics*. In his work as a plastic surgeon, Maltz was intrigued to learn that after

FIGURE 7.4

BOX 7.4 Technology and Personality

The Internet has opened a whole new avenue to explore personality traits. Take a glance at any page from Facebook, Twitter, Match.com, or the domains that include personal avatars and Internet video games, and you are likely to see more than simple lifestyle preferences. Similar to a Halloween costume, what appears on the computer screen is likely to be different than what meets the eye during a face-to-face exchange. Internet games give a whole new meaning to the term *role playing*. However, changes to or magnifications of one's personality are not new to the Internet generation. Long ago, psychologists noticed that people behave differently behind the wheel of a car than they might in an aisle of a grocery store. With two tons of metal behind one's persona, aggressive behaviors are more common. Before caller ID, people could also hide anonymously behind the voice piece of a telephone. In each of these cases, Freud would say the alter ego has taken center stage. Has the Internet expanded the bandwidth of the alter ego? That's the opinion of Robbie Cooper and Tracy Spaight (2007), co-authors of the book *Alter Ego: Avatars and Their Creators*.

Things have come a long way since the days of Dungeons and Dragons. In a piece aired on National Public Radio, commentator Ketzel Levine reported that online games such as Everquest and Star Wars Galaxies include players who use avatars with different genders, races, and physical attributes. Personalities are certainly more complex than what we reveal to others on a day-to-day basis. In a unique way, the Internet not only allows us to try on different personalities or magnify our best characteristics, but also levels the playing field regarding race, ethnicity, gender, and many disabilities. In this regard, virtual personalities open the potential to augment one's sense of confidence and perhaps even courage, traits associated with a stress-resistant personality. There is also concern regarding the transfer effect of war-based video games and how this may trigger neural responses during episodes of anger. Perhaps the real question is, what beneficial transfer effect, if any, occurs from the virtual world to the actual world we live in? The jury appears to be out on this issue. Across the country, however, it is not uncommon to hear conversations in middle school and high school staff lounges bemoaning the negative change in students' interpersonal communication skills in tandem with the proliferation of Internet activity, where comfort level with one's online persona does not transfer to face-to-face encounters. This, unlike the virtual world, is where the greatest percentage of stressors exists.

Omar is a recent graduate of Metro State University in Denver, Colorado. He believes there are pros and cons to online video games. He is no stranger to spending time playing X-Box 360, poker on Full Tilt, and first-person shooter games such as his favorite, Team Death Match.

"There certainly can be an addictive quality to these games. I lost a semester of school due to my [Everquest] video habit. I kept putting off my homework to a point where I had to drop all my classes for a semester. On the plus side, I ended up meeting some neat people from Florida and Las Vegas."

performing scores of nose jobs and facelifts, his clients didn't seem all that much happier with their new appearance. (Similar results have been observed with participants in the television reality shows *Extreme Makeover*, *Dr. 90210*, and *The Swan*.) After scores of interviews with patients, he came to the realization that before any external changes take place, the real change first has to take place inside. In other words, if people change their physical image but their self-image remains poor, no amount of surgery will change how one feels about oneself. The changes have to come from within first, changes that nurture and cultivate our inner resources such as confidence, courage, love, compassion, and willpower. If your level of self-esteem is low, so, too, will be your self-image. Through his principles of psycho-cybernetics, Maltz suggests that we first work within before changing external features. Working within means focusing on our positive aspects; shedding old beliefs, attitudes, and perceptions that trap us in the mindset of low self-esteem; and learning to use our inner resources to move out of crisis into creative opportunity.

High self-esteem is considered the best defense against stress; strategies used to combat stress are useless without a strong feeling of self-worth or self-value. Although an abstract concept, your self-esteem should be attended to regularly, every day, like brushing your teeth and eating. It is that important.

SUMMARY

- Personality comprises several traits, characteristics, behaviors, expressions, moods, and feelings as perceived by others.
- Personality is thought to be molded at an early age by genetic factors, family dynamics, social influences, and personal experiences.
- Personality is thought to be a fixed entity, not subject to significant changes; however, the most likely part of personality to change is behavior.
- Personalities can be classified as either stress prone (seeming to attract stress) or stress resistant (providing a buffer against various stressors).
- Type A, codependency, and helpless-hopeless are three personalities that have been associated with both acute and chronic stress. They have one common factor: low self-esteem.
- Type A personality, "the hurried sickness," was first observed by cardiologists Rosenman and Friedman as a major risk factor for heart disease. Later studies revealed that the trait of hostility is most closely linked with hypertension and coronary heart disease.
- Type A behavior is not gender specific; as many-females demonstrate Type A behavior as males. However, desire for higher social status is thought to be strongly correlated with Type A behavior.
- Codependency, first observed in the spouses and children of alcoholics when recovery programs began to include family members, is now thought to apply as well to children of broken homes and those with emotionally repressive parents. Codependents are people who validate their existence by serving others at their own expense. Codependents typically operate from fear of rejection, failure, and the unknown.
- The helpless-hopeless personality develops as a result of repeated bouts of failure over time, to the point where individuals no longer feel competent to try things they really do have control over. Low self-esteem and an external locus of control appear to be significant factors in this type of personality.
- The hardy personality and the sensation seeker are two personalities currently believed to be stress resistant. The commonality between the two is high self-esteem.
- The hardy personality was identified by Kobasa and Maddi, who observed that some people under severe stress did not succumb to stress-related ailments while others did. People who showed a strong sense of commitment, control, and challenge were labeled hardy personalities.
- The survivor personality uses biphasic personality traits to endure danger with a level head. Everyone has the ability to access these traits.
- Zuckerman identified the sensation-seeking personality as those people who seek thrills and sensations but take calculated risks in their endeavors.
- Self-esteem is a crucial cornerstone of personality. Low self-esteem attracts stress; high self-esteem seems to repel it. Clemes states that self-esteem consists of four components: connectedness, uniqueness, power (control), and models. The strength or weakness of these components is highly correlated with level of self-esteem.

STUDY GUIDE QUESTIONS

1. List the stress-prone personalities and give an example of each.
2. List the stress-resistant personalities and give an example of each.
3. Define resiliency.
4. Describe self-esteem and explain what role it plays in promoting and resolving stress.
5. List several ways to help promote self-esteem.

REFERENCES AND RESOURCES

Associated Press. Attention-Deficit Drug OK'd, *Denver Post,* August 2, 2000.

Baker, L. J., Dearborn, M., Hastings, J. E., and Hamberger, K. Type A Behavior in Women: A Review, *Health Psychology* 3:477–497, 1984.

Barefoot, J. C., Dahlstrom, W. G., and Williams, R. B., Jr. Hostility, CHD Incidence, and Total Mortality: A 25-Year Follow-Up Study of 255 Physicians, *Psychosomatic Medicine* 45:59–63, 1983.

Barefoot, J. C., et al. Predicting Mortality from Scores on the Cook-Medley Scale: A Follow-Up Study of 118 Lawyers, *Psychosomatic Medicine* 49:210 (abstract), 1987.

Barry, C. R. *When Helping You Is Hurting Me: Escaping the Messiah Trap.* HarperCollins, New York, 2003.

Beattie, M. *Beyond Codependency.* Harper/Hazelton Press, New York, 1989.

Beattie, M. *Codependent No More.* Harper/Hazelton Press, New York, 1987.

Branden, N. *The Power of Self-Esteem.* Health Communications, Deerfield Beach, FL, 1992.

Branden, N. *The Six Pillars of Self-Esteem.* Bantam Books, New York, 1994.

Cheng, N. *Life and Death in Shanghai.* Penguin Books, New York, 1986.

Cheng, N. Personal communication, June 26, 2003.

Clemes, H., Bean, R., and Clark, A. *How to Raise Teenagers' Self-Esteem.* Price Stern Sloan, Los Angeles, 1990.

Cook, W., and Medley, D. Proposed Hostility and Pharisaic-Virtues Scale for the MMPI, *Journal of Applied Psychology* 38:414–418, 1954.

Cooper, R., and Spaight, T. *Alter Ego: Avatars and Their Creators.* Chris Boot Books, London, 2007.

Degennaro, G., Personal conversation and tour. School of Nursing, University of Virginia, Charlottesville, VA. April 25, 2013.

Friedman, M. Type A Behavior Pattern, *Bulletin of the New York Academy of Medicine* 53:593–603, 1977.

Friedman, M., and Rosenman, R. H. *Type A Behavior and Your Heart.* Knopf, New York, 1974.

Friedman, M., and Ulmer, D. *Type A Behavior and Your Heart,* 2nd ed. Knopf, New York, 1984.

Friedman, M., et al. Alteration of Type A Behavior and Reduction in Cardiac Recurrences in Post-myocardial Infarction Patients, *American Heart Journal* 108:237–248, 1984.

Galloway, J. Coordinator Affiliate Services. Personal conversation, February 21, 2008.

Gonzales, L. *Deep Survival.* Norton Books, New York, 2003.

Holmes, T. H., and Rahe, R. H. The Social Readjustment Rating Scale, *Journal of Psychosomatic Research* 11:213–218, 1967.

Jenkins, D., et al. Development of an Objective Test for the Determination of the Coronary Score Behavior Pattern in Employed Men, *Journal of Chronic Diseases* 20:371–379, 1967.

Jenkins, M. The Hard Way: Between a Rock and a Hard Place, *Outside Magazine* August: 51–54, 2003.

Johnson, J. H., Sarason, I. G., and Siegel, J. M. Arousal Seeking as a Moderator of Life Stress, *Perceptual and Motor Skills* 49:665–666, 1979.

Katz, S., and Lieu, A. *The Codependency Conspiracy.* Warner Books, New York, 1991.

Kobasa, S. Commitment and Coping in Stress Resistance among Lawyers, *Journal of Personality and Social Psychology* 42:707–717, 1982.

Kobasa, S. Stressful Life Events, Personality, and Health: An Inquiry into Hardiness, *Journal of Personality and Social Psychology* 37:1–11, 1979.

Kobasa, S., Maddi, S., and Courington, S. Personality and Constitution as Mediators in the Stress-Illness Relationship, *Journal of Health and Social Behavior* 22:368–378, 1981.

Kobasa, S., Maddi, S., and Kahn, S. Hardiness and Health: A Prospective Study, *Journal of Personality and Social Psychology* 42(1):168–177, 1982.

Kobasa, S., and Puccetti, M. Personality and Social Resources in Stress Resistance, *Journal of Personality and Social Psychology* 45(4):839–850, 1983.

Kristol, E. Declarations of Codependence, *American Spectator,* June 20–23, 1990.

Larsen, E. *Basics of Codependency.* E. Larsen Enterprises, Brooklyn Park, MN, 1983.

Leftcourt, H. M. *Locus of Control: Current Trends in Theory and Research.* Hillsdale, NJ, Earlbaum, 1976.

Levine, K. Alter Egos in a Virtual World, *National Public Radio*, July 31, 2007. www.npr.org/templates/story/story.php?storyId=12263532.

Locke, S., and Colligan, D. *The Healer Within.* Mentor Books, New York, 1986.

Maddi, S. Hardiness: An Operationalization of Existential Courage, *Journal of Humanistic Psychology*, 44(3):279–298, 2004.

Maddi, S. Salvatore R. Maddi. http://socialecology.uci.edu/faculty/srmaddi.

Maddi, S., et al. The Personality Construct of Hardiness, *Journal of Research in Personality*, 36(1):72–85, 2002.

Maddi, S. R. Hardiness and Optimism as Expressed in Coping Patterns, *Consulting Psychology Journal* 51:95–105, 1999.

Maddi, S. R. *Personality Theories: A Comparative Analysis,* 6th ed. Waveland Press, Prospective Heights, IL, 2002.

Maltz, M. *Psycho-Cybernetics.* PocketBooks, New York, 1960.

McKay, M. *Self-Esteem.* New Harbinger Publications, Oakland, CA, 4th ed. 2016.

Miller, M. C. The Dangers of Chronic Distress, *Newsweek,* October 3, 2005: 58–59.

Minchinton, J. *Maximum Self-Esteem: The Handbook for Reclaiming Your Sense of Self-Worth.* Arnford House Publishers, Vanzant, MO, 1993.

Monte, C. *Beneath the Mask: An Introduction to Theories of Personality.* Wiley, NY, 8th ed. 2008.

National Association for Children of Alcoholics. Homepage. www.nacoa.org.

Ornish, D. Love Is Real Medicine, *Newsweek,* October 3, 2005: 56.

Ragland, D., and Brand, R. J. Type A Behavior and Mortality from Coronary Disease, *New England Journal of Medicine* 318:65–69, 1986.

Reivich, K. *The Resilience Factor.* Broadway Books, New York, 2003.

Rice, P. *Stress and Health,* 2nd ed. Brooks/Cole, Pacific Grove, CA, 3rd ed. 1998.

Rosenman, R. H. Type A Behavior Pattern: A Personal Overview, *Journal of Social Behavior and Personality* 5:1–24, 1990.

Rosenman, R. H., and Friedman, M. Modifying Type A Behavior Pattern, *Journal of Psychosomatic Research* 21: 323–331, 1977.

Rosenman, R. H., et al. A Predictive Study of Coronary Heart Disease: The Western Collaborative Groups Study, *Journal of the American Medical Association* 189:15–22, 1964.

Rotter, J. B. Generalized Expectancies for Internal versus External Control of Reinforcement, *Psychological Monographs* 609:80, 1966.

Schaef, A. W. *Codependence–Misunderstood, Mistreated.* Harper & Row, San Francisco, 1986.

Schaef, A. W. *When Society Becomes an Addict.* Harper & Row, San Francisco, 1987.

Schafer, W. *Stress Management for Wellness,* 2nd ed. Harcourt Brace Jovanovich, Fort Worth, TX, 1992.

Schmale, A., and Iker, H. Hopelessness as a Predictor of Cervical Cancer, *Social Science and Medicine* 5:95–100, 1971.

Schultz, D. *Theories of Personality,* 10th ed. Cengage Learning, 2012.

Seligman, M. *Authentic Happiness.* Free Press, New York, 2002.

Seligman, M. Happy Days (Positive Psychological Movement), *Psychology Today* 33(3):32, 2000.

Seligman, M. *Learned Optimism: How to Change Your Minds and Life.* PocketBooks, New York, 2006.

Seligman, M. E. *Helplessness: On Depression, Development, and Death.* Freeman, San Francisco, 1975.

Shackleton, E. *South: The Last Antarctic Expedition of Shackleton and the Endurance.* Lyons Press, New York, 1919.

Shiraldi, G., and Kerr, M. H. *The Anger Management Sourcebook.* Contemporary Books, New York, 2002.

Shekelle, R. B., Schoenberger, J. A., and Stamler, J. Correlates of the JAS Type A Behavior Pattern Score, *Journal of Chronic Disease* 29:381–394, 1976.

Siebert, A. *The Resiliency Advantage.* Berrett-Koehler Publishers, San Francisco, 2005.

Siebert, A. *The Survivor Personality.* Perigee Books, New York, 2010.

Smith, E. Fighting Cancerous Feelings, *Psychology Today* 22(5):22–23, 1988.

Sorenson, G., et al. Relationships among Type A Behavior, Employment Experiences, and Gender: The Minnesota Heart Survey, *Journal of Behavioral Medicine* 10:323–336, 1987.

Steffenhagen, R. *Self-Esteem Therapy.* Praeger, New York, 1990.

Steffenhagen, R. *The Social Dynamics of Self-Esteem: Theory to Therapy.* Praeger, New York, 1987.

Taylor, S. E. *Health Psychology,* 9th ed. McGraw-Hill, New York, 2014.

Turnipseed, D. L. An Exploratory Study of the Hardy Personality at Work in the Health Care Industry, *Psychological Reports* 85(3, pt 2):1199–1217, 1999.

Underwood, A. The Good Heart, *Newsweek,* October 3, 2005: 49–55.

Wegscheider-Cruse, S. Codependency: The Therapeutic Void. In *Codependency: An Emerging Issue.* Health Communications, Pompano Beach, FL, 1984.

Wegscheider-Cruse, S. Personal conversation, February 20, 2008.

Whitfield, C. *Co-dependence.* Health Communications, Deerfield Beach, FL, 1991.

Williams, R. B., et al. Type A Behavior Hostility and Coro-nary Atherosclerosis, *Psychosomatic Medicine* 42:539–549, 1980.

Zuckerman, M. Dimensions of Sensation Seeking, *Journal of Consulting and Clinical Psychology* 36:45–52, 1971.

Stress and Human Spirituality

The winds of grace are blowing perpetually. We only need raise our sails.

—Sri Ramakrishna

Laura Wellington was less than a half a mile from the finish line when she heard a loud explosion. Stunned, she stopped to ask someone what had happened and learned that the location where her family was waiting in downtown Boston was bombed. She was quickly diverted away from the marathon route. Once she made contact with her brother, Bryan, via cell phone and learned everyone in her family was safe, she sat down and cried. At that moment a married couple walking by stopped to comfort her. The man asked if she had finished the race. Laura shook her head no, whereupon he took his coveted Boston Marathon medal, placed it around her neck, and said, "You are a finisher in my eyes." In between her tears and sobs, she said thanks. Laura never learned this stranger's name, but will forever be indebted to his random act of kindness. That afternoon, hundreds of similar acts were performed for total strangers across the city, all in the name of compassion. Equally amazing were the scores of runners who crossed the finish line after running 26-plus miles only to continue running a few more miles to the nearest hospital to donate blood. In the words of Mother Teresa, "We can do no great things, only small things with great love." Times of stress may seem anything but spiritual, yet there is always a choice; the ego reacts, the soul responds.

To write a book about stress without addressing the concept of human spirituality would be a gross injustice to both topics. In my quest for understanding and personal journey of enlightenment, I have met these two at the junction of many a crossroad. I know I am not alone. Human spirituality and stress seem to be as inseparable as the Taoist yin and yang, earth and sky, and, quite literally, mind and soul. I became aware of this relationship in my first year of teaching stress management in 1984. Many of the topics I taught, and several of the issues I was asked to address by students, had strong parallels with the cornerstones of several (if not all) religions: relationships, values, the meaning of life, and a sense of connectedness—the common denominator of these four being a unique level of human consciousness known as human spirituality. British author Aldous Huxley called this the perennial philosophy, or a transcendent reality beyond the limitations of cultures, politics, religions, and egos.

The association between eustress (those moments of exhilaration and ecstasy) and spirituality, those cosmic moments Maslow called "peak experiences," is so profound that it is often taken for granted or overlooked. The converse, distress, is quite another matter. I have learned that, in many cases, stress (specifically, unresolved anger and fear) can be a roadblock to spiritual well-being, and that a strong human spirit can be a vital asset to dismantling roadblocks, resolving stress, and promoting a greater sense of inner peace. In turn, the resolution of life's stressors can actually enhance the strength and health of the human spirit if we choose to learn from our experiences. Although stress and the human spirit appear, on the surface, to be at opposite poles, they are quite literally partners in the dance of life (FIG. 8.1).

It is no coincidence that as the topic of stress grabs headlines across the nation, Americans seem to be on the verge of a new spiritual awareness. In fact, in the past decade alone, the word spirituality has begun to take on a greater level of comfort in the vocabulary of the media and the population in general. This new awareness of human spirituality, promoted by a nucleus of individuals with grass-roots inspiration, goes by several names—the human potential movement, the consciousness movement, and the New Age movement, among others—all of which imply both spiritual bankruptcy and spiritual awakening in humankind, at least in the Western hemisphere. In his classic book As Above, So Below, Ronald Miller describes a collective search for new forms of spirituality with which to make our lives more meaningful and relevant in a world of global social upheaval. With an appetite greater than that which can be satisfied by their existing institutions, people have begun to look beyond their own backyards to answer questions about how they fit into the bigger picture. As indicated by the title of Miller's book (which is an axiom from ancient Egypt), there is a growing appreciation and understanding that no separation exists between the two worlds. Rather, the divine essence "above" resides within ourselves, making the two one.

Perennial philosophy: A term used by Aldous Huxley to describe human spirituality, a transcendent reality beyond cultures, religions, politics, and egos.

FIGURE 8.1 In times of stress, people often search for answers to life's most difficult problems. This search is known as a spiritual hunger and often leads to a deeper search for life's meaning. A spiritual hunger can progress to a spiritual exploration, thus allowing for a deeper soul growth learning process.

The speed of this movement has also been fueled by a growing concern about ecology and the protection of the environment—a wake-up call of sorts. For example, the 2010 oil disaster in the Gulf of Mexico, the dramatic effects of global warming, and the rapid depletion of our natural resources, including the tropical rainforests—all issues on the discussion table at the 2012 United Nations "Earth Summit" in Rio de Janeiro—are fire alarms beckoning us to set aside our cultural and political differences and work together as one people. This was most clearly stated by 2007 Nobel Laureate Al Gore in his best-selling book Earth in the Balance: Ecology and the Human Spirit, in which he wrote, "The ecological perspective begins with a view of the whole, an understanding of how the various parts of nature interact in patterns that tend toward balance and persist over time. But this perspective cannot treat the earth as something separate from human civilization; we are a part of the whole too." This message was echoed once again as a moral imperative in his best-selling book An Inconvenient Truth based on his Academy Award–winning documentary. His message is as pertinent today as it was when it was originally written in 1993—perhaps even more so.

A Spiritual Hunger?

Genetic engineering. Global terrorism. Cloning. Global warming. Stem cell research. Extraterrestrial life. In times of crises and uncertainty, people of every generation and every culture have been known to seek help from a divine source. In the past, people took spiritual refuge in their religious traditions, and to a large extent this remains true today. However, at the beginning of the twenty-first century, new questions have emerged that are not so easily addressed by ancient texts, particularly as humans start to play God. Although the fear associated with the terrorist attacks on September 11, 2001, coupled with a perceived moral decay of the American culture, has sent many people running back to their religious roots, others seem a little disenchanted with the standard religious practices because they do not seem to provide adequate answers to the problems looming on the horizon of humanity. According to a 2012 Pew Research Center (PRC) study, the fastest growing religious group in the United States is made up of people who say they are not religious. Referred to as the "nones" (because when asked about their religious affiliation they reply "none"), the PRC estimates this group to be 46 million people and growing. Nones come from all walks of life, but are primarily under the age of 30. A PRC spokesperson noted that although some nones identify themselves as atheists or agnostics, the majority often describe themselves as "spiritual, but not religious," suggesting a shifting demographic within the United States (Glenn, 2013).

In what is being referred to by some as the post-denominational age, many people do not feel a loyalty to one particular religion; rather people seek a host of sacred traditions, blending various practices to form their own spiritual path. There are Catholics who practice Buddhist meditation, Jews who participate in American Indian sweatlodges, and Methodists, Lutherans, and Protestants who participate in Sufi dancing. Even hell has gotten a makeover: The biblical conception of the most dreaded place in the universe has moved from a literal to a figurative interpretation. Once described as eternal flames of death, the Vatican currently describes hell as "a state of those who freely and definitively separate themselves from God." Many of those who claim to have already been to hell (on earth, that is), as well as those who have come close, are seeking a better understanding of God.

The expression used today is spiritual hunger, a term that describes a searching or longing for that which cannot be attained by traditional religious practices. Another term used in conjunction with spiritual hunger is spiritual bankruptcy, a concept that suggests a sense of moral decay, perhaps caused by an emptiness that cannot be filled with material possessions. Yet a strong element of human nature (the ego) encourages us to try anyway. One only need reflect on the shootings on several college campuses, or other similar horrific events, to see that something is terribly amiss.

A third phrase commonly heard today is spiritual dormancy. It refers to people who for one reason or another choose not to recognize the importance of the spiritual dimension of health and well-being at both an individual and a societal level. The result of such inaction often leads to a state of dysfunction (a term many now call the "national adjective"). Like a person who hits the snooze button on the alarm clock, falling asleep on the spiritual path can have real consequences because one is ill equipped to deal not only with the problems at hand, but also with potential problems down the road.

A Turning Point in Consciousness

A number of factors have come together to raise human consciousness to today's current level of awareness. They include but are not limited to the following:

- Vatican II, which in the 1960s changed the Catholic mass from Latin to various indigenous languages around the world, thereby opening the doors to a wealth of knowledge of Christianity (which had pretty much remained known only to a chosen few because Latin is not a contemporary language).
- The invasion of Tibet by China in 1959, which not only forced thousands of Tibetans into exile around the world, but ultimately allowed for the sharing of their sacred knowledge, which had been largely inaccessible for thousands of years.
- The Apollo Space Project, with its mission to land Americans on the moon in 1969, allowed us for the first time to see planet Earth as a whole,

Spiritual hunger: A term to illustrate the quest for understanding of life's biggest questions, the bigger picture, and how each of us fits into it.

Spiritual bankruptcy: A term to convey the lack of spiritual direction, values, or less than desirable behaviors, suggesting moral decay.

Spiritual dormancy: A state in which someone chooses not to recognize the importance of the spiritual dimension of life, individually and socially.

suspended in space, a planet without borders. This view altered many minds with regard to the future of the planet and her many inhabitants.

- The proliferation of self-help groups that use variations of the twelve-step program, as outlined by Alcoholics Anonymous, that provide for relinquishing control of addiction to a higher power. Self-help membership is nondenominational.
- The American Indians, particularly the Lakota and Hopi, who for decades have been told by their elders not to share various aspects of their cultural heritage and spirituality because of lack of trust, have now been told this is the time to reveal their sacred knowledge, and they have done so. The Lakota Sioux prophecy foretold of the age of the white buffalo, when a shift in consciousness would appear. A white buffalo named Miracle was born in Janesville, Wisconsin, on August 20, 1994.
- The Hebrew Kabalah, the sect of Jewish mysticism held only by a chosen few for the past several millennia, has recently been made available to anyone who has an interest in this topic.
- A growing interest in Sufism, a mystical sect of Islam (often symbolized by the photographs of whirling dervishes) with republished and retranslated works of Rumi, Hafiz, and several others.
- Since the early 1970s, near-death experiences (NDEs) have been studied in earnest to learn more about the survivor's recollection. Research compiled by critical care physician Sam Parnia reveals that advances in modern medicine over the past several decades have resulted in a new phenomenon in which millions of documented NDEs have been reported by people from all religious denominations (Parnia, 2013). Those who recall their experience describe a new mission of compassion and inner peace. Children, many of whom have not been exposed to various spiritual matters, come back to consistently describe experiences of a divine mystical nature.
- In the 1990s, South American shamans for the first time shared their wisdom of healing with "their younger brothers" in the Northern hemisphere.
- The Telecommunications Revolution opened the door of information to anyone with access to the Internet. Knowledge from around the world in all its many sources suddenly has become accessible without the censorship of intellectuals, religious leaders, or politicians, who for centuries have played a major role in keeping people in the dark about a great many issues and facts. Access to information has become a major stepping stone toward higher consciousness.
- The official acceptance of global warming and climate change (Engel, 2002) has become a new wake-up call for planetary citizens to unite in a global effort to reduce greenhouse gases or face potentially catastrophic consequences due to dramatic shifts in population and utilization of natural resources.
- The collaboration between media giant Oprah Winfrey and best-selling author Eckhart Tolle in spreading the message of higher consciousness through his book, A New Earth, via her television show, Web site, online chat rooms, and podcasts to millions of people around the world.

Unthinkable right after September 11, 2001, today it is not uncommon to see universities and corporate health-promotion programs including courses on spiritual well-being as well as more traditional programs on physical well-being. Today, as the information age of the twenty-first century unfolds, concepts from all cultures, religions, and corners of the globe are now accessible to us. As the pieces of this jigsaw puzzle called the human spirit are assembled, it becomes increasingly obvious that despite subtle nuances and obvious differences, there are common denominators that tie and bind the integrity of the human spirit. First and foremost is a desire to learn, a personal quest of self-exploration. Be it instinctual or a learned trait, human behavior is often inspired by self-improvement, and herein lies the first step of the journey. In the words repeated by many Zen masters in the spirit of Chinese philosopher Lao Tzu, "There are many paths to enlightenment. The journey of each path begins with the first step."

The material in this chapter is a synthesis of several different perspectives on human spirituality. Some of these ideas may resonate with your way of thinking, whereas others may seem foreign, perhaps even intimidating, to your attitudes, beliefs, and values. The purpose of this chapter is not to intimidate you, but to show that despite our varied backgrounds and religious differences, there are elements common to all of us. I ask you to focus on these common elements, not the differences, as you read. It would serve you best to respect and be receptive to all ideas different from your own because, as you will see, an open attitude will ultimately strengthen your own beliefs and the integrity of your spiritual well-being.

Definition of Spirituality

It would be fair to say that human spirituality has been the focus of countless conversations dating back to antiquity. Yet, despite the millions of words and hundreds of philosophies exploring this concept, human spirituality is still a phenomenon for which no one definition seems adequate. Undoubtedly, it includes the aspects of higher consciousness, transcendence, self-reliance, self-efficacy, self-actualization, love, faith, enlightenment, mysticism, self-assertiveness, community, and bonding, as well as God, Allah, Jesus, Buddha, and a multitude of other concepts. Yet no aspect alone is sufficient to describe the essence of human spirituality. In various sources, the human spirit has been described as a gift to accompany one through life, an inner drive housed in the soul, and even a living consciousness of a divine-like presence within us and around us. These descriptions are poetic and profound, but they don't bring us any closer to a concrete understanding of what human spirituality really is. In many cultures, the word spirit means "first breath": that which enters our physical being with our first inhalation at birth. The Hebrews called this ruah, and even as the word is spoken, you can hear the rush of wind pass through your lips. Among some Eastern cultures, pranayama, or diaphragmatic breathing, is thought to have a spiritual essence that enhances physical calmness by uniting the body and mind as one, by breathing the universal energy. The ancient Greeks used the words pneuma to connote spirit and psyche to describe the human soul, the latter of which is now commonly associated with the study of human behavior, psychology. More recently, the World Health Organization (WHO) defined human spirituality as "that which is in total harmony with the perceptual and nonperceptual environment."

Sometimes defining what a concept is not becomes a type of definition in itself. For instance, human spirituality is neither a religion nor the practice of a religion (FIG. 8.2). Religions are based on a specific dogma: an active application of a specific set of organized rules based on an ideology of the human spirit. Being actively involved in a religion is considered enhancing of one's spirituality. This is one of religion's primary goals, and on the whole, religions are very effective in this. But now and again it has been noted by several psychologists that, like too much of anything at one time, too much religion can impede the growth of the human spirit for some people, leading to what psychologists Anne Wilson Schaef (1987) and Leo Booth (1991) call an addiction to religion. By the same token, elements of spirituality pushed to the extreme are considered unhealthy, too. Comedian Steven Wright jokingly states, "My girlfriend and I had conflicting attitudes. I wasn't into meditation and she wasn't into being alive." There is no doubt that religion can promote spiritual evolution; the two are very compatible. But individuals can be very spiritual, and not "religious" (in the sense of attending services), just as they can be very religious but have poor awareness of their spirituality. It is often said that where religion separates, spirituality unites. In the words of psychiatrist Viktor Frankl, "Spirituality does not have a religious connotation, but refers specifically to the human dimension." Spirituality, like water, and religions, like the various containers that attempt to hold it, are related yet separate concepts (FIG. 8.3). Like a Venn diagram (FIG. 8.4), spirituality and religion share common ground, but they are not the same thing.

FIGURE 8.2 When people hear the word spirituality, many think of religion. Although spirituality and religion share common ground, they are not the same thing. Spirituality is inclusive whereas religions are exclusive.

To define a term or concept is to separate and distinguish it enough from everything else to gain a clear focus and understanding of what it really is. All nonrelated aspects must be factored out to reach a clear and undiluted meaning.

Transcendence: A means to rise above the mundane existence to see a higher order to things, often used to describe human spirituality.

FIGURE 8.3 Although no language can adequately describe the concept of spirituality, the language of metaphor works the best. Spirituality is often described as being like water. Religions are similar to containers (some beautiful, some questionable) that hold water.

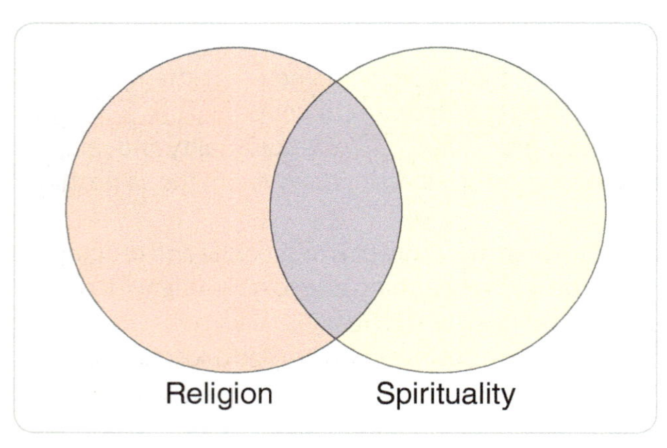

FIGURE 8.4 A Venn diagram depicts the concepts of spirituality and religion nicely, where the two circles contain common ground but are not the same.

This is where the difficulty lies when one attempts to formulate an adequate definition of the word spirituality. It appears that human spirituality encompasses so many factors, possibly everything, that to separate anything out denies a full understanding of the phenomenon. On the other hand, perhaps at this time, we just don't possess the vocabulary to express it to our complete comprehension. Sometimes, to understand a concept, you just have to experience it, and experiences will certainly vary, as will their interpretation. Typically, people tend to describe their collective spiritual experiences as a journey or path. Most important, for a path to enhance the maturation or evolution of the soul, it must be creative, not destructive; progressive, not regressive. It must stimulate and enhance, not stifle, spiritual well-being. Given this premise, remember, too, that there are many paths to enlightenment. No one path is superior to the others, so it doesn't matter which path you take, but only that you keep moving forward (growing) on the path you have chosen. To quote Carlos Castaneda in The Teachings of Don Juan, "Look at every path closely and deliberately. Try it as many times as you think is necessary. Then ask yourself, and yourself alone, one question. Does this path have a heart? If it does, the path is good; if it doesn't, it is of no use."

Theories of Human Spirituality

Human spirituality has been studied by several academic disciplines—most notably, philosophy, theology, sociology, and psychology. More recently, this topic has begun to be investigated in the fields of physics, nursing, and clinical medicine as well. Thus, human spirituality will be described henceforth in terms of the various theories devised to provide a better understanding of this concept in several different disciplines.

In the scientific disciplines, theories give rise to operational (working) definitions. From these definitions come conceptual models. From models come tools to assess and measure, and from measurements come a holistic picture of understanding. More often than not, the synthesis of a number of theories offers a mosaic that, up close, may look confusing, and even incomprehensible, but from a distant perspective, it closely approaches a representation of this mystical phenomenon. If human spirituality were compared to a huge mountain, then the individuals who created these theories are the ones who have bushwhacked a path to the top by articulating their own perspectives. Metaphorically speaking, what follows is an aerial view of this mountain, capturing but a few of the many paths reaching toward the summit. The paths described here are by individuals who have encountered and studied matters of the soul with various prophets, sages, and masters. Their personal perspectives, which arise from a range of disciplines and cultures, contribute pieces of the mosaic we call human spirituality. But they only begin to illustrate the nature of this unique human characteristic.

The Path of Carl Jung

Typically, when individuals first consider the source of the human spirit, their search leads them to external things, like nature and the heavens above. It was the work of psychiatrist Carl Jung who, as a pioneer in psychology, turned the search inward to explore the depths of the mind, as a means to understand the spiritual nature of humanity. Jung was fascinated with the human psyche, especially the relationship between the conscious mind and the unconscious mind. He spent much time learning about intuition, clairvoyance (dreams foretelling events that later actually happened), seemingly bizarre coincidences, and supernatural occurrences. His fascination led him to explore the mystical side of the mind, and for this reason he was ridiculed by many of his contemporaries. Yet, with time, perceptions have changed. Although Jung is still considered ahead of his time by many, today his theories are recognized as the cornerstones of not only mental and emotional well-being, but also spiritual well-being. And although Jung did not advocate any particular religion, his work is studied, taught, and cited by psychologists, theologians, and spiritual leaders around the world. Moreover, his work has given impetus to a new discipline of healing called transpersonal psychology or psychospirituality, the study of the relationship between the mind and the soul.

Unlike his mentor, Freud, an atheist who hypothesized that humans functioned at an instinctual level, Jung proposed that there was a spiritual element to human nature, a spiritual drive located in the realm of the unconscious mind, which manifests itself when it bubbles to the conscious level. As a man who studied the myths and belief systems of many cultures on virtually every continent, Jung observed similarities in the symbols in dreams and art by various races of people who had no possible way of communicating them to one another. From research conducted during his professional experiences as well as intensive self-reflection, Jung theorized that these similarities were often represented in symbolic forms he called archetypes. Archetypes are primordial images or concepts originating in the unconscious mind at a level so profound that they appear to be common elements, or elements of unity, among all humankind.

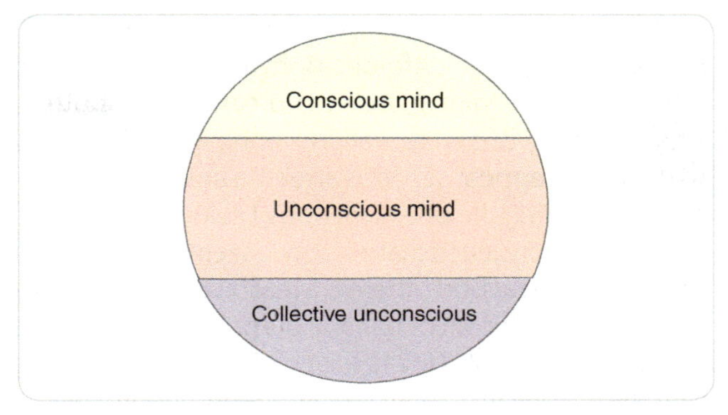

FIGURE 8.5 A symbolic representation of Jung's view of the mind with the collective unconscious residing in the depths of the unconscious mind. This aspect of the mind surfaces to consciousness through intuition, creativity, and dreams.

Jung proposed a dichotomy of levels constituting the unconscious mind: the personal unconscious and the collective unconscious (FIG. 8.5). The latter he described as universal consciousness: a unifying force within all individuals, or the collective soul. He believed that the collective unconscious was divine in its nature, the essence of God within all of us. According to Jung, this divine essence manifests in the conscious mind through several cognitive functions, including intuition, creativity, and the interpretation of dreams.

In his exploration of dreams, Jung discovered several people who dreamed of events they could have no possible knowledge of at a conscious level, only to discover that their dreams emerged as crystal-clear predictions of circumstances yet to come. In addition, sometimes during

Carl Jung: A twentieth-century psychiatrist who, under the initial tutelage of Sigmund Freud, forged a new premise of psychology honoring the importance of the human spirit. He became the second greatest influence in the field of psychology.

Transpersonal psychology: A discipline in the field of psychology that recognizes the spiritual dimension of the human condition.

Psychospirituality: A focus in the field of psychology, influenced by Carl Jung, to acknowledge the spiritual dimension of the psyche.

Archetypes: A Jungian term to describe primordial images that become symbolic forms with an inherent understanding among all people.

his counseling sessions, Jung would find himself in awe of coincidences that unfolded right in front of him. One example was listening to a client's dream about spotting a fox while the two were walking along a dirt road, only to have a fox appear seconds after the animal was mentioned. Studying the phenomenon of coincidences more closely, Jung concluded that when two seemingly unrelated events happen at once, there is a reason and purpose for it, whether significant or banal, a purpose that cannot be explained rationally by cause and effect. He coined the term synchronicity to explain this phenomenon. He also hypothesized that in reality there is no such thing as coincidence; rather, everything is connected, and events unfold simultaneously for a reason. His study of Taoism and the I Ching led him to believe that there is a connectedness extending beyond the individual throughout the entire universe, a concept not well accepted in the West during his lifetime (FIG. 8.6).

Synchronicity: A term coined by Carl Jung to explain the significance of two seemingly unrelated events that, when brought together, have a significant meaning.

"Look, I've got a really busy day planned. I don't have TIME for a complete shakedown of my belief system!"

FIGURE 8.6

Jung was once quoted as saying that "every crisis a person experiences over the age of 30 is spiritual in nature." While some only credit Jung with addressing the midlife-crisis phenomenon, Jungian psychologists have maintained the importance of spirituality to the individual, especially at midlife. With regard to this spiritual crisis, Jung further believed that modern men's and women's inability to get in touch with their inner selves provided fertile ground for life's stressors. He added that sickness is a result of not being whole—that is, never connecting with the divine qualities of the unconscious mind to clarify values and gain sharp focus on one's life's meaning.

Another of Jung's theories is that there are characteristics of the personality called the shadow that individuals keep hidden, even from themselves, but which they usually project onto other people. Confronting the shadow of the soul, or attaining profound self-awareness, allows individuals to come to terms with several issues that form the undercurrents for stress in their own lives so that they may become whole.

In a story recounted in his autobiography, Memories, Dreams, Reflections, Jung tells of a young boy who asked an old wise man why no one in this day and age ever sees the face or hears the voice of God. The wise old sage replied that man no longer lowers himself enough to God's level. Jung tells this story to reinforce the idea that people in "civilized" cultures have become distant from the wisdom and knowledge seated in the fathoms of the unconscious mind. Instead, they see God primarily as an external force or supreme being in the clouds. By contrast, Jung suggested that God is a unifying force that resides in all of us, in the depths of the unconscious mind. Like the ancient Asian mystics he studied, who practiced meditation to attain spiritual enlightenment, Jung advocated personal responsibility to examine the conscious and unconscious mind in an effort to find what he called psychic equilibrium. In Modern Man in Search of a Soul, he further warned that the advancement of technology and materialism, now accepted by many to be stressors, would further widen the gap between the conscious and unconscious minds. Jung believed that as technology and materialism increased, people would spend less and less time cultivating their inner selves. This observation, made in 1933, has come to pass at the beginning of the twenty-first century. It is interesting to note that Jung advised one of his clients that psychoanalysis alone would not cure him of his chronic alcoholism. In a letter to this client, Jung suggested that his best chance for cure was a "spiritual conversion." After Roland H.'s recovery, which he attributed to spiritual enlightenment, he and a friend, Bill W., started the now well-known organization for problem drinkers called Alcoholics Anonymous. Although this program is not tied to any particular religion, it is based on a very strong sense of spirituality.

Shortly before his death in 1961, Jung was interviewed by John Freeman of the British Broadcasting Corporation. When asked if he believed in God, Jung replied, "No." Then he paused for a moment, and stated, "I know."

The Path of M. Scott Peck

In 1978, M. Scott Peck ushered in a new age of spiritual awareness in American culture with a seminal book entitled The Road Less Traveled, now considered to be a classic. As a psychiatrist who spent many years counseling clients with neurotic and psychotic disorders, Peck became aware of a commonality among virtually all of them: either an absence or immaturity of spiritual development. He also noted that not all people were at the same level of spirituality, which made it a challenge to treat his clients.

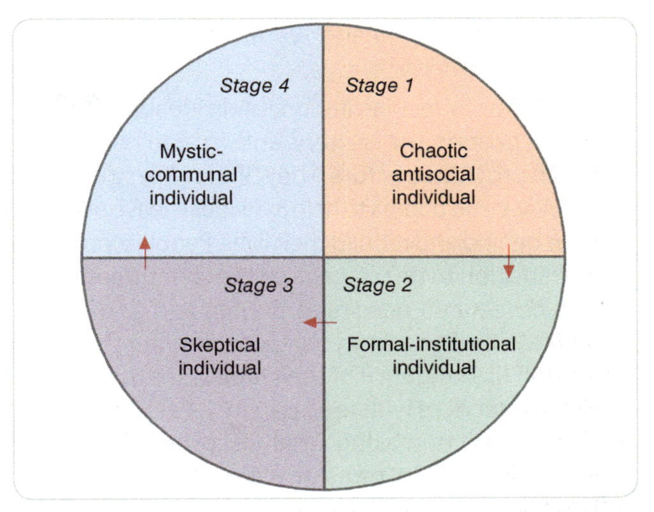

FIGURE 8.7 A symbolic representation of Peck's conception of human spirituality as a maturation process with four hierarchical stages.

Upon intense reflection on his own spiritual beliefs, coupled with what he observed in his clients, Peck developed a framework he called the road to spiritual development. This framework consists of four systematic, hierarchical stages of spiritual growth and development (FIG. 8.7): chaotic antisocial, formal-institutional, skeptical, and mystic-communal. (These stages are similar to James Fowler's stages of faith.) Admittedly, as Peck states in his book The Different Drum, not everyone falls neatly into one of these four categories. Some people hover between stages, and others migrate back and forth from one stage to another. Despite its shortcomings, which Peck admits to, this model provides a basis from which we can begin to understand the maturation of the human spirit. The stages are described as follows:

Stage 1: The chaotic antisocial individual. The first stage of Peck's road to spiritual development is an undeveloped spirituality or, in some cases, a spiritual absence or bankruptcy. As a rule, young children fall into this category because of their immaturity, but among adults, the chaotic antisocial individual is someone whose life is in utter chaos. This chaos can be represented by various attitudes and behaviors, including drug or alcohol addiction, codependency, or a helpless-hopeless attitude. Chaotic antisocial individuals can be very manipulative and unprincipled, and they often find that controlling others is easier than taking responsibility for their own lives. Individuals at this stage have a poor self-relationship; completely avoid self-awareness; maintain poor relationships with family, friends, and co-workers; hold a weak value system with many unresolved conflicts; and show an absence of a meaningful purpose in their lives. Some people remain at this stage their whole lives. A life-threatening situation, however, can act as a catalyst to move to the next stage. In preparation to leave this stage, the chaotic antisocial individual looks for some kind of structure to make order out of the chaos, and to

M. Scott Peck: A contemporary psychiatrist who reintroduced the aspect of human spirituality and psychology with his classic book, The Road Less Traveled.

Chaotic antisocial: The first stage of Peck's hierarchy of spiritual growth in which one's spiritual essence is lacking (spiritual bankruptcy).

Formal-institutional: The second stage of Peck's hierarchy of spiritual growth where one tends to find comfort in the guidelines of religious institutions.

Skeptical: The third stage of Peck's spiritual hierarchy where one shuns all religious dogma.

Mystic-communal: The fourth stage of Peck's spiritual hierarchy in which one perpetually and joyfully seeks life's answers in the mystical divine universe.

help slay some personal dragons masking themselves as chronic stressors.

Stage 2: The formal-institutional individual. Institutions such as prisons, the military, and, in many cases, the church provide structure. They offer rules, structured guidelines, and dogma to help individuals leave personal chaos behind and rebuild their lives. People who make the transition to this stage from the chaotic antisocial stage desperately need rules, dogma, and guidance to survive. Although many young people enter this stage through the influence of their families (e.g., going to religious services with their parents), Peck found that adults enter it by making an almost overnight conversion, a "born-again" transformation. In essence, they adopt the dogma of an institution as a means of personal survival. Peck observed that when an individual advances to this stage, it may be not only very sudden but also perhaps unconscious. A relationship with God parallels the parent–child relationship, where God is a loving but punitive God. In the words of Peck, "God becomes an 'Irish cop' in the sky." A supreme being is personified in human terms, and perhaps most important, God is purely an external figure who rewards and punishes one's behavior. People who advance to this stage come looking for personal needs to be met and for life's answers. Quite often they find what they are looking for. Comfortable with this stage, many people stay at this level for the rest of their lives. Some, however, may slip back into the first stage, and then oscillate between the two. Others eventually leave this stage because of unmet needs. They become skeptical of (perhaps) all institutions, yet remain spiritually stable enough to avoid slipping back to stage 1. At this point, such people begin a free-floating process, unanchored to anything.

Stage 3: The skeptical individual. When a person questions the dogma and rules necessary to maintain membership in a church or other organization that has provided some security, and becomes skeptical about the answers (or lack of answers) received, he or she may eventually leave the safety the organization once provided. Peck said that this is a crucial stage of spiritual development, when one begins to question the understanding the institution represents. This is also a very risky stage because there are no guaranteed answers elsewhere. Tongue in cheek, Peck calls people in this stage born-again atheists. People become skeptical when they find that the institution they joined does not fulfill or answer all their needs or expectations. Frustration turns into distrust, and they often leave the institution they once joined for refuge, becoming very cynical about it and perhaps about life in general. The skeptical individual is looking for truth, and according to Peck, is more spiritually developed than many devoted churchgoers. Some college students, and even more college graduates, reach this stage after years of following their parents' religious lead, and then finding that the beliefs on which they were raised no longer seem adequate for the situations in which they currently find themselves. The skeptical individual finds him- or herself in a very tenuous position, however, because everyone needs sure footing or an anchor eventually. Two outcomes are possible at this stage. Either one samples other church institutions and makes a half-hearted compromise along the way, or the individual progresses to the next and final stage of spiritual development.

Stage 4: The mystic-communal individual. In the continual search for answers to life's questions, some people eventually come to the realization that there are questions that have no answers. Unlike the skeptical individual who fights this premise, the mystic-communal individual takes delight in life's paradoxes. These people find comfort in the unanswerable, yet like sleuths, they seek out the continuing challenge, ever hungry for clues and possible answers. People in this stage of spiritual development love a good mystery, and they love to explore. Mystic-communals begin to depersonify God and come to the realization that God is an internal source (the power of love, faith, and will) as much as an external source (an unexplained energy or consciousness). Mystic-communals begin to see an outline of the whole picture even though several pieces are missing. These people see spirituality as a living process, not merely an outcome or heaven-oriented goal. Perhaps as important, they see the need to build and maintain a sense of community by developing quality relationships built on acceptance, love, and respect. They see and feel the need to be connected. Upon arrival at this stage, individuals realize that it is only the beginning of a very long but fruitful journey.

Like Jung, Peck hints that the continued inability to deal with psychological crises often manifests itself as spiritual immaturity, or not progressing through these stages of spiritual growth. And, similar to Maslow's hierarchy of needs, Peck agrees that individuals regress when stressful situations cause them to lose their footing on this road. For example, a person in the mystic-communal stage who experiences the death of a loved one may feel anger or guilt if the death is perceived as a form of punishment (Why me?). Many stressful situations cause individuals to focus on the external side of "God" (or lack thereof), often causing them to slip back into stage 2 or 3. Although the road to spiritual development is an independent one, Peck suggests that we are not alone on this journey. Love and grace are the guides that lead the way, when we choose to listen.

The Path of Hildegard von Bingen

The word spirit often conjures up the expression mystic for many, and in the case of Hildegard von Bingen this adjective is most accurate. However, the word mystic alone is not enough to describe this unique woman who lived in Germany at the turn of the twelfth century (1098–1179). Visionary, poet, composer, healer, artist, and saint are also words used to describe her, yet even these seem inadequate to capture the essence of Hildegard von Bingen. Born of a noble family near the town of Mainz, Hildegard was 8 years old when she first experienced a vision of light, followed by a period of intense illness. At first not familiar with the meaning of her experience, she soon understood that this vision was in some way a message from God. Not long after her first vision, she acquired a remarkable psychic ability, which left her family rather puzzled. As was the custom of her day, Hildegard, the tenth child in her family, was brought to a monastery to be looked after and raised in the hope that her work and accomplishments would please the church.

The first vision was actually one of many to occur throughout her life. Hildegard was encouraged by members of her order to write what she saw in these visions.

> What I write is what I see and hear in the vision. I compose no other words than those I hear, and I set them forth in unpolished Latin just as I hear them in the vision, for I am not taught in this vision to write as philosophers do. And the words of the vision are not like words uttered by the mouth of many but like a shimmering flame, or a cloud floating in a clear sky.

In what is considered to be her most impressive writing, Scivias, she describes a series of visions illustrating the story of creation, the dynamic tension between light and darkness, the work of the holy spirit, and several words of encouragement to ponder and savor as we each journey on the human path. Her writings didn't go unnoticed. Word soon traveled to Pope Eugenius III, who sent for copies of these writings. So impressed was he that he not only gave his blessings, but also sent words of support to Hildegard to continue her writings, thus making her a celebrity.

In the time of the Dark Ages, the vision Hildegard saw wasn't just a ray of light in the shadows—it became a philosophy that breathed life into a people with a spiritual hunger. And in a time when women took a back seat to the dominance of male authority, Hildegard's presence and renown demonstrated a higher order of humanity.

Her message was simple: There is a holistic nature to the universe, just as there is a holistic nature to humanity. And just as man and woman are essential parts of the universe, so too is the universe an essential part to be found within each individual. In other words, this message is similar to the axiom, "As above, so below," or "As the microcosm, so the macrocosm." As if extending an invitation into nature, she encouraged the "greening" of the soul, a process whereby one engages with the natural world as a part of it, instead of shutting oneself off from it. Hildegard also spoke to the principle of each soul. She routinely emphasized that our soul is not to be found in our body; rather, it is our body that resides in our soul. The body, she said, is the instrument of the soul, a means by which our divine essence can function in the material world. The soul, a unique aspect of our divine nature, is boundless and contains our dreams, hopes, wishes, and desires. Can all things be spiritual? This, indeed, was the message of Hildegard von Bingen. From her visions described in Scivias she learned that all things are sacred, "Every creature is a glittering, glistening mirror of divinity."

In times of spiritual hunger, people often look back to those in earlier times who were able to hold the light of divine essence and in turn share it. Perhaps this is why today, after nearly 1,000 years, the music composed by Hildegard von Bingen has been recorded in a popular CD entitled Vision, along with a similar best-selling recording of Benedictine monks entitled Chant.

The Path of Black Elk

American Indians in the United States number some several hundred tribes. Although cultural differences abound among them, from the Algonquins in the Northeast to the Navajo in the Southwest, their spirituality is fairly

Hildegard von Bingen: An early Christian mystic who added a feminine voice to a male-dominated Christian theology.

consistent regardless of tribe. One voice that ascended the heights of consciousness in American Indian culture was that of Black Elk, a medicine man of the Ogalala Sioux (Lakota) nation. His mystical visions, recorded by John G. Neihardt in the book Black Elk Speaks, have galvanized the understanding and appreciation of American Indian spirituality, also referred to as Mother Earth spirituality. Despite the devastation of his culture by European traditions and values, Black Elk's vision was quite profound and elaborate with respect to the essence and integrity of the human spirit and the bonding relationship between the two-legged (man) and his natural environment.

Perhaps the features that most distinguish American Indian spirituality from that of other cultures are its set of values demonstrating respect for and connectedness to Mother Earth. Black Elk is not alone in voicing this philosophy; it has been expressed by a great many American Indians. In the words of Shoshone shaman Rolling Thunder, who describes the earth as a living organism, "Too many people don't know that when they harm the earth they harm themselves" (Boyd, 1974). In his book, Mother Earth Spirituality, Ed McGaa (Eagle Man) both expounds on Black Elk's vision and augments this knowledge with additional insights of the American Indian culture to provide a more profound understanding of Black Elk's enlightenment. The following is a brief synopsis of Black Elk's influence on spiritual healing.

First, despite the conviction of Christian missionaries that Indians were pagans, American Indians had established a very profound relationship with a divine essence. Unlike Europeans, who personified this higher power, American Indians accepted divine power as the Great Mystery, with no need to define or conceptualize God in human terms. In the words of Chief Seattle, transcribed for a letter to President Franklin Pierce in 1855, "One thing we know, our God is the same God. You may think you own Him as you wish to own land, but you cannot. He is the God of man; and his compassion is equal for the red man and the white. The earth is precious to Him, and to harm the earth is to heap contempt on its creator. Our God is the same God. This earth is precious to Him" (Gore, 1993) (BOX 8.1). This preciousness was and continues to be represented in the bonding relationship between each American Indian and the earth's creatures, the wind, the rain, and the mountains.

North American indigenous peoples see Mother Earth as a symbol of wholeness and represent it with a medicine wheel. Just as the seasons are divided into quarters, so too are many concepts of American Indian spirituality. Some, for example, identify four elements: earth, fire, water, and air; four earth colors: red, yellow, black, and white; four directions: east, west, north, and south; and four cardinal principles or values of the Red Way: to show respect for Wankan Tanka (the Great Mystery or Great Spirit), to demonstrate respect for Mother Earth, to show respect for each fellow man and woman, and to show respect for individual freedoms. The American Indian medicine wheel is a symbol of Mother Earth spirituality from which the lessons of nature are used to better understand oneself (FIG. 8.8). To people of these cultures, each quadrant of the wheel represents a specific aspect of spiritual growth and various lessons to learn. The eastern quarter represents the Path of the Sun, where respect is shown for ourselves, others, and the environment. The southern quarter is the Path of Peace and is characterized by the traits of youth, innocence, and wonder. The western quarter is referred to as the Path of Introspection, where time is allocated for the soul-searching process and striving for a balance between physical substance and spiritual essence within oneself. The northern quarter represents the Path of Quiet, which symbolizes the importance of mental health, in which the intellect is stimulated by the lessons of nature.

Although there are several ceremonies to celebrate American Indian spirituality—the most famous being a feast of Thanksgiving taught to European settlers nearly 400 years ago—one practice, called the vision quest, exemplifies the strong bond with Mother Earth especially well. The vision quest is recognized as a time of self-reflection, which helps one to understand one's purpose in life, to become grounded in the earth and centered with the Great Spirit, and to reach a clearer understanding of one's contribution to the community. During a vision quest, an individual isolates him- or herself in the wilderness, on a hilltop, a large meadow, or any area that provides privacy. The vision quest creates an opportunity for emptying the mind (meditation) and body

Black Elk: An early twentieth century Native American elder whose perspective of spirituality is often cited as the clarion vision of our relationship with Mother Earth.

Mother Earth spirituality: The expression used to describe the American Indian philosophy with the divine through all of nature.

Vision quest: An American Indian custom of a retreat in nature where one begins or continues to search for life's answers.

BOX 8.1 A Letter from Chief Seattle (1855)

The president in Washington sends word that he wishes to buy our land. But how can you buy or sell the sky? the land? The idea is strange to us. If we do not own the freshness of the air, and the spark of the water, how can you buy them? Every part of this earth is sacred to my people. Every shining pine needle, every sandy shore, every mist in the dark woods. All are holy in the memory and experience of my people. We know the sap that courses through the trees as we know the blood that courses through our veins. We are part of the earth and it is part of us. Perfumed flowers are our sisters. The bear, the deer, the great eagle; these are our brothers. The body heat of the pony and man belong to the same family. The shining water that moves through the streams and rivers is not just water, but the blood of our ancestors. If we sell you our land, you must remember it is sacred.

Each ghostly reflection in the clear water of the lakes tells of the event and the memory in the life of my people. The water's murmur is the voice of my father's father. The rivers are my brothers. They quench our thirst, they carry our canoes and feed our children. So you must give to the river the kindness that you would give any brother. If we sell you our land, remember that the air is precious to us. The air shares its spirit with all life which it supports. The wind that gave our grandfather his first breath also receives his last sigh. The wind also gives our children the spirit of life.

So if we sell you our land, you must keep it apart and sacred as a place where man can go to taste the wind that is sweetened by the meadow's flowers. Will you teach your children what we have taught our children; that the earth is our Mother? What befalls the earth, befalls all the sons of the earth. This we know: the earth does not belong to man, man belongs to the earth. All things connect, like the blood that unites us all. Man did not weave the web of life, he is merely a strand in it. Whatever he does to the web, he does to himself. One thing we know: our God is your God. The earth is precious to him and to harm the earth is to heap contempt on the creator.

Your destiny is a mystery to us. What will happen when the buffalo are all slaughtered, the wild horses tamed? What will happen when the secret corners of the forest are heavy with the scent of many men and the view of the ripe hills is blotted with talking wires? Where will the thicket be? Gone! Where will the eagle be? Gone! And what is it to say good-bye to the swift pony and the hunt—the end of living and the beginning of survival. When the last red man has vanished in his wilderness, and his memory is only the shadow of a cloud moving across the prairie, will these shores and forests still be here? Will there be any spirit of my people left? We love the earth as a newborn loves his mother's heartbeat. So if we sell you our land, love it as we love it. Care for it as we have cared for it. Hold in your mind the memory of the land as you received it. Preserve the land for all children, and love it as God loves us all. As we are part of the land, you too are part of the land. It is precious to us, it is also precious to you. One thing we know: there is only one God. No man, be he red man or white, can be apart. We are brothers after all.

Modified by Ted Perry, loosely based on Chief Seattle's 1854 oration, "The Great Ecology" as it appeared in the Seattle Sunday Star, Oct. 29, 1887.

(fasting). The emptying process allows the human spirit to be filled with energy from the Great Spirit, leading the individual toward a path of self-enlightenment and self-improvement. Typically performed as a rite of passage from adolescence into adulthood, a vision quest can also be taken any time there is a need for spiritual growth or guidance.

Nearly extinguished by Christian missionaries a century or more ago, many elements of American Indian spirituality are now beginning to be recognized and respected, particularly in light of concerns about the poor "health status" of the planet (the environment). Ironically, it is now the "white man" who is adopting this value from the American Indian.

The Path of Matthew Fox

Matthew Fox is a former Roman Catholic theologian who, much like American Indians in the centuries before, was silenced by the Vatican in 1989 for his "progressive" views on human spirituality and has since been excommunicated from the church. The premise of Fox's theory is that the

Matthew Fox: A Christian theologian renowned for his theory of creation spirituality and many other concepts. He was silenced by the Vatican in 1989 for one year followed by excommunication in 1999. He is now an Episcopal minister in California.

FIGURE 8.8 The Native American medicine wheel, which honors the four directions and the four seasons (Mother Earth spirituality).

Judeo-Christian concept of spirituality, formulated when it was believed that the earth was the center of the universe, has not kept pace with scientific discoveries of the earth as but a piece of the whole universe and by no means its center. Fox has attempted to unite many concepts of theology with the laws and theories of physics in what he terms creation spirituality. Creation spirituality suggests that divinity can be found in any act of creation, from the atom to the far reaches of the cosmos, and every particle in between. The seed of creativity is energy, an element that binds all things together. And, as stated in the first law of thermodynamics, energy is neither created nor destroyed.

Fox was inspired by the work of the thirteenth-century German theologian Meister Eckhart, many American Indians, Albert Einstein, and a divine presence he terms the cosmic Christ. Through these influences, he has developed four paths or attitudes of creation spirituality (FIG. 8.9), which in his opinion raise individual consciousness and thus the spiritual level of humankind as a whole. These paths are as follows:

Creation spirituality: A term coined by theologian Matthew Fox to describe the paths of human spirituality blending the laws of physics and theology.

Via positiva: Fox's term to describe a sense of awe and wonder of creation.

Via negativa: Fox's term to describe the act of emptying and letting go of unnecessary thoughts and feelings.

Via creativa: Fox's term to describe a breakthrough or moment of enlightenment.

Via transformativa: Fox's term to describe the euphoria from the realization of insights and the responsibility to share these with others.

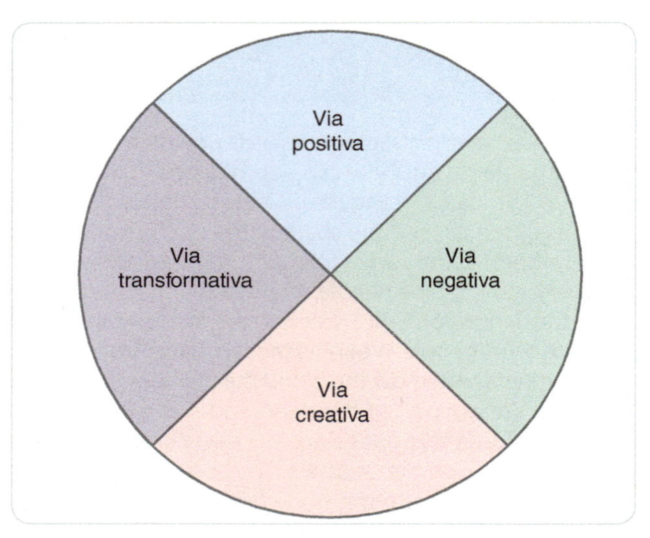

FIGURE 8.9 A symbolic representation of Fox's creation spirituality.

Path 1: *Via positiva.* A sense of awe and wonder at the design and creation of all that surrounds us. Like the wonder of a young child, via positiva is a continual awareness and appreciation of all things, from the simplicity of a blade of grass to the mechanical complexity of the space shuttle. All creation should be celebrated, not feared or shamed.

Path 2: *Via negativa.* The process of emptying or letting go of thoughts, feelings, values, even possessions that weigh down, enclose, and smother the soul, depriving it of nutrients for growth. Via negativa is a period of darkness, silence, even fasting of the soul, for only when emptiness occurs is there room for new growth. This stage also goes by a less favorable name, "the dark night of the soul." This process may be emotionally painful at times, yet it is necessary for the maturation of the human spirit.

Path 3: *Via creativa.* A breakthrough or explosion of enlightenment, which fills the space vacated through the cleansing process of via negativa. This enlightenment may come in the form of divine inspiration, intuitive thoughts, or imagination. Via creativa is human creativity, which increases the quantity and quality of awe in the universe.

Path 4: *Via transformativa.* Fox calls via transformativa the path of struggle, compassion, and celebration. With this path comes the responsibility to act on the enlightenment and inspiration from via creativa by channeling divine energy into personal acts of creation, and using this positive creative energy for the betterment of humankind.

Fox suggests that all people see themselves as acts of creation, deserving of awe and wonder. In turn, the ability to use one's imagination and creativity will add to the awe of the universe. These four paths align themselves in what Fox calls a sacred hoop, or a circle symbolizing wholeness, with each path nourishing the others to their full potential. The connection between each element of this hoop is compassion. Compassion, as defined by Fox, is a continual celebration of life and includes the fulfillment of love, forgiveness, and a personal as well as public display of one's spirituality. Thus, human spirituality involves the integration of all four paths into one road, or what Fox refers to as a "'personal cosmology'—a relationship to the divine presence that dwells in us." When asked how to cultivate this divine relationship, Fox in turn asks these questions: What poets do you read? What music moves you? What acts of creation are you involved with? What social issues are your passion? What work do you most love doing? What pain is in your emptiness? When do you feel a connection to the universe? From Fox's perspective, the fulfillment of these answers nurtures the growth of the human spirit.

The Path of Joan Borysenko

New to the emerging discipline of psychoneuroimmunology, Joan Borysenko hit the ground running as cofounder, therapist, and director of the Mind/Body Clinic affiliated with the Harvard Medical School in Boston, Massachusetts. Through working with her mentor, stress physiologist Dr. Herbert Benson, her patients, and her personal journey of self-enlightenment, Borysenko began to synthesize an understanding of the connections among the body, mind, and soul. One observation inspiring her journey was that some of her clients' personal faith seemed to be stronger than any clinical medicine—faith that caused cancerous tumors to go into spontaneous remission, healed several illnesses, or simply brought inner peace in the last moments of life.

But just as faith can heal, so its absence can quicken the pace of physical illness and even death. Borysenko is among a growing number of clinical specialists who believe that the mechanistic approach to medicine is very much outdated. As explained in Guilt Is the Teacher, Love Is the Lesson, the mind and spirit play a crucial role in the health and healing process of the body. For example, for a new medicine to be proven clinically effective, it must cure more than 35 percent of the people who use it. Below this point of demarcation, cures are considered the result of the placebo effect, or healing by faith alone (Brody, 2000). That is, sugar water and sugar pills have a healing rate of 35 percent (and in some cases up to 70 percent) among people who believe they will cure them of their disease. In addition, in a now-famous study cited by Borysenko, patients who had a view of nature outdoors from their rooms were released from the hospital sooner, indicating a significantly faster recovery rate, than those patients who had either no view or a view of adjacent brick buildings (Ulrich, 1984). These facts and several others indicated to Borysenko that a significant factor in the human equation has been ignored regarding the treatment of illness and disease—the factor of human spirituality.

In her campaign of health promotion, which has included several books, interviews, and national presentations, Borysenko advocates healing the human spirit as an integral part of physical healing and emphasizes the important role of spirituality in the self-healing process. Spirituality is defined by Borysenko (1990) as "a reconnection (remembrance) of our eternal connection with a lifeforce or power that we are a part of." Strongly influenced by the works of Jung, Larry Dossey, and others, Borysenko advocates the importance of building a relationship with the inner self and taking the time to get to know the real self. The distance that people keep from this self-center—distance created by shame, guilt, and the expectations of who we should be rather than who we really are—is fertile ground upon which to sow the seeds of stress. She also believes that through the ability to know the self we strengthen the bonds with higher consciousness as well as with the people within our community. In her original definition, influenced by Richard Lazarus, she believed stress to be the inability to cope, but she now proposes that stress is a lack of connectedness.

Personal cosmology: Fox's term to explain one's personal relationship with the divine that dwells in each of us.

Joan Borysenko: An early pioneer in the field of psychoneuroimmunology who emphasized the importance of spirituality as part of the mind-body concept.

Borysenko (1990) describes two possible attitudes relating to the development of the human spirit: spiritual optimism and spiritual pessimism. She defines spiritual optimism as "an intuitive knowledge that love is the universal energy and the human condition is ripe for learning experiences in which love manifests." Conversely, spiritual pessimism she describes as an attitude that nurtures low self-esteem, guilt, and all that impedes the way of love. Borysenko adds that spiritual pessimism is directly tied to low self-esteem, which produces psychological helplessness. In her work, she has observed many emotional roadblocks that not only impede spiritual development, but also appear to wreak havoc on the physiological systems of the body, leading to the onset of disease and illness. These emotions are commonly seen in the stress response: fear, anger, worry, and guilt, with guilt (in her opinion) as one of the largest obstacles to spiritual growth. Like Fox, Borysenko emphasizes the importance of compassion: "the flower of psychospiritual growth." To access this and other spiritual components of human nature, Borysenko advocates the practice of meditation to calm the mind and find peace in the soul. Stress, she says, is an obstacle to the spiritual nature of humankind. Meditation, like a warm wind that clears the sky of clouds to allow a view of the heavens, clears the mind of the taxing and toxic thoughts that obstruct the pathway of nutrients to the soul. Meditation, she believes, is a process for emptying the mind and making way for new insight into the real self, an insight that can guide one around the obstacles of life.

In her book A Woman's Journey to God, Borysenko notes that women constitute the greatest percentage of Americans she labels as "religious drop-outs"—those women who leave the institution of their religious upbringing to wander, drift, and possibly reconnect to another affiliation with more acceptance. One reason for this apathy can be found in the language of several religions where male pronouns describing God exclude the female gender—a big issue to many women in an age of equal rights. She states that the white-male hierarchy has become a huge roadblock on the spiritual path to women of the baby-boomer generation and their children.

Spiritual optimism: Joan Borysenko's description of an intuitive knowledge that love is the universal energy.

Spiritual pessimism: Joan Borysenko's description of an attitude that nurtures low self-esteem, guilt, and other less-than-becoming behaviors.

Deepak Chopra: A contemporary physician and metaphysician originally from India, he presents and integrates the ageless wisdom of spirituality, quantum physics, and medicine.

Borysenko describes each woman's quest for a relationship to the divine as a spiritual pilgrimage. Although not outlining a systematic progression of steps on this pilgrimage, Borysenko shares her insights on how a woman might journey through various stages of the feminine quest. Borysenko suggests that each woman connect to the creative aspect of the divine and not see God entirely as a male entity. She cites menses and childbirth as examples of the creative process. Next she conveys the importance of resolving anger issues that develop (some as early as childhood) in what she terms as the first step to healing. Borysenko then speaks of the practice of rituals as a means to remember the divine connection. Rituals may include baby showers, candle ceremonies, retreats—anything to place one in the conscious recognition of God or Goddess. A final aspect of the feminine path Borysenko talks about is the connection to other women through support groups, prayer circles, or other venues where women can share their stories. For generations upon generations, stories have been the vehicle by which women have passed on spiritual truths to each other and their children.

In A Woman's Journey to God, Borysenko writes, "A quiet awakening is under way as women are coming together to worship, to tell stories, and find their place spiritually, if not always religiously, in the household of God. Women's spirituality groups are popping up everywhere. . . . Women often report a deep sense of connection to God as part of friendship, or mothering. We see God in others." It is this aspect of the feminine path that Borysenko shares in the hopes of inclusiveness and healing of the human spirit.

The Path of Deepak Chopra

One might think that spirituality and medicine would go hand in hand because both honor the essence of life, but that is not how Dr. Deepak Chopra or any of his physician colleagues and peers were introduced to the science of medicine. An endocrinologist by training, Chopra came to the United States from India and landed a job in New Jersey in 1970. With his sights set on a bigger hospital, he soon ended up outside of Boston, working as chief of staff at New England Memorial Hospital. Frustrated at the limitations of Western medicine, Chopra returned to his Indian roots and began to explore Ayurvedic medicine, an ancient form of holistic health care, which, when translated, means the Science of Life where mind, body, and spirit connect as one. On a path that led him from allopathic to holistic medicine, Chopra soon discovered that mind-body medicine, or psychoneuroimmunology as it is referred to clinically, is really mind-body-spirit medicine, in which the human spirit plays an integral role in the healing process. His search into psychoneuroimmunology and the essence of spirituality led him to study with the founder of Transcendental Meditation (TM), Maharishi Mahesh Yogi, where he began to understand the concepts of mind and consciousness. This exposure to consciousness began to galvanize his understanding of the intricacies of the human condition in states of disease and health and matters of the soul.

But Chopra didn't rest there. An avid reader, he, like a child with a crayon, began to connect the dots of wisdom from all corners of the earth, including the writings of Einstein, Blake, Rumi, the Bhagavad Gita, the Bible, the Koran, Lao Tzu, Tagore, and others to synthesize a comprehensive if not universal understanding of the nature of God and the laws that govern all creation.

The author of several books, including Quantum Healing, Perfect Health, and Ageless Body, Timeless Mind, Chopra has now focused his attention on the matters of the soul. In his book The Seven Spiritual Laws of Success, Chopra presents a simple guideline of seven principles for embracing the spirit of life in everyday living.

The Law of Pure Potentiality. Understanding that at the core of our essence is pure consciousness, the law of pure potentiality reminds us to enter in silence the core of our being and tap the universal wisdom in which to create and reach our potential. In the Western culture, it is common to seek validation through external objects. The law of pure potentiality reminds us that we only need look inside to find our divine essence. Once this source is accessed, we become co-creators and active participants, rather than passive victims on the human journey.

The Law of Giving. According to this law, the universe is a dynamic cornucopia. Nothing is static. Energy flows freely. In support of the axiom, "As you give, so shall you receive," the law of giving reminds us to keep open the channels of our heart, for when the heart is closed, the energy becomes blocked and the stagnation of universal energy leads to an atrophy of the spirit. Chopra points out that the derivation of the words affluence and currency has nothing to do with money. Rather, it means to flow, a lesson the law of giving teaches. Nature abhors a vacuum; however, she is not fond of gluttony either. The law of giving reminds us to walk in balance.

The Law of Karma (or Cause and Effect). As if taken from a law of physics stating that every action has an equal and opposite reaction, the law of karma invites us to become more responsible for our thoughts and actions. The law of karma, similar to the Christian expression, "As you sow, so shall you reap," invites us to shed the habits that inhibit our growth, break the bonds of conditioned thoughts, and become responsible (the ability to respond) for our every action.

The Law of Least Effort. Nature teaches us that water finds its own level. The universe unfolds in its own time and place. If we try to rush it, we only tire ourselves. The law of least effort invites us to go with the flow, not resist what we cannot change or influence. Chopra writes that nature's intelligence functions effortlessly. To be in harmony with nature means to go with the flow. One aspect of least effort is to accept those things we cannot change. A second aspect of least effort is to initiate self-responsibility rather than cast blame on others. The law of least effort asks us to travel the human path lightly, discarding those opinions, beliefs, and attitudes that are defensive in nature, for when we carry these, the human journey becomes a struggle, rather than a delightful sojourn.

The Law of Intention and Desire. We attract what we submit to the universal consciousness through intention. "Intention," writes Chopra, "grounded in the detached freedom of the present, serves as the catalyst for the right mix of matter, energy, and space-time events to create whatever it is that you desire." The Buddha once said that all suffering comes from desire. What is implied in the teachings of the Buddha is that the partner of desire is

The Law of Pure Potentiality: A reminder to be silent and look within for guidance and insights rather than validation through external means.

The Law of Giving: A reminder to live life with an open heart to give and receive freely.

The Law of Karma (or Cause and Effect): A reminder that we reap what we sow.

The Law of Least Effort: A reminder to go with the flow with things that we cannot control as well as to live in harmony with nature.

The Law of Intention and Desire: A reminder to set our intentions for both big and small goals, yet not become encumbered by the ego's desires.

detachment or letting go. Attachment to our desires most likely will create suffering when our intentions are not fully realized. As you intend, so must you detach, and let the universe take care of the details.

The Law of Detachment. The law of detachment is an invitation to let go of our desires, wishes, and dreams. It's not that we don't want the desired outcome, but detachment allows the desire to stand on its own two feet. This law serves as a reminder that we are co-creators in the universe of our lives, but not codependent on it. Detachment means to let go of the emotions that align with our desires—fear and anger, if our desires go unfulfilled. The law of detachment is one of the hardest laws to honor because we often place our security in those things we keep near us. Implicit in the law of detachment is the concept of trust. When we let go of thoughts, wishes, and desires, we are trusting that whatever the outcome, it is in our best interest. So if we apply for a job (intention) and we don't get it, we must realize that at a higher level of consciousness, this was in our best interest. Those things in our best interest will come back to us as intended.

The Law of Dharma or Life Purpose. Each of us has a unique gift and talent to share with the community of humanity. This law invites us to realize what our life purpose or mission is, and to act on it, so that we help raise consciousness for one and all. Dharma is the ancient Sanskrit word for purpose or mission. The acceptance of life on Earth requires that we not only realize our purpose, but also act to fulfill it so that all may benefit from it.

In his acclaimed book How to Know God, Chopra uses the template of the seven chakras as a way to expand one's level of awareness to a higher level of consciousness. It is Chopra's thesis (and he is not alone in this thought) that each person must journey back to the divine source by cultivating a relationship through mind and heart.

The Law of Detachment: A reminder to release and let go of all thoughts that hold back our human potential.

The Law of Dharma or Life Purpose: This law invites contemplation of one's purpose in life.

Jesus of Nazareth: A remarkable spiritual leader with a timeless message of compassion, forgiveness, and integrity.

Unconditional love: An altruistic love expressed by Jesus of Nazareth, where nothing is expected in return.

In doing so, we come to realize that we partner with God in the creation process of our own lives.

Chopra has become a bridge that unites not just spirituality and medicine, but many facets of humanity that have become divided through ego and fear. If asked, he and others like him will tell you that we, the human species, stand on the precipice of great change. For us to weather this change and become self-realized, we must work to evolve our soul growth, and this can be done by honoring and practicing the seven universal laws of spirituality.

The Path of Jesus of Nazareth

More than 2,000 years ago, a unique man appeared in the Middle East, and his presence has since left an indelible mark on humanity. His teachings were profound, his healings miraculous, and his death a mystery. Some people called him a prophet, others called him the Messiah, and still others called him a heretic. Little is known about Jesus of Nazareth other than that he was born in a barn, worked as a carpenter, shared his philosophies with others, and died a cruel death. He never wrote down any of his teachings; rather, he shared his simple yet profound wisdom with followers who yearned to understand his enlightenment, and they in turn created a community years later called Christianity. Decades after his death, in an effort to remember those teachings, his followers recorded his wisdom, stories, and healing practices in a collection of manuscripts now known as the New Testament of the Holy Bible. Scholars and theologians continue to study and interpret his words of wisdom today. It may be difficult, if not impossible, to separate the messenger from the message, but if we focus on the fundamental principle taught by Jesus, we find that his basic premise is the power of unconditional love (FIG. 8.10). What follows is a small sampling of insights and reflections on this theme (Borg, 2008).

When Jesus began teaching in the Middle East, there was much civil conflict and strife. The Hebrews in Jerusalem were oppressed by the Romans and in essence were treated as second-class citizens in their own country. Many were searching for a political leader to save them and return them to a life of undisturbed peace. In this time of ambivalence and hatred, Jesus preached and practiced the power of unconditional love. He was charismatic, his style was uniquely humble, and he attracted many followers who in their hearts believed he possessed the qualities of a great political leader. But Jesus of Nazareth regarded himself as a spiritual leader only. By his example and teachings, he showed men and women

FIGURE 8.10 A symbolic representation of human spirituality from the perspective of Jesus of Nazareth.

how to restore and maintain inner peace through a loving relationship with God. Beyond all else, he believed that through love all things were possible.

Based on the inspirational words of Jesus and his followers, many people have since attempted to illustrate the concept of love on the canvas of their own hearts. Scottish theologian Henry Drummond described love as a spectrum of several attributes, including patience, kindness, generosity, humility, unselfishness, and sincerity. Theologian Thomas Merton wrote in his book The Ascent to Truth that love is the source of one's merit, and as such, it is in love that God resides. Psychiatrist Gerald Jampolsky defines love as an experience absent from fear and the recognition of complete union with all life. To Jesus, the expression of love was like a passageway. For love to be effective as a channel of communication or healing energy, there must be no obstructions and no conflicting thoughts to pollute it. In other words, there must be no conditions or expectations placed on the expression of love. Like a child who acts spontaneously, the expression of love must be uninhibited, not filtered by conscious (ego) thought. As Jesus elaborated, people under oppression, whether by foreign rulers or the perceptions of their own minds, begin to close and harden their hearts. Their ability to feel and express love is overridden by critical, judgmental, and conditional thinking, thought processes often rooted in fear. But as described by Ken Carey in the book Starseed, these two concepts are mutually exclusive: You cannot experience love and fear at the same time. From the writings of Jesus' followers, we see that it is fear, expressed in terms of hatred, greed, and guilt, that is the greatest obstacle to love.

Love has an inherent healing power all its own, and it was this power that Jesus demonstrated in performing his miracles of giving sight to the blind and health to the infirm. Inspired by the book A Course in Miracles, Jampolsky cites love as a divine energy that knows no bounds. In his own book, Teach Only Love, Jampolsky explains that when love is undiluted it becomes the most powerful source of healing energy. When there is a conscious shift from the motivation of fear to the motivation of love, then nothing real is impossible.

Once while teaching, Jesus was asked about the greatest rule to live by. His reply was to love unconditionally—specifically, to love God and to extend this love to each human being as you would to yourself. Jesus further explained that God resides in each and every one of us: "The Kingdom of God is within you." These words, although not new, were novel in their meaning. Given the hatred and fear in the hearts of the Hebrews at the time, it seemed incongruous to love one's enemy as Jesus suggested. His message here was that forgiveness is a crucial element of unconditional love. To elaborate on this theme, he shared the story of the prodigal son, a young man who wasted his inheritance on foolish pleasures and then came crawling back home destitute. Yet his father welcomed him back and forgave him completely. This was an example of the depth of God's unconditional love for all people.

Jesus also spoke about faith and its relationship to love. Faith, a confident belief and conviction in the power of God's love, is the intent or desire to express love. Jesus explained the concept of faith through metaphors and parables. In one such case, he compared faith to a tiny mustard seed, implying that a small seed of faith could expand to phenomenal proportions and overcome the trials of human experience. To paraphrase the words of theologian C. S. Lewis, faith is a necessary virtue to complete the will of God. And in the words of President John F. Kennedy, "God's work must truly be our own."

Paul, one of Jesus' earliest followers, in a letter to friends in the city of Corinth (which has since been recited at many weddings), described love this way:

> Love is patient and kind, never jealous or envious, never boastful or proud, never haughty or selfish or rude. Love does not demand its own way. It is not irritable or touchy. It does not hold grudges and

> will hardly ever notice when others do it wrong. It is never glad about injustice, but rejoices whenever truth wins out. Above all there are three things that remain, faith, hope, and love. The greatest of these is love. Let love be your greatest aim.

The Path of Joseph Campbell

The word myth comes from an ancient Sanskrit word, meaning the source of truth. Today the word myth has become synonymous with the word fallacy, but it is fair to say that every myth is based on a source of truth, perhaps exaggerated to make a point, but truth nevertheless. Joseph Campbell is the most respected scholar in the study of mythology. For more than 60 years, he studied myths, legends, and stories from all cultures, from the ancient Hindus to several American Indian tribes. Campbell left no stone unturned when it came to looking behind the message of each story. What he found was not only astonishing parallels (e.g., virgin births, resurrections, healings), but remarkable patterns, regardless of the story's origin, which speak to the nature of the human spirit. His own quest brought him to the front door of psychologist Carl Jung, mystic Jiddu Krishnamurti, poet Robert Bly, and scores of luminaries over the world, all of whom added to his collective wisdom.

Campbell's work went largely unrecognized outside of academic circles during the twentieth century until PBS television host Bill Moyers aired a six-part special, titled The Power of Myth, with Joseph Campbell in the spring of 1987. Campbell died soon thereafter on October 30. Despite his death, his work grows increasingly popular as people discover the links between mythology and spirituality—a legacy for all to share.

In the first episode with Bill Moyers, Campbell explained the connection between mythology and human spirituality like this:

> Myths are clues to the spiritual potentialities of the human life. Our problem today is that we are not well acquainted with the literature of the spirit.

Joseph Campbell: Renowned for his wisdom about human mythology gathered from all cultures over time, Campbell's greatest work illustrates the human experience as the hero's journey as exemplified in the template of every great story.

Hero's journey: Mythologist Joseph Campbell's classic template of the human journey with three stages: departure, initiation, and return.

Having studied the myths and legends of every culture throughout the ages, from Zeus to Star Wars (George Lucas was a student of Campbell's), Campbell noticed an interesting trend. In each myth there is a hero, and although the face of the hero may change over time, the story line remains consistent. In his book The Hero with a Thousand Faces, Campbell highlights the progression of the hero's journey, which, as it turns out, mirrors our own life sojourn. The stages include departure, initiation, and return. Let's take a closer look at each one.

- Departure: The first step in any adventure is to leave your place of origin. Whether one travels like Ulysses on a ship or like Luke Skywalker on a spacecraft, every hero must leave home to go and find him- or herself. The departure stage is also referred to as severance or separation, where the reluctant hero is forced into a situation unwillingly. Campbell cites Adam and Eve as examples of reluctant departure. Stepping outside of the classic myth tale, departure may begin with the first year in college away from home, the death of a parent, or the end of a marriage. Departures can occur in a great many ways. With the first step out the door and across the threshold, the journey has begun.
- Initiation: Traveling down the road far away from home, the hero is put to the test. Campbell calls this stage "the road of trials." It can be observed in nearly every story from Frodo Baggins in Lord of the Rings to each Harry Potter book. For some heroes, the test may be dragons (the symbol of fear); for others, it may be a symbolic river to cross (the River Styx). For still others, it may be an evil witch, a wicked stepmother, a rescue, or the betrayal of a close friend. In the legend of King Arthur, it began with the apprenticeship with Merlin. In the life of a college student, initiation can manifest itself in thousands of ways, including the roommate from hell or the abusive alcoholic parent. In every mythological story, the hero must demonstrate strength, courage, patience, and willpower. If she fails the first test, another will appear until she is strong enough to conquer it and move on.
- Return: At some point in the journey, usually upon success with the initiation process, the hero must return home. Upon crossing the threshold of return, the hero shares the wealth of riches acquired on the road. Symbolically, the return home is accompanied with a trophy of sorts: magical runes, the golden fleece, a broomstick, or Medusa's head. Campbell

Stress with a Human Face

In 1960, at the invitation of renowned anthropologist Louis Leakey and the government of Tanzania, a young British woman named Jane Goodall ventured into the forests of Africa, known then as the "Dark Continent." Her assignment was to observe and study the behaviors of the chimpanzee, one of the great apes whose behavior in the wild was virtually unknown at the time. Today, Goodall is recognized not just for her discovery that humans are not the only species to make and use tools, but also for her tireless efforts as an environmental activist to save wildlife habitats around the globe. In her autobiography Reason for Hope, she shares both her life's work and her spiritual insights, for Goodall is a very spiritual person.

Every once in a great while a person enters the world stage and makes an indelible mark in the minds of the entire world. Even rarer is the person who touches our hearts in a way that leaves us inspired to reach our highest potential. Goodall is one such person. Through her unyielding inspiration, compassion, humility, vision, and unceasing effort to make the world a better place, she has been compared to such luminaries as Gandhi, Einstein, the Dalai Lama, and Mother Teresa. In recognition of her achievement and world influence, former United Nations Secretary General Kofi Annan appointed her a UN Messenger of Peace in 2002, a title balanced with honor and responsibility. By all counts, Goodall demonstrates the traits of a leader, hero, and role model. She embodies the expression "Live simply, so that others (including all of God's creatures) may simply live." In doing so, she reminds us that we, too, must do the same.

Through a wonderful path of serendipity, I found myself having breakfast with Goodall in spring 2004 to collaborate on a project. Despite the clouds of uncertainty, she shared with me her conviction to make planet Earth a better world in which to live and her reasons for hope in achieving this result—symbols of achievement that transcend the limitations of ego. The first was a California condor feather given to Goodall by those who were responsible for bringing this magnificent bird back from the brink of extinction—a symbol of what is possible. The second was a piece of rock from the prison quarry where Nelson Mandela was confined for more than 26 years under the rule of apartheid. Goodall carries it with her as a sign of both forgiveness and powerful, peaceful transformation. The third reason for hope was a mystical experience in Nebraska watching the migration of the sandhill cranes—the same day war broke out in Iraq in 2003. Goodall viewed the experience as a sign that in a world of chaos, there is still beauty, and that beauty is worth saving.

To sit in the presence of Jane Goodall is to experience grace firsthand. She is a very spiritual individual. Moreover, to see her work take root around the world through her youth-based programs like "Roots & Shoots" is proof that one person can, indeed, make a difference. In Goodall's words, "Each of us has a role to play. Each one of us must take responsibility for our lives and, above all, show respect and love for living things around us, especially each other. Together we must reestablish our connection with the natural world and with the spiritual power that is around us. Despite signs of imbalance, I believe in the power of the human spirit, but we must act now," she says.

points out that there may be a reluctance to go home, caused either by feelings of shame or the lust for additional conquests. But return we must to complete the story. The stage of return is also called incorporation, where the returning hero is accepted by his family and peers as an equal, and everyone benefits from his wisdom as a master of two worlds: the one he conquered and the one he has returned home to. The return phase offers a promise that all ends well.

There was a time when the sharing of myths was passed down from parent to child, not merely for entertainment purposes but as wisdom to guide the child on his or her own life journey. Stories from the Bible, the Bhagavad Gita, and other sacred scriptures as well as scores of legends, fairy tales, and folklore all serve the same purpose. However, for the most part the tradition of finding wisdom from these stories has vanished in the American culture. In his discussion in The Power of Myth, Campbell drew a connection between the rising state of spiritual hunger and the absence of our connection to mythological stories. As he explained, when a society forgoes the power of myth, instead replacing it with information, technology, or perhaps nothing, the society becomes less civilized and more destructive.

Knowing the power of myth himself, Campbell had ever the optimistic outlook on the journey of humanity itself, for he knew the end of the story: "We are at this moment participating in one of the very greatest leaps of the human spirit—to a knowledge not only of outside nature, but also our own deep inward mystery—the greatest leap ever!"

The Path of Lao Tzu

Around 500 B.C., the writings of China's most famous philosopher, Lao Tzu, were first published under the title of Tao Teh Ching. Originally written primarily for the leaders of his country, this collection of 5,000 words soon became the doctrine of Chinese living, outlining the path to spiritual enlightenment through inner peace. Lao Tzu used the word Tao to describe the movement, path, or way of universal energy. The literal translation of the title of Tzu's book is "the path that leads straight from the heart," and the Chinese character for this title symbolizes "walking wisdom." Tzu's writings speak of building a peaceful world through inner peace. Only when peace is created within yourself can you move in tandem with the energies that circulate within and around you and to establish world peace.

The concept of Taoism suggests that all things connect with a flow of energy called chi. To move along with the patterns of flow allows a peaceful coexistence with both oneself and the environment. Movement against the flow causes internal as well as external disturbances, often with far-reaching consequences. This movement of life energy goes in cycles, like the ebb and flow of the ocean tide. One of the many concepts the Tao Teh Ching teaches is balance between the opposing forces of yin and yang, which provides harmony, patience, and timing of the events of life. That is, to move with rather than against the flow promotes and maintains inner peace. Tzu's Tao invites the individual to look inward, beyond the superficial facade of humanness, and sense the inner rhythms that move in harmony with the universal rhythms. By doing this, not only is inner peace achieved, but also harmony with nature and all relationships. Tzu also spoke of the importance of self-reliance: "Wise people seek solutions, the ignorant only cast blame." Although initially Taoism may seem like a foreign concept, it can be found in many Western writings as well. Perhaps the best example of it is the Taoist mannerisms and character of Winnie the Pooh, described by Benjamin Hoff in the renowned best-seller, The Tao of Pooh. In fact, with a closer look, Taoist principles can be found virtually everywhere.

Lao Tzu: An ancient Chinese philosopher and writer. He is the author of the acclaimed book Tao Teh Ching, a manifesto for human spirituality based on the concept of balance with nature. Lao Tzu is believed to be the creator of the concept of Taoism.

The Principle of Oneness: A Taoist concept of oneness with nature serving as a reminder of our oneness with it.

The Principle of Dynamic Balance: A Taoist concept revealing the opposites that make up the balance of life.

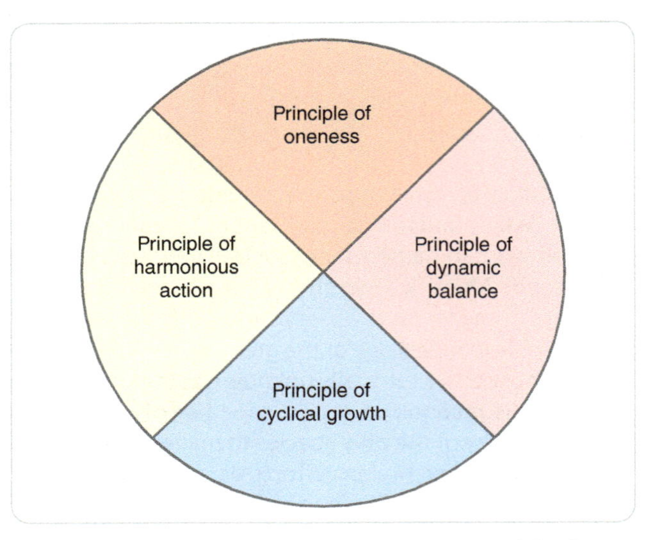

FIGURE 8.11 A symbolic representation of the four principles of Taoism created by Lao Tzu.

In her book The Tao of Inner Peace, Diane Dreher explains that Tzu outlined four "great disciplines" to help achieve inner peace through the way of the Tao: oneness, dynamic balance, cyclical growth, and harmonious action (FIG. 8.11).

The Principle of Oneness. The principle of oneness suggests that we are part of the whole, connected to a dynamic network of universal energy. Oneness means to be one with, or a part of, nature, not above or apart from it. When we see ourselves as separate from the whole, we distance ourselves from other people and the natural elements. This distance weakens our spiritual strength. Just as there is strength in numbers, there is also strength in oneness.

The Principle of Dynamic Balance. Taoist philosophy speaks of the composition of all creation as two complementary opposites: yin and yang. In simple terms, yin comprises the quiet, feminine, receptive elements of nature, while yang is seen as active, dynamic, and masculine. Alone, each side is overbearing. The union of yin and yang within the individual provides a perpetual movement that strives for balance and harmony. After rain comes sunshine. After disaster comes calm. To live in dynamic balance in the world, one must move with the flow through the mountains and valleys of life. To stay always static or always dynamic goes against the laws of nature of which both men and women are very much a part.

The Principle of Cyclical Growth. The natural world consists of many cycles: day and night, birth and death, winter and summer. Each human life is also filled with cycles, from the life cycle of a red blood cell to the highs and lows of our emotions. The wisdom of the Tao advocates that these cycles be recognized and appreciated. Too often, impatience blinds human vision to the natural cycles of which we are a part. The universe is not still. The Tao encourages patience.

The Principle of Harmonious Action. As a part of nature, we must work in cooperation with it and not try to dominate, monopolize, or destroy it. The wisdom of the Tao advises individuals to live in harmony with nature, respecting her many components, including the lives of others. To live in harmony means to live in moderation, not excess; to live with simplicity, not complexity; and to slow down, know oneself, and make wise choices. One concept of harmonious action is called the wu wei, which means knowing when to wait for the right moment, and knowing when to be spontaneous, moving with the rhythms of life.

There are many ways to reinforce the attitudes of Taoist philosophy behaviorally. The most commonly known techniques are yoga, meditation, and T'ai Chi ch'uan.

The characteristics of a Tao person are very similar to those of the self-actualized individuals described by Maslow, and those of the hardy personality described by Kobasa and Maddi. These characteristics include self-acceptance, humor, creativity, commitment, challenge, and self-control, and they serve as buffers against the perceptions of stress. Tao individuals have faith in themselves and what they do. They carry no illusions about who they are. They embrace life joyously. This is what it means to be "one with the Tao."

The Path of Albert Einstein

It may seem rather strange to include a physicist among the several people noted here who have speculated on the nature of human spirituality, yet at the same time it would be a gross oversight to omit this perspective. The fields of physics and theology, which were so bitterly divided more than 300 years ago, are finding they have more commonalities than differences today. These commonalities were first brought to scientific light about 100 years ago by a physicist named Albert Einstein, who took it upon himself to challenge the accepted principles of natural physics developed by Isaac Newton. Like an earthquake, Einstein's concepts of the physical laws of nature rocked the foundations of the scientific community. But as can be seen today, the ramifications of this challenge actually parallel, and may eventually validate, the concept of a higher power, albeit somewhat differently from the way that many people currently perceive it. In 1999, Time magazine named Einstein "Man of the Century," not solely for his scientific theories or Nobel Prize, but rather for changing the paradigm of thought of humanity in a nonthreatening way.

Curious about the nature of the universe and the laws that govern it, Einstein was convinced that all matter is made up of energy, and that time and space are not locked into a continuum as previously thought, giving way to his famous theory of relativity: $E = mc^2$. Very simply put, this suggests that all matter is energy that is not confined to the "local" concept involving space and time. Although the complexities of this theory are beyond the scope of this book, the premise of Einstein's theory, once rejected by his peers, is now completely accepted by the scientific community, as well as those mystically inclined individuals who see Einstein's theory as a stepping stone toward higher consciousness. Moreover, the impact of Einstein's work has reached far beyond science to the fields of poetry, art, and even psychology. (It was Einstein's theory of relativity that

The Principle of Cyclical Growth: A Taoist concept that suggests that everything is cyclic: the moon, tides, seasons, and all aspects of human life.

The Principle of Harmonious Action: A Taoist concept that reminds us to work in harmony with nature, not in opposition to it or control over it.

Albert Einstein: A world-renowned theoretical physicist who revolutionized perceptions of reality with the equation $E = mc^2$, suggesting that everything is energy. His later years focused on a spiritual philosophy including pacifism.

gave Jung the idea for the collective unconscious.) With energy being the word that opened the door to understanding, theologians also gravitated toward Einstein's theories, making the concept of light a solid foundation from which to explore the divine nature of the universe. Compare, for example, the concept of universal energy with the following description (Dreher, 1991):

> We Look at it and we do not see it;
> Its name is The Invisible.
> We Listen to it and we do not hear it;
> Its name is The Inaudible.
> We Touch it and don't find it;
> Its name is The Subtle.
>
> —Lao Tzu, Tao Teh Ching, 14

Stepping out of the scientific box that Newton had created centuries earlier, Einstein paved the way for others to follow. With the initial theoretical basis constructed, other physicists (Heisenberg and Chew) quickly added corollaries to Einstein's theory, leading the way to the field of quantum physics. Today, pioneers in the field of energy medicine credit Einstein with building a conceptual model from which to understand the human energy field and even human consciousness (FIG. 8.12). Biophysicist Itzhak Bentov expounded on Einstein's concept that "energy equals matter" in his widely acclaimed book, Stalking the Wild Pendulum. From his added insight we begin to see that consciousness is actually a form of energy that surrounds, permeates, and connects all living objects. Like the atom's electrons, which vibrate to give off an energy field, so too does the human body produce an oscillation and energy field, which Bentov refers to as subtle energy. He hypothesized that this subtle energy comprises many layers or "frequencies," which he suggests constitute various layers of human consciousness (and the soul itself).

FIGURE 8.12 A glimpse of the universe depicting Einstein's perspective where everything is energy and the universe is indeed a friendly place.

Since the introduction of the theory of relativity, physicists have discovered that subatomic particles called photons appear to travel at or greater than the speed of light. Renowned quantum physicist Dave Bohm has combined this knowledge with that of emotional thought, neuropeptide activity, and coherence. He too postulates that thoughts are a form of energy: Negative thoughts (e.g., fear and anger) are expressed by electrons, and positive thoughts (e.g., love and peace) are conveyed through the movement of photons. This idea has gained momentum among those who have taken a scientific look at the power of prayer and clairvoyant "coincidences" (McTaggart, 2008). For instance, in the landmark double-blind study designed by cardiologist Randolph Byrd (1986), more than 300 hospital patients were randomly assigned to either a "prayed for" group or control group. Results demonstrated a statistically significant difference on various health parameters between those who received prayer and those who did not, suggesting that there may actually be a healing power in prayer. Even more significant, the people doing the praying lived hundreds if not thousands of miles away from the hospital where the patients were located. Additional studies of prayer have been conducted by the Spindrift Organization in Lansdale, Pennsylvania, using both direct and indirect prayer on the metabolic rate of plants. These studies have produced results similar to those found by Byrd. An analysis of case studies by psychiatrist Jean Bolen in her book The Tao of Psychology indicates that distance (time and space) was not a factor among people who experienced a clairvoyant "coincidence," but that love (a positive emotion) was.

Dr. Larry Dossey—author of the books Space, Time, and Medicine; Recovering the Soul; and Healing Words—applauds Einstein for his "quantum leap" of new understanding regarding both the universe and its relevance to human consciousness. Dossey, a former internist at the Dallas Diagnostic Association, synthesized the theories of quantum physics and medicine in an attempt to validate that human spirituality is a vital element in the healing process. Borrowing a term from the field of physics, Dossey refers to the spiritual-healing nature of humankind as the nonlocal mind, meaning thoughts that are not bound by time or space. Dossey also explains that there is a connectedness to all things in the universe and that this connectedness has a spiritual quality to it. It is this same spiritual quality that Pelletier referred to as the "missing piece" of the stress and disease model, and why he suggested that the principles of quantum physics be included in the study of psychoneuroimmunology. In the words of Dr. Richard Gerber, "With respect to his theory of relativity, Einstein was more right than even he imagined."

With a greater understanding of the theory of relativity, several physicists have noted connections between the world of physics and the spiritual nature of the universe. In his book The Tao of Physics, Fritjof Capra outlined many similarities and parallels between the disciplines of physics and the Eastern mystical philosophies of Buddhism, Hinduism, and Taoism, suggesting that there is an incredible linkage between them and that whether it is called "energy," the "Tao," or the "Holy Spirit," its essence appears to be very similar. Capra writes, "Physicists and mystics deal with different aspects of reality. Physicists explore levels of matter, mystics levels of mind. What their explorations have in common is that these levels, in both cases, lie beyond ordinary sensory perception." Capra suggests that these two disciplines, in effect, are looking at the same mountain, but from different vantage points and through different binoculars. To Capra, the paradigm shift that occurred in physics with Einstein's theory of relativity is currently rippling through other Western disciplines, including clinical medicine and psychology. In his autobiography Memories, Dreams, Reflections, Jung wrote, "There are indications that at least part of the psyche is not subject to the laws of space and time." The collective unconscious and subtle energy in which all things connect may, in fact, be the same component of human spirituality. As science continues to explore the realm of human energy and consciousness, the fields of physics and theology may not only connect but someday become one and the same (Radin, 2006).

Those who knew him and studied his works say that Einstein was a spiritual man but not a religious one. Yet these same people note that he appeared to be driven by a spiritual quest to understand the nature of the universe. One of Einstein's most famous quotes speaks to this fact: "I want to know the thoughts of God, the rest are just details." And although some people infer from his theory of relativity that his view of the cosmos is impersonal at best (with the order of the universe simply calculated by mathematical equations), Einstein retorted, "God does not play dice with the universe." From his own writings it becomes very obvious that he was not only a scientific genius, but a world-class philosopher as well. A person who spent much time in deep personal reflection, he once wrote,

> A human being is part of the whole, called by us "universe," a part limited in time and space. He experiences his thoughts and feelings as something separate from the rest, a kind of optical delusion of his consciousness. This delusion is a kind of prison for us, restricting us to our personal decisions and to affection for a few persons nearest us. Our task must be to free ourselves from this prison by widening our circle of compassion to embrace all living creatures and the whole of nature in its beauty.

Einstein spent the better part of his later years conceiving his unified field theory (a thesis to explain the relationship of gravity and electromagnetic energy), as well as playing a more subtle role as pacifist for world peace—a moral position in which he took great pride. Yet through it all, it was light, symbolically and literally, that fascinated Einstein.

"For the rest of my life, I want to reflect on what light is," he said.

Common Bonds of Human Spirituality

Although no one path seems to offer complete insight into the mystery of the human spirit, some common themes run through the various paths. Specifically, these common themes are four processes that collectively nurture the growth of the human spirit: centering, emptying, grounding,

Nonlocal mind: A term given to consciousness that resides outside the brain (possibly outside the human energy field), which may explain premonitions, distant healing, and prayer.

Centering: A time for soul searching, cultivating one's internal relationship.

Emptying: Also known as the "dark night of the soul" and the winter of discontent. The emptying process is a time to release, detach, and let go of thoughts, attitudes, perceptions, and beliefs that no longer serve you.

Grounding: The point at which new insights may be revealed to assist a person to move from point A to point B.

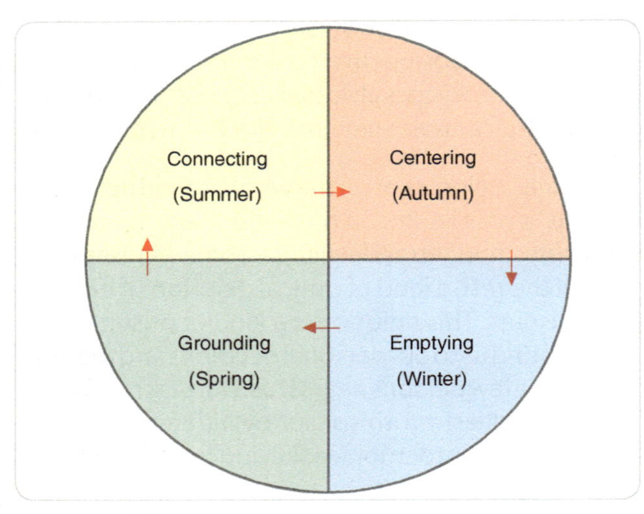

FIGURE 8.13 A symbolic representation of the common themes among approaches to human spirituality referred to as "seasons of the soul."

FIGURE 8.14 The centering process (like the autumn season) is a time to go inside and explore the landscape of the soul.

and connecting (FIG. 8.13). These processes provide a nurturing enlightenment to our own spiritual growth. And some or all of these processes are found in virtually every form of relaxation and several coping techniques used to deal with stress.

In its simplest terms, the common bonds of human spirituality can be viewed as a cycle of seasons (seasons of the soul): centering (autumn), where one goes inside to do some soul searching; emptying (winter), a process of letting go of thoughts, perceptions, and frustrations to make room for new insights; grounding (spring), where new insights are sought and received; and connecting (summer), a time of sharing and celebration. Let's take a closer look.

Centering Process (Autumn)

The centering process involves deep reflection on one's real self: who we are and what our purpose in life is. Jung devoted much of his professional as well as personal life to understanding the centering process. He was deeply committed to the idea that centering our thoughts—or more specifically, accessing the powers of the unconscious mind—was imperative to mental, emotional, spiritual, and even physical well-being. The American Indian vision quest is also an exercise in centering. It is uninterrupted time devoted to addressing those questions that can only be answered by the soul in the midst of deep solitude. Likewise, Lao Tzu was an advocate of the centering process: "Be still, and discover your center of peace. Returning to the center is peace." Fox's creation spirituality theory also extolls the virtue of centering: the ability to appreciate the creative process within and to initiate the emptying process, which plants the seeds of personal transformation. Borysenko advocates centering to unite the body, mind, and soul as one. She suggests many ways this can be done, including journal writing, yoga, and meditation (FIG. 8.14). As Borysenko points out, the purpose of virtually every relaxation technique is to create an opportunity for centering.

Connecting: A realization that we are all connected, and the connection is made and nurtured through love.

Emptying Process (Winter)

It appears that for spiritual growth to continue there must be a continual process of emptying, or cleansing, of our consciousness. Some people refer to this as entering the void. Emptiness typically occurs as a result of sustained centering, where the individual discovers and makes peace with the real self by an act similar to spring cleaning: getting rid of old ways of thinking, toxic thoughts, and perceptions and feelings that inhibit spiritual growth. Jung referred to this process as confronting the shadow of our unconscious mind. Peck's stage 3 is an emptying process, where one tosses out the old concept of an authoritarian

God, the "Irish cop in the sky," and questions any divine existence at all. The American Indian vision quest is a time of fasting and removing oneself from the community to find a deep sense of self-awareness and self-purpose. Via negativa, as Fox stated, is also a period of emptiness, when one edits out of one's life the thoughts, feelings, and even possessions that obstruct the path of spiritual growth. Darkness symbolizes this emptiness. The wisdom of the Tao also advises emptying oneself. To quote Lao Tzu, "Close your mouth, shut your doors and live close to the Tao. Open your mouth, be busy all day and live in confusion." Borysenko, as well as many others, cites the practice of meditation (clearing the mind of thoughts) as a vehicle for the emptying process. Journal writing also serves this purpose.

FIGURE 8.15 The emptying process (winter) is a time of cleansing, releasing, and letting go to make room for new insights. Of all the four seasons, this can be the most painful. Like a cold waterfall, it feels refreshing once you are out.

This emptying process can be painful. Peck compares it to a walk in the desert. Fasting will make one's stomach growl just as Jung's shadow and Fox's darkness will promote their respective growls. Chopra reminds us that detachment is the cornerstone of the emptying process. Regardless of how it is done, this emptying must be a conscious process. It is not a process you fall into by chance, but rather one that is intentionally created.

FIGURE 8.16 The grounding process (spring) is the "eureka" moment. An epiphany, a streak of intuition, or some insight helps you get from where you are to where you need to go.

A Zen story illustrates the concept of emptiness. Years ago, an American professor toured Asia. One day he came upon a Buddhist monk and sat down to talk with him over a cup of tea. The professor graciously held out his cup while the Zen monk poured—and continued to pour, until the cup was overflowing. The professor, baffled, asked, "Why do you keep pouring?" The monk smiled kindly and replied, "Your mind is like this cup. It is so full of concepts that there is no room for new wisdom." The emptying process is a cleansing of the spirit (FIG. 8.15). Just as the body needs exercise to rid itself of chemical waste, and the mind exhibits laughter and tears as emotional catharsis, so too the soul needs to empty and cleanse itself.

Grounding Process (Spring)

The grounding process quickly follows the emptying process. In this stage, the soul or spirit is filled with new insight and knowledge made possible by the "space" made available during emptying. This insight may occur immediately, as an intuitive thought, or it may be synthesized over a short period of time and unfold right in front of you (FIG. 8.16). If the emptying process is like plowing a field, the grounding process is planting and harvesting. During grounding comes the vision of the vision quest, answers to life's most difficult questions, and light to replace the darkness of the emptiness stage. It is a time of revelation and resolution with regard to life purpose and value conflicts, respectively. In Eastern cultures (from India to Tibet), the grounding process is referred to as enlightenment. To be grounded also means to feel secure with the insight received during this process. In a literal sense, groundedness means being connected to the earth and feeling a part of nature. In a figurative sense, grounding is the ability to feel comfortable in your surroundings, in your own environment. Grounding also means establishing clear paths of communication between the conscious and unconscious mind, thereby giving focus to one's life. From a Taoist perspective, to be grounded

FIGURE 8.17 The connecting process (summer) is a celebration with friends, family, and colleagues in the realization that we truly are all connected to something much bigger and more powerful than ourselves.

means to be in touch with the cycles of nature (the phases of the moon, the seasons of the earth) and to move in rhythm with these cycles. In the vision quest, a new name (e.g., Walking Rainbow) is chosen to symbolize the vision and is "worn" proudly upon return to the community.

Connecting Process (Summer)

In the Taoist philosophy, all things connect; nothing is separate. This is the premise of the principle of oneness. Quantum physics, likewise, has reached this conclusion. Jung proposed that we are all connected by a universal soul he called the collective unconscious. Peck cites connectedness as a crucial element in the development of both inner and world peace (FIG. 8.17). In a process described as community building, he explains that bonding with others in one's environment builds a community of oneness and is the manifestation of the spiritual nature of humankind. This connecting process is what some people refer to as social well-being, and it is best manifested by participation in formal or informal support-group activities. Originally, a vision quest was completed only when the individual returned to the community, reunited with friends and family, and shared insight gained from his or her unique vision. But American Indians believe in connecting not only with other people, but with all creations on Mother Earth, from trees and lakes to animals, birds, and fish. Chief Seattle wrote, "What is man without beasts? If all the beasts were gone, men would die from great loneliness of spirit, for whatever happens to beasts, soon happens to man. All things are connected." Thus, connecting is based on respect for all creation. Borysenko also cites the importance of the connecting process as the foundation of support groups for individuals overcoming addictions. The strength of the connecting process is related to the power of centering, emptying, and grounding oneself. Finally, the work of Jesus of Nazareth was about building bonds of love between persons so that all may become one people.

Clearly, the order of the four steps is important to the effectiveness of the process as a whole. Each step alone confers strength, but the dynamics of the four steps in sequence is an unparalleled strategy to nurture inner strength and enhance spiritual well-being.

A Model of Spirituality for Stress Management

In my efforts to integrate spiritual well-being into the wellness paradigm of total well-being for corporate health promotion, I created an integrative theoretical model to emphasize the dynamic relationship between stress and human spirituality. I synthesized this spiritual well-being model from the psychological theories of Jung, Maslow, Frankl, Peck, Fox, Selye, Schaef, and Borysenko, as well as several other influences from American Indian and Asian cultures. In this model, human spirituality is defined as the maturation process of our higher consciousness as developed through the integration of three facets: an insightful, nurturing relationship with oneself and others; the development of a strong personal value system; and a meaningful purpose in one's life. These facets, each tightly integrated with the other two, constitute a dynamic configuration that, when attended to and nurtured, will advance human consciousness to a higher level of understanding—that is, seeing oneself as a part of a larger whole.

Let us take a closer look at the three facets.

Internal and External Relationships

Internal and external relationships involve a twofold process whereby one explores, confronts, and resolves one's inner thoughts, feelings, and perceptions, as well as strengthens ties or connectedness with others in one's environment. In some ways, human spirituality can be thought of as a form of self-government. It consists of both a domestic policy, or a personal philosophy and behavioral guidelines for the relationship with oneself, or the self, and a foreign policy concerning relationships with all other people in one's environment. A weak domestic policy will carry over into a weak foreign policy. Human spirituality works the same way: A poor internal relationship carries over into weak relationships with family, friends, co-workers, and other people with whom you come in contact. For optimal spiritual well-being, there must be a healthy balance between internal and external relationships. In other words, love your neighbor as yourself.

An Insightful Internal Relationship. The internal relationship begins with the practice of centering, or discovering and nurturing your real self. Some ancient mystics referred to the centering process as "entering the heart." According to Lao Tzu, "The way of inner peace begins with self-acceptance, to seek peace outside is to leave it behind." This process of centering involves dedicating quality alone-time to self-discovery, and separating who you are from what you do, as well as from your relationships with other people. Centering means coming to terms with the constituents of your identity and going beyond asking "What?" during the process of internal dialogue to ask "Why?" Similarly, in the process known as individuation, Jung emphasized the importance of self-reflection to bridge the gap between the conscious and the unconscious mind, thereby accessing the divine power within to help resolve spiritual crises. Jung was convinced that continual soul searching strengthened one's internal resources, including intuition, creativity, willpower, faith, patience, optimism, and humbleness. A strong internal relationship is characterized by improving and maintaining honesty in your inner thoughts, feelings, and even dreams, through introspection and exploration of your conscious and unconscious mind. The quest for self-knowledge is a soul-searching effort that leads to awareness of inner wisdom from the unconscious mind. It is this quest that develops the strength of your human spirit. In both accepting your fixed personal limitations and expanding your conscious barriers, you are led to new heights of spiritual development and consciousness, or what Jung referred to as spiritual evolution. The result of increased self-awareness, and ultimately the most powerful of inner resources, is the ability to accept and love yourself.

Divine Personification. Consensus among leaders in the emerging field of psychospirituality suggests that as you develop your own internal relationship, you also strengthen the bond to a higher power residing both within and beyond your physical domain. This, in fact, is a necessary part of the internal relationship: to see yourself as whole, yet a part of a bigger whole. In the words of Fox, this bond is "a personal cosmology—a relationship to the divine presence that dwells in us." Thus, a strong internal relationship also includes a comfortable and nurturing relationship with a higher power, however you might perceive that to be. Perceptions, however, need to be refocused, perhaps even changed, as this relationship matures. At a young age, our first introduction to a higher power is often through personification. A higher power of consciousness is given a name (e.g., God, Yahweh, Allah, Supreme Being) and described with human features, which are easy for children to identify, understand, and find comfort in. More often than not, however, this image does not develop or keep pace with a person's physical, emotional, and intellectual maturation into adulthood. In fact, Fox notes that many adults still envision God as a wise old man in a white robe resting on a cloud.

A comparable example is the American personification of the spirit of Christmas, in which the concept of loving kindness is symbolized by the human figure of Santa Claus. For those children who were introduced to the jolly fat man in a red suit, a new reality seeps in somewhere between the ages of 6 and 10 years. With the death of the personification, so wither away other elements of the essence of Christmas, and sometimes these elements are lost forever. Likewise, many adults experiencing a painful emptiness choose not to find their "God," but rather elect to leave this relationship underdeveloped. In theology circles, the phrase "killing off the old gods" is used to describe the depersonification process at this stage of maturation, as individuals are counseled to strengthen their internal relationship. Sometimes even the word God can be too limiting to conceptualize this mystical phenomenon. In fact, for many people, the word God carries with it a lot of baggage. Be that as it may, a strong and maturing relationship with a higher power is the anchor of the soul in the rough seas of crises. It provides a means of connectedness on a very personal and special level. Internal relationships are augmented by activities of solitude, meditation, reflection or prayer, and vision quests, where quality alone-time is allocated

An insightful internal relationship: How well do you know and love yourself? What is your relationship with your higher self?

Divine personification: A term signifying one's evolving perception or image of the divine, whatever this happens to be.

for the purpose of strengthening this relationship with the real self. Many relaxation techniques and coping skills are rooted in the premise of centering to nurture this relationship.

External Relationships. External relationships constitute a healthy bonding with anyone or anything outside the relationship with the inner self, including family, friends, acquaintances, and the creations of Mother Earth such as animals, trees, lakes, and the planet itself. External relationships are improved and maintained through your expression of acceptance, peace, compassion, communication, and respect for all individuals in your environment as well as your sense of connectedness with nature on the planet Earth. More specifically, strong external relationships include open tolerance, acceptance, and respect for other people's opinions, beliefs, and values, even when they don't agree with your own. This aspect of spirituality includes a forgiving (accepting) attitude toward others when their behavior is different from or inconsistent with your own ideals. Remember the saying espoused by all major religions: Do unto others as you would have them do unto you.

To Peck, this element of human spirituality also involves building community. Community is defined as the bonding and belongingness of supportive individuals in your collective environments. Building community means reaching out to other people to raise the level of human consciousness and human potential, for in the face of stress there is strength in numbers. Some scholars have designated social well-being as a fifth and separate component of well-being. However, a sound understanding of spirituality includes this social aspect in the framework of external relationships and community building. Finally, healthy external relationships necessitate the continual nurturing of the spiritual growth and love of other individuals in your environment through behaviors that will raise your human consciousness and human potential to new heights.

Both internal and external relationships require continuous work to further your spiritual evolution. Relationships are living organisms that, like plants and animals, need nutrients to survive. Neglect leads to starvation, atrophy, root rot, and eventual death of the human spirit. A loss of connectedness is detrimental to the health of the human spirit. Peck once remarked that true evil is masked as laziness and apathy. With regard to human spirituality, there is a consensus among his colleagues that he is right.

> **External relationships:** One's relationships with others (e.g., family, friends, and colleagues) as well as the earth, water, and air we breathe.

Personal Value System

The identification, clarification, and implementation of a personal value system is tantamount to spiritual well-being. Values, as described by Lewis (1990), are constructs of importance: personal beliefs based on the concepts of goodness, justice, and beauty that give meaning and depth to our thoughts, attitudes, and behaviors. Values, including love, honesty, self-esteem, independence, leisure, education, privacy, forgiveness, and respect for Mother Earth, to name a few, typically dictate our attitudes and behaviors. As suggested by the research of Milton Rokeach (1972), values—both basic or core, such as love and honesty, and supporting, or those that support the core values, including trust and creativity—constitute a collection of ideals, or hierarchy of values, specific to each person. Individuals adopt many values unconsciously throughout their lives; however, most values are acquired in early childhood. Values such as acceptance, love, respect, and trust are learned from our parents, teachers, and respected individuals when there is strong interaction and the development of emotional bonds with them. These and other values are adopted as a means of acquiring approval from role models, or figures of importance, whom one chooses to emulate in the development of one's own identity.

Values that are adopted consciously or unconsciously lay the developmental groundwork for personality traits and behaviors. In addition, they construct a framework for self-validation and development of moral judgment of right and wrong, good and bad, and pain and pleasure. Values are abstract in nature, yet are often symbolized by material objects or possessions that represent a specific thing. For example, a diploma is a symbol of the value of education, and a television set is a symbol of leisure. As we mature, our value system also changes, but it continues to account for the way we think and behave. Like earthquakes caused by movements of the earth's tectonic plates, our values shift in importance as we mature, causing our own earth to quake. These shifts are called value conflicts, and they can result in a great deal of stress. Jung referred to this type of stress as a spiritual crisis, because these conflicts rock the foundations of the soul. Examples of value conflicts abound, ranging from those on the personal level all the way up to the governmental level. The abortion controversy is an example of a values conflict at the governmental level. Another example is the preservation of national wetlands versus the push for housing and industrial development. Both of these issues have caused much stress in the national consciousness. On a more personal level, leisure versus work, integrity versus wealth, and fame versus privacy are just a few examples of value conflicts causing stress at a spiritual level.

According to psychiatrist Viktor Frankl, "We are our values." Frankl observed that stress arises when values conflict with each other, leading to an arousal of inner tension, thus disturbing the homeostasis of the mind. But Frankl saw opportunity where others saw disaster, believing that resolution of value conflicts brings with it incredible strength of inner resources. The challenge is to assume responsibility for bringing these conflicts to resolution. Maslow (1976) considered the ultimate disease of our time to be "valuelessness," the condition wherein society's traditional value systems have proven ineffective and value conflicts at all levels go unresolved. He believed that a new valid, usable system of human values must be created, initially by the individual, and then adopted by society. This new value system, he argued, must be based on trust rather than on the false hopes and ignorance inspired by laziness, greed, and inability to know oneself. Conflicts in values can be helpful in our own maturation process if we work through the conflict to a full resolution. But this takes work, which many people would rather avoid. However, a strong personal value system is one in which the hierarchy of basic and supporting values is regularly assessed and reorganized, allowing conflicts of values to be resolved so as to promote inner peace.

Meaningful Purpose in Life

A major facet of the spiritual well-being model is represented by one's meaningful purpose in life. According to Frankl (1984), a life mission can be accomplished through the design and achievement of a series of life goals, and through the experience of a value conflict or emotional suffering. Frankl asserted that the health of the human spirit rapidly declines with the loss of meaning in one's life, while a continual search for and fulfillment of one's aim in life are essential to spiritual development. He was convinced that the search for meaning was a primary force, instinctual in nature, and not merely a rationalization by humans, for humans (FIG. 8.18).

In my work with Olympic athletes, I was introduced to the concept of the "Olympic blues," a period of time directly after the Olympic Games when non–medal winners lost

FIGURE 8.18

all sense of meaning in their lives. The rebound time could be months or even years. Similarly, mothers suffer the empty-nest syndrome when their last child leaves home, creating a vacuum of life purpose. Men and women who retire after 30 to 40 years of employment may also suffer from feelings of lack of purpose. Frankl suggested that there is no ordained life purpose for each person; rather, a series of progressive life goals culminates in a life mission. He believed that emotional suffering at the completion of a goal is an essential part of the process of moving to the next ambition and continuing with one's purposeful meaning. The premise behind his logotherapy was to help people move beyond the suffering and thereby find a new meaning on which to focus. Finding a new life purpose in the ashes of suffering is not impossible, but this, too, takes work. One must create new goals and ambitions to aim for and accomplish.

Hans Selye, renowned for his work in stress physiology, later turned his attention to matters of the spirit as well. In his book Stress Without Distress, he stated that one's health status is dependent on the ability to maintain a purpose in life that commands self-respect and pride. As a result of his research on the effects of perceived stress and the physiological manifestations of the stress response, Selye theorized that the most significant strategy for conquering stress is to pursue what he called the aim of life. This aim, or meaningful purpose, of one's life is the foundation of health, and is built on both short-term and long-term attainable goals. The process of pursuing and completing the aim of life is initiated by self-reflection, giving strength to the individual's internal relationship.

In this model of spiritual well-being, all components are so tightly integrated they are difficult to separate. Each facet—nurturing, insightful, and bonding relationships; a strong personal value system; and an assessment of progress in one's meaningful purpose in life—is mutually inclusive of the other two. Moments of solitude and self-reflection lend themselves to the assessment of personal values and steps toward conflict resolution, as well as toward refinement of one's purpose in life. Values influence the direction of life's meaningful purpose. For example, the expression of love, perhaps the strongest spiritual value, not only nurtures self-growth, but also influences the strength of external relationships and inspires the direction of one's life mission. This integration of components is exemplified by the works of Nobel Peace Prize winners Martin Luther King, Jr., Mother Teresa, and the Dalai Lama, as well as thousands of lesser known but equally inspiring individuals (FIG. 8.19).

FIGURE 8.19 Dr. Martin Luther King, Jr., Mother Teresa, and the Dalai Lama are among the recipients of the Nobel Peace Prize, the highest possible honor for humanitarian achievement in the world.

The Divine Mystery

There is a fourth pillar of human spirituality that is often neglected in the discussion of psychology and theology—the mystical aspect. If for no other reason than looking foolish (another type of stress), many people rarely talk about the mystical side of spirituality. Yet this pillar is equally important to the full understanding and appreciation of the divine aspect in which we are all connected. Jung was so impressed by the mysteries of the divine that he spent many years devoted to their study, and for this reason was shunned and ridiculed by many of his colleagues. Under the cloud of Descartes's reductionistic paradigm, things that cannot be explained are often ignored. Yet the mystical side of life begs our attention, if only to better appreciate the complexity of life in the universe. Peck addressed the mystical side of the spiritual path as a yearning to understand the bigger picture of life, even though several pieces will be missing. The mystery begins where science fails to explain any or all dynamics of the unexplainable.

Spontaneous remissions are not merely miracles, but qualify as mystical experiences. Synchronistic moments, divine apparitions, premonitionistic dreams, and perhaps some crop-circle formations qualify as mystical moments. The popularity of this topic, as depicted by Oprah Winfrey on her TV specials, Coast to Coast AM radio show, and many national conferences, supports the concept that spiritual hunger is very real in terms of trying to understand the bigger picture of which each of us is a part. The lack of scientific evidence does not invalidate the divine mystery. Rather, it supports the idea that the human mind will never understand everything in the universe by using just the five senses. Furthermore, to be a good mystic doesn't mean to be able to rationally explain the supernatural; it merely means to appreciate the fact that we will never fully understand all aspects of the cosmos. In essence, to be a good mystic means to see the supernatural as natural and the ordinary as extraordinary.

Spiritual Potential and Spiritual Health

This spiritual well-being model suggests that the configuration of the four components to promote higher consciousness yields a host of personality traits specific to the integrity of the human spirit. I call these traits or inner resources spiritual potential, and they can be either dormant or active parts of one's personality. Creativity, will, intuition, faith, patience, courage, love, humility, and optimism are examples of these human spiritual traits. The manifestation of spiritual potential, which I label spiritual health, is expressed as specific emotional responses and behaviors that often expand the limits of human potential as a whole. Employing faith or an optimistic attitude in the face of diversity exemplifies spiritual health. In addition, Maslow might have considered creative acts or peak experiences to be examples of spiritual health; Peck cites community building, while Schaef would describe it as a "living process." Spiritual potential is like a group of instruments (e.g., violin, cello, and piano), and spiritual health is the music created by the individual with the instrument in hand. With practice, we are all capable of making beautiful music.

Roadblocks and Interventions

In Eastern philosophies, the division between the conscious and unconscious mind is considered the major obstacle to spiritual enlightenment. In Western philosophies, the walls of the ego, serving to protect one's thoughts, feelings, and identity, can hinder one's spiritual growth and human potential (FIG. 8.20). Although the ego wall is an abstract concept, elements that constitute its bricks and mortar are more easily recognized. These obstacles, some specific and concrete, others quite general and abstract, might include the following: laziness, greed, despair, anger, fear, low self-esteem, unresolved loss, substance addictions, and codependency. Roadblocks, both specific characteristics and/or related behaviors, undermine the maturation process of human spirituality to the detriment of spiritual health and total well-being. Roadblocks actually perpetuate the stress response rather than minimize it. Whereas roadblocks impede the progress

Spiritual potential: A term coined by the author to describe the potential we all have as humans to cope with stress through the use of our inner resources (e.g., humor, compassion, patience, tolerance, imagination, and creativity).

Spiritual health: A term to describe the use of our inner resources to help us cope with stress and dismantle the roadblocks on the path of life.

Roadblocks: A metaphor to explain how stressors act as obstructions on the human journey or spiritual path, yet these are not meant to be avoided—rather they are meant to be dismantled, circumnavigated, or transcended so that one can move on with one's life.

Photo courtesy of Mietek and Margaret Wirkus, www.mietekwirkus.com.

FIGURE 8.20 Divine mysteries are best defined as those unexplained happenings that often reveal a bigger picture of life than that observed through the five senses. This photograph of the Virgin Mary, taken in Medjugorje, Bosnia, emerged on a roll of film by a visitor to the shrine where her apparition appeared only to three teenagers.

of our spiritual journey, distractions actually pull you off the path, sometimes indefinitely. Distractions begin as attractions. A beer is an attraction; alcoholism is a distraction. Campbell indicates that each story depicting the hero's journey is loaded with distractions disguised as temptations that the hero must learn to overcome. Like the story of Rip Van Winkle, many people fall asleep on the spiritual path because of distractions. Like behavioral changes to influence physical well-being (e.g., aerobics, smoking cessation, balanced diet), intervention techniques can be utilized to enhance the development of inner resources and behaviors associated with spiritual health. The most common technique mentioned as an intervention is meditation. Meditation includes many styles of increasing self-awareness. In line with the idea that all things are connected, you will see that most, if not all, of the coping skills and relaxation techniques described in this book have some tie to the concepts discussed in this chapter. Art therapy, music therapy, humor therapy, communication skills, and several others include many aspects of spiritual well-being that integrate the concepts of centering, emptying, grounding, and connecting. They reinforce the importance of internal and external relationships, value systems, and the search for a meaningful purpose in life. In many Eastern cultures, relaxation techniques and coping skills were originally created as vehicles to enhance spiritual enlightenment and inner peace. Western cultures adopted several of these techniques and even created a few more, but lost in the translation were their true meaning and purpose. Slowly, this purpose is being rediscovered and recognized as an essential factor in these techniques, integrating the spiritual component with total well-being.

Distractions: Material possessions (greed or wealth) and/or behaviors (addictions) that distract one from making progress on the spiritual path. Distractions begin as attractions, pulling one off the spiritual path indefinitely.

As we begin to understand the dynamics of human nature, it becomes increasingly obvious how important spiritual well-being is to total well-being. Spirituality involves many academic disciplines, including theology, psychology, and quantum physics. The theories presented here are only a handful of concepts describing personal insights into the elements associated with human spirituality and the soul. Because of the sensitive relationship between spirituality and religion, this area of health promotion, particularly as it applies to stress management, has often been neglected altogether, or not incorporated fully, as a significant aspect of the wellness paradigm. As researchers continue to explore and measure human consciousness, they may reveal that the mind and the soul play integral roles in both the understanding of human stress and the most effective ways to deal with it (BOX 8.2).

Current Research on Spirituality and Health

What was once a taboo subject in academia (FIG. 8.21) has now become a hot topic of study, particularly with regard to prayer, faith, and the outcomes for healing (Levin, 2001; Koenig and Cohen, 2002; Miller and Thoresen, 2003). In large part because of the synthesis of work presented by Dr. Larry Dossey, prayer has become a bona fide field of study in medicine. Moreover, several medical schools

BOX 8.2 Stress and Human Spirituality

Here is a series of questions based on the work of several luminaries in the field of human spirituality. Take a moment to proceed through each question as a means to help resolve one or more issues in your life.

Are you aware of coincidences that go beyond chance?
—Carl Jung

What stage of spiritual growth are you at now?
—M. S. Peck

Are you open to questions that have no earthly answers?
—Hildegard von Bingen

What is your relationship with Mother Earth?
—Black Elk

Are you stuck in the dark night of the soul?
—Matthew Fox

Do you employ the skills of spiritual optimism?
—Joan Borysenko

Do you live within the seven laws of spirituality?
—Deepak Chopra

Do you approach situations from a place of fear or love?
—Jesus of Nazareth

Where are you on your hero's journey?
—Joseph Campbell

What aspect of your life is out of balance?
—Lao Tzu

Do you see yourself as a single entity or connected to all of life?
—Albert Einstein

What "season of the soul" do you avoid?
—Common Bonds of Human Spirituality

What stressors in your life involve relationships, values (value conflicts), and a meaningful purpose in life?
—Three Pillars of Human Spirituality

FIGURE 8.21 To some, authentic crop circles suggest a divine mystery.

now offer lectures, seminars, and courses on the topic of spiritual health and healing. Unfortunately, because the concept of spirituality is difficult to define and perhaps impossible to measure, many researchers have opted instead to measure the relationship between religiosity (going to church) and several health parameters, adding to confusion about the distinction between the concepts of spirituality and religion. Nevertheless, spirituality and health continue to be a topic of academic inquiry (Vaillant et al., 2008; Blumenthal et al., 2007). Although faith or church attendance may or may not be associated with health and healing, community support within church groups (connectedness) appears to be a significant factor in one's health status. What is interesting to note is that the abyss between science and spirituality, which formed during the Renaissance period, is narrowing, particularly as a greater appreciation of quantum physics unfolds to reveal aspects of ageless wisdom shared by spiritual luminaries over the past 2,000 years (McTaggart, 2008). So important is the spiritual aspect of health that the governing body that provides accreditation for hospitals across the country, the Joint Commission, has now mandated that each person who is admitted to any hospital be given a "spiritual assessment" as part of the admission process (Goliath, 2006).

The timeless insights of the perennial wisdom-keepers remind us that stress and human spirituality are partners in the dance of life. The following is a letter from one of my college students who asked me to share it with others:

Dear Professor Seaward,

> Ahoy from the peaceful shores of Seattle! This is a long overdue letter from one of your American University students, class of '93, your last semester I believe. I should have written much sooner, there's been something I've been meaning to tell you.

Remember when you told us that the things you were teaching might take on greater significance as we aged and matured (or failed to mature)? That was a major understatement! In fact, you may have saved my life. This is my story:

I'm an alcoholic. I've been one since I was in my teens, and I was headed for more advanced stages when we crossed paths. I had a DWI and was charged with another misdemeanor before I reached twenty. And that's when they caught me. But my legal difficulties were the least of my problems. I was becoming a vicious, animalistic monster, the very antithesis of who I really was. I was alienating everyone I loved and lost all self-respect. But try to tell me that back then and you would've been treated to the work of a master manipulator with true genius toward rationalization and self-deceit.

And then, I had the beginnings of what I now see to be a spiritual awakening. It was suggested that I go to Alcoholics Anonymous. I went and my first instinct was to run out the door. They used words like God and spirituality. What the hell did God and spirituality have to do with my problems? I am sure you know the answer to this question better than I. But of course my ego told me that these people were freaks thinking that spirituality was the answer for them.

When was the last time I heard of talk like this? It was from you. And you certainly weren't a freak. You possessed a sincere inner calm. You helped people and I believed you were behind the concepts you taught. I remembered how impressive some of your presentations were. How you could get a group of students to open their minds and try meditation. I remember when you had a Native American shaman visit the class and how impressed I was with what he shared. I remembered when you told us that drugs and alcohol did not enhance spiritual development, they put up walls. I did feel a spiritual link back then for all my faults and I saw some of the things you covered in the Twelve Steps. So maybe there was something to this spiritual angle they talked about in AA, I thought. And I stayed.

I celebrated four years of sobriety on December 10th, 1999, and am still sober as I write this letter. I have gained a deep and very personal appreciation for the concepts you introduced me to and promised would become important further down the road. Thank you.

Sincerely,

Steven M.

SUMMARY

- The term spirituality is becoming a more comfortable one in the Western world. Although stress seems to be omnipresent in American lifestyles, there also appears to be a spiritual awakening taking place, from seeds planted by the human consciousness movements of the late 1960s. The World Health Organization cites spiritual well-being as critical to overall well-being.
- Spirituality has proved elusive to define because its essence seems to permeate everything. Harmony with self, others, earth, and a higher power is often considered a description of this concept. Spirituality and religion are related, but separate, concepts.
- Several viewpoints of human spirituality by intellectuals from Eastern and Western cultures representing several disciplines, including psychology, theology, philosophy, physics, and medicine, were described.
- Jung postulated that there is a profound, divine level of unconsciousness, the collective unconscious, which unites all people. Poor spiritual health results from the inability to access this source within us.
- Peck outlined the road to spiritual development, a systematic path consisting of four stages: chaotic antisocial, formal-institutional, skeptical, and mystic-communal.
- Hildegard von Bingen was a mystic who reminds us of the mystical side of human nature and highlights that every aspect of creation is spiritual and sacred in its own way.
- American Indian spirituality, called Mother Earth spirituality, was described to Anglo-Americans by Black Elk. It includes four cardinal principles: respect for the Great Spirit, respect for Mother Earth, respect for fellow men and women, and respect for individual freedoms. The vision quest, a soul-searching retreat, is one of the most profound experiences of Mother Earth spirituality.
- Fox synthesized several concepts of theology and physics into creation spirituality, which consists of four phases: via positiva, via negativa, via creativa, and via transformativa.
- Borysenko outlines a categorical difference between spiritual optimism and spiritual pessimism: the former, an asset to total well-being; the latter, a significant contributing factor to the stress-and-disease relationship.
- Deepak Chopra reminds us to continually explore our consciousness and live in harmony with the spiritual laws of the universe. These include the laws of pure potentiality, giving and receiving, karma, least effort, intention and desire, detachment, and Dharma or life purpose.
- Jesus spoke of love as a divine source that resides in every one of us. It is this source that longs to bond with all others. His message was to love ourselves and then share this love with each member of humanity.
- Campbell stated that the hero's journey involves three distinct phases: (1) departure, (2) initiation, and (3) return.
- Lao Tzu described spirituality as the Tao. He outlined four principles of the Tao that help to clarify human interaction with the universe: oneness, dynamic balance, cyclical growth, and harmonious action. Many of the traits associated with these principles can be seen as parallels to Maslow's characteristics of self-actualization.
- Einstein's theory of relativity brought new light to the concept of energy and mass and properties of the nonlocal mind. His theory bears a remarkable resemblance to Jung's theory of the collective unconscious.
- Four common themes among theories of human spirituality constitute a systematic series of processes to strengthen the human spirit: centering, emptying, grounding, and connecting.
- Human spirituality can be defined operationally as the maturation process of higher consciousness as developed through the integration of three facets: an insightful, nurturing relationship with oneself and others; the development of a strong personal value system; and a meaningful purpose in life.
- A fourth but often unmentioned aspect of human spirituality is the mystical aspect of life—that which can be experienced but cannot be measured scientifically, and perhaps not completely understood in rational terms.

- The explosion in research regarding spirituality and health actually measures religious factors, not spirituality. Nevertheless, the connectedness of religiosity appears to be a major factor in optimal well-being.
- There are many roadblocks to spiritual evolution, perhaps the most significant being the stress emotion, fear.
- Many coping and relaxation techniques share characteristics that foster the spiritual process of centering, emptying, grounding, and connecting.

STUDY GUIDE QUESTIONS

1. Define human spirituality (as best you can).
2. Select four theories of human spirituality and explain each (e.g., the theory of Jung, Peck, Black Elk, Campbell, or Jesus of Nazareth).
3. Define and explain the common bonds (seasons) of human spirituality.
4. Explain how relationships, values, and a meaningful purpose in life are affected by stress.
5. Define spiritual potential and spiritual health.
6. Describe roadblocks and distractions in terms of stressors of spiritual health.

REFERENCES AND RESOURCES

Bellingham, R., et al. Connectedness: Some Skills for Spiritual Health, American Journal of Health Promotion 4:18–31, 1989.

Benedictine Monks. Chant. Angel Records, 1993.

Bentov, I. Stalking the Wild Pendulum. Destiny Books, Rochester, VT, 1988.

Blumenthal, J. A., et al. Spirituality, Religion, and Clinical Outcomes in Patients Recovering from an Acute Myocardial Infarction, Psychosomatic Medicine 69(6):501–508, 2007.

Bobko, J. Vision: The Life and Music of Hildegard von Bingen. Penguin Studio Books, New York, 1995.

Bohm, D. Toward a New Theory of the Relationship of Mind and Matter, Frontier Perspectives 1(9), 1990.

Bolen, J. S. The Tao of Psychology. Harper & Row, San Francisco, 25th Anniversary ed. 2005.

Bonham, T. Humor: God's Gift. Broadman Press, Nashville, TN, 1988.

Booth, L. When God Becomes a Drug. Tarcher Press, Los Angeles, 1991.

Bopp, I., et al. The Sacred Tree: Reflections on Native American Spirituality. Four Worlds Development Press, Wilmot, WI, 1985.

Borg, M. Jesus: Uncovering the Life, Teachings, and Relevance of a Religious Revolutionary. Harper One, New York, 2008.

Borysenko, J. Fire in the Soul: A New Psychology of Spiritual Optimism. Warner Books, New York, 1993.

Borysenko, J. Guilt Is the Teacher, Love Is the Lesson. Warner, New York, 1990.

Borysenko, J. The Ways of the Mystic: Seven Paths to God. HayHouse, Carlsbad, CA, 1997.

Borysenko, J. A Woman's Journey to God. Riverhead Books, New York, 1999.

Borysenko, J., and Dveirin, G. Your Soul's Compass. HayHouse, Carlsbad, CA, 2008.

Boyd, D. Rolling Thunder. Delta, New York, 1974.

Brody, H. The Placebo Response. Cliff Street Books, New York, 2000.

Byrd, R. C. Cardiologist Studies Effect of Prayer on Patients, Brain/Mind Bulletin, March 7, 1986.

Byrd, R. C. Positive Therapeutic Effects of Intercessory Prayer in a Coronary Care Unit Population, Southern Medical Journal 81(7):826–829, 1988.

Cousineau, P. The Hero's Journey. Element, Shaftsbury, UK, 1999.

Campbell, J. The Hero with a Thousand Faces, 3rd ed. Princeton Bollinger, Princeton, NJ, 2008.

Campbell, J. The Power of Myth (with Bill Moyers). Doubleday Books, New York, 1988.

Campbell, J. Radio interview on New Dimension Radio. San Francisco, CA, 1988.

Capra, F. The Tao of Physics, 4th ed. Shambhala Publications, Berkeley, CA, 2010.

Carey, K. Starseed: The Third Millennium. HarperCollins, San Francisco, 1991.

Carlson, R., and Shield, B. (eds.). Handbook for the Soul. Little, Brown, Boston, 1995.

Carlson, R., and Shield, B. Healers on Healing. Tarcher, Los Angeles, 1989.

Castaneda,C.TheTeachingsofDonJuan:AYaquiWayofKnowledge. Pocket Books, New York, 1968.

Catford, L., and Ray, M. The Path of the Everyday Hero: Strategies for Finding Your Creative Spirit. Tarcher, Los Angeles, 1991.

Chapman, L. Developing a Useful Perspective on Spiritual Health:Wellbeing,SpiritualPotential,andtheSearchfor Meaning, American Journal of Health Promotion 1: 31–39, 1987.

Chapman, L. Spiritual Health: A Component Missing from HealthPromotion,AmericanJournalofHealthPromotion 1(1):38–41, 1986.

Chopra, D. The Higher Self. Nightengale-Conant, Chicago, 1996.

Chopra,D.HowtoKnowGod:TheSoul'sJourneyintotheMystery of Mysteries. Harmony Books, New York, 2000.

Chopra, D. Personal communication, October 14 & 15, 1996.

Chopra, D. The Seven Spiritual Laws of Success. New World Library, San Rafael, CA, 1995.

Cimino, R., and Lattin, D. Choosing My Religion, American Demographics, April 1999: 60–65.

Clark, R. W. Einstein: The Life and Times. Avon Books, New York, 1971.

Cochran,T.,andZalenski,J.Transformations:Awakeningtothe Sacred in Ourselves. Bell Tower, New York, 1995.

Course in Miracles (3rd ed.). Foundation for Inner Peace, Farmingdale, NY, 2008.

Coutuier,L.SpeakinginSilence,NewWomenMagazine,March 1992:58–61.

Crow-Dog, M., and Erdoes, R. Lakota Woman. Harper Perennial Books, New York, 1990.

Dossey, L. Healing Words. HarperCollins, San Francisco, 1993.

Dossey,L.RecoveringtheSoul:AScientificandSpiritualSearch. Bantam New Age Books, New York, 1989.

Dossey, L. Reinventing Medicine. HarperSanFrancisco, San Francisco, 1999.

Dossey,L.Space,Time,andMedicine.BantamNewAgeBooks, New York, 1982.

Dreher, D. The Tao of Inner Peace. (Revised ed.) Harper Perennial Books, New York, 2000.

Drummond, H. Drummond's Address. Henry Altemus Company, Philadelphia, 1891.

Einstein, A. Ideas and Opinions. Crown, New York, 1954.

Eley, G., and Seaward, B. L. Health Enhancement of the Human Spirit. National Center for Health and Fitness, Spiritual Well-Being Symposium, Washington, DC, April 16–17, 1989.

Elliot, W. Tying Rocks to Clouds. Image Books–Doubleday, New York, 1996.

Engel, M. It's Official, Global Warming Does Exist, Says Bush. The Guardian, June 4, 2002. www.guardian.co.uk /environment/2002/jun/04/usnews.globalwarming.

Fahlberg, L. L., and Fahlberg, L. A. Exploring Spirituality and Consciousness with an Expanded Science: Beyond the Ego with Empiricism, Phenomenology, and Contemplation,AmericanJournalofHealthPromotion5:273–281, 1991.

Fields, R., et al. Chop Wood, Carry Water: A Guide to Finding Spiritual Fulfillment in Everyday Life. Tarcher Books, Los Angeles, 1984.

Foster,S.,withLittle,M.VisionQuest:PersonalTransformations in the Wilderness. Prentice-Hall, New York, 1988.

Fowler,K.StagesofFaith:ThePsychologyofHumanDevelopment andtheQuestforMeaning.Reviseded.HarperSanFrancisco, San Francisco, 1995.

Fox, M. Creation Spirituality. Harper, San Francisco, 1991.

Fox,M.IlluminationsofHildegardvonBingen.2nded.Bear and Company, Santa Fe, NM, 2003.

Fox, M. One River, Many Wells. Tarcher Books, New York, 2000.

Fox,M.ASpiritualityNamedCompassion.WinstonPress,Minneapolis, MN, 1999.

Frankl, V. Man's Search for Meaning. Pocket Books, New York, 1984.

Freeman, J. Interview with Carl Jung. British Broadcasting Corporation, 1959. Film.

Galanter, M. Healing Through Social and Spiritual Affiliation, Psychiatric Services 53(9):1072–1074, 2002.

Gerber, R. Personal communication, November 25, 1991.

Glenn, H. Losing Our Religion: The Growth of the "Nones." NPR,January13,2013.www.npr.org/blogs/thetwo-way /2013/01/14/169164840/losing-our-religion-the-growth-of -the-nones.

Gore, A. An Inconvenient Truth. Rodale Press, Emmaus, PA, 2006.

Gore,A.EarthintheBalance:ForgingANewCommonPurpose (Revised ed.). Plume Press, New York, 2007.

Grof,C.TheThirstforWholeness:Attachment,Addictionandthe Spiritual Path. HarperCollins, New York, 1993.

Hammerschlag,C.TheTheftoftheSpirit:AJourneytoSpiritual Healing. Fireside Books, New York, 1994.

Hand, F. Learning Journey in the Red Road. Learning Journey Communications, Toronto, 1998.

Hodges, S., et al. Effect of Spirituality on Successful Recovery fromSpinalSurgery,SouthernMedicalJournal95(12):1381–1385, 2000.

Hoff, B. The Tao of Pooh. Penguin Books, New York, 1982.

Hoyman, H. The Spiritual Dimension of Man's Health in Today's World, Journal of School Health, February 1966.
Hunt, S. Spring Cleaning, Spiritual Healing, Black Issues Book Review 4(3):51–53, 2002.
Huxley, A. The Perennial Philosophy. Perennial Library, New York, 1945.
Jampolsky, G. Teach Only Love. (Expandeded.) Bantam Books, New York, 2000.
Jung, C. G. Man and His Symbols. Anchor Books, New York, 1964.
Jung, C. G. Memories, Dreams, Reflections. Vantage Press, New York, 1964.
Jung, C. G. Modern Man in Search of a Soul. Harvest/HBJ Books, San Diego, CA, 1933.
Jung, C. G. The Undiscovered Self. Mentor Books, New York, 1958.
Kennedy, J. F. Inaugural Address, January 20, 1961, Department of State Bulletin, February 6, 1961.
Klivington, K., et al. Does Spirit Matter? Four Commentaries, Advances 8(1):31–48, 1992.
Koenig, H., and Cohen, H. (eds.). The Link Between Religion and Health: Psychoneuroimmunology and the Faith Factor. Oxford Press, New York, 2002.
Koerner, B., and Rich, J. Is There Life After Death? U.S. News & World Report, February 23, 1997.
Krebs, K. The Spiritual Aspect of Caring—An Integral Part of Health and Healing, Nursing Administration Quarterly 25(3):55, Spring 2001.
Krishnamurti, J. On God. HarperSanFrancisco, San Francisco, 1992.
Lao Tzu. Tao Teh Ching, trans. J. C. H. Wu. Shambhala, Boston, 1990.
Larson, D. B. The Faith Factor. National Institute for Healthcare Research, Bethesda, MD, December 1993.
Leichtman, R. Einstein Returns. Ariel Press, Columbus, OH, 1982.
Lerner, M. Spirit Matters. Walsh Books, Charlottesville, VA, 2000.
Leskowitz, E. The Relationship of Spirituality to Coronary Heart Disease, Alternative Therapies 7(5):96–98, 2001.
Lesser, L. The New American Spirituality. Random House, New York, 1999.
Levin, J. God, Faith and Health: Exploring the Spirituality–Healing Connection. John Wiley & Sons, New York, 2001.
Lewis, C. S. Mere Christianity. Collier Books, New York, Revised 2015.
Lewis, H. A Question of Values. Harper & Row, San Francisco, Revised 2007.
Maslow, A. H. The Farther Reaches of Human Nature. Penguin Books, New York, 1976.
Maslow, A. H. Religion, Values, and Peak Experiences. Penguin Books, New York, 1964.
McFadden, S. Profiles in Wisdom: Native Elders Speak about the Earth. Bear and Company, Santa Fe, NM, 1991.
McGaa, E. (Eagle Man). Mother Earth Spirituality: Native American Paths to Healing Ourselves and the World. HarperCollins, San Francisco, 1990.
McGaa, E. Nature's Way: Native Wisdom for Living in Balance with the Earth. Harper, San Francisco, 2004.
McTaggart, L. The Field: The Quest for the Secret Force of the Universe, 2nd ed. HarperCollins, New York, 2008.
Merton, T. The Ascent to Truth. Harcourt Brace Jovanovich, San Diego, CA, 1951.
Miller, W., and Thoresen, C. Spirituality, Religion, and Health: An Emerging Research Field, American Psychologist 58(1):24–36, 2003.
Millman, D. The Laws of Spirit. H. J. Kramer, Tiburon, CA, 1995.
Moore, T. Care of the Soul. HarperCollins, New York, 1992.
Muller, W. Sabbath: Restoring the Sacred Rhythm of Rest. Bantam Books, New York, 1999.
Naranjo, C., and Ornstein, R. On the Psychology of Meditation. Esalen Books, New York, 1971.
Neihardt, J. G. Black Elk Speaks. University of Nebraska Press, Lincoln, Complete ed. 2014.
O'Murchu, D. Quantum Theology. Crossroad, New York, Updated ed. 2004.
O'Murchu, D. Reclaiming Spirituality. Crossroad, New York, 1998.
Parnia, S. Erasing Death. Harper One, New York, 2013.
Peck, M. S. The Different Drum: Community Making and Peace. Simon & Schuster, New York, 2nd ed. 1998.
Peck, M. S. The Road Less Traveled. Simon & Schuster, New York, 1978.
The Pew Forum on Religion and Public Life. U.S. Religious Landscape Survey. http://religions.pewforum.org/reports.
Piedmont, R. Spiritual Transcendence and the Scientific Study of Spirituality, Journal of Rehabilitation 67(1):4–14, 2001.
Pilch, J. Wellness Spirituality, Health Values 12(3):28–31, 1988.
Powell, L., et al. Religion and Spirituality: Linkages to Physical Health, American Psychologist 58(1):36–53, 2003.
Radin, D. Entangled Minds. Paraview Pocket Books, New York, 2006.
Redwood, D. Rediscovering the Soul: A Scientific and Spiritual Search (interview with Larry Dossey), Pathways, Spring 1992:19–29.
Remen, R. N. On Defining Spirit, Noetic Sciences Review 8:7, 1988.
Remen, R. N. Spirit: Resource for Healing, Noetic Sciences Review 8: 4–9, 1988.

Rifkin, I., ed. Spiritual Innovators. Starlight Paths, Woodstock, VT, 2002.

Rokeach, M. Beliefs, Attitudes, and Values. Jossey-Bass, San Francisco, 1972.

Roman, S. Spiritual Growth: Being Your Higher Self. H. J. Kramer, Tiburon, CA, 1989.

Rosewall, A. Drawing Out the Spirit, EAP Association Exchange 31(3):14, 2001.

Schaef, A. W. When Society Becomes an Addict. Harper & Row, New York, 1987.

Seaward, B. L. From Corporate Fitness to Corporate Wellness, Fitness in Business 2:182–186, 1988.

Seaward, B. L. Giving Wellness a Spiritual Workout, Health Progress 70:50–52, 1989.

Seaward, B. L. Health of the Human Spirit, (2nd ed.) Jones & Barlett, Burlington, 2012.

Seaward, B. L. Quiet Mind, Fearless Heart. John Wiley & Sons, New York, 2005.

Seaward, B. L. Reflections on Human Spirituality at the Worksite, American Journal of Health Promotion 9(3):165–168, 1995.

Seaward, B. L. Spiritual Wellbeing, a Health Education Model, Journal of Health Education 22(3):166–169, 1991.

Seaward, B. L. Stand like Mountain, Move like Water. Health Communications, Deerfield Beach, FL, Revised ed., 2007.

Seaward, B. L., Meholick, B., and Campanelli, L. Introducing Spiritual Wellbeing in the Workplace: A Working Model for Corporations, Wellness in the Workplace National Conference, Baltimore, MD, March 21, 1990.

Seaward, B. L., Meholick, B., and Campanelli, L. A Program in Spiritual Wellbeing at the United States Postal Service, Wellness Perspectives 8(4):16–30, 1992.

Selye, H. Stress without Distress. Signet Books, New York, 1974.

Schmidt, L. E. Restless Souls. 2nd ed. Harper, San Francisco, 2012.

Shield, B., and Carlson, R., eds. For the Love of God: New Writings by Spiritual and Psychological Leaders. New World Library, San Rafael, CA, 1990.

Siegel, B. Peace, Love, and Healing. Walker, New York, 1990.

Spindrift Inc. Century Plaza Bldg., 100 W. Main St, Suite 408, Lansdale, PA 19446, (215) 361–8499.

Spirituality, Happiness, and Health. Christian News Notes. New York, 1991.

Storr, A. Solitude: A Return to the Self. Ballantine Books, New York, 1988.

Sweeting, R. A Values Approach to Health Behavior. Human Kinetics, Champaign, IL, 1990.

Tatsumura, Y., et al. Religious and Spiritual Resources, CAM and Conventional Treatment in the Lives of Cancer Patients, Alternative Therapies 9(3):64–71, 2003.

Taylor, E. Desperately Seeking Spirituality, Psychology Today, Nov/Dec 1994:54.

Taylor, K. Living Bible. Tyndale, Wheaton, IL, 1971.

Thompson, I. Mental Health and Spiritual Care, Nursing Standard 17(9):33–39, 2002.

Thorton, L., Gold, J., and Watkins, M. The Art and Science of Whole-Person Caring: An Interdisciplinary Model for Health Care Practice, International Journal of Human Caring 6(2):38–47, 2002.

Ulrich, R. L. View Through a Window May Influence Recovery from Surgery, Science 224:420–421, 1984.

Vaillant, G., Templeton, J., Ardelt, M., and Meyer, S. E. The Natural History of Male Mental Health: Health and Religious Involvement, Social Science Medicine 66(2):221–231, 2008.

von Bingen, H. Scivias, Bruce Hozeski, trans. Bean & Company, Santa Fe, NM, 1986.

von Bingen, H. Vision. The Music of Hildegard von Bingen. Angel Capitol Records, Los Angeles, CA, 1995.

Walsh, R. The Practice of Essential Spirituality, Noetic Science Review 58:8–15, 2002.

Williams, R. Social Ties and Health, Harvard Mental Health Letter, April 1999: 4–5.

World Health Organization, as quoted in "Spirituality, Happiness and Health." Christian News Notes. New York, 1991.

Young-Sowers, M. Spiritual Crisis: What's Really Behind Loss, Disease, and Life's Major Hurts. Stillpoint Publishing, Walpole, NH, 1993.

Zeckhausen, W. Spirituality and Your Practice, Family Practice Management 8(5):60, 2001.

Glossary

ABC rank-order method A time-management technique for which things are prioritized by order of importance.

Absurd or nonsense humor This type of humor is best exemplified by the works of Gary Larson's *The Far Side*. The comedian Steven Wright is also a prime example.

Acceptance Often the final outcome of reframing a situation: Accepting that which you cannot change and moving on with your life.

Acetylcholine A chemical substance released by the parasympathetic nervous system to help the body return to homeostasis from the stress response.

ACTH axis A physiological pathway whereby a message is sent from the hypothalamus to the pituitary and then on to the adrenal gland to secrete a flood of stress hormones for fight or flight.

Active imagination A term coined by Carl Jung describing a mental imagery process in which, in a lucid dream state or relaxed state, you consciously imagine (and resolve) the end of a recurring dream. Active imagination is a form of visualization.

Active meditation A term given to a physical activity (e.g., walking, swimming) that promotes a cleansing of the mind through repetitive motion.

Acute stress Stress that is intense in nature but short in duration.

Adaptation A behavior and attitude considered the epitome of the acceptance stage of grieving, in which a person adapts to the new situation and no longer views him- or herself as a victim.

Adaptors The most difficult type of nonverbal communication to decode, such as the folding of one's arms across the chest or the crossing of one's legs.

Adenosine-triphosphate-creatine Chemical compound in muscles that produces energy (anaerobically) for muscle contraction.

Adrenal cortex The portion of the adrenal gland that produces and secretes a host of corticosteroids (e.g., cortisol and aldosterone).

Adrenal gland The endocrine glands that are located on top of each kidney that house and release several stress hormones including cortisol and the catecholamines epinephrine and norepinephrine. The adrenal gland is known as "the stress gland."

Adrenal medulla The portion of the adrenal gland responsible for secreting epinephrine and norepinephrine.

Aerobic exercise Rhythmic physical work using a steady supply of oxygen delivered to working muscles for a continuous period of not less than 20 minutes (e.g., jogging).

Affect displays Facial expressions used to express a particular emotion (e.g., amazement).

Aggressive behavior style An aggression-based behavior that employs intimidation and manipulation.

Agility Maneuverability and coordination of gross and fine motor movements.

Agnostics Individuals who do not know if there is a higher source.

Alarm reaction The first stage of Selye's general adaptation syndrome, in which a threat is perceived and the nervous system is triggered for survival.

All-or-none conditioning principle A principle of exercise that states that to benefit from physical training, you must have the right intensity, frequency, and duration for each component of fitness challenged.

Allostatic load A term coined by stress researcher Bruce McEwen to replace the expression "stressed out"; the damage to the body when the allostatic (stress) response functions improperly or for prolonged states, causing physical damage to the body.

Altered state of consciousness A shift in one's thought process, typically from left-brain to right-brain thinking, to become more aware and more receptive.

Alternative medicine Modalities of healing (homeostasis) that include nearly all forms of stress management techniques. Also known as complementary or integrative medicine.

American Massage Therapy Association The governing body that accredits massage therapy schools and certifies graduates in massage therapy.

Anabolic functioning A physiological process in which various body cells (e.g., muscle tissue) regenerate or grow.

Anaerobic exercise Physical work done in the absence of oxygen; activity that is powerful and quick but does not last more than a few minutes (e.g., weightlifting).

Archetypes A Jungian term to describe primordial images that become symbolic forms with an inherent understanding among all people.

Aromatherapy The use of essential oils to promote relaxation through the sense of smell, often used in many types of body work as a complementary relaxation method.

Art of balance A term in hatha yoga that requires a balance of *asanas* on both the right and left sides of the body.

Art of breathing A term in hatha yoga that honors the importance of the pause of the breath (*pranayama*).

Art of conscious stretching An expression that suggests to yoga participants to be fully mindful as they assume and maintain an *asana*.

Art therapy A coping technique of self-expression and self-awareness employing various media to describe feelings and thoughts in ways that verbal language cannot.

Arteriosclerosis The third and final stage of coronary heart disease, wherein the arteries become hardened by cholesterol buildup, calcium deposits, and loss of elasticity.

Artist Von Oech's term to identify the second stage of the creative process, in which one plays with or incubates ideas that the explorer has brought back.

Artistic roadblocks The perceived inability to express oneself though creative expression (often based on fear).

Aspartame Two amino acids that combine to make an artificially sweet taste, including one that is documented to affect brain chemistry and cognitive function. Like MSG, this substance is known as an "excitotoxin." (Aspartame is also marketed as Nutrasweet.)

Assertive behavior style A behavior style that is neither passive nor aggressive, but one that is tolerant and considerate in the quest for individual rights.

Assertiveness The term given to a behavior that is neither passive nor aggressive, but proactively diplomatic.

Atheists Individuals who do not believe in a higher source.

Atherogenesis The first stage of coronary heart disease, wherein a fat streak appears on the inner lining of artery walls.

Atherosclerosis The second stage of coronary heart disease, wherein artery walls slowly become occluded by cholesterol-plaque buildup.

Attitudes These are beliefs about our values, often expressed as opinions.

Auditory imagery A term representing a means to imagine or recall a song or melody in one's head to promote relaxation.

Autogenic discharge Physical sensations such as muscle twitching, numbness, and perhaps some emotional responses (tears) released by the unconscious mind from autogenic training sessions.

Autogenic training Introduced by Schultz and Luthe; a relaxation technique in which the individual gives conscious messages to various body parts to feel warm and heavy; effects are thought to result from vasodilation to the specified body regions intended for warmth and heaviness.

Autoimmune diseases Diseases that occur because of an overactive immune system, which "attacks the body." Examples include lupus and rheumatoid arthritis.

Autonomic dysregulation Increased sensitivity to perceived threats resulting from heightened neural (sympathetic) responses speeding up the metabolic rate of one or more organs.

Autonomic nervous system (ANS) Often referred to as the automatic nervous system, the ANS consists of the sympathetic (arousal) and parasympathetic (relaxed) nervous systems. This part of the central nervous system requires no conscious thought; actions such as breathing and heart rate are programmed to function automatically.

Avoidance versus confrontation A dichotomy to describe how some people deal with stress.

Awareness Learning to become aware of a specific behavior in the effort to change it.

Awfulizing A mindset wherein one tends to see (or hope for) the bad in every situation.

Balance The ability to maintain equilibrium in motion.

Bandha A series of breathing exercises to unlock chronic pain.

Bathroom humor A form of humor often described as vulgar, crude, and tasteless, it derives its name from the use of various bodily functions known to occur in the bathroom.

Beginning position From the starting position, one begins to move his or her hands upward to eye level, palms facing down.

Behavior modification model A model that illustrates the steps taken to change a negative behavior into a positive one.

Behavioral changes One of three categories used in mental imagery (e.g., quitting smoking, improved athletic performance, weight-loss programming).

Behavioral substitution Substituting a new (positive) behavior for a less desirable one.

Behavioral therapy A therapy based on the work of John B. Watson, in which coping and relaxation techniques are used to desensitize oneself to stress.

Behaviors Actions (direct or indirect) that are based on conscious (sometimes unconscious) thoughts.

Belly breathing The most common form of relaxation by means of placing the emphasis of one's breathing on the lower stomach area (belly or diaphragm) rather than the upper chest (thoracic area), thereby decreasing sympathetic response and inducing a greater sense of relaxation.

Bhakti yoga One of five yogic paths; the path of devotion.

Binary One of two categories used to describe biofeedback; an example might include a device that lets one know of an effect of biofeedback on a specific biological function that results in lights appearing on a panel.

Biochemical theory A theory suggesting that music is received internally through the eardrum with sounds converted into neurochemicals that are registered by the brain, which one then finds either pleasant or unpleasant.

Bioflavonoids Nonnutrients found in foods (fruits and vegetables) that contain antioxidants and seem to provide a means of fighting cancer and other illnesses. Bioflavonoids provide the colors in foods.

Biophilia Human beings' affiliation to other living organisms (e.g., plants, trees, animals, birds, dolphins and whales) and planet earth, as well.

Bioplasma Another term for the etheric layer of energy closest to the physical body.

Biphasic Survivor personality traits; the ability to use both right-brain and left-brain thinking processes to successfully deal with a problem or stressors.

Bisociation The ability to perceive two aspects to a situation, in this case, resulting in a laugh.

Black Elk An early twentieth-century Native American elder whose perspective of spirituality is often cited as the clarion vision of our relationship with Mother Earth.

Black humor Humor about death and dying; thought to decrease fear of death.

Blaming Shifting the responsibility of a problem away from yourself.

Blog A term depicting someone's Internet journaling practice. Unlike a personal journal that is kept confidential, a blog is a public document to express opinions, beliefs, and newsworthy items of the author.

Blueprint aspect A term to suggest that the visualization has a goal to complete or accomplish; thus, the blueprint is the template for completion (e.g., a healed wound).

Borysenko, Joan An early pioneer in the field of psychoneuroimmunology who emphasized the importance of spirituality as part of the mind–body concept.

Bow Pose (Dhanurasana) A classic yoga *asana* intended to promote balance with the muscles of the lower back and stomach as well as neck and shoulders.

Boxing A scheduling technique used in time management for which the day is divided into 3- to 5-hour chunks of time devoted to accomplishing big projects.

Brief grief A concept that suggests that some grieving is appropriate and healthy versus unhealthy, prolonged grieving.

Broken heart syndrome A name given to the condition in which symptoms of a heart attack occur as a result of emotional stress; when stress hormones temporarily overwhelm heart tissue cells.

Buffer theory A theory suggesting that people invited to a support group act to buffer the participants from stress to lessen the impact.

Buzan writing style A specific journal approach to access the powers of both the right and left hemispheres of the brain through words and images.

Campbell, Joseph Renowned for his wisdom about human mythology gathered from all cultures over time, Campbell's greatest work illustrates the human experience as the hero's journey as exemplified in the template of every great story.

Cannon, Walter Twentieth-century Harvard physiologist who coined the term "fight or flight."

Cardiovascular (EKG) biofeedback Biofeedback that measures the electrical activity of the heart muscle in terms of amplitude and frequency of each heartbeat.

Cardiovascular endurance The ability of the heart, lungs, and blood vessels to supply oxygenated blood to the working muscles for energy metabolism.

Catabolic functioning A metabolic process in which metabolites are broken down for energy in preparation for, or in the process of, exercise (fight or flight).

Catastrophizing Making the worst out of every situation.

Catharsis Emotional release through crying, yelling, laughing, and the like.

Centering A time for soul searching, cultivating one's internal relationship.

Central nervous system (CNS) Consists of the brain and spinal column, whereas the peripheral nervous system (PNS) comprises all neural pathways to the extremities.

Cerebration A term used to describe the neurological excitability of the brain, associated with anxiety attacks and insomnia.

Chakras Chakra (pronounced "shock-ra") is a Sanskrit word for spinning wheel. Chakras are part of the subtle anatomy. The seven major chakras align from the crown of the head to the base of the spine and connect to various endocrine glands. Each major chakra is directly associated with various aspects of the mind-body-spirit dynamic. When a specific chakra is closed, distorted, or congested, the perception of stress, disease, or illness may ensue.

Chaotic antisocial The first stage of Peck's hierarchy of spiritual growth in which one's spiritual essence is lacking (spiritual bankruptcy).

Chi The universal life force of subtle energy that surrounds and permeates everything.

Chondromalacia Chronic knee pain, typically from excessive running and improper foot placement.

Chopra, Deepak A contemporary physician and metaphysician originally from India, he presents and integrates the ageless wisdom of spirituality, quantum physics, and medicine.

Chronic stress Stress that is not as intense as acute stress but that lingers for a prolonged period of time (e.g., financial problems).

Circadian rhythms Biological rhythms that occur or cycle within a 24-hour period (e.g., body temperature) that create the body's internal clock, also known as chronobiology. These can be affected by stress, causing a disruption that is even more stressful to the body.

Civility The practice of good manners and appropriate behavior.

Classical conditioning A learned behavior to a stimulus with regard to involuntary functions, such as becoming hungry when the clock strikes 12 noon.

Clinical biofeedback A process using one or more specially designed machines to amplify body signals (e.g., heart rate, muscle tension) and display these signals in a way that can be interpreted so that their intensity can be changed for the health of the individual.

Closed-loop feedback system A term used to describe the dynamics of biofeedback with its sensors attached to various parts of the human body.

Clustering A scheduling technique used in time management for which errands are grouped by location (e.g., dry cleaners, post office, pharmacy).

Cobra (Bhujanghasana) A classic yoga *asana* intended to promote balance with the lower back.

Codependency A stress-prone personality with many traits and behaviors that seem to increase the likelihood of perceived stress and the inability to cope effectively with it; addictive in nature; based on the need to make others dependent to receive self-validation.

Cognitive-dissonance theory A theory suggesting that the collective energy of one's support group supersedes any individual's negative experience of stress.

Cognitive distortion Distorting a situation beyond how bad it actually is.

Cognitive restructuring A coping technique; substituting negative, self-defeating thoughts with positive, affirming thoughts that change perceptions of stressors from threatening to nonthreatening.

Collective unconscious A term coined by psychologist Carl Jung; the deepest level of consciousness, which connects all people together as one; divine consciousness.

Color therapy A type of mental imagery exercise for which color is imagined as an agent for tranquility (e.g., green) or healing (e.g., blue).

Combative versus preventive Another dichotomy to describe how some people deal with stress.

Compensation The ability to cultivate and utilize one's strengths in times of need rather than claim victimization.

Compensation theory A theory suggesting that support groups compensate for various emotional losses one experiences during stress.

Concentric contraction A muscle contraction during which the length of the muscle shortens.

Conditional response A learned response (in this case through biofeedback) to control various biological functions such as heart rate and blood pressure.

Conditioned response A response learned over time to a particular (negative) situation, such as displaying caution or apprehension about something perceived as stressful.

Conflict-management styles There are five conflict-management styles: withdrawal, surrender, hostile aggression, persuasion, and dialogue.

Conflict resolution The resolution of arguments displayed as three styles: content conflict, value conflict, and ego conflict.

Connecting A realization that we are all connected, and the connection is made and nurtured through love.

Conventional sense of humor A term to describe more than one person laughing at the same thing, all agreeing to its humor.

Cool-down period A designated time right after the stimulus period to decrease circulation to the body's periphery and return to a resting state.

Coping responses Positive skills to cope with stress.

Corpse Pose (Shavasana) This is the typical position assumed at the close of each yoga session to restore energy.

Corticosteroids Stress hormones released by the adrenal cortex, such as cortisol and cortisone.

Cortisol A stress hormone released by the adrenal glands that helps the body prepare for fight or flight by promoting the release of glucose and lipids in the blood for energy metabolism.

Corumination Stress-based conversations between women as a means of coping by finding support among friends.

Cousins, Norman (1915–1990) An author of the classic book *Anatomy of an Illness* (1976), he used humor to help heal himself from a serious disease and brought the importance of humor to the national consciousness in terms of mind-body-spirit healing, paving the way for the field of psychoneuroimmunology.

Creation spirituality A term coined by theologian Matthew Fox to describe the paths of human spirituality blending the laws of physics and theology.

Creative problem solving A coping technique utilizing creative abilities to describe a problem, generate ideas, select and refine a solution, implement the solution, and evaluate its effectiveness.

Creative sense of humor This describes a person who thinks of jokes or funny things, but may be too shy to share them.

Cultural roadblocks Cultural thinking patterns that limit our ability to take in new ideas, leading to asymmetrical thinking.

Daily life hassles Occasional hassles, like locking your keys in your car; when combined with many other annoyances in the course of a day, these create a critical mass of stress.

Deceptive procrastinator Someone who attempts to work on projects, but only scratches the surface, stalling on the completion of tasks.

Decibels A unit of measurement (named in honor of Alexander Graham Bell) to denote the level of sound/noise measured as pressure through air.

Decoding A process in which the listener attempts to understand what the speaker has encoded in his or her verbal message.

Defense mechanisms Described by Sigmund Freud; unconscious thinking patterns of the ego to either decrease pain or increase pleasure.

Delegation Relinquishing control of a responsibility by turning it over to someone else.

Denial In some cases, this is the first step toward changing a negative behavior; one of the primary defense mechanisms noted by Freud in which one disbelieves what occurred when personally threatened.

Depression A state of mind in which thoughts are clouded by feelings of despair. Physiologists suggest that depression is caused by a chemical imbalance; psychologists suggest that depression is the result of unresolved stress emotions (anger turned inward).

Descartes, René A seventeenth-century scientist and philosopher credited with the reductionistic method of Western science (also known as the Cartesian principle). He is equally renowned for his influential philosophy of the separation of mind and body as well as the statement, "I think, therefore I am."

Desires In the Buddhist perspective of stress, desires are conditions and expectations that are associated with goals. Desires with attachments cause stress.

Detached observation A term derived from inclusive meditation during which the individual observes him- or herself meditating, in essence detaching from the ego's desire.

Diaphragmatic breathing The most basic relaxation technique; breathing from the lower stomach or diaphragm rather than the thoracic area.

Direct approach A term used in autogenic training when you not only suggest the words *warm* and *heavy* but also imagine the flow of blood to these body regions such as hands or feet.

Direct-effect theory A theory suggesting that social contact serves to provide uplifting aspects to the individual and thus pleasure to the ego.

Displacement The transference of emotional pain (usually anger) from a threatening source (one's boss) to a nonthreatening source (one's cat).

Distractions Material possessions (greed or wealth) and/or behaviors (addictions) that distract one from making progress on the spiritual path. Distractions begin as attractions, pulling one off the spiritual path indefinitely.

Distress The unfavorable or negative interpretation of an event (real or imagined) to be threatening that promotes continued feelings of fear or anger; more commonly known simply as stress.

Divine personification A term signifying one's evolving perception or image of the divine, whatever this happens to be.

Divinity theory The belief that humor is a gift from God.

Double entendre A joke that has two meanings.

Dream incubation A process in which an idea to be used as dream material is consciously seeded to prompt the unconscious mind during sleep; a technique effective to help resolve stressors.

Dream therapy A coping technique in which dreams, including recurring dreams, are explored and deciphered to help understand acute or chronic stressors.

Dry humor Often found in storytelling (e.g., Garrison Keillor, Mark Twain), in which the humor is subtle and clever.

Eccentric contraction A muscle contraction during which the size of the muscle lengthens.

Ecotherapy A method of restoring optimal health and well-being through routine exposure to and experience in the natural world.

Effleurage The first of five progressive steps/hand maneuvers in the Swedish massage that consists of long strokes along the length of the muscle tissue.

Ego A term coined by Freud naming the part of the psyche that not only triggers the stress response when threatened, but also defends against all enemies, including thoughts and feelings generated from within.

Egosyntonic A visualization expression meaning that images created/suggested in the visualization process must fit with the values and ideals that are most beneficial.

Einstein, Albert A world-renowned theoretical physicist who revolutionized perceptions of reality with the equation $E = mc^2$, suggesting that everything is energy. His later years focused on a spiritual philosophy including pacifism.

Electrodermal (EDR) biofeedback Biofeedback that measures the sweat response from skin.

Electroencephalographic (EEG) biofeedback Biofeedback that measures the electrical activity of the brain.

Electromyographic (EMG) biofeedback Biofeedback that measures the electrical impulses from specific muscles.

Emblems Physical gestures that tend to replace words, such as the thumbs-up signal.

Emotional literacy A term used in reference to one's ability to express oneself in an emotionally healthy way. Someone who routinely "goes ballistic" would be said to lack emotional literacy.

Emotional roadblocks Obstacles to the creative process, in the guise of fear, such as the fear of making a mistake (failure), rejection, or the unknown.

Emotional well-being The ability to feel and express the full range of human emotions and to control these feelings, not be controlled by them.

Emptying Also known as the "dark night of the soul" and the winter of discontent. The emptying process is a time to release, detach, and let go of thoughts, attitudes, perceptions, and beliefs that no longer serve you.

Enablers A term coined in the alcohol recovery movement, referring to a person who enables a spouse, parent, or child to continue either a substance or process addiction.

Encoding The process in which the speaker attempts to frame his or her thoughts and perceptions into words.

Endogenous-overreactive An overreactive immune system affected by internal pathogens (e.g., rheumatoid arthritis and ulcers).

Endogenous-underreactive An underreactive immune system affected by internal pathogens (e.g., cancer).

Energy psychology A term used to describe the collaboration of subtle energy (chakras, meridians, and the human energy field) with psychological issues and trauma involving certain aspects of stress.

Enhanced receptivity In the practice of meditation, one's mind opens to become more receptive to ideas that are often censored by the ego during normal consciousness.

Entrainment In physics, the mutual phase locking of like oscillations; in human physiology, organs or organisms giving off strong vibrations influencing organs or organisms with weaker vibrations to match the stronger rate of oscillation; thought to conserve energy.

Environmental disconnect A state in which people have distanced themselves so much from the natural environment that they cannot fathom the magnitude of their impact on it.

Environmental roadblocks Personal constraints such as time, money, or a host of responsibilities that impede the creative process.

Epigenetic theory A theory subscribed to by cell biologist Bruce Lipton. The theory states that DNA is greatly affected by the cell's environment, not just the unfolding of the genetic code. Lipton states that emotional stress is part of the cell's environment.

Epinephrine A special neurochemical referred to as a catecholamine that is responsible for immediate physical readiness for stress including increased heart rate and blood pressure. It works in unison with norepinephrine.

Essentic forms Musical patterns (vibrations) that are thought to influence neuropeptide activity and thus metabolic activity in the body.

Etheric energy The layer of energy closest to the physical body (also known as the etheric body).

Eustress Good stress; any stressor that motivates an individual toward an optimal level of performance or health.

Evaluation The process of observing and analyzing a newly adopted behavior, to see if the new behavior works.

Exclusive meditation A form of meditation wherein concentration is focused on one object (e.g., *mantra*, *tratak*) to the exclusion of all other thoughts, to increase self-awareness and promote relaxation.

Execution The third of three aspects essential for effective time management, in which tasks are actually completed.

Exogenous-overreactive An overreactive immune system affected by external pathogens (e.g., allergies).

Exogenous-underreactive An underreactive immune system affected by external pathogens (e.g., colds and flu).

Exploders People exhibiting a mismanaged-anger style by exploding and intimidating others as a means to control them.

Explorer Von Oech's term to identify the first stage of the creative process in which one begins to look for new ideas by venturing outside one's comfort level.

Exposure desensitization A process of learning to destress from something by brief, yet safe, encounters with the stressor.

External relationships One's relationships with others (e.g., family, friends, and colleagues) as well as the earth, water, and air we breathe.

Faith An optimistic attitude adopted to cope with stress for which one perceives a connection to something bigger than oneself (e.g., a divine source).

Fasting the heart A T'ai Chi term that explains the flow of one's life energy as a moving essence, and finding comfort in solitude.

Fear of death Anxious feelings about death and the dying process.

Fear of failure Anxious feelings of not meeting your own expectations.

Fear of isolation Anxious feelings of being left alone.

Fear of rejection Anxious feelings of not meeting the expectations of others.

Fear of the loss of self-dominance Anxious feelings of losing control of your life.

Fear of the unknown Anxious feelings about uncertainty and future events.

Fight-or-flight response A term coined by Walter Cannon; the instinctive physiological responses preparing the body, when confronted with a threat, to either fight or flee; an evolutionary survival dynamic.

Fish (Matsyasana) A classic yoga *asana* intended to promote balance with the lower back.

Fist over Head (Araha Chakrasana) A classic yoga *asana* intended to promote balance with arms and shoulders.

Flexibility The ability to use a muscle group throughout its entire range of motion.

Flexible optimism A term coined by Seligman to convey that we can all harness the power of optimism into positive thinking.

Flotation tanks A moderate sensory deprivation tank in which a person floats on his or her back in warm water to calm the nervous system through decreased stimulation.

Focusing The ability to recognize the body signals of oncoming stress (e.g., muscle tension, increased breathing, sweating).

Forgiveness A coping technique for anger-related stressors for which a shift in attitude is adopted toward those against whom a grudge was previously held.

Formal-institutional The second stage of Peck's hierarchy of spiritual growth, in which one tends to find comfort in the guidelines of religious institutions.

Fox, Matthew A Christian theologian renowned for his theory of creation spirituality and many other concepts. He was silenced by the Vatican in 1989 for one year followed by excommunication in 1999. He is now an Episcopal minister in California.

Frankenfood A name coined in Europe to promote the hidden dangers of genetically modified organisms (GMOs). GMOs are currently banned in Europe.

Frankl, Viktor (1905–1997) World-renowned psychiatrist and survivor of the Nazi Auschwitz Concentration Camp who coined the term "logo therapy" to describe a purpose in life focus. Author of the best-seller *Man's Search for Meaning*.

Free radicals Highly reactive oxygen molecules with an aberrant electron that can cause damage to cell membranes and DNA.

Freeze response Part of the stress response wherein the individual neither fights nor flees but freezes like a deer caught in headlights, paralyzed as if the person has forgotten to run.

Frequency The number of exercise sessions per week; the ideal number is three.

Friction The third of five progressive steps/hand maneuvers in the Swedish massage, also known as kneading the muscle tissue.

General adaptation syndrome A term coined by Hans Selye; the three distinct physiological phases in reaction to chronic stress: the alarm phase, the resistance phase, and the exhaustion phase.

Genetically modified organisms (GMOs) DNA manipulation of foods whereby the gene from one species is spliced into the DNA of a different species to enhance quality or shelf life. GMOs are currently associated with a host of food allergies. An example of this would be taking the genes from a flounder and splicing them into the DNA of a tomato.

Glucocorticoids A family of biochemical agents that includes cortisol and cortisone, produced and released from the adrenal gland.

Good-sport sense of humor This describes someone who can take a practical joke without suing.

Grasp the bird's tail The fifth (roll back and press) and sixth (push) steps in the classic T'ai Chi movement with a specific series of hand motions and feet placement.

Grounding The point at which new insights may be revealed to assist a person to move from point A to point B.

Guided mental imagery An exercise in which one is guided through a series of suggestions provided by an instructor, therapist, or counselor to enhance one's imagination.

Hardy personality A term coined by Maddi and Kobasa; personality characteristics that, in combination, seem to buffer against stress: control, commitment, and challenge.

Hatha yoga One of five yogic paths; the path of physical balance.

Head of Cow (Gomukhasana) A classic yoga *asana* intended to promote balance with arms and shoulders.

Helpless-hopeless personality Describes a person who has given up on life, or aspects of it, as a result of repeated failure.

Hero's journey Mythologist Joseph Campbell's classic template of the human journey with three stages: departure, initiation, and return.

Hertz (Hz) A physics term describing the number of oscillations or vibrations produced per second.

Hierarchy of needs Maslow's concept of a stair-step approach of consciousness (thoughts and behaviors), ranging from physiological needs to self-transcendence.

Hobby A pleasurable pursuit or interest outside one's daily work responsibilities through which one begins to make order out of chaos (e.g., botanical gardening).

Holistic medicine A healing approach that honors the integration, balance, and harmony of mind, body, spirit, and emotions to promote inner peace. Every technique used in stress management is considered to support the concept of holistic medicine.

Homeostasis A physiological state of complete calmness or rest; markers include resting heart rate, blood pressure, and ventilation.

HPA axis The hypothalamic-pituitary-adrenal axis, a term synonymous with the ACTH axis.

Human energy field Subtle human anatomy that goes by many names, from the electromagnetic field around an object to a colorful aura. The human energy field is thought to be composed of layers of consciousness that surround and permeate the physical body.

Human Triangle (Trikonasana) A classic yoga *asana* intended to promote balance with the upper torso.

Humor A perception of something funny or comical; not a mood, but a perception that can trigger a feeling or mood of joy and happiness. Also, the defense mechanism noted by Freud that both decreases pain and increases pleasure.

Humor therapy A coping technique; the use of humor and comic relief as a means to relieve and reduce emotional stress by focusing on the funny, humorous, and positive aspects of life.

Hydrotherapy The use of baths, hot tubs, Jacuzzis, and flotation tanks to augment the sense of touch to promote relaxation.

Hypothalamus Often called the "seat of the emotions," the hypothalamus is involved with emotional processing. When a thought is perceived as a threat, the hypothalamus secretes a substance called corticotrophin-releasing factor (CRF) to the pituitary gland to activate the fight-or-flight response.

Idiosyncratic A term meaning self-generated, such as images used in visualization that are created by the person performing the visualization.

Illusion of control A term used in association with codependent behavior, thinking that one can control (manipulate) things/others that one really cannot.

Illustrators Movements or postures used in combination with verbal conversation, such as various hand motions.

Immediate (effects of stress) A neural response to cognitive processing in which epinephrine and norepinephrine are released, lasting only seconds.

Immune dysregulation An immune system wherein various functions are suppressed; now believed to be affected by emotional negativity.

Immunoenhancement A term used to describe various stress management techniques that appear to boost the immune system.

Important-versus-urgent method A prioritization time-management technique in which tasks are categorized.

Inclusive meditation A form of meditation in which all thoughts are invited into awareness without emotional evaluation, judgment, or analysis. Zen meditation is an example.

Incongruity theory A theory that states the reason we laugh is because when two concepts come together in our head and they don't make sense, we get a chuckle.

Increased awareness The first step of an effective coping technique when one becomes more aware of the situation.

Indirect approach A term used in autogenic training when you suggest to yourself that various body parts are warm and heavy.

Individuation A term coined by Carl Jung to describe self-realization, a process leading to wholeness.

Ineffability Experiences that cannot be expressed verbally; especially common during meditation.

Information processing The second step of an effective coping technique when one works toward resolution of the problem.

Information-processing model A model that reveals how we potentially perceive sensory information, for better or worse.

Information seeking A common coping technique; searching for detailed information to increase awareness about a situation that has become a perceived threat.

Infradian rhythms Biological rhythms that occur less than once in a 24-hour period (e.g., women's menstrual period). These can be affected by stress.

Insightful meditation An expression given to any type of meditation (inclusive or exclusive) whereby a person, after clearing the mind of interrupting thoughts and ego chit-chat, begins to expand his or her awareness to the intuition, or the deep-seated wisdom of the collective unconscious, thus giving insight into the person's life.

Insightful internal relationship How well do you know and love yourself? What is your relationship with your higher self?

Insomnia Poor-quality sleep, abnormal wakefulness, or the inability to sleep.

Instinctual tension A Freudian term used to highlight the tension between the mind's impulses and the body's response, suggesting that stress is humanly inherent.

Instrumental coping The implementation of a series of effective coping skills to alter one's reaction to stress.

Intellectual/expressive roadblocks Obstacles to the creative process; in this case, created by the language we use that gives bias to our way of thinking (e.g., doorway versus entrance).

Intensity The physical challenge (stress) placed on a specific physiological system for exercise.

Intercessory prayer One style of prayer for which the individual seeks assistance from a higher (divine) source to intervene or assist with his or her problems.

Intermediate stress effects The hormonal response triggered by the neural aspects of the adrenal medulla that are released directly into the blood, lasting minutes to hours.

Internal body images One of three categories used in mental imagery for the purpose of healing disease or illness (e.g., shrinkage of cancerous tumors, mending broken bones).

Irony A type of humor in which the opposite from what was originally expected occurs.

Irrational An overwhelming feeling of anxiety based on a false perception.

Isometric contraction A muscle contraction during which there is no visible change in the length of the muscle fiber.

Jesus of Nazareth A remarkable spiritual leader with a timeless message of compassion, forgiveness, and integrity.

Jnana yoga One of five yogic paths; the path of knowledge.

Jonah complex A term coined by Abraham Maslow to illustrate the fear of not maximizing one's potential.

Journal writing A coping technique; expression of thoughts, feelings, memories, and ideas in written form, either prose or poetry, to increase self- awareness.

Judge Von Oech's term to identify the third stage of the creative process in which one selects the best idea and prepares it for manifestation.

Jung, Carl A twentieth-century psychiatrist who, under the initial tutelage of Sigmund Freud, forged a new premise of psychology honoring the importance of the human spirit. He became the second greatest influence in the field of psychology.

Karma yoga One of five yogic paths; the path of action.

Kinesthetic A visualization expression meaning the actual involvement through the five senses in the practice of this technique.

Kirlian photography A technique developed by Russian Semyon Kirlian enabling the viewer to see the electromagnetic energy given off by an object such as the leaf of a tree or human hand. This technique is one of several technologies that substantiates the human energy field.

Kneading Also known as friction in Swedish massage, when hands knead the muscle tissue to promote relaxation.

Koan An unsolvable riddle that aims to shift one's consciousness from analytical thoughts to profound contemplation.

Kübler-Ross (MD), Elisabeth (1926–2004) Psychiatrist renowned for her stages of grieving (denial, anger, bargaining, withdrawal, and acceptance) and death with dignity.

Kundalini yoga One of five yogic paths; the path of spiritual awakening.

Lactic acid A by-product of the breakdown of ATP, which can also be used as a source of energy (anaerobic).

Law of Detachment A reminder to release and let go of all thoughts that hold back our human potential.

Law of Dharma or Life Purpose This law invites contemplation of one's purpose in life.

Law of Giving A reminder to live life with an open heart to give and receive freely.

Law of Intention and Desire A reminder to set our intentions for both big and small goals yet not become encumbered by the ego's desires.

Law of Karma (or Cause and Effect) A reminder that we reap what we sow.

Law of Least Effort A reminder to go with the flow with things that we cannot control as well as to live in harmony with nature.

Law of Pure Potentiality A reminder to be silent and look within for guidance and insights rather than validation through external means.

Lazarus, Richard Renowned stress researcher credited with the concept of daily life hassles.

Left-hand ward-off The third step in the classic T'ai Chi movement with a specific series of hand motions and feet placement.

Leftover guilt A term coined by psychologist Wayne Dyer explaining the ill effects of unresolved guilt left over from an early childhood experience.

Leukocytes The family of cells that constitute the major component of the immune system.

Life-change units A unit of measurement that corresponds to items on the Social Readjustment Rating Scale.

Life-of-the-party sense of humor The class clown, the person who gets all the laughs.

Lifestyle behavior trap A behavior in which people have a hard time saying no and end up overwhelmed with multiple responsibilities.

Lift hands The eighth step in the classic T'ai Chi movement, incorporating a series of specific hand motions and foot placement to facilitate optimal *Chi* movement.

Light therapy An extension of color therapy for which full-spectrum lighting or one color from the light spectrum is used to promote homeostasis and healing.

Limbic system The midlevel of the brain, including the hypothalamus and amygdala, which is thought to be responsible for emotional processing.

Locus of control A sense of who or what is in control of one's life; people with an internal locus of control take responsibility for their actions; those with an external locus of control place responsibility on external factors like luck or the weather; the latter is associated with the helpless-hopeless personality, a stress-prone personality.

Logotherapy A term coined by psychiatrist Viktor Frankl describing the search for meaning in one's life.

Love The emotion studied and advocated by Leo Buscaglia as being the cornerstone to self-esteem and ultimately altruism.

Lymphocytes Immune system cells that are housed throughout the lymphatic system, with two percent in circulation at any one time.

Magnifying A term to describe blowing things out of proportion.

Mandala A circular-shaped object used as a visual mantra for the purpose of clearing the mind of unnecessary (ego-based) thoughts.

Mantra Typically a one-syllable word (e.g., *om*, *peace*, *love*) or a short phrase that acts like a broom to sweep the mind of nonessential (ego-based) thoughts.

Massage therapy A relaxation technique; the manipulation of skin, muscles, ligaments, and connective tissue for the purpose of releasing muscle tension and increasing physical comfort of musculature and surrounding joints.

Mechanistic model A health model based on the concept that the body is a machine with parts that can be repaired or replaced.

Meditation A practice of increased concentration that leads to increased awareness; a solitary practice of reflection on internal rather than external stimuli.

Melatonin A hormone secreted in the brain that is related to sleep, mood, and perhaps several other aspects of physiology and consciousness.

Mental imagery Using the imagination to observe, in the first person, images created by the unconscious mind; falls into three categories: (1) images that replicate peaceful scenes to promote relaxation, (2) images that substitute a less desirable behavior with a more healthy one, and (3) images that help to heal damaged body tissue.

Mental well-being The ability to gather, process, recall, and communicate information.

Meridian A river of energy with hundreds of interconnected points throughout the body, used in the practice of acupuncture and shiatsu massage.

Metadisease A concept by Maslow that depicts origins of physical disease as being based in unresolved emotional issues.

Metamessages The underlying intention of verbal communication when people are indirect with their comments thus adding to miscommunication.

Metaphysical theory A theory that suggests that music is a gift from God.

Methylated xanthine The active ingredient in caffeine, which triggers a sympathetic response.

Mindfulness A type of meditation in which all senses concentrate on the activity being performed during the present moment, like eating an apple or washing the dishes.

Mineralocorticoids A class of hormones that maintain plasma volume and electrolyte balance, such as aldosterone.

Misoneism A term coined by Carl Jung to explain the fear or hatred of anything new (fear of the unknown).

Modeling The ability to emulate or imitate our behaviors from the observation of others we respect (e.g., parents, schoolteachers, and peers).

Modified behaviors The third step of an effective coping technique when one works toward a sense of resolution.

Monosodium glutamate (MSG) A food brightener that is documented to affect brain chemistry and cognitive function. Like aspartame, this substance is known as an "excitotoxin." MSG is merely listed as "spice" on many condiments.

Mother Earth spirituality The expression used to describe the Native American philosophy with the divine through all of nature.

Mountain Pose (Tadasana) A classic yoga *asana* intended to promote balance and stability.

Mozart effect A term coined by renowned music therapist Don Campbell to illustrate the lifelong effect of classical music on healing, learning, and behavior.

Multitasking Acting on many responsibilities at one time (driving and talking on a cell phone) to save time, yet potentially compromising the integrity of both outcomes.

Muscular endurance The ability to sustain repeated contractions over a prolonged period of time.

Muscular strength The ability to exert a maximal force against a resistance.

Music therapy The ability to listen to, sing, or perform music as a means to promote relaxation and homeostasis.

Myofascial release Deep-tissue massage created by John Barnes to release tension by working with the myofascial (soft connective) tissue.

Mystical (peak) sensation A euphoric experience during which one feels a divine or spiritual connection with all life.

Mystic-communal The fourth stage of Peck's spiritual hierarchy in which one perpetually and joyfully seeks life's answers in the mystical divine universe.

Nadam An auditory mantra for which a repetitive sound is used to help clear the mind of unnecessary (ego-based) thoughts.

Natural killer (NK) cells Large lymphocytes that can detect endogenous antigens, thus helping to destroy mutant cells.

Nature Deficit Disorder A term coined by Richard Louv to describe a now-common behavior (affliction) in which people (particularly children) simply don't get outside enough, hence losing touch with the natural world and all of its wonder.

Neoplasms Another term for cancerous tumors.

Networking Establishing and nurturing personal and professional relationships to assist with the completion of personal responsibilities.

Neurolinguistic programming (NLP) A program designed to look at how our thoughts control our language and how our language influences our behavior.

Neuropeptides Unique messenger hormones produced in the brain (and other organs of the body) that fit into the receptor sites of lymphocytes.

Neurotheology A name coined to describe how the brain is hardwired to perceive metaphysical or mystical experiences of a divine nature.

Neustress Any kind of information or sensory stimulus that is perceived as unimportant or inconsequential.

Newton, Issac An eighteenth-century physicist who advocated the mechanistic paradigm of the universe, which was then adapted to the human body.

Nocebos A bona fide, effective medicine that does *not* work because the patient doesn't believe that it will.

Nonlocal mind A term given to consciousness that resides outside the brain (possibly outside the human energy field), which may explain premonitions, distant healing, and prayer.

Nonverbal communication All types of communication that do not involve words, including body language and facial expressions.

Nonverbal expression Many thoughts and feelings cannot be expressed verbally, giving rise to art therapy as a means of nonverbal expression.

Noo-dynamics A term coined by Viktor Frankl describing a state of tension, a spiritual dynamic, that motivates one to find meaning in life. The absence of noo-dynamics is an existential vacuum.

Norepinephrine A special neurochemical referred to as a catacholamine that is responsible for immediate physical readiness to stress, including increased heart rate and blood pressure. It works in unison with epinephrine.

Occupational stress Job-related stress, which often comes from occupational duties for which people perceive themselves as having a great deal of responsibility yet little or no authority or decision-making latitude.

Oncogene A gene in the DNA double-helix strand thought to be responsible for producing a mutant (cancerous) cell.

One Knee to Chest (Pawan Muktasana) A classic yoga *asana* intended to promote balance with the lower back.

Opening-up meditation *See* Inclusive meditation.

Operant conditioning A learned behavior that stems from a voluntary function or something about which we make a conscious decision.

Palliative coping A positive emotional regulation process during a stressful encounter (e.g., responding, not reacting).

Paradigm shift Moving from one perspective of reality to another.

Paralanguage A term used to describe speaking aspects such as volume, tone, and pitch that actually color verbal language.

Parasympathetic The branch of the central nervous system that specifically calms the body through the parasympathetic response.

Parasympathetic rebound The parasympathetic effect of relaxation (homeostasis) after physical exercise. Typically the response is such that parameters such as heart rate and blood pressure dip below preexercise levels.

Pareto principle Also known as the 80/20 Rule, this time-management technique prioritizes tasks by the satisfaction factor.

Parody A style of humor in which something or someone is made fun of. Self-parody is thought to be the best type of humor to reduce stress.

Passive-aggressive A mismanaged-anger style (*see* Underhanders) in which people seek revenge while at the same time fronting a smile.

Passive behavior style A behavior influenced by intimidation that can often lead to feelings of resentment and victimization.

Passive concentration A term coined by the creators of autogenic training to denote the conscious receptivity of self-generated thoughts.

Peaceful resolution The ultimate goal of any effective coping technique allowing one to move on with life.

Peck, M. Scott A contemporary psychiatrist who reintroduced the aspect of human spirituality and psychology with his classic book, *The Road Less Traveled*.

Perception distortion A sense during meditation (an altered state) in which, for example, one's arms and legs seem extremely heavy.

Perceptual roadblocks Obstacles to the creative process, placed by the ego, in the role of the judge.

Perennial philosophy A term used by Aldous Huxley to describe human spirituality, a transcendent reality beyond cultures, religions, politics, and egos.

Perfectionism Perpetually imposing above-human standards on oneself.

Perfectionist A person who is obsessed with the details of every task, aiming for quality, yet who ends up getting caught up with the details and missing the whole picture.

Personal cosmology Fox's term to explain one's personal relationship with the divine that dwells in each of us.

Personal unconscious A repository of personal thoughts, perceptions, feelings, and memories.

Personality traits Thoughts and behaviors that combine to form or color one's personality; in this case, cognitive traits associated with survival.

Pessimism Looking at the worst of every situation.

Pet therapy The use of hand contact with pets to promote relaxation among hospital patients, nursing home patients, and now everyday pet owners who claim better health through decreased resting heart rate and blood pressure values.

Petrissage The second of five progressive steps/hand maneuvers in the Swedish massage, it consists of a series of rolls, rings, and squeezes made by the fingertips or palm of the hand.

Phases of a workout Warm-up, stimulus period (target zone), and cool-down.

Physical well-being The optimal functioning of the body's eight physiological systems (e.g., respiratory, skeletal).

Pitch The human ear detects vibrations or oscillations as pitch.

Pituitary gland An endocrine gland ("master gland") located below the hypothalamus that, upon command from the hypothalamus, releases ACTH and then commands the adrenal glands to secrete their stress hormones.

Placebos A nonmedicine (e.g., sugar pill) that can prove to be as effective as the medicine it is supposed to represent. Healing occurs as a matter of belief.

Poetry therapy A therapeutic tool; a modality of writing poetry to enhance both increased awareness and emotional catharsis of a variety of issues.

Polarized thinking A condition in which things are always viewed in extremes, either extremely good or horribly bad.

Polyphasia A trait of thinking or doing many activities at once, also known as multitasking. This is also a trait of the Type A personality.

Positive psychology A field of modern psychology emphasizes the brighter side of human behavior with a specific focus on (1) positive emotions, (2) positive personality traits, and (3) positive institutions.

Post-traumatic stress disorder (PTSD) The mental, emotional, and physical repercussions experienced after an extremely stressful experience (e.g., war combat, natural disasters, rape and sexual abuse, car accidents).

Poverty consciousness A term used to describe an attitude or perception held by a person reinforcing the idea that he or she never has enough money, which in turn becomes a self-fulfilling prophecy.

Power Force multiplied by distance over time.

Pranayama A Sanskrit term to describe diaphragmatic breathing that restores one's vital life force of energy.

Pranayama A yogic term describing the concept of breath control during each of the *asanas* (yoga postures).

Predictive encoding A mental training strategy to utilize the unconscious mind for better performance; an academic term for *mental imagery*.

Present-centeredness An altered state in which one is fully aware of the present moment with no regard to past or future time periods.

Primary creativity Maslow's term for the first stage of the creative process in which ideas are conceived.

Principle of Cyclical Growth A Taoist concept suggesting that everything is cyclic: the moon, tides, seasons, and all aspects of human life.

Principle of Dynamic Balance A Taoist concept revealing the opposites that make up the balance of life.

Principle of Harmonious Action A Taoist concept that reminds us to work in harmony with nature, not in opposition to it or control over it.

Principle of Oneness A Taoist concept of oneness with nature serving as a reminder of our oneness with it.

Prioritization The first of three aspects necessary in effective time management, for which tasks are given priority for completion.

Process addiction The addiction to a behavioral process such as shopping, intercourse, gambling, television watching, cutting, and codependent behaviors.

Procrastinator Someone who employs diversions and avoidance techniques rather than tackling a host of responsibilities.

Progressive muscular relaxation (PMR) A relaxation technique; tensing and then relaxing the body's muscle groups in a systematic and progressive fashion to decrease muscle tension.

Projection The act of attributing one's thoughts and feelings to other people so that they are less threatening to the ego.

Prolonged effect of stress Hormonal effects that may take days or perhaps more than a week to be fully realized from the initial stress response.

Proportional One of two categories used to describe biofeedback; an example might be a device that lets one know the amount of physiological change, as determined by the pitch of a noise.

Psychic equilibrium A term coined by Carl Jung to describe the balance of thought (and subsequent health-wholeness) between the conscious and unconscious minds, by having the conscious mind become multilingual to the many languages of the unconscious mind (e.g., dream interpretation).

Psychoneuroimmunology The study of the effects of stress on disease; treats the mind, central nervous system, and immune system as one interrelated unit.

Psychophysiology A field of study based on the principle that the mind and body are one, where thoughts and perceptions affect potentially all aspects of physiology.

Psychosomatic A term coined from Franz Alexander's term *organ neurosis*, used to describe a host of physical illnesses or diseases caused by the mind and unresolved emotional issues.

Psychospirituality A focus in the field of psychology, influenced by Carl Jung, to acknowledge the spiritual dimension of the psyche.

Puns A type of wordplay that may leave people sighing rather than laughing.

Qigong A form of Chinese energy exercise and energy healing, in which *Qi* or *Chi* is directed through the body as a means to balance one's energy. Qigong healing may involve a Qigong healer to facilitate the energy healing process.

Quick-witted humor A style of humor that is based on quick wit without using sarcasm. Quick-witted humor often involves clever wording or phrasing that catches you off guard and leaves you impressed. Examples include the works of Mark Twain and NPR's "Car Talk" radio show.

Rage reflex A concept coined by Darwin that reflects the aggressive (fight) nature of all animals as a means of survival.

Rational emotive behavior therapy (REBT) Developed by Albert Ellis as a means to help people cope with anxiety by changing the perceptions associated with the stressor.

Rational A term to mean useful, as in rational fear of poisonous snakes.

Rationalization The reinterpretation of the current reality to match one's liking; a reinterpretation of the truth.

Reactionaries A term associated with the codependent personality illustrating a behavior of reacting, rather than responding, to stress.

Reconstruction The reinterpretation (from negative to neutral or positive) of a stressor (also known as reframing).

Reframing The name given to the thought process by which a negative perception is substituted for a neutral or positive one, without denying the situation.

Regulators Nonverbal messages used to regulate or even manipulate a conversation, including eye movements and other types of body language.

Relaxation response A term coined by Dr. Herbert Benson, who Americanized TM to make it more accessible to the Western world.

Release/relief theory Freud's theory of laughter is based on his concept that all laughter is the result of suppressed sexual tension, thus relieving it through humor.

Repression The involuntary removal of thoughts, memories, and feelings from the conscious mind so they are less threatening to the ego.

Residual tension A slight degree of muscle tension visible in some people who think they are relaxed.

Restrictive meditation A form of meditation wherein concentration is focused on one object (e.g., *mantra*, *tratak*) to the exclusion of all other thoughts, to increase self-awareness and promote relaxation.

Retail therapy The behavior attributed to people who go shopping to alleviate their stress. The consequence is buying things they don't really need or cannot always afford.

Reticular activating system (RAS) The neural fibers that link the brain to the spinal column.

Return to nature A T'ai Chi expression to explain the joys of childhood: innocence, laughter, and play.

Right-hand ward-off The fourth step in the classic T'ai Chi movement with a specific series of hand motions and feet placement.

Roadblocks A metaphor to explain how stressors act as obstructions on the human journey or spiritual path, yet these are not meant to be avoided—rather they are meant to be dismantled, circumnavigated, or transcended so that one can move on with one's life.

Rolfing Deep-tissue massage created by Ida Rolf to promote better posture by working with the soft connective tissue around and between muscles.

Runner's high The euphoric feeling generated from beta-endorphins released from cardiovascular exercise.

Salute to the Sun (surya namaskar) One of the most classic and symbolic series of hatha yoga *asanas*, often performed at the beginning and/or end of each yoga session.

Sapir-Whorf hypothesis The idea that our perception of reality is based largely on the words we use to communicate or express ourselves.

Sarcasm Thought to be the lowest form of humor, the word *sarcasm* means to tear flesh. Because sarcasm is a latent form of anger, it promotes rather than reduces stress.

Satire A written or dramatic form of parody. Examples include the works of Bill Maher, Louis C. K., and the movie *Shrek*.

Scheduling The second of three aspects necessary in effective time management, for which prioritized tasks are scheduled for completion.

Schismogenesis A term coined by Deborah Tannen suggesting that exaggerated conversation styles become intensified under stress, thus adding to miscommunication.

Schumann's resonance A physics term given to the actual vibration of the planet Earth: 7.8 Hertz.

Seasonal affective disorder (SAD) The physiological response to lack of sunlight that results in feelings of depression.

Secondary creativity Maslow's term for the last stage of the creative process in which a strategy is played out to have the selected idea come to fruition.

Secondary PTSD The emotional and financial stress of the family members and friends of those with PTSD.

Selected awareness The receptivity of the conscious mind to acknowledge and receive specific thoughts or messages.

Self-actualization The fifth level of Maslow's hierarchy of needs, at which one experiences a sense of personal fulfillment.

Self-disclosure The process in which a person reveals various aspects of him- or herself that are not readily apparent.

Self-efficacy A term coined by Albert Bandura to describe a sense of faith that produces a "can-do" attitude.

Self-esteem The sense of underpinning self-values, self-acceptance, and self-love; thought to be a powerful buffer against perceived threats.

Self-hypnosis A form of relaxation; an individual provides him- or herself with suggestions to relax (as with the suggestions of autogenics) as opposed to having someone else provide the suggestions.

Self-imposed guilt A term coined by psychologist Wayne Dyer to describe the guilt one places on oneself when a personal value has been compromised or violated.

Self-punishers People exhibiting a mismanaged-anger style by denying a proper outlet of anger, replacing it with guilt. Self-punishers punish themselves by excessive eating, exercise, sleeping, cutting, or even shopping.

Self-regulation The ability to control various aspects of human physiology; a self-produced or self-generated activity (e.g., self-hypnosis).

Self-talk The perpetual conversation heard in the mind, usually negative and coming from the critical (ego), which rarely has anything good to say.

Self, *the* (two versions, Tibetan psychology) The *Self* is the higher self or the true self; the *self* is identified as the false self or the ego-driven self.

Self-transcendence A sense of becoming one with something bigger than oneself; a mystical experience that occurs in meditation. Also the sixth and highest stage of Maslow's hierarchy of needs, at which one offers oneself altruistically to the service of others. Mother Teresa, Jane Goodall, Jimmy Carter, and Desmond Tutu serve as examples of this stage.

Seligman, Martin Renowned psychologist and proponent of the field of Positive Psychology.

Sensation seeker Also known as Type R personality, these courageous people confront stress by calculating their risks in extreme situations and then proceeding with gusto.

Senses of humor A frame of mind as part of one's personality in how one uses humor and laughter in one's life.

Sensory overload An inundation of information that overwhelms the mind.

Serenity Prayer A popular short prayer encouraging acceptance and wisdom, attributed to Reinhold Niebuhr.

Serotonin A neurotransmitter that is associated with mood. A decrease in serotonin levels is thought to be related to depression. Serotonin levels are affected by many factors including stress hormones and the foods you consume.

Seville Statement A statement drafted in Seville, Spain, endorsing the belief that aggression is neither genetically nor biologically determined in human beings.

Shallow effect A shallow understanding of complicated issues that is caused by information grazing. Jumping from website to website and cherry-picking information compromises one's ability to concentrate or focus on something long enough to fully understand all of its implications.

Shiatsu A type of massage, also known as acupressure, for which pressure is placed on various points (*tsubos*) to release blocked energy and thus promote relaxation.

Should-ing Reprimanding yourself for things you "should" have done.

Single whip The seventh step in the classic T'ai Chi movement characterized by a specific series of hand motions and feet placement.

Sit and Reach (Paschimottasana) A classic yoga *asana* intended to promote balance with the hamstrings and lower back.

Skeptical The third stage of Peck's spiritual hierarchy, at which one shuns all religious dogma.

Slapstick Originating from vaudeville, a physical farce such as getting a pie thrown in the face or slipping on a banana peel.

Sleep hygiene Factors that affect one's quality of sleep, from hormonal changes and shift-work to excessive caffeine intake.

Social orchestration A coping technique; either (1) changing stress-producing factors in the environment or (2) changing the entire stress-producing environment; the path of least resistance (as distinguished from avoidance).

Social Readjustment Rating Scale An inventory of life events that may be perceived to be stressful, used to determine one's level of stress.

Social support A coping technique; those groups of friends, family members, and others whose company acts to buffer against and dissipate the negative effects of stress.

Sociology The study of human social behavior within families, organizations, and institutions; the study of the individual in relationship to society as a whole.

Solitude The intentional act of seeking alone time in a quiet space, away from family, friends, and daily distractions as a means of seeking inner peace.

Somatizers People exhibiting an anger style by suppressing rather than expressing feelings of anger. *Soma* means body, and when anger is suppressed, unresolved anger issues appear as symptoms of disease and illness.

Spinal Twist (Ardha Matsyendrasana) A classic yoga *asana* intended to promote balance with the upper and lower back and hips.

Spiritual bankruptcy A term to convey the lack of spiritual direction, values, or less than desirable behaviors, suggesting moral decay.

Spiritual dormancy A state in which someone chooses not to recognize the importance of the spiritual dimension of life, individually and socially.

Spiritual health A term to describe the use of our inner resources to help us cope with stress and dismantle the roadblocks on the path of life.

Spiritual hunger A term to illustrate the quest for understanding of life's biggest questions, the bigger picture, and how each of us fits into it.

Spiritual nutrition A term to suggest that the colors of specific fruits and vegetables augments the flow of subtle energy to the respective *chakras* represented by these colors (e.g., foods with the color red are beneficial for the root *chakra* and organs associated with this area).

Spiritual optimism Joan Borysenko's description of an intuitive knowledge that love is *the* universal energy.

Spiritual pessimism Joan Borysenko's description of an attitude that nurtures low self-esteem, guilt, and other less-than-becoming behaviors.

Spiritual potential A term coined by the author to describe the potential we all have as humans to cope with stress through the use of our inner resources (e.g., humor, compassion, patience, tolerance, imagination, and creativity).

Spiritual well-being The state of mature higher consciousness deriving from insightful relationships with oneself and others, a strong value system, and a meaningful purpose in life.

Spontaneous remission The sudden (sometimes gradual) disappearance of a nonmedically treated disease, most often observed with cancerous tumors, but other diseases, as well.

Sports massage A combination of Swedish massage, shiatsu, and some type of deep-tissue body work now popular among professional and amateur athletes.

Stage of exhaustion The third and final stage of Selye's general adaptation syndrome, in which one or more target organs show signs of dysfunction.

Stage of resistance The second stage of Selye's general adaptation syndrome, in which the body tries to recover.

Stages of grieving A process outlined by Elisabeth Kübler-Ross regarding the mental preparation for death, including denial, anger, bargaining, depression, and acceptance.

Starting posture The stance that begins the first of many positions in the flow of the T'ai Chi exercise; balancing your weight on both feet and looking straight ahead.

Stimulus period Called the "meat" of the workout, during which one targets the specified intensity toward heart, lungs, and muscles (e.g., heart rate, sets, reps for weight lifting).

Straightforward procrastinator A person who knowingly avoids completing a task.

Stress The experience of a perceived threat (real or imagined) to one's mental, physical, or spiritual well-being, resulting from a series of physiological responses and adaptations.

Stressor Any real or imagined situation, circumstance, or stimulus that is perceived to be a threat.

Stress reaction The body's initial (central nervous system) reaction to a perceived threat.

Stress response The release of epinephrine and norepinephrine to prepare various organs and tissues for fight or flight.

Substance addiction The addiction to a host of substances, from nicotine and caffeine to alcohol and various drugs.

Subtle anatomy Also called energy anatomy, subtle anatomy comprises the human energy field (aura), the *chakra* system, and the meridian system of energetic pathways that supply energy (also known as *chi* or *prana*) to the organs and physiological systems with which they connect.

Subtle energy A series of layers of energy that surround and permeate the body; thought to be associated with layers of consciousness constituting the human energy field.

Superiority theory First coined by Plato describing the reason why people laugh is at other people's expense.

Supportive-expressive group therapy A term coined by Dr. David Spiegel for women with breast cancer to share their experiences, grief, and healing with others going through the same experience.

Survival skills A term associated with codependency in which certain behaviors are adopted in adolescence to "survive" demanding, alcoholic, or abusive parents.

Survivor personality The traits that comprise a unique winning attitude to overcome adversity and challenges, no matter what the odds may be, so that one comes out the victor, not the victim.

Swedish massage The most common and well-known type of massage in Western culture that uses a variety of hand motions (e.g., kneading, stroking, and karate-type chops) to relieve the tension for muscle tissue, often expressed as knots.

Sympathetic The branch of the central nervous system that triggers the fight-or-flight response when some element of threat is present.

Sympathetic resonance A resonating vibration given off by one object that is picked up by another object in close proximity. Tuning forks are a classic example.

Synchronicity A term coined by Carl Jung to explain the significance of two seemingly unrelated events that, when brought together, have a significant meaning.

Synesthesia A cross-wiring of one's senses (during an altered state) during which one smells sounds or sees noises.

Systematic desensitization A term coined by psychologist Joseph Wolpe to describe a process of progressive tolerance to stress by gaining a greater sense of comfort with the unknown through repeated exposure and visualization.

T'ai Chi ch'uan A relaxation technique originating among the Chinese; a succession of movements to bring the body into harmony with the universal energy (*Chi*); a moving meditation.

Tapotement The fourth of five progressive steps/hand maneuvers in the Swedish massage that look like karate chops on the belly of the muscle.

Target heart rate The ideal heart rate or target zone in which to identify the intensity of cardiovascular activity.

Target organs Any organ or tissue receiving excess neural or hormonal stimulation that increases metabolic function or abnormal cell growth; results in eventual dysfunction of the organ.

T-cytotoxic cells Best known as the cells that attack and destroy tumorous cells by releasing cytokines.

Technostress A term used to define the result of a fast-paced life dependent on various means of technology, including computers, cell phones and smartphones, personal digital assistants, texting, and email—all of which were supposed to give people more leisure time. Instead, people have become slaves, addicted to the constant use of these devices and technologies.

Tend and befriend A theory presented by Shelley Taylor stating that women who experience stress don't necessarily run or fight, but rather turn to friends to cope with unpleasant events and circumstances.

T-helpers Also known as CD4, these cells help in the production of antibodies released by T-cells.

Theory of motivation Maslow's theory associated with personality and behavior, based on his theory of the hierarchy of needs.

Therapeutic touch An energy-based healing modality using the science of subtle energy to restore homeostasis (also similar to Reiki and healing touch).

Thermal biofeedback Biofeedback that measures the response from skin temperature. These can be affected by stress.

Thigh Stretch (Bandha Konasana) A classic yoga *asana* intended to promote balance with the leg muscles.

Thought stopping A coping technique by which one consciously stops the run of negative thoughts going through one's head.

Thyroxine axis A chain of physiological events stemming from the release of thyroxine.

Tickler notebook A personal collection of humorous items (e.g., cards, letters, JPEGs, jokes) to lighten your spirits.

Time (duration) The number of minutes of exercise in one session; the ideal number is 30 minutes in the target zone, not including a warm-up or cool-down.

Time distortion As an altered state, one's perception of time is changed or distorted so that a segment of time seems either longer or shorter than it actually is.

Time juggler Someone who multitasks, overbooks, and double-books oneself and bargains for time, often dropping responsibilities in the process.

Time management The prioritization, scheduling, and execution of daily responsibilities to a level of personal satisfaction. Effective time management does not mean you have more time; it means you make better use of the time you have.

Time mapping A time-management technique; breaking down the day into 15- to 30-minute segments and assigning a task or responsibility to each segment.

Time urgency A characteristic or behavior of someone who displays Type A personality, someone who is constantly time conscious.

Time-trap procrastinator A person who does other tasks, such as laundry, thus keeping busy while still avoiding the more important responsibilities.

Tinnitus The clinical name given to the symptom of ringing, hissing, or buzzing in the ears.

Toxic thoughts Repeated negative thought processing that tends to pollute our view of our lives and ourselves.

Tragic optimism A term coined by psychiatrist Viktor Frankl to explain the mindset of someone who can find value and meaning in the worst situation.

Tranquil natural scenes One of three categories used in mental imagery (e.g., ocean beach, mountain vista, old-growth forest, lavender gardens).

Transcendence A means to rise above the mundane existence to see a higher order to things, often used to describe human spirituality.

Transcendental Meditation (TM) This meditation is the epitome of exclusive meditation in which all thoughts are eliminated save the mantra itself.

Transpersonal psychology A discipline in the field of psychology that recognizes the spiritual dimension of the human condition.

Transpsychological A term used to describe the therapeutic effects of self-discovery through active awareness in journaling.

Tratak A visual type of mantra, such as a seashell, a colorfully designed mandala, or any object that is used by the eyes to focus attention and ignore distracting thoughts.

Trigger point therapy Applied pressure to and manipulation of hyper-irritable points of the muscle that are causing radiating pain in a region; used in sports massage.

Tsubos The specific point on the meridian that is used in acupressure to release tension.

T-suppressors Also known as CD8, these cells decrease the production of antibodies, thus keeping a healthy balance of T-cells.

Two Knees to Chest (Apanasana) A classic yoga *asana* intended to promote balance with the lower back.

Type A personality This personality, once associated with time urgency, is now associated with unresolved anger issues.

Type of exercise The type of activity one chooses to engage in to work one or more physiological systems (e.g., walking, jogging, cycling).

Tzu, Lao An ancient Chinese philosopher and writer. He is the author of the acclaimed book *Tao Teh Ching*, a manifesto for human spirituality based on the concept of balance with nature. Lao Tzu is believed to be the creator of the concept of Taoism.

Ultradian rhythms Biological rhythms that occur many times in a 24-hour period (e.g., hunger pangs).

Unconditional love An altruistic love expressed by Jesus of Nazareth, for which nothing is expected in return.

Underhanders People exhibiting a mismanaged anger style by seeking revenge and retaliation. This passive-aggressive anger style is a means to control others, but in a very subtle way.

Unwarranted fear Similar to an irrational fear, an instance when anxiety overcomes one's thoughts based on a nonphysical threat to one's existence.

Values Abstract, intangible concepts of importance or meaning, such as time, health, honesty, and creativity, that are symbolized by material possessions.

Vasopressin axis A chain of physiological events stemming from the release of vasopressin or antidiuretic hormone (ADH).

Via creativa Fox's term to describe a breakthrough or moment of enlightenment.

Via negativa Fox's term to describe the act of emptying and letting go of unnecessary thoughts and feelings.

Via positiva Fox's term to describe a sense of awe and wonder of creation.

Via transformativa Fox's term to describe the euphoria from the realization of insights and the responsibility to share these with others.

Vibration The fifth of five progressive steps/hand maneuvers in the Swedish massage that resembles a type of shaking gesture to promote increased circulation.

Victimization A mindset of continually seeing yourself as a victim.

Vision quest A Native American custom of a retreat in nature during which one begins or continues to search for life's answers.

Visualization A directed exercise in mental imagery; consciously creating images of success, healing, or relaxation for the purpose of self-improvement.

Vitamin supplements Processed pills containing various vitamins (e.g., A, B complex, C, E).

von Bingen, Hildegard An early Christian mystic who added a feminine voice to a male-dominated Christian theology.

Warm-up period The first phase of the workout, during which circulation is increased to the large muscles with some time for flexibility.

Warrior The last stage in von Oech's creative process template, in which the idea is taken to the street and campaigned to the rest of the world for its merits.

Wellness paradigm The integration, balance, and harmony of mental, physical, emotional, and spiritual well-being through taking responsibility for one's own health; posits that the whole is greater than the sum of the parts.

Winning by losing A T'ai Chi expression that explains the benefits of failure as a stepping stone toward success.

Workaholism A personality style that inhibits good time-management skills with excessive hours devoted to work, often at the expense of other responsibilities.

Writer's block The inability to write down one's thoughts and feelings, usually attributed to fear (e.g., fear of failure).

Wu-wei A T'ai Chi term that signifies doing nothing, or action through nonaction, moving with the simple, subtle flow of nature.

X-factor A term coined by psychologist Leo Buscaglia to describe that special quality that makes each one of us unique. By focusing on our X-factor and not our faults and foibles, we enhance our self-esteem.

Yang Those complementary components in the Taoist philosophy of yin/yang expressed as light, masculine, day, hard, and so on.

Yerkes-Dodson principle The theory that some stress (eustress) is necessary for health and performance but that beyond an optimal amount, both will deteriorate as stress increases.

Yin Those complementary components in the Taoist philosophy of yin/yang expressed as dark, feminine, night, soft, and so forth.

Yoga A Sanskrit word that means union, specifically the union of mind, body, and spirit.

Yoga Sutras The ancient yogic text attributed to Patanjali, who described each of the yoga *asanas*.

Zen (Zazen) meditation A form of meditation wherein one learns to detach from one's emotional thoughts by becoming the observer of those thoughts.

Zero firing threshold A term to signify complete muscular relaxation with no tension.